MW01122452

Inside Arbitration

How an Arbitrator Decides
Labor and Employment Cases

Related Arbitration Titles From Bloomberg BNA

The Common Law of the Workplace

Discipline and Discharge in Arbitration

Elkouri and Elkouri: How Arbitration Works

Fairweather's Practice and Procedure in Labor Arbitration

Grievance Guide

How ADR Works

How to Prepare and Present a Labor Arbitration Case

Inside Arbitration: How an Arbitrator Decides Labor and Employment Cases

Just Cause: The Seven Tests

Labor Agreement in Negotiation and Arbitration

Labor Arbitration: Cases and Materials for Advocates

Labor Arbitration: A Practical Guide for Advocates

Labor Arbitrator Development: A Handbook

National Academy of Arbitrators (NAA) Proceedings

Winning Arbitration Advocacy

Inside Arbitration

How an Arbitrator Decides Labor and Employment Cases

Roger I. Abrams

Richardson Professor of Law
Northeastern University School of Law

**Bloomberg
BNA**

Arlington, VA

Library of Congress Cataloging-in-Publication Data

Abrams, Roger I., 1945-
   Inside arbitration : how an arbitrator decides labor and employment cases /
Roger I. Abrams, Richardson Professor of Law, Northeastern University.
   pages cm
   Includes index.
   ISBN 978-1-61746-272-6
   1. Arbitration, Industrial--Law and legislation--United States. I. Title.

KF3424.A73 2013
344.7301'89143--dc23

                                                             2013026881

Published by Bloomberg BNA
1801 S. Bell Street, Arlington, VA 22202
bna.com/bnabooks

ISBN 987-1-61746-272-6
Printed in the United States of America

To my colleagues in the
National Academy of Arbitrators

"[A]rbitration is an integral part of the system of self-government. And the system is designed to aid management in its quest for efficiency, to assist union leadership in its participation in the enterprise, and to secure justice for the employees. It is a means of making collective bargaining work and thus preserving private enterprise in a free government."

—Harry Shulman, Dean of the Yale Law School
and the leading labor arbitrator of his day, in
Reason, Contract and Law in Labor Relations,
68 HARVARD LAW REVIEW 999, 1024 (1955)

"Do I believe in arbitration? I do. But not in arbitration between the lion and the lamb, in which the lamb is in the morning found inside the lion."

—Samuel Gompers, ROCKY MOUNTAIN NEWS,
February 10, 1888

Preface

For those of us who have been privileged to serve as neutrals in labor-management and employment disputes, the practice of arbitration has offered a wealth of learning experiences and opportunities to connect with men and women in an everyday working environment. In each of the 2,500 cases to which I have been appointed over 40 years as an arbitrator, I have learned how people interact within their own "special-purpose" communities. With each new case, the learning continues.

In the process, I have also been instructed on how to make glass, cardboard boxes, and the orange drink of the astronauts. I have visited sawmills, slaughterhouses, and aircraft factories. I have made some baseball players very wealthy in salary arbitration—and those are the players who lost their cases! I have learned about the telephone industry, the Internal Revenue Service, and over-the-road trucking. As a young academic, there was a risk that my work life would only be filled with theories, research, and hypotheticals. Arbitration has offered me a lesson plan in real life.

There is a rich literature on labor arbitration, much of it published by Bloomberg BNA. Many of the books explain how parties ought to prepare and present cases in arbitration. Others, such as *How Arbitration Works*,[1] the monumental text originally authored by Frank Elkouri and Edna Asper Elkouri and now maintained by the ABA Section of Labor and Employment Law, relate what arbitrators say in their decisions. No one, however, has written a book about arbitration from the perspective of the arbitrator. How does an arbitrator actually make a decision? How does an arbitrator react to the conduct of the parties at the hearing? One would think it would be quite valuable to understand how the decision maker goes about actually deciding a case. And so I have tried to discuss this and many other matters in this book.

---

[1] ELKOURI & ELKOURI: HOW ARBITRATION WORKS (Kenneth May, ed., 7th ed. 2012).

Admittedly, this text presents my perspective. I do not pretend to speak for all arbitrators—no one can. My guess is that most of my colleagues who are labor arbitrators would agree with my conclusions, which are consistent with what I have learned from my colleagues in discussions at the National Academy of Arbitrators meetings for more than 30 years. I have participated in, led, and witnessed innumerable presentations by arbitrators on many of the issues raised in this book. Some arbitrators will disagree with my opinions and analysis, and they will be free to present their own thoughts in rebuttal.

In this text, I use the terms *arbitrator* and *neutral* interchangeably. I also use the terms *advocate* and *representative* in the same way— he or she is the person who will speak for a party in an arbitration proceeding.

I first began to think about this book when I reread the work of Judge Frank M. Coffin of the U.S. Court of Appeals for the First Circuit. It was my great good fortune to have clerked for Judge Coffin in 1970–71. He was a remarkable man and an inspirational mentor. His book about how an appellate judge makes a decision—*The Ways of a Judge*[2]—inspired my work in trying to understand how an *arbitrator* makes a decision. If I am half as successful as Judge Coffin was in his explanation, I will be very pleased.

When I began work on this project, I asked my research assistant, Joshua Nadreau, to contact union and management lawyers to seek their assistance. I wanted to know what questions they had always wanted to ask an arbitrator. Joshua compiled the questions they submitted but kept them anonymous. These questions formed the backbone of this work. I have also added some questions of my own to make the text more complete. Yet the book is not intended to be comprehensive, like the Elkouris' work. There may be questions that readers have that are not answered here—send them to me at r.abrams@neu.edu, and they will be answered in the next edition.

This text is designed for advocates and representatives with all levels of experience. Some of the material that explains the process of arbitration may seem basic to those more experienced in arbitration, but it is better to be inclusive rather than exclusive, particularly because of the influx of new advocates in the past several years, especially on the union side. Advocates for parties in arbitration must learn how their arbitrator reacts to certain issues and behaviors. There is an old saying

---

[2]Frank M. Coffin, The Ways of a Judge: Reflections from the Federal Appellate Bench (1980).

that applies to arbitration as well as to litigation: A good lawyer knows the law, but a great lawyer knows the judge. A great arbitration advocate may not know the particular arbitrator who will hear his or her case, but the advocate should know how arbitrators approach the hearing and the issues to be resolved.

Books such as this one require many hands. I should make special mention of my friend and law school classmate Dennis R. Nolan. During the 1980s and 1990s, Dennis and I collaborated in writing 19 law review articles about various topics in labor arbitration. He helped me to understand the nature of this process that we both have administered for almost four decades. My editors at Bloomberg BNA, Tim Darby and Joanne Nobile, also have been of great help. My wife of 44 years, Frances Elise Abrams, has made this book better, as she has made my life better.

Inside Arbitration is not a tell-all memoir. Rather, it is a tell-you-more-than-you-know-now look from the perspective of one arbitrator. This wondrous process of arbitration in the workplace is the star of this enterprise, as we try to understand the various elements that come together to make it work so well.

ROGER I. ABRAMS
BOSTON, MA
June 2013

Summary Table of Contents

Detailed Table of Contents

Chapter 1

Introduction

1

I. ARBITRATION

Arbitration is a remarkable institution, not without its flaws but almost universally praised by members of the labor-management community. It provides employers, employees, and labor organizations with an alternative dispute resolution (ADR) system that works, no small benefit to productivity and fairness in the workplace.[1]

The practice of labor arbitration by union and management lawyers requires the representatives of the parties to apply the skills of a trial advocate in a setting that is very different from a court proceeding. Presenting an effective case before a neutral labor arbitrator obviously involves an understanding of how arbitrators decide cases. Arbitrators are adjudicators, like judges, but in a very specialized forum. Although the finished product of labor arbitration—opinions and awards on procedural and substantive matters—fills hundreds of volumes, no one has described how an arbitrator actually goes about reaching a decision. This book will fill that important gap in the literature.[2]

In recent years, many nonunion employers have created arbitration systems to resolve disputes with their employees, most importantly cases that involve termination of employment. The National Academy of Arbitrators (NAA), the premier association of labor arbitrators, recently recognized the growth of employment arbitration by adding experienced employment arbitration neutrals to its membership. The challenges faced by those who participate in employment arbitration— either as a representative of a party or as a neutral—differ from those involved in traditional labor arbitration. Little analytical work has been done in this allied field regarding how employment arbitrators decide cases, and this lacuna is addressed in Chapter 17.

In addition, resolving employment disputes in both unionized and nonunionized workplaces involves using nonadjudicatory tools of ADR other than arbitration, in particular mediation. Neutrals in the labor relations field are often called on to mediate either pending grievance disputes or disputes concerning the establishment of new terms and conditions of employment. In such situations, the neutral is no longer the "decider," but becomes a facilitator whose task is to assist the parties

---

[1] *See generally* ROBBEN FLEMING, THE LABOR ARBITRATION PROCESS (1965).

[2] The best existing work on labor arbitration is that written by two splendid full-time arbitrators, Arnold Zack and Richard Bloch. *See* ARNOLD ZACK & RICHARD BLOCH, LABOR AGREEMENT IN NEGOTIATION AND ARBITRATION (2d ed. 1995).

in reaching their own resolution of their differences. Although some of the same interpersonal skills are needed in both mediation and arbitration, the neutral must recognize the differences between the two processes and be prepared to "change gears" at the appropriate moments, exhibiting the appropriate nimbleness in moving from one process to the other. We discuss in Chapter 18 how "med-arb" makes that possible.

An estimated 30,000–40,000 labor arbitration cases are filed each year. In most of these cases, the employer and the union are each represented by attorneys, although many nonattorneys also serve as advocates, in particular in representing labor organizations. It is obvious that these advocates must understand how neutral arbitrators decide cases. Currently, there are no resources that explain the decisional process from the perspective of the arbitrator. Similarly, there are a growing number of employment arbitrations each year and, as noted earlier, many labor arbitrators hear nonunion employment cases. These cases present distinctive challenges, and a thoughtful examination of the grounds for these decisions is also needed.

The real purpose of the arbitration process—both under union collective bargaining agreements (CBAs) and individual employment contracts—is to bring the unbiased voice of a private, informed, and neutral adjudicator into the workplace. The arbitrator is charged with resolving the dispute with finality. Disputes are certain to arise within the special purpose communities that produce products and supply services. Employers will terminate or discipline employees. Problems will arise concerning the operation of the workplace, the allocation of work responsibilities, and the layoff of workers. Management manages and, until arbitration, management's decision in any dispute is the final word. The neutral changes the workplace dynamic, even if the award ultimately affirms management's decision.

When labor and management reach agreement on the provisions of their CBA, they know what arrangements they have made to control the workplace. They should also know in some general sense how arbitrators are likely to read, interpret, and apply the provisions of the CBA as disputes arise during the contract term. It is more likely, however, that the parties are so focused on avoiding the costs of disagreement that they use flexible and ambiguous language to embody their understandings and may even ignore the possibility that disputes will arise that they cannot settle themselves. Nonetheless, they are wise enough to create within their agreements mechanisms for resolving the disputes that are certain to occur. They create grievance and arbitration procedures.

Over the years, arbitrators have formulated—and parties have tacitly accepted—what might be termed a "common law of the labor agreement," principles that neutrals will use to resolve disputes if and when they arise.[3] These rules of contract interpretation and dispute resolution do not lead to precise predictions as to how each case will come out in arbitration, but they do offer the parties a projected range of outcomes that are most likely to occur.

Some who are new to arbitration may wrongly believe that arbitrators simply decide cases based on purely subjective values. Some think that arbitrators flip a coin or split the difference. That is most unlikely among experienced arbitrators, especially those who are members of the NAA. Arbitrators are guided by well-understood neutral principles of adjudication;[4] otherwise, the arbitration process would simply be a roulette wheel that spins anew for every case. An ADR system based on the vagaries of arbitrator temperament and disposition would be intolerable to the parties to a CBA.

The parties expect their neutrals to decide cases accurately. In most disputes, an arbitrator must determine what actually happened that gave rise to the grievance. He or she must resolve disputes about the facts. Once the arbitrator has "found the facts," the neutral applies the well-understood principles of the common law of the labor agreement and ultimately reaches an award that resolves the dispute. Under virtually every CBA, that award is final and binding.

It is critical that a neutral stay faithful to the provisions of the contract to which the parties agreed. The arbitrator's power comes from those provisions. The contract guideposts are unyielding, even if the arbitrator thinks them unwise. He or she must fulfill the expectations of the parties as they are evidenced in the terms of their agreement.

---

[3] *See* Roger Abrams, *The Nature of the Arbitral Process: Substantive Decision-Making in Labor Arbitration*, 14 U.C. Davis L. Rev. 551 (1981). The only truly comprehensive collection of what arbitrators say in their decisions was written by Frank Elkouri in 1952 as his doctoral thesis. *How Arbitration Works* became the preeminent text in the field. Elkouri was an emeritus professor on the faculty of the University of Oklahoma Law School and passed away on January 18, 2013. His wife, Edna, joined the book for the second, third, and fourth editions. The text is now in its seventh edition. *See* Elkouri & Elkouri: How Arbitration Works (Kenneth May, ed., 7th ed. 2012).

[4] The best restatement of those principles was written by members of the NAA and edited by Professor Emeritus Ted St. Antoine. *See* National Academy of Arbitrators, The Common Law of the Workplace: The Views of Arbitrators (Theodore J. St. Antoine, ed., 2d ed. 2005). *See also* Dennis R. Nolan, Labor Arbitration Law and Practice in a Nutshell (1979).

The neutral in arbitration is selected by the parties to the dispute pursuant to the procedures set forth in the controlling documents. A CBA typically provides for the selection of the arbitrator under the procedures of an appointing agency—either the American Arbitration Association (AAA) or the Federal Mediation and Conciliation Service (FMCS). The selected arbitrator enters the dispute with the imprimatur of the parties, enhancing the legitimacy of the process in the eyes of the disputants.

The agreement negotiated by labor and management sets the rules for the organized workplace.[5] As part of that agreement, the parties write their own ticket when it comes to the arbitration process. They should exercise their control over the process by tailoring the procedures to meet their particular needs, although it may take some time until they understand the benefits and costs of deviating from what might be called "standard arbitration." If they want grievances to be filed within a particular period of time after an event occurs, the contract should so provide. If they want an arbitration hearing conducted in a timely manner, the contract should so specify. The parties own the arbitration process; they only "rent" the neutral.

Some parties to an arbitration may see the system in purely adjudicatory terms—as a courtroom with a private judge. Others understand that labor arbitration is a continuation of the collective bargaining process. Their CBA is necessarily incomplete. It could not always anticipate the precise issues that will arise and offer a negotiated resolution. The arbitrator steps into the shoes of the parties, as they intended would happen. He or she will "finish" the agreement, at least insofar as the particular dispute requires. Acting like an adjudicator but operating in a distinctive context, the arbitrator fulfills the parties' needs and expectations.

II. Arbitrators

When the parties to a CBA provide in their contract for an arbitration process to decide unresolved grievances, they count on the availability of experienced neutrals who will be willing to serve as arbitrators. There is an abundance of persons who call themselves labor

---

[5]In addition to the Elkouris' volume, Owen Fairweather's *Practice and Procedure in Labor Arbitration,* now in its fourth edition, is a very useful compendium on the substance and the process of arbitration. *See* Fairweather's Practice and Procedure in Labor Arbitration (Ray J. Schoonhoven, ed., 4th ed. 1999).

arbitrators and are willing to serve in that capacity. Their primary responsibility is to the parties who appoint them, but they also are fiduciaries for the process of labor arbitration. Arbitration's success as a private ADR procedure depends on how well these arbitrators perform their roles.

1.   Who are these labor arbitrators?

There are thousands of professionals nationwide who call themselves labor arbitrators. In fact, only a very small group—300 or so experienced neutrals—hear 90 percent of all labor arbitration cases. Most of these men and women are trained in the law, but some bring to arbitration what they have learned in labor relations matters over the years. Many of these men and women are full-time arbitrators with a comprehensive docket of disputes to resolve; others are part-timers who combine labor arbitration with an academic appointment or with the practice of law in other fields.[6] In general, members of the corps of labor arbitrators follow the same or similar approaches to decision making, an approach we discuss in Chapter 14.

The most experienced arbitrators may be elected to the NAA, an honorary and professional organization of labor and employment arbitrators. About 650 arbitrators are elected members of the organization. They meet twice annually to discuss major issues that affect arbitration.

In the Introduction to the AAA's Labor Arbitration Rules,[7] the Association extols the virtues of labor arbitration but notes its limitations: "When abused or made to do things for which it was never intended, the outcome can be disappointing."[8] The critical difference, it says, is who arbitrates the case: "In the hands of an expert, [arbitration] produces useful results."[9]

---

[6]Mario Bognanno's and Charles Coleman's book on the arbitration profession, although somewhat out of date, offers an interesting profile, based on empirical data, of those who serve in the role of arbitration neutrals. *See* LABOR ARBITRATION IN AMERICA: THE PROFESSION AND PRACTICE (Mario F. Bognanno & Charles J. Coleman, eds., 1992).

[7]AMERICAN ARBITRATION ASSOCIATION, LABOR ARBITRATION RULES (amended and effective July 1, 2013), *available at* http://www.adr.org/aaa/faces/rules/searchrules/rulesdetail?doc=ADRSTG_012406&_afrLoop=422248314580768&_afrWindowMode=0&_afrWindowId=7og4tr6be_1#%40%3F_afrWindowId%3D7og4tr6be_1%26_afrLoop%3D422248314580768%26doc%3DADRSTG_012406%26_afrWindowMode%3D0%26_adf.ctrl-state%3D7og4tr6be_57 (reproduced in Appendix D).

[8]*Id.*

[9]*Id.*

2.   *How are arbitrators trained?*

There are no arbitrator schools where someone completes a course of study on how to be an arbitrator. There is no official arbitrator certification, except for that provided in effect by the appointing agencies—the AAA and the FMCS—when they decide whether to add an applicant to their rosters of arbitrators. Periodically, but not regularly, there have been labor arbitrator training programs normally co-sponsored by law schools, unions, and management organizations.

Most arbitrators come from decades of labor relations or labor law experience that included work appearing before arbitrators. Other arbitrators come from academia. Traditionally, senior arbitrators have employed and mentored future arbitrators—a system reminiscent of how lawyers were trained in the nineteenth century.

Yet, despite the absence of formal training, there is available a corps of arbitrators ready, willing, and, most importantly, able to serve the parties.

3.   *What are the qualities and characteristics that make a good arbitrator?*

We focus on the qualities of a good labor arbitrator in Chapter 2. It should suffice to state at this point that a good arbitrator must understand the context of the workplace, be absolutely neutral, and have the personal ability to run a hearing and write an understandable and timely decision.

4.   *Are arbitrators bound by precedent like a court?*

One fundamental premise of arbitration is that the decision makers in arbitration are not bound by precedent in the same way as judges in courts would be. There is no binding *stare decisis*. That is an oversimplification, however, both with regard to judicial and arbitral decision making. In court disputes, judges are often presented with conflicting precedent from which to choose, especially if there is no ruling on point from an appellate court in the same jurisdiction. Although judges like to state in their opinions that they had "no choice" but to follow a prior decision and, as a result, reach the outcome they did, there often is a choice in deciding whether the case at hand is similar enough to the prior case to make that holding applicable. Judges readily distinguish precedent, and arbitrators enjoy similar flexibility.

III. The Collective Bargaining Agreement

The parties to a CBA create the arbitration process to resolve disputes they anticipate will arise during the term of their contract, which normally lasts for three years. If they attempted to answer all possible questions that might arise, they would never finish negotiating. Instead, they reach agreement on the most important matters, provide reasonable direction on a host of other matters, and create a process whereby the disputes that do arise can be resolved. That process is labor arbitration.

1. *What is the collective bargaining agreement?*

The CBA is a contract negotiated by management and by the union that represents the employees. It sets forth the parties' understandings on a broad spectrum of employment issues, such as what employees should be paid, how a promotion should be filled, what rights management reserves, and how benefits—such as vacations, paid holidays, pensions, and such—will be earned and allocated.

No one is hired as a result of the agreement, but when management hires an employee, his or her terms and conditions of employment are already established by the provisions of the CBA.

2. *Are there other documents that should be considered part of the parties' binding understandings?*

It is not uncommon for other documents to bind the parties. Side letters, memoranda of agreements, letters of understanding, or other supplemental agreements are part of the complete written and enforceable deal. They normally will be attached as an appendix to the CBA.

3. *What about unwritten understandings?*

As discussed in Chapter 13, by virtue of a consistent and long-standing pattern of conduct, parties create "past practices" that may also be binding. Arbitrators will use past practices as a helpful gloss in interpreting ambiguous contract language. In addition, past practice may serve as an independent source of employee rights on matters involving benefits.

Thus, the CBA must be understood to include all of these elements—both written documents and unwritten practices. All are part of the agreement that the arbitrator is asked by the parties to read, interpret, and apply.

IV. THE "LAW" OF ARBITRATION

1. What is the "common law of the labor agreement," and how do you find it?

Much like the common law system of civil court adjudication, the principles of labor arbitration have evolved over time as arbitrators elaborated what might be termed the "common law of the labor agreement." This is a set of rules and principles that are generally applied by arbitrators in grievance cases. Every experienced arbitrator knows those rules and principles.

The common law of the labor agreement controls in arbitration. To claim that an arbitrator is free to exercise his or her own personal judgment in reading and applying the terms of a CBA is absurd. Such a system of total ad hoc decision making would be far too risky for the parties—it would be intolerable roulette. It would also make it impossible for parties to settle a matter before a hearing, because there would always be a chance that the selected neutral could create a whole new approach to decision making that might favor one side or the other in the case under consideration. That would be lawless.

Parties can find these prevailing common law principles of labor arbitration the same way they would research the law in a court case. There are thousands of reported arbitration decisions published by Bloomberg BNA, CCH, Westlaw, and Lexis. Secondary sources such as *Elkouri and Elkouri: How Arbitration Works*[10] have collected and summarized the common law of the labor agreement, which makes research far more convenient. Although all experienced neutrals know these doctrines, just as with courts they may differ as to precisely which principles are applicable in any given case.

Although many arbitrators and parties choose not to submit their opinions for publication, there is no indication that published awards are atypical. In addition, there are some, but not many, law review articles that report, analyze, and criticize particular approaches taken by arbitrators in certain areas.

2. Are arbitration outcomes predictable?

The essence of any system of law is that outcomes are predictable, at least within a reasonable range of variance. Civil court disputes are almost all settled before trial. That is because the legal principles that

---

[10]ELKOURI & ELKOURI: HOW ARBITRATION WORKS (Kenneth May, ed., 7th ed. 2012).

would be applied in court are generally known and applied uniformly within limits. The availability of appellate courts that can correct errors gives the parties in civil litigation confidence that ultimately the law will be applied correctly.

Similarly, it is important that arbitration decisions be generally predictable to the parties. Advocates may dream of winning a losing case, but such aberrations do not serve the legitimacy of the process in the long run. It is best for the arbitration process that losing cases lose and winning cases win. That does not always happen, of course, but, within a range of outcomes, parties should be able to predict how a case will come out. This is why at least half of all cases scheduled for arbitration are settled before or at the hearing. The party that understands it will likely lose after adjudication may seek the best settlement before incurring the expenses of using a neutral.

Arbitration law outside the federal public sector does not provide for appellate review of the merits for reasons we will discuss later. Thus, it is critical that the arbitrator get it right the first time. The autonomous nature of labor arbitration makes the selection of the neutral a critical step.[11]

A different issue is presented when the parties have received a previous arbitration award on the issue at hand. In such a situation, arbitrators should follow the established law of the shop, as long as the earlier case is not clearly wrong. Stability and continuity are important variables in the workplace, especially when the parties are always free to alter their agreement's terms during negotiations and, in effect, amend any previous arbitration ruling. Even without a prior arbitration opinion on point, the arbitrator is not free to roam: He or she is bound by the reasonable expectations of the parties that the dispute will be resolved consistent with the established principles of labor arbitration.

V. THE HISTORY OF LABOR ARBITRATION

Arbitration has been a fixture of labor-management relations since before World War II.[12] The relationship between the ADR systems established through collective bargaining and the established judicial system was not set until 1960 in the Supreme Court's *Steelworkers Tril-*

---

[11] See Chapter 2.

[12] *See* Dennis Nolan & Roger Abrams, *American Labor Arbitration: The Early Years*, 35 U. FLA. L. REV. 373 (1983) *and* Dennis Nolan & Roger Abrams, *American Labor Arbitration: The Maturing Years*, 35 U. FLA. L. REV. 557 (1983).

ogy cases,[13] where the U.S. Supreme Court ruled that labor arbitration should be autonomous and a court's role was to facilitate the process.

1.   *What is the origin of modern labor arbitration?*

The growth of labor arbitration as the preferred procedure for resolving disputes that arise during the terms of CBAs followed the successful effort by industrial labor organizations to unionize the manufacturing sector in the 1930s. Unions and management realized that it was too costly to leave grievance disputes for resolution through the use of strikes or lockouts. Unions and management needed to ensure that the provisions of their agreements would be followed, and courts were not only too slow, but too risky a mechanism. Instead, parties devised private systems of arbitration to resolve their disputes in a final and binding manner consistent with their contract terms.

Arbitration received a significant boost during the Second World War when the War Labor Board wrote arbitration clauses into CBAs as an alternative to work stoppages that might have a negative impact on war production. Unions relinquished their right to strike, and in exchange they accepted neutral arbitral intervention to review management decisions. The major problem the parties faced, however, was that there were not enough arbitrators available to hear grievance disputes. Staff members of the War Labor Board filled the need, leaving the agency to hear and resolve these disputes.

Following the Second World War, a profession of labor arbitrators began to emerge, including highly skilled adjudicators who devoted full time to the practice. In 1947, the NAA was formed and established a code of ethics to ensure that labor arbitrators would uphold high standards of skill and integrity. Membership in the Academy was by invitation only. Academy membership today remains the premier credential of the labor arbitration profession.

Congress added its imprimatur to the arbitration process in 1947 by including in the Labor-Management Relations Act[14] two provisions in support of dispute resolution according to the system negotiated by the parties; thus, arbitration carried out national labor policy.[15]

---

[13] Steelworkers v. American Mfg. Co., 363 U.S. 564 (1960); Steelworkers v. Warrior & Gulf Navig. Co., 363 U.S. 574 (1960); Steelworkers v. Enterprise Wheel & Car Corp., 363 U.S. 593 (1960). See Appendix A.

[14] 29 U.S.C. §§203(d) and 301.

[15] Congress declared in §203(d) of the Labor-Management Relations Act that "final adjustment by a method agreed upon by the parties is declared to be the desirable method for settlement of grievance disputes."

It was not until the 1950s that arbitration took its modern form, but since then the process has remained fairly constant. By 1965, Robben Fleming, an arbitrator who also served as chancellor of the University of Wisconsin and president of the University of Michigan, could describe arbitration as the greatest invention of the American labor movement.[16] An arbitration hearing in the mid 2010s would look very much like one in the mid 1950s, except for the fact that arbitrators in the mid 1950s were virtually all white men, and today the corps of arbitrators better reflects the workforce, with women and people of color among established neutrals.

2.   *Do courts favor labor arbitration?*

In May 1960, the U.S. Supreme Court decided three cases involving the United Steelworkers of America union: *Steelworkers v. American Manufacturing Co.,*[17] *Steelworkers v. Warrior & Gulf Navigation Co.,*[18] and *Steelworkers v. Enterprise Wheel & Car Corp.*[19] These cases are generally referred to as the *Steelworkers Trilogy*. In three opinions written by Justice William O. Douglas, the Court solidified the place of arbitration in the pantheon of national labor policy. With effusive praise for the process and for the arbitrators who operated it, Justice Douglas firmly set the role courts were to play in supporting, and not interfering with, the private dispute resolution procedures chosen by labor and management. More than half a century later, the *Trilogy* remains the guiding text for the arbitration process. We will return to Douglas' opinions throughout this text.

Congress ordained this special role for arbitration in Section 203 of the Taft-Hartley Amendment of 1947, declaring the parties' chosen method of settling disputes as the "desirable method."[20] It also provided in Section 301 that federal courts had jurisdiction to enforce CBAs. Those agreements almost universally contain arbitration as the parties' dispute resolution mechanism of choice.

Throughout the *Trilogy*, Justice Douglas made much of the supposed expertise of labor arbitrators, repeatedly emphasizing that judges were not equally equipped to resolve industrial labor disputes. Judges would, according to Justice Douglas, be ignorant of the context of the

[16] ROBBEN FLEMING, THE LABOR ARBITRATION PROCESS (1965).
[17] 363 U.S. 564 (1960).
[18] 363 U.S. 574 (1960).
[19] 363 U.S. 593 (1960).
[20] 29 U.S.C. §203(d).

plant, and it is that setting that might give meaning to the words the parties used in their agreement. With regard to some judges, such as Douglas' colleague Justice William Brennan, who was a longtime labor lawyer in New Jersey before appointment to the bench, a judge might be equal to an arbitrator in the eyes of the court. Yet Douglas cautioned against generalist judges substituting their adjudicatory skills for that of the labor arbitration specialist, because an arbitrator is better at doing this type of job. Even if an arbitrator were not better, Justice Douglas stated, the parties to a CBA have chosen the arbitration process as their method for resolving grievance disputes.

The *Trilogy* is an interesting example of the Supreme Court rejecting established doctrine on the enforcement of executory arbitration promises. Courts had exhibited a history of animosity toward arbitration, perhaps out fear that their power might be threatened. Justice Douglas turns this history on its head, enforcing arbitration promises as long as the party seeking arbitration is making a claim that on its face is governed by the contract. Courts are not to examine the merits; that is for the arbitrator to do.

Justice Douglas expounded on the very nature of the CBA. It is a "generalized code to cover a myriad of cases which the draftsmen cannot wholly anticipate."[21] Unlike an ordinary contract, the CBA called into being a new "common law" that operated under a system of "industrial self-government." Arbitration is, in effect, the judiciary of this new self-government, applying the agreement and the customs of the shop to the disputes that are certain to arise. The terms of the CBA simply cannot have an express rule on every possible permutation of dispute; arbitration and the arbitrators will fill in the gaps. The grievance procedure capped by an arbitration conducted by an outside neutral will, in effect, continue the negotiation process by resolving contract disputes. Of course, the parties in subsequent negotiations can continue to fill in the gaps in their agreement and, in the process, alter the conclusions reached in arbitration.

Justice Douglas tells us that the labor arbitrator, as part of this system of self-government of the workplace, can find his or her sources of law in the practices of the industry and the shop. It is the parties, however, that supply the neutral with this data. It is not the labor arbitrator's responsibility to investigate. Douglas also tells us that the skilled arbitrator understands the impact of his or her decision on the workplace in matters of productivity, morale, and the easing of tensions. That is

---

[21] *Warrior & Gulf Navigation,* 363 U.S. at 578–79.

a broad charter, indeed. In some general sense this may be true, but Douglas' hymn of praise for labor neutrals may be overdrawn. Douglas might be correct in his assessment comparing arbitrators to judges, but that does not mean that labor arbitrators possess such celestial skills.

The *Steelworkers Trilogy* makes labor arbitration autonomous. Courts will compel parties to use their process and will enforce the results of that process without review on the merits. In effect, Douglas tells parties to an arbitration procedure to stay out of the courtroom, and, for the most part, they do.

3.   *Do the parties in arbitration cite the* Steelworkers Trilogy?

Representatives of parties in arbitration frequently misapply the lessons of the *Steelworkers Trilogy* in cases where issues of arbitrability are raised. In the *Trilogy*, the U.S. Supreme Court addressed the proper approach of the judiciary toward arbitration. When a party (typically management) refuses to proceed to arbitration and the union brings suit to enforce the contract promise to arbitrate, the court's role is to order the parties to follow the procedures to which they have agreed. This approach applies even if some (including judges) might consider a grievance to be frivolous. In more difficult cases where the arbitration clause excludes certain matters from the procedure, a court is to apply a presumption of arbitrability. After an arbitrator renders an award, the court's job is to enforce the decision as long as the award draws its "essence" from the contract. Taken as a whole, the Supreme Court sought a norm of noninterference with the arbitration process. Although later cases have modified that stance with regard to grievances that raise matters that involve clear public policy concerns, in large measure the *Trilogy* stands strong after half a century.

The error sometimes made in arbitration is confusing the role of a court, as set forth in the *Trilogy*, with the role of an arbitrator in ruling on issues of arbitrability. The Court did *not* say that an arbitrator should apply a presumption in favor of finding a matter arbitrable. An arbitrator should do what he or she always should do—read and interpret the provisions of the CBA—including the provisions on the scope of arbitration—and determine whether a grievance is or is not arbitrable in fact. Presumptions do not play a role unless the parties have so provided in their CBA.

When the parties agree to an arbitration provision, they do not necessarily agree to arbitrate every difference that may arise between them. It is the contract that will control, and it will inform the arbitrator of the scope of his or her jurisdiction. Some agreements expressly exempt certain classes of grievances from the arbitration procedure, such as differences about the operation of the pension system, which may have its own internal arbitration procedure to resolve such disputes. Management may resist arbitrating a dispute, and it is understandable. Until an arbitrator takes jurisdiction, management's decision stands. Under the *Steelworkers Trilogy*, of course, management's resistance may prove short-lived.

4.   Labor relations have changed substantially in the past half century. Is there a better way to understand the Steelworkers Trilogy today?

Upon reflection more than half a century later, one can question some of Justice Douglas' characterizations of labor arbitration and labor arbitrators. In general, arbitrators understand the workplace, as Douglas wrote, but it is most likely that, in any given case, the arbitrator is serving the parties for the first time. Almost certainly, however, the neutral knows little, if anything, about the particular workplace involved in the dispute or even the industry in which it operates, unless the arbitrator is on an industry panel or has a long history of dealing with a specific company and union. Arbitrators are certainly specialists in their field of functioning as neutral deciders, but they are not all-knowing.

Threaded throughout the *Trilogy*, Justice Douglas expressed the concern of the Court that the failure to support the institution of arbitration would destabilize the unionized workplace. Courts should order even frivolous grievances to be arbitrated, because otherwise unions might feel compelled to strike. Because federal policy was designed to promote industrial peace, courts should apply a presumption of arbitrability and order the parties to arbitration in the absence of a specific and clear exclusion of the dispute at hand from the arbitration promise. Courts should enforce arbitration awards because finality enhances the legitimacy of the process. When the court carries out its job of supporting the arbitral process, industrial peace is served.

The rationale of the *Steelworkers Trilogy* should be updated. In 1960, Justice Douglas focused on labor arbitration as the substitute for industrial strife. In 1960, Douglas was writing in a very different context. More than 50 years ago, almost 30 percent of all private sector employees were organized. Today, that number has decreased to less than 7 percent. More importantly, in 1960 there were 222 work stoppages involving 1,000 or more employees. In the five-year period ending in 2013, that number has been reduced to an average of 11 large work stoppages per year. This dramatic change in circumstances warrants a rethinking of the anchors that hold the *Trilogy* in place. Today, when strikes are rare and unionization no longer is the norm in the private economy, there must be a better justification for the remarkable autonomy enjoyed by the labor arbitration system.

Arbitration deserves its autonomous status as ordained in the *Trilogy* because it is part of collective bargaining regimes that remain favored by national labor policy. Until Congress changes that policy, that policy should govern the proper relationship between courts and arbitration. Justice Douglas was focusing not on negotiation-related work stoppages, but rather on industrial disruptions during the terms of CBAs over grievance disputes. Following the *Trilogy*, the Supreme Court in *Boys Markets, Inc. v. Retail Clerks Local 770*[22] announced that an employer could seek an injunction to halt a union strike over a matter that could have been brought to arbitration. As a quid pro quo, if management can compel the union to arbitrate and not strike, a union should be able to force management to arbitrate as well. The *Trilogy* has become woven into the fabric of national labor policy, and, as such, it deserves continued respect.

5.   *Why can't there be an appeal from an arbitrator's decision? Are arbitrators infallible?*

Justice Douglas did not claim that an arbitrator's decision is always correct. In fact, in later cases the Supreme Court maintained its position of no review on the merits even if the arbitrator was wrong![23] Although the *Steelworkers Trilogy* makes much of the comparative attributes of a judge and an arbitrator, that is not really an adequate basis for the Supreme Court's rather remarkable support for the autonomy of labor arbitration.

In a ground-breaking law review article,[24] Professor Ted St. Antoine, a leading labor arbitrator and legal academic, explained the theoretical underpinnings of the *Trilogy:* The arbitrator is a contract reader who speaks for the parties. The arbitrator's award is their contract. There can be no appeal from an arbitrator's decision on the merits because of what the decision actually is: a pronouncement from the parties

---

[22]398 U.S. 235 (1970).

[23]*See, e.g.,* Major League Baseball Players Ass'n v. Garvey, 532 U.S. 504, 509 (2001).

[24]*See* Theodore J. St. Antoine, *Judicial Review of Labor Arbitration Awards: A Second Look at* Enterprise Wheel *and Its Progeny,* 75 MICH. L. REV. 1137 (1977).

themselves through their alter ego, the arbitrator. If two parties voluntarily enter into a contract, there is no appeal to a court about what was agreed to. The agreement is what it is—an agreement. If two parties agree to arbitration as a method to fill in the gaps in their contract, there is no appeal on the merits to a court, because the arbitrator is acting for the two contracting parties.

On some infrequent occasions, the losing party in arbitration will bring suit to have the arbitration award vacated, or the prevailing party will bring suit to enforce the award. Parties sometimes make the error of suing the arbitrator, but courts have clearly and repeatedly stated that arbitrators enjoy the same immunity as court judges.[25] The suit should be brought against the opposing party, but under prevailing law the arbitrator's award will likely be quickly enforced.

6. *Because virtually every collective bargaining agreement contains an arbitration provision, does everyone involved in arbitration think the process is just wonderful?*

Those who are privileged to serve as labor arbitrators are quick to defend the process they administer as neutrals. They offer the free market defense of arbitration: If there were problems with the process, why would the parties continue to include arbitration in their CBAs? If arbitrators were unsuited to the task, certainly parties would find better arbitrators. Arbitrators successfully meet the test of the marketplace by virtue of party selection, but is that a sufficient justification?

The problem with these assertions is that they are normally expressed by arbitrators extolling their own virtues. There have been contrary views. Judge Paul Hays served as a labor arbitrator for 23 years while he was a professor of law at Columbia University before ascending the federal bench. In his controversial 1966 book on labor arbitration, *Labor Arbitration: A Dissenting View,*[26] Judge Hays presented a decidedly negative view of labor arbitrators and the labor arbitration process. Some of his insights and conclusions are worth noting, because they may have validity and, more importantly, can direct our attention to improving the operation of the process. In fact, some parties may believe along with Judge Hays that the arbitration process is fatally flawed, although they are unable to obtain the consent of the opposing parties to remove the procedure from their CBAs.

---

[25] Dennis Nolan & Roger Abrams, *Arbitral Immunity*, 11 INDUS. REL. L.J. 228 (1989).
[26] PAUL R. HAYS, LABOR ARBITRATION: A DISSENTING VIEW (1966).

Judge Hays' views were first presented as the Storrs Lectures on Jurisprudence at Yale Law School a few years after the Supreme Court rendered its decisions in the *Steelworkers Trilogy*. In large measure, Hays spoke in response to the pronouncements of Justice William O. Douglas. Douglas had based his conclusions for the Supreme Court on the superior skills of labor arbitrators, a conclusion Hays felt was unwarranted. Hays bemoaned the absence of any objective studies of arbitrators or the arbitration process that could support the Court's grand conclusions. Here his criticism was on solid ground.

Judge Hays believed that the partisan parties selected their arbitrator based solely on whether they thought the neutral was likely to decide the dispute in their favor. It is hard to imagine anything else. Would parties select a neutral who they think would definitely rule against them? Although Hays may be correct that parties are motivated by a desire to win, the way the selection process normally operates makes it difficult to select a decidedly pro-management or pro-union arbitrator. The opposing party will simply veto the choice.

Judge Hays' conclusion that parties only play to win at arbitration also ignores the process values that arbitration provides the parties. Unions may appreciate that they are likely to lose a case on the merits but are willing to accept an arbitrator who will make the process meaningful, thus serving the needs of their membership. Similarly, management will accept the neutral who they know will hear their arguments with care even if it ultimately might not prevail in arbitration.

Judge Hays believed that the arbitration process worked best when it mirrored the judicial process. He abhorred the very thought of settlements that masqueraded as decisions on the merits, so-called consent awards. Hays insisted on calling them "rigged" awards, and his concerns were well-founded. He was sure that it constituted "a shocking distortion of the administration of justice."[27] Hays posited as examples situations where parties used the consent award as a way to do harm to a third party not involved in the deal making or the arbitration: Any procedure that would countenance such a compromise must be rotten to the core. Judge Hays did not suggest how often such a travesty occurred, but its very existence was sufficient for him to condemn labor arbitration.

He applauded those arbitrators who adhered strictly to the terms of the CBA, which assumed, of course, that those provisions were clear enough to apply mechanically. Regretfully, in fact, contracts always contain provisions that require some interpretation.

---

[27] *Id.* at 65.

Judge Hays was correct, however, when he criticized that portion of the *Steelworkers Trilogy* that said that an arbitrator could bring to bear in making a decision the effect on productivity of the given result. This is far beyond the skill level of labor arbitrators. Similarly, Hays had harsh words for any arbitrator who attempted to consider the effect of an arbitral determination on the "tensions" in a plant—the neutral simply does not have enough information to know whether his or her award will have that kind of impact, even assuming that it would be appropriate to consider that factor. Reaching beyond the contract to do good things for the parties (in the mind of the neutral, at least) has always been misguided.

Judge Hays wanted arbitrators to apply the same rules of law that a court would apply in interpreting ordinary contracts. For example, he stood in staunch opposition to any modification of the parol evidence rule. There are good reasons for a court to apply the parol evidence rule, which bars consideration of evidence of the interaction between parties before they reached a complete contractual agreement. Here Judge Hays demonstrated his lack of understanding of the labor relations context, a failure shared by other judges. Deals reached at the bargaining table should be embodied in the terms of the CBA, but sometimes clear arrangements between the parties never find their way into the provisions of a new contract. These understandings may be barred from evidence under the parol evidence rule, but they are part of the web of binding arrangements that make up the controlling principles of the workplace.

Judge Hays saved his harshest criticism for nonlawyer arbitrators. How could they possibly conduct a hearing? How could they control the parties? These criticisms seem to blanket a large number of arbitrators who had demonstrated their skills and abilities and were perfectly acceptable to the parties.

Judge Hays was mostly concerned about the Supreme Court giving private labor arbitration a special place in the panoply of American dispute resolution. Under prevailing court rulings, parties were forced to go to arbitration if they included such a procedure in their CBA. The decisions of arbitrators would be enforced as a regular matter without review on the merits by the courts. Arbitrators themselves were given judicial immunity. How could all of this happen, Hays reasoned, when so many of the arbitration deciders were not even lawyers?

Hays did recognize a few arbitrators—he cited Archibald Cox and Harry Shulman—as the "best exemplars" of the profession. He asserted, however, that many (or perhaps most) arbitrators were incompetent frauds. How did Hays reach that judgment? He made use of the published biographies of arbitrators and examined their past experiences. Here is where Hays' prejudices were revealed. Although more than half of the labor arbitrators at the time were attorneys, their experiences were simply insufficient, according to Judge Hays, to justify the special role they were to play under national law. He found no basis in the published biographies to support the assumption that these arbitrators had any unique expertise in labor relations that would justify their autonomous role. In addition, there were arbitrators who Hays claimed were "pure rascals," although he did not name names or cite any empirical basis for his conclusion.

The heart of the Hays' indictment of the labor arbitration process was saved for the method of appointment of labor arbitrators. Because parties select their neutrals, the neutral must please these parties in order to obtain return business. Arbitrators, he said, were afraid to displease any party. This critical aspect of the arbitration process—that parties select their own private judge—is a primary reason why Hays condemned the process.

What then should the courts do under Judge Hays' approach? At the very least, they should review awards on the merits. Courts know a thing or two about contract interpretation, and their judgment should be respected in contract cases as it is elsewhere. This way the parties would receive a correct decision, according to Hays. The problem, of course, is that no decision would ever be final until after what could be years of litigation.

Hays also had ideas about how arbitrators could do their jobs better, in particular by using precedent. He did appreciate the fact that arbitrators do look to reported arbitration decisions and regularly cited other arbitrators' decisions in making their determinations. He thought, however, that arbitrators resisted the notion of using prior reported decisions as precedent because a system of binding precedent would lessen the need for additional arbitrator appointments!

Nothing could be farther from the truth. If the parties could agree on which precedent applied in any given case, they would have no need to call on the services of the neutral. The problem is not the absence of precedent, but the existence of a disagreement. Judge Hays did not appreciate the fact that the language found in many contracts is generally interpreted the same way by experienced neutrals. They may not call this precedent, but it has an equivalent influence.

In sum, Judge Hays relies on anecdotal rather than empirical evidence for his indictment of arbitration. He demonstrated disdain for any nonjudicial approaches to dispute resolution. He supported his arguments by proffering truly evil cases where arbitrators misstepped. He would have liked all arbitrators to have shared his own extraordinary background. Hays wanted arbitration to be purely voluntary without the judicial support it enjoyed. Courts would not act as rubber stamps. He suggested that courts set aside awards that were wrong or the product of corruption, fraud, or undue means. He saw arbitration hearings as potential anarchy, filled with surprise evidence and lacking in procedural fairness, with an arbitrator's decision rendered based on a record overflowing in irrelevant evidence.

Most importantly, Hays was convinced that there was a need for uniformity in arbitration procedures and outcomes. He would be pleased almost 50 years after his Yale lecture to find that the process has achieved on its own many of the outcomes he wanted. Shortcomings that Hays identified, however, have not proven to be fatal. Arbitrators wholly unfit for the job have been weeded out by the parties themselves. The process is not "vicious," as he claimed. Arbitrators are not incompetents as a general matter. Those who are better at the process are the busiest. The procedures they regularly follow are not intolerable.

Although Hays appears to be too harsh in his broad indictment of the process and the persons who serve as neutrals, his criticisms cannot be ignored or rebutted simply through self-praise. Other than the cursory review provided by the NAA when it votes to accept a candidate into membership who has issued the requisite number of awards, there is no systematic, nonpartisan evaluation of the performance of arbitrators.[28]

VI. An Arbitrator's Acceptability

It is very difficult to become a successful labor arbitrator. Although it is somewhat cumbersome to be admitted to the arbitrator rosters of the AAA and the FMCS, it is the easiest step in the process of actually becoming an arbitrator. Fully competent neutrals only become arbitrators when parties select them to serve in that capacity.

Those in the labor relations field refer to the critical characteristic of a neutral as his or her "acceptability." If either management or labor has objections to the appointment of a person as an arbitrator, he or she

---

[28] Selection of an arbitrator is discussed in more detail in Chapter 2.

lacks acceptability. A junior arbitrator just seeks a chance to prove that he or she has the "right stuff" to make it as a neutral.

1.   When rendering his or her decision, how concerned is a labor arbitrator about being appointed by one or both of the parties to hear subsequent cases?

Arbitrators understand that future appointments to hear grievance cases depend on their reputation as a neutral. It would be nonsense to suggest that a labor arbitrator does not think about future appointments when rendering a decision. The question is not whether these thoughts enter an arbitrator's mind, but whether they affect his or her decision.

Although parties may think that arbitrators purposefully issue split decisions, most arbitration cases are not so evenly divided. In clear cases, an arbitrator who decides the case against the side that presented a winning case only to enhance the chances of another appointment from the opposing party is acting foolishly as well as unethically. A party that wins a losing case, after a brief period of rejoicing, will realize that the arbitrator is unreliable. The next case may be a presumptive winner, and that neutral has already demonstrated his or her ability to ignore the merits.

In a truly evenly divided case, it is not impossible that a neutral will decide the case in favor of the large nationwide employer or the national union with many locals simply to win favor. If indeed the case could go either way, the parties need a resolution that only the arbitrator can provide. However, to consider factors extraneous to the merits in making an award in any case is simply intolerable.

2.   Does the arbitrator keep track of wins and losses for each party and try to make them balance over time?

Once again, it is possible that arbitrators do keep track of outcomes over time. Most arbitrations are ad hoc, however, meaning that the arbitrator will not preside over a long string of cases between the same parties. The exception is a permanent arbitrator or a member of a permanent panel. Appointed to resolve a broad spectrum of cases over a period of time, it is likely that some disputes would be decidedly pro-union and others pro-management. That need not be the case, however. If management regularly discharges employees and carefully follows announced policies and established procedures, it will likely prevail in arbitration. Deciding an occasional discharge case for the union in any instances where that would not be warranted may result in a swift departure from a permanent role as neutral.

3.　*Is an arbitrator concerned that if too many decisions go in favor of management that the arbitrator minimizes the chances of being selected by labor, and vice versa? Does someone keep score?*

An arbitrator who develops a reputation as being pro-management or pro-labor will not last long in the profession. That said, an arbitrator is not given a choice regarding the cases to which he or she is appointed. The arbitrator can, of course, turn down an appointment, but there is simply no way to know how a case is destined to turn out from the name of the employer or the union.

An arbitrator's reputation and acceptability should not be based on the outcome of one or a handful of decisions. Parties, especially parties that lose a case, can decide that they do not want to appoint the neutral to hear another case. There are many labor arbitrators from whom to select. On the other hand, deciding "too many" cases in favor of management or labor suggests that the arbitrator has sided with one side or the other even in the face of an overwhelming record supporting a contrary result.

An arbitrator should worry about whether he or she is serving the parties well. That includes not only considering the ultimate award in a case, but also the way a hearing is handled. Some arbitrators have been told by losing parties that they appreciated the way the neutral handled a case even though they did not prevail. Acceptability is a multi-factor construct.

4.　*What do arbitrators do to market themselves except write good decisions?*

Arbitrators generally do not "market" themselves. Writing good decisions and seeking the permission of the parties to submit those decisions for publication is one way arbitrators can demonstrate proficiency. Most arbitrators do most of their arbitrating in a particular geographic region. For those neutrals, being involved in local labor relations organizations, like the Labor and Employment Relations Association, offers arbitrators an opportunity to meet management and union people in a bipartisan setting. The next time the arbitrator's name appears on a list supplied by an appointing agency, these people will know who that arbitrator is.

VII. A Typical Grievance and Arbitration System

Every arbitration case is a little different. The parties' advocates bring different skills to the arbitration hearing. Every case has unique facts, although patterns emerge over time. We can offer a general overview of a typical grievance and arbitration process.

1. What is the role of the grievance procedure?

Before disputes are brought to arbitration, they are normally processed through grievance procedures that the parties establish in their CBA. A grievance procedure normally has three or more steps. It normally starts at the shop floor level, with a meeting between an aggrieved employee and a supervisor. Grievance procedures vary as to whether the union must be involved at this first step, but normally a shop steward participates. Most problems are resolved at this stage. If the employee or the union is not satisfied with the supervisor's response to the complaint, the matter can be brought to the next step. The complaint will likely have to be put in writing. A higher-level supervisor might be involved at this stage. Once again, management can simply deny the grievance, and the union may process the matter further to be heard by higher levels of management and union officials. If the dispute is not resolved through the grievance procedure—and most are—the union can decide whether to invoke arbitration and have the facts of the dispute heard by an outside neutral.

The grievance procedure is a glorious invention that provides an avenue of redress for workers. In the absence of any procedure, management decisions are not reviewable in an easy, fairly low-cost manner. During a grievance procedure, management can simply say no and allow the matter to be processed to a higher step. When it works well, a grievance procedure can be a source of industrial democracy, and it can help management keep aware of what happens on the shop floor.

The key for efficient management is to resolve grievances at the lowest level on the grievance pyramid. The procedure normally imposes time limits on the filing of complaints. Time limits are also set with regard to responding to grievances at each step. The CBA will provide when the grievance must be put in writing. Putting grievances in writing crystallizes the complaint so that it can be resolved. On the other hand, it does make the process more cumbersome to use for employees. However, it may also deter the filing of frivolous grievances. Management often insists that the grievance reference a particular contract article that was allegedly violated, but unions have avoided this trap by specifying in the grievance document some relevant contract clauses plus "all other applicable provisions."

Who should be able to bring the grievance? Should an individual employee be allowed to file on his or her own? Must the union representative sign off on the grievance before it is processed? These are choices the parties make during negotiations.

2.   *Please describe a typical labor arbitration.*[29]

When the parties appoint a neutral to hear a grievance dispute, they supply him or her with virtually no information about the case. Unlike a court proceeding, there are no pleadings in arbitration. At best, the neutral learns the names of the parties and their representatives and, perhaps, the general category of the case. Is it a discharge or discipline case? Is it a contract interpretation? Normally, the neutral must wait until the hearing to find out what the case is all about.

To address this lack of data, some arbitrators ask the parties to supply a copy of the grievance and the CBA. That strategy is only partially successful: The grievance often simply protests management's action in the most general terms, and the CBA may supply the nature of the company's business, but little more. Experienced arbitrators proceed without these documents and schedule a hearing. This part of the process is discussed in more detail in Chapter 2.

Upon arriving at the hearing room at the appointed time, the neutral begins two processes that are critical parts of the assignment: developing a cordial relationship with the parties and accumulating the information that he or she needs to resolve the dispute. Both are vital steps if the hearing is going to proceed efficiently and if the ultimate award will prove acceptable to the parties—even to the party that loses the case. For many parties—and even for some representatives of the parties—this may be their first introduction to arbitration. The arbitrator may serve as their teacher.

Even before commencing the hearing, the arbitrator might chat informally with those in attendance while awaiting the arrival of other participants. The discussion, of course, is not about the case, but about any small talk topic—baseball and football, if not the weather. It is

---

[29] *See* Roger Abrams, *The Integrity of the Arbitral Process*, 76 MICH. L. REV. 231 (1977).

critical that the parties appreciate who they have selected as their neutral. An arbitrator is not a judge wearing a black robe and sitting above the parties on the bench. The arbitrator is a decision-making specialist in labor relations who the parties chose to hear and decide their case.

Once the hearing begins, the arbitrator moves into fact-gathering mode. He or she is the only person in the room who knows nothing about the dispute. That is why in opening arguments advocates must first educate the neutral before beginning to persuade. One critical variable in arbitration cases is whether there is any conflict in the facts. In a contract interpretation case, the parties often agree that the basic facts are not in dispute—the only dispute is the proper meaning of contract language. That may also be the case in a discipline or discharge case, but it is more likely that there will be facts in controversy as well.

The minute the neutral learns the nature of the case, he or she begins the analytic process of deciding the dispute. This reality is contrary to the myth that arbitrators do not begin to decide a case until after the parties' briefs are filed months later and all arguments are completed. When the neutral learns that a case involves a discharge, he or she is already thinking about "just cause" and whether the alleged misconduct rises to a level that would warrant termination of employment. What did the grievant do? We spend time discussing discharge and discipline cases in Chapter 10.

In addition to accumulating factual data at the hearing both in testimony and in documents, the neutral also begins to form less tangible but equally important feelings about the parties and the witnesses. Does a witness' story make sense? Credibility is critical, and not only with regard to witnesses: Can the arbitrator trust what the advocate for a party is saying? Does it match up with the testimony presented under oath?

The parties typically present the arbitrator with sworn testimony from witnesses presented in a question-and-answer format. Direct examination of a witness is followed by cross-examination by the opposing party. That is normally followed by redirect examination and re-cross-examination until the advocates have exhausted their questions. The arbitrator keeps control over the process and keeps the parties moving forward. Advocates stay seated while asking questions, and the arbitrator will not allow the badgering of a witness.

Better arbitrators personally engage in the hearing process to clarify matters as they arise. One common impediment to the neutral's understanding is the use of jargon distinctive to that workplace. For example, government agencies use the numbers of forms as part of their lingua franca. The arbitrator must inquire what a term means the first time it is mentioned. On the other hand, the arbitrator must let the parties present their cases, even if he or she could do it better. The parties own the process—it does not belong to the neutral. Patience by the arbitrator is critical, followed in a timely manner by a question or two from the neutral.

The arbitrator must seek to decide a case accurately. That requires, in the first instance, that the arbitrator learn exactly what actually happened to give rise to the dispute, focusing on the evidence presented. Parties may have very different views as to what occurred. Memories fade, and sometimes, albeit rarely, witnesses will fabricate their stories to aid their side of the case.

Better arbitrators often share with the parties what they are learning about a dispute during the hearing to make sure they are accurately digesting the material presented. By the close of the hearing, the arbitrator should know everything he or she needs to make a decision. Although the parties are likely to want to submit briefs—and briefs can be valuable, as we will discuss later—the case is likely over. Arbitrators are unlikely to admit it, but typically the neutral knows with certainty how a case will come out when the hearing is over. In some rare situations an arbitrator will change his or her mind as an opinion takes shape and form, but, for the most part, the hearing is determinative.

3. If experienced arbitrators are as accomplished as Justice Douglas claims, does it really matter how good a party's advocate is?

Experienced arbitrators know enough about arbitration, collective bargaining, and the common law of the labor agreement to avoid being "hoodwinked" by an advocate. That does not mean that arbitrators do not make mistakes—they do, and every arbitrator has made mistakes. In any adjudicatory system where an arbitrator is expected to issue a comprehensive opinion with just a few days of work, mistakes are inevitable.

Even when arbitrators do their jobs well, a good advocate can make a substantial difference. First, a good advocate knows what information an experienced arbitrator needs, how that evidence can be presented in an orderly fashion, and how to make arguments that the arbitrator can use. A good advocate can avoid many of the mistakes that will be discussed in this text. A good advocate can also tip the scales in close cases.[30]

4. Does the individual grievant have rights in arbitration?

One fundamental premise of labor arbitration is that the process belongs to the employer and the union. Sometimes a dispute arises between the grievant and the union as to their respective roles. Unless the contract provides otherwise, it is the union that controls the grievance and arbitration process. The union can, consistent with its duty of fair representation, decide not to bring a dispute to arbitration or to cut short the process.

By comparison, in employment arbitration, where there is no union, the employee has control over the process when he or she represents himself or herself. The problem, as discussed in Chapter 17, is that the employee may not have the resources to hire an attorney to present the case. In labor arbitration, there may be some rough parity between the parties in terms of financial resources—a parity that may not exist in employment arbitration.

Many contract interpretation cases involve conflicts between employees, for example, when a junior employee receives a promotion and a grievance is filed by a more senior employee who also applied for the job. If the grievant prevails in arbitration, the job belongs to him or her and not to the junior employee. Normally management returns the junior employee to his or her prior position. The junior employee is not even present at the arbitration.

A union takes a matter to arbitration to defend rights that it negotiated for all employees in the CBA. In the process, it may side with one worker over another. For example, the union commonly negotiates clauses that benefit senior employees over junior employees. That is the union's responsibility—to make choices—and, as long as it does so in a reasonable and not arbitrary fashion, its decisions must stand.

---

[30] A comprehensive discussion of how an advocate should go about his or her job is beyond the scope of this book, but that type of information and the topics discussed here should obviously be coordinated. There are some fine sources of advice specific to advocates and representatives. Among the best is *How to Prepare and Present a Labor Arbitration Case* by Charles S. Loughran, now in its second edition. Loughran's book covers many, but not all, of the issues addressed here, but it also adds insight based on the author's years as a practitioner of arbitration before he became a neutral. His chapter on exploring settlement addresses a topic not explored here because arbitrators rarely have any involvement in that process. At the same time, Loughran's book does not cover how an arbitrator drafts an opinion, something parties are not directly involved in. *See* CHARLES S. LOUGHRAN, HOW TO PREPARE AND PRESENT A LABOR ARBITRATION CASE (2d ed. 2006).

VIII. ARBITRATION IN CONTEXT

Arbitration is just one forum where labor and management interact. It is important to see the process in context in order to understand the important role it plays in labor-management relations.

1. How do negotiations and arbitration interrelate? [31]

Collective bargaining is a process that creates many of the rules of the workplace. Management normally retains the right to make determinations on operations, but that prerogative can be limited through negotiations. Whether by design or by happenstance, every business has an industrial relations system, as Professor John Dunlop wrote more than half a century ago.[32] Each workplace has a technological context as well as market and budgetary constraints. In order to operate, management must employ workers to assist in production while complying with an employer's standards of conduct. Each of these operational and labor relations contexts is dynamic. They change over time. The actors within the industrial relations system represent both parties: managers and their hierarchy as well as workers and their hierarchy. They establish a system of rules through their interaction within the limits set by legal constraints.

The labor arbitration and collective bargaining processes might be compared to a marriage. The parties formally enter into a collective relationship. Negotiations are not a one-time-only event; the parties continue to live together, at least during working hours. When foreseeable disputes arise, the parties have provided for a system within which to resolve them. Arbitration is a continuation of the collective bargaining process—it is designed to fill in the inevitable gaps that the parties leave in the CBA in a manner consistent with what they have agreed to and with their previous practice.

In fact, collective bargaining and labor arbitration might be seen as family meetings, albeit at times dysfunctional, as are some families. Personalities often control over legal constraints—they are part of a very human process.

Parties have to understand the relationship between collective bargaining and the grievances that arise during the term of the agreement. Although it is clearly foreseeable that some disputes will arise, it is not foreseeable exactly what issues will be raised. The ambiguities in

---

[31] *See* Roger Abrams, *Negotiating in Anticipation of Arbitration: Some Guideposts for the Initiated*, 29 CASE W. RES. L. REV. 428 (1979).

[32] JOHN DUNLOP, INDUSTRIAL RELATIONS SYSTEMS (1958).

CBAs—and some ambiguities are inevitable and, at times, purpose-ful—will find their way to arbitration. The arbitrator will clarify what the parties have written, and if the result does not meet the needs of the parties, they can negotiate around the awards. Although it is but a goal, parties should attempt to bargain in anticipation of arbitration and seek clarity in draftsmanship, as far as that is humanly possible.

2. How is arbitration different from court adjudication?

The arbitration process is a cousin of court adjudication, but no one should confuse the two processes. Although lawyers are involved in both procedures, the skills needed to achieve success differ in the two forums. The tone and character of the advocacy in each forum is different, and the rules differ, as does the nature of the adjudicators.

A court applies public law established by federal and state statutes or constitutions or on a case-by-case basis under the common law. Parties to a CBA are bound by public law, but by negotiation they create their own private law to operate within the workplace. They even create their own court system—arbitration—with the expectation that the neutrals they select as their arbitrators will apply their law to disputes that arise during the terms of their CBAs.

There are significant differences between labor arbitration and court adjudication. First, the parties to the arbitration dispute select their adjudicator, and that does not happen in court. (It is true that parties in court may attempt to find a favorable venue by filing suit in one jurisdiction or another, but judges are assigned at random.) Self-selection of the decision maker generally enhances the legitimacy of the arbitration process.

Second, arbitration is normally final and binding, and court adju-dication is not until the parties reach the court of final resort. That does not mean that a losing party cannot contest an arbitration award, but the grounds for setting awards aside are quite narrow under U.S. Supreme Court precedent. Trial court decisions are always subject to appellate review. This means that prevailing in arbitration is critical, because there is no review on the merits.

Third, normally the procedure in arbitration is informal, albeit orderly. Courts are formal and always quite orderly. Disruption in a courtroom can lead to a contempt citation, whereas misbehavior before an arbitrator might lead, at worst, to a scolding by the neutral out in the hallway. The norm in arbitration is not to abide by the strict rules of evidence; the contrary is the case in courts. As a result, the arbitration setting feels more comfortable to working men and women.

Fourth, arbitration differs from court adjudication because normally those involved at the arbitration hearing will go to work with one another the following day. Court adjudication normally involves people who will go their separate ways after the trial. This difference will prove important—winning a case in arbitration without the exercise of restraint may taint the workplace, causing problems that make victory quite expensive.

These distinctive characteristics of labor arbitration may not be present in nonunion employment arbitration. Most of the employment cases involve persons who are no longer employed, and the dispute rarely involves whether they can return to their jobs. After the close of the employment arbitration hearing, the parties may never see each other again, depending on the arbitrator's ruling. In that regard, it is much more akin to court litigation. Employment arbitration can be as informal as labor arbitration, but it is likely to be much more court-like, especially if the neutral is a former judge. In Chapter 17, we discuss the distinctive issues regarding the selection of the neutral, the conduct of the employment arbitration proceeding, and the enforceability of employment arbitration awards.

3.   Why is arbitration preferable to litigation?

Arbitration enjoys advantages over other means of resolving disputes. It is certainly speedier than court litigation, although no one would rightfully characterize arbitration as expeditious in itself. The most recent figures compiled by the FMCS show that the grievance and arbitration processes normally take at least a year to resolve a dispute.[33] That is still much shorter than the multi-year judicial process.

Arbitration is also cheaper than litigation, although arbitration is not free. In addition to the cost of the neutral's time, both to hear the case and write an award, parties normally have to pay for their advocates and even a court reporter for the most important matters.

Although Justice William O. Douglas might have been willing to call an arbitrator an "expert," it is preferable to refer to the neutral as a "specialist" in the field. The experienced arbitrator brings to an unresolved dispute an abundance of knowledge about what parties to a collective relationship normally mean when they use certain terms in

---

[33] For fiscal year 2012, the FMCS reports an average of 306 days between the time the parties request a panel of arbitrators from the agency and the issuance of the award. In addition, an average of 139 days passes between the filing of a grievance and the request for an FMCS panel. FMCS statistics are available at www.fmcs.gov.

CBAs or when they behave toward each other in a certain way over time. The experienced arbitrator has a good sense what the parties normally mean when they limit management's right to discipline or discharge an employee to situations where the employer has "just cause." The labor arbitrator will fill in the gaps, and the parties can always modify the ruling through negotiations.

IX. THE ROLE OF A GOOD ARBITRATOR

Parties may have different ideas of what makes a good arbitrator. An advocate who is comfortable in a court setting may prefer a legalistic arbitrator who conducts a proceeding as a judge would. Other advocates might prefer an arbitrator who will give the parties substantial leeway in presenting their cases. One would think that a good arbitrator could do a little of both at a hearing.

Parties will agree, however, that an arbitrator must afford both parties a full opportunity to present their evidence and make their arguments. Although one party will not prevail in the proceeding, as long as its advocate had a fair opportunity to make the case, the outcome is likely to be acceptable.

1. What are the requirements of good arbitrating?

In 1951, the NAA, the AAA, and the FMCS jointly drafted the Code of Professional Responsibility for Arbitrators of Labor-Management Disputes.[34] Substantially revised in 1972 and again in 2007, the Code sets forth the principles of good arbitrating.

The Code of Professional Responsibility provides that an arbitrator must possess honesty, integrity, impartiality, and competence. One could not imagine a successful neutral who does not possess these qualities. He or she must protect the process from those who would undermine it, ensure that both parties have a fair opportunity to present their evidence and arguments, and render a decision that is generally consistent with the expectations of the parties.

An arbitrator must possess other qualities not mentioned in the Code. A successful arbitrator must have courage. The parties select a

---

[34]NATIONAL ACADEMY OF ARBITRATORS, AMERICAN ARBITRATION ASSOCIATION, & FEDERAL MEDIATION & CONCILIATION SERVICE, CODE OF PROFESSIONAL RESPONSIBILITY FOR ARBITRATORS OF LABOR-MANAGEMENT DISPUTES (as amended and in effect Sept. 2007), *available at* http://www.naarb.org/code.html (reproduced in Appendix B).

neutral because they want his or her decision, and that decision could make one party quite upset. The neutral cannot make everyone happy and must be willing to accept the consequences of that reality.

An arbitrator must exhibit an openness to the parties and the process. Whereas a judge sweeps into the courtroom adorned in a black robe just before the proceeding begins, the better neutral arbitrators arrive at the hearing room long before the hearing commences and introduces himself or herself to the parties and others in attendance. Reticent neutrals may not last long.

An arbitrator must have good work habits and be prompt in issuing awards. The parties' most common complaint about neutrals is that they take too long to issue their awards. Delays of many months or even a year in issuing an award are simply unacceptable. Similarly, labor arbitrators must provide the parties with a reasoned decision that resolves their dispute. Although it may be true that parties turn first to that last page of the opinion to find out who won, it is critical that the parties understand how the neutral reached that decision.

Finally, an arbitrator must be balanced in his or her conduct at the hearing. Showing partiality, even in the face of obnoxious conduct by one party, is also unacceptable conduct by the neutral. Moreover, the hearing must be productive. The arbitrator must be able to collect enough information at the hearing to decide the case and make an intelligent disposition.

2. Do arbitrators meet this norm? If not, how can the quality of neutrals be improved?

For the most part, the 300 or so arbitrators who hear most arbitration cases do meet this high standard. They are elected members of the NAA. They provide the parties with a hearing that meets the norms of due process, and they render informed and intelligible decisions in a relatively prompt fashion.

The practice of labor arbitration would benefit from increasing the number of better trained and more diligent arbitrators. Parties continue to appoint the same arbitrators to hear and resolve disputes because they think those neutrals are the best available. Some would argue that, because these arbitrators have met the "test of the marketplace," the system works reasonably well. However, if there were more arbitrators who were trained to meet this high standard, that would reduce the delays that are part of the present system while not substantially reducing the caseload of the current core of neutrals who hear most of the disputes.

Chapter 2

Selecting a Labor Arbitrator

I. OVERVIEW

In a paper delivered at the 1962 National Academy of Arbitrators (NAA) annual meeting on how arbitrators decide cases, Arbitrator Peter Seitz said: "Arbitrators differ as much as race horses, concert fiddlers, and proctologists."[1] Seitz was correct in his characterization of arbitrators as different from one another. They each have their own style.

Some administer a labor arbitration hearing as if it were a court; others are more attuned to the informality that distinguishes the arbitration process. Although it is likely that most experienced labor arbitrators will ultimately decide the same case the same way, they differ substantially in how they conduct and control a hearing. Some labor arbitrators emulate the demeanor of trial judges; others see themselves as avuncular workplace professionals. Others may play the role of teachers at an arbitration, and still others sit back and let the parties present their cases without interruption or questions. Some combine these characteristics, conducting a labor arbitration with an ordered informality that

---

[1] Peter Seitz, *How Arbitrators Decide Cases: A Study in Black Magic,* in COLLECTIVE BARGAINING AND THE ARBITRATOR'S ROLE: PROCEEDINGS OF THE 15TH ANNUAL MEETING, NATIONAL ACADEMY OF ARBITRATORS 159 (Mark L. Kahn, ed., 1962).

provides a comfortable setting for the parties to present to the arbitrator the evidence in their cases.

Some arbitrators write long and learned decisions, providing much more than the parties either want or need. Others provide the parties with an award long on facts but short on reasoning. Still others write opinions that demonstrate that they paid attention to the evidence and arguments presented and then reasoned to a judgment about the dispute. With this preferred approach, the parties receive what they wanted—arbitration, although they may not agree that the arbitrator's ultimate conclusion was correct.

Arbitrator Seitz's witty comment ignores a critical fact about labor arbitration that distinguishes it from court litigation. The parties to the dispute have the right to choose their neutral, and they give that arbitrator virtually unreviewable power to resolve their dispute. Arbitration decisions are normally final and binding with no review on the merits. In a court, by comparison, parties to an adjudication do not select their decision makers, and trial court decisions are subject to appeal. Thus, who the parties select as their labor arbitrator is vitally important. How the parties should make that selection is the subject of this chapter.

II. Picking Your Labor Arbitrator

Choosing an arbitrator may be the most important step the parties take in the arbitration process. If parties select the wrong person to serve as the neutral, the hearing may be a virtual nightmare, and the resulting award may be delayed for months. When the arbitrator's decision finally arrives, it may be devoid of reasoning and fail to adequately resolve the dispute.

On the other hand, selecting a better arbitrator will mean that the hearing will be a useful process, even if it does not ultimately result in a victory for your side. A good labor arbitrator will keep the process moving along and under control. He or she will positively engage in the proceeding and ask questions to clarify issues that arise in his or her mind. The resulting award will be issued in a timely fashion and will explain the basis for the decision.

Parties can choose their neutral, but it is often difficult to get enough information to make the right selection. Parties cannot always pick the perfect labor arbitrator, but they can avoid choosing someone who will ill-serve their needs.

1. Who are these labor arbitrators?

In the not-too-distant past, virtually all labor arbitrators were very senior, white men. The average age of arbitrators remains in the mid 60s. Some arbitrators continue to hear cases well into their 80s. Today, a significant portion of the corps of arbitrators is made up of women and persons of color, a diversity that better reflects the American workforce.

There are thousands of professionals who hold themselves out as capable of hearing and deciding arbitration cases. The most telling statistic about these arbitrators is that most of them are rarely appointed to hear a case. Ninety percent of all labor arbitration cases are heard by about 300 arbitrators.[2] Most arbitrators are attorneys, but not all. Some have a business or union background and serve ably as neutrals in most cases. Most arbitrators are full-time neutrals, and some are part-time arbitrators who also hold academic appointments in law or business schools.

2. Don't each of the parties just select an arbitrator because the party thinks that person will decide the case in its favor?

We can say with some certainty that a party does not choose an arbitrator who it thinks will decide the dispute against its side. Of course, each party would want an arbitrator who would be predisposed to its side's arguments: management would want a pro-management arbitrator, and the union would want a pro-union arbitrator. They obviously are not talking about the same person. It is rare to find an arbitrator who holds such partisan favor with both labor and management.

In fact, if someone actually were pro-management or pro-union, he or she would not last long as a neutral. What each party truly seeks is a neutral who will listen to the evidence and the arguments and then render a decision consistent with the record and the collective bargaining agreement (CBA). Rather than being predisposed to one side or the other, the perfect arbitrator is someone who will listen and learn. As we shall explore below, as part of the typical selection process, parties should be able to remove from consideration persons who they believe—correctly or incorrectly—are partisan against them.

---

[2] Don A. Banta, *Arbitrator Selection: A Management View,* in LABOR ARBITRATION: A PRACTICAL GUIDE FOR ADVOCATES 93 (Max Zimny, William Dolson, & Christopher Barreca, eds., 1990). *See* CHARLES S. LOUGHRAN, HOW TO PREPARE AND PRESENT A LABOR ARBITRATION CASE 67–94 (2d ed. 2006) (discussion on selecting an arbitrator and arranging the hearing).

3. Why select someone to serve as arbitrator who you are not confident will decide the case in your favor?

As just explained, under the typical selection process it is virtually impossible to select someone who you are sure will decide the dispute in your favor. If you are so certain that a neutral will decide for you, the opposing party is likely to be just as certain of the opposite conclusion. On the other hand, it is possible for both parties to believe that the neutral they jointly select will listen to the case they present and render an award consistent with the evidence and the arguments made.

Winning and losing is only one of the reasons parties select a particular neutral. In fact, an attitude of "win at all costs" can be quite shortsighted because of the lingering impact of the arbitration procedure on the workplace. One critical circumstance that distinguishes labor arbitration from court adjudication and employment arbitration is that the individuals involved in the labor arbitration—except for the arbitrator, a discharged employee, and likely the advocates—will be working with one another the next day and beyond. Court cases involve parties that only met at the scene of the car accident or when they negotiated a commercial contract under dispute. After their case is over, they will have nothing further to do with one another. The same is likely true for an employment arbitration case. A labor arbitration, on the other hand, involves people from the workplace who will arrive for the 7 a.m. shift tomorrow morning. Justice William O. Douglas, in the *Steelworkers Trilogy*,[3] spoke about the labor arbitrator's knowledge about productivity and morale being part of the decision-making process. More to the point, an arbitrator can do harm to the productivity and morale of the workplace by the way the hearing is conducted.

In most instances, the merits of the dispute will determine the outcome of a case. The labor arbitration process, however, is also an important event in the continuing relationship between management and the union that represents its employees. Selecting the right arbitrator can enhance the positive impact of that process. The parties' choice of a neutral will determine the quality of the arbitration experience, win or lose. For management, a successful arbitration experience can ease tensions in the workplace. For labor, pursuing arbitration can demonstrate to the membership how well the union can serve their interests. Parties benefit (or suffer) from arbitration in a variety of ways.

---

[3] Steelworkers v. American Mfg. Co., 363 U.S. 564 (1960); Steelworkers v. Warrior & Gulf Navig. Co., 363 U.S. 574 (1960); Steelworkers v. Enterprise Wheel & Car Corp., 363 U.S. 593 (1960). See the discussion of Justice Douglas' *Steelworkers Trilogy* analysis in Chapter 1, §V. The *Steelworkers Trilogy* decisions are reproduced in Appendix A.

4. How does the typical labor arbitrator selection process operate?[4]

The parties to a CBA normally address in their arbitration provision how they will select their neutral. Normally, they will specify that the party seeking arbitration—almost always the union—should file with the American Arbitration Association (AAA) or the Federal Mediation and Conciliation Service (FMCS) and request a panel of labor arbitrators. Both of these appointing agencies maintain rosters of labor arbitrators, some with decades of experience and others who are fairly new to the profession. Arbitrators on the rosters complete a form indicating their experience, education, and fees.[5] The parties can request that the appointing agency only submit to them the names of labor arbitrators who live in their state or who have certain qualifications, such as a law degree or special abilities in engineering.

The appointing agencies select at random the names of seven neutrals and transmit the list with the arbitrators' biographies to the parties. Unless the parties have specified in their agreement how the actual selection will be made, the appointing agencies suggest the following methods. Under the FMCS system, parties generally alternately strike the names of unacceptable candidates. The candidate who is left after the others are stricken is then appointed the arbitrator by the agency. Under the AAA system, each party strikes the names of unacceptable arbitrators from the list and then rank orders the remaining names. The AAA tribunal administrator then compares the two lists and appoints as the arbitrator the acceptable person with the highest mutual rank. If none of the names listed by the appointing agencies is mutually acceptable, the agencies will supply a second list.

Parties will strike a name from a panel for a variety of reasons. Previous negative experience with the neutral will have the greatest impact on the decision to strike a name. Although one might think that experienced and talented arbitrators would be each party's first choice, some advocates are concerned about bringing what they fear is a losing case to a star arbitrator. They will (and should) likely lose. Before a less experienced neutral, the party may have a chance to prevail.

Under a system of alternate striking, the party that makes the last strike in effect chooses the arbitrator. It may be that the other party is satisfied with the choice because the truly unacceptable neutrals were

---

[4]*See* Fairweather's Practice and Procedure in Labor Arbitration 89–116 (Ray J. Schoonhoven, ed., 4th ed. 1999) (discussing the procedures for selecting an arbitrator).

[5]For a sample form, *see* Loughran, *supra* note 2, at 77–78.

dispatched earlier in the selection process. In any case, it is preferable to choose second and not first. The parties' agreement may provide a method for determining which party strikes first. For example, the parties may flip a coin, and the winner strikes second.

As we can see, although the parties select their arbitrator, under these systems the arbitrator appointed is actually the least offensive choice among the persons on the list. That is hardly a ringing endorsement. Alternately, the representatives of the parties may review the list together and agree on one of the persons on the list to be their arbitrator. The arbitrator never knows why he or she has been selected. Every appointed arbitrator likes to think that he or she was the first choice of both parties.

5.   *What are the characteristics of a good labor arbitrator?*

A good labor arbitrator is someone who knows the common law of the labor agreement, can administer a fair hearing consistent with due process, and resolve the dispute in a timely manner through an opinion that is well written and reasoned.[6] That is what the parties want and can expect, but how do they get there?

The two major appointing agencies, the AAA and the FMCS, supply the parties with biographical sketches of the neutrals whose names they propose to the parties. Most labor arbitrators, but certainly not all, will have a law degree. Others generally will hold a business degree or an advanced degree in economics. Still others may come directly from the labor relations community with years of service either for employers or unions. Selecting the best arbitrator from this scant data regarding background and work experience is difficult. Formal credentials may be a proxy for ability and expertise, but they do not necessarily tell you much about an arbitrator's performance.

At times, the best choice from among the available neutrals might depend on the nature of the grievance dispute in question. A complicated technical case involving statistics and calculations would benefit from an arbitrator who has skills to work with that data. A simple discipline case, however, does not require selection of an arbitrator with an advanced degree in economics or nanotechnology. It might not even require a very experienced neutral. Parties should select an arbitrator

---

[6]Regarding the selection of arbitrators from the union's viewpoint, one commentator emphasizes two criteria: objectivity and competence. Ira R. Mizner, *Arbitrator Selection: A Union View,* in LABOR ARBITRATION: A PRACTICAL GUIDE FOR ADVOCATES 99–103 (Max Zimny, William Dolson, & and Christopher Barreca, eds., 1990).

with legal training to hear a complicated public sector arbitration case involving the potential intersection of various contract provisions and statutes, regulations, and other administrative documents. Although experienced nonlawyer neutrals do work their way through a maze of legalisms, an inexperienced nonlawyer arbitrator may find it more difficult to accomplish the tasks that will be required.

In general, a good arbitrator will be able to quickly learn what the parties will teach him or her about the subject matter of the dispute. The neutral may never have actually built a jet plane but in fairly short order will learn enough about the C-130 to resolve a dispute about job assignments on the aircraft. Admittedly, this shallow expertise in esoteric fields will not be sufficient to trust the neutral to design a new jet engine, but an aeronautical engineer would not likely be able to apply a seniority provision in a promotion case.

The cases that parties present to arbitrators arise in different industries and fields as varied as a shipyard and a university. Although the settings differ, the labor relations issues do not. Holiday pay, vacations, wage rates, and layoff disputes do not depend on the nature of what the employer does. The parties are not hiring a plumber—they are appointing an experienced specialist in labor arbitration.

Formal credentials, such as membership in the NAA, may be relevant and may be all the parties have, but there are more important abilities that should be kept in mind and, if possible, discovered before a party makes a choice among arbitrators. The Code of Professional Responsibility speaks to the "essential personal qualifications" of an arbitrator.[7] A complete dossier on a neutral would talk about the arbitrator's "honesty, integrity, impartiality and general competence in labor relations matters."[8] Equally important are the arbitrator's interpersonal skills, which will be demonstrated at the hearing. Similarly, a good arbitrator must appear to the parties to genuinely care about the dispute they have asked the neutral to resolve. Regretfully, all of this essential information is not easily obtained. None of these qualities requires a law degree or an advanced degree from an Ivy League school. An arbitrator must have "good judgment," according to the Code.[9] Assessing these qualities is a significant challenge.

---

[7]NATIONAL ACADEMY OF ARBITRATORS, AMERICAN ARBITRATION ASSOCIATION, & FEDERAL MEDIATION & CONCILIATION SERVICE, CODE OF PROFESSIONAL RESPONSIBILITY FOR ARBITRATORS OF LABOR-MANAGEMENT DISPUTES §1.A.1 (as amended and in effect Sept. 2007), *available at* http://www.naarb.org/code.html (reproduced in Appendix B).
[8]*Id.*
[9]*Id.*

III. THE APPOINTING AGENCIES

Many parties use the services of the two major appointing agencies in the selection of their labor arbitrator for a particular case. These so-called "ad hoc" arbitrators hear one dispute. If the parties like the arbitrator's work, they can select him or her directly to resolve future disputes. By one estimate, however, over 40 percent of the parties do not use an appointing agency in the selection of their arbitrators.[10]

The American Arbitration Association (AAA) is a private, non-profit organization committed to dispute resolution in all fields, including workplace disputes.[11] Within the AAA's regional offices, tribunal administrators will serve parties by providing names of both labor and employment arbitrators, appointing the neutrals they select and administering the proceeding. In some parts of the country, such as New England, the AAA is the predominant labor arbitration appointing agency. In most areas, however, the Federal Mediation and Conciliation Service (FMCS) is the preferred agency.[12] A small and efficient office in the federal government, FMCS provides lists of experienced labor arbitrators to disputing parties. Once the parties select their labor neutral, the FMCS is no longer involved in the proceeding. FMCS also employs full-time labor mediators, providing services to parties in both the public and private sector regarding collective bargaining and grievance disputes.

1.   Why would the parties designate in their collective bargaining agreement the selection of arbitrators through the AAA or the FMCS? Why would they choose one agency and not the other?

The AAA roster contains the names of thousands of arbitrators, many of whom have not heard many cases. Hundreds of those arbitrators have not received an appointment in years. By comparison, the FMCS roster contains the names of far fewer arbitrators, all of whom have at least heard arbitrations. Virtually everyone on the FMCS roster is also on the AAA roster.

The AAA and the FMCS see their roles quite differently, and that has an impact on the parties and the proceeding. The AAA administers the entire arbitration process. A "tribunal administrator" handles each case. He or she transmits the panel of names to the parties and receives

---

[10] DENNIS NOLAN, LABOR AND EMPLOYMENT ARBITRATION IN A NUTSHELL 33 (2007).
[11] *See* AMERICAN ARBITRATION ASSOCIATION, www.adr.org.
[12] *See* FEDERAL MEDIATION & CONCILIATION SERVICE, www.fmcs.gov.

their responses. The administrator then contacts the selected arbitrator, obtains possible dates for a hearing from the neutral, sends out notices to the parties and the arbitrator confirming the date and the place of the hearing, and ultimately exchanges the briefs and issues the award received from the arbitrator. Parties new to arbitration may find this hands-on system to be more comfortable.

The AAA administers alternative dispute resolution (ADR) systems in a variety of fields—from commercial arbitration to international arbitration to construction disputes. Although it is particularly prominent in the labor field in some geographic regions, it is not the preferred choice of experienced parties throughout much of the country for selecting a labor arbitrator.

By comparison, the FMCS focuses only on labor disputes. It is an efficient federal agency that also employs full-time government mediators who are available to help parties reach agreements on bargaining disputes in key industries and in the public sector. Once the parties select their labor arbitrator, the FMCS notifies the neutral. He or she contacts the parties and arranges for the hearing; after that point the agency is no longer involved in the process. For parties that are experienced in the arbitration process, the FMCS would seem a better option for selecting an arbitrator.

2.   *Are FMCS arbitrators better than AAA arbitrators?*

The AAA roster is much larger than the FMCS roster. Because of the substantial overlaps of the rosters, virtually all arbitrators on the FMCS list are also on the AAA list. There are great arbitrators on the AAA roster who are not yet listed by the FMCS, but it is difficult to determine who they are. There are also arbitrators on the FMCS roster who, for one reason or another, will not serve the parties well. It is hard to generalize, but parties seem to prefer using the FMCS in most regions, perhaps because they find the AAA hands-on process to be unnecessary and cumbersome.

IV. RESEARCHING ARBITRATORS

1.   *How do you know whether a person will be a good arbitrator?*

An arbitrator's biography can only tell you so much. What schools did the neutral attend? What jobs did the neutral hold? In what industries has the neutral arbitrated? What kinds of issues has the neutral resolved? Is he or she a member of the NAA? You might be able to infer from the biography how old the arbitrator is. The biography does give you information about the breadth of the neutral's experience, but it does not tell you whether the arbitrator resolved the cases correctly, how the arbitrator conducts a hearing, or how timely the arbitrator's awards have been. A party needs more information.

Researching arbitrators can present a substantial challenge to a practitioner. Management can purchase the Simpson sheets—the "Arbitrators Qualifications Reports" with data compiled by R.C. Simpson, Inc.[13]—but they may not be reliable predictors of success in arbitration. In addition to biographical information, the sheets present information about how many cases the arbitrator has decided for management and how many for labor. This information is worthless without knowing more about the facts of the cases where the arbitrator ruled. The sheets also contain the subjective evaluations offered by management advocates, who are likely to praise arbitrators who issued decisions in their favor and castigate those who did not.

Unions, typically at the international level, accumulate data on arbitrator performance, and local unions may have access to this information. Reading published opinions written by a neutral can give you a good idea of how his or her mind works, but only a very small percentage of arbitration cases are even submitted for publication. Some arbitrators never submit their decisions for publication. Reading the published arbitration decisions that are available can offer a party insight into how an arbitrator goes about expressing a judgment in writing.

Perhaps the best source of information in the labor or management community is word of mouth from those who have tried cases before the particular neutral. Seeking input from colleagues in the field may be useful, although it may also reflect a bias borne of having won or lost a case before a particular neutral.

This means that the parties may be left with subjective evaluations and unreliable information in making their choices. The best that can be accomplished in the selection process is eliminating the names of those neutrals that a party knows will not serve well and trying to piece together enough information to end up with an acceptable neutral.

2.   *Should an arbitrator make available to the parties copies of his or her prior unpublished decisions for purposes of aiding in the selection of a neutral?*

Unpublished arbitration decisions are private. On the other hand, in the absence of firsthand knowledge about the neutral, they are the best evidence of how an arbitrator goes about his or her job, other than

---

[13] *See* R.C. SIMPSON, INC., www.rcsimpson.com.

an in-depth interview, which few parties are willing to pursue outside of the process of appointing a permanent umpire. Upon request, however, an arbitrator should make available to requesting parties prior unpublished decisions with all identifying information redacted.

3. What is the benefit of selecting an experienced arbitrator?

An experienced arbitrator knows the common law of the labor agreement or at least knows where and how to find it. When he or she finds out the nature of the dispute at the start of the hearing through opening statements, the arbitrator is ready to learn about the presence or absence of key facts the neutral knows will be relevant and essential in resolving the dispute. After about two decades, a fully acceptable and experienced arbitrator will have heard cases in just about every unionized industry. Thus, selecting an experienced neutral allows the parties to choose someone who has likely heard a case in the particular industry in the past—a useful criterion, but not absolutely essential.

An experienced arbitrator knows how to gather information through the hearing process. A junior arbitrator may not yet have the grounding in the broad spectrum of potential labor disputes to make the best use of the hearing. With time, junior arbitrators become experienced arbitrators if they demonstrate an ability to conduct a hearing and issue timely and thoughtful awards.

4. Are all arbitrators truly neutral?

It is impossible to vouch for the neutrality of all arbitrators, although experienced neutrals who are elected members of the NAA have passed the test of acceptability. It is difficult to survive as an arbitrator unless the selecting parties believe the adjudicator is neutral.

Arbitrators come to the profession from very different backgrounds. If they are lawyers who practiced labor relations, they almost always represented either employers or unions. Although a few individuals are able to practice on both sides, that is the exception rather than the rule. Others came from union or management positions. In order to be placed on the rosters of an appointing agency, they need to establish their neutrality. That usually is done by having advocates on the other side vouch that they can decide a case without bias. The parties will make the ultimate judgment as to whether the arbitrators are, in fact, neutral.

Neutrality does not mean that an arbitrator decides half the cases for management and half for the union. The arbitrator has no control over the cases the parties appoint him or her to decide. It could be that

the distribution of appointments favored the union side or the management side. In that case, an arbitrator who would divide the outcomes
evenly would not really be neutral.

Neutrality also does not mean that an arbitrator does not hold distinct views about the common law of the labor agreement. Management
manages; employees are entitled to due process and the benefits of the
deal negotiated in collective bargaining. There are limitations on management's discretion contained in and implied by the CBA and based
on prior practice. These principles are not biased. They are neutral,
because the parties over the years have made them an inherent part of
their arrangement.

V. ALTERNATIVE SYSTEMS OF ARBITRATION SELECTION

The most common form of arbitrator selection discussed earlier
involves the selection by the parties of an arbitrator for a particular
case—an ad hoc selection. Obviously, the transaction costs of starting
with a new list of neutrals for each case can be high. In addition, the
parties may not know very much about the persons on the lists.

1.   *Are there other ways for parties to select their arbitrator?*

Parties can design whatever arbitration system they wish, although
the norm is to use an ad hoc single neutral selected through one of the
appointing agencies. However, there are downsides to using this default
process. Selecting an ad hoc arbitrator for a particular case takes time.
The neutral ultimately selected may not be familiar with the parties' industry and so will have a steep learning curve at the hearing. As a practical matter, the parties may be stuck with selecting one of the names on
the first or second panel submitted by the appointing agency, and none
of those arbitrators may be completely acceptable to the parties.

One alternative that labor and management have used since the
1930s is to select one person as the parties' permanent arbitrator, sometimes called an *umpire,* who will serve either for a certain period of
time or for the duration of the CBA. The arbitration clause in their
CBA likely contains a provision about either party removing the permanent arbitrator. The obvious advantage is that the permanent arbitrator knows the parties and is acceptable to both sides. The downside
is that the arbitrator may know too much about the parties and begin
to think that his or her role is not simply to adjudicate disputes but to
guide the parties toward a more productive relationship.

Many parties that have a full docket of arbitration cases use a variation of the permanent arbitrator scheme: They agree to appoint a panel of permanent arbitrators who they then appoint in rotation as cases arise. The contractual description of their system often states that, to be appointed, the arbitrator must be able to hold a hearing within a certain period of time. If that is not possible, the parties move on to the next name on the list. This system also provides for a method for either party to remove an arbitrator from the panel. The advantage of the panel system is that it substantially reduces the time needed to appoint an arbitrator and all the neutrals on the panel are familiar with the particular workplace.

The permanent panel approach has great advantages. These arbitrators get to know the nature of the work performed, and they learn the jargon and the methods of operation. At the same time, the parties learn the work habits and the decision-making approaches of the members of a panel. Using a panel may allow the parties to avoid the downsides of using a single arbitrator, who may hold too much power in a collective relationship.

2.   *What about tripartite boards? What do arbitrators think about serving in those systems?*

Some CBAs provide for a tripartite board of arbitration to hear unresolved grievances. One partisan arbitrator is appointed by management, a second is appointed by the union, and a neutral arbitrator who serves as chair of the board is selected by both parties. The neutral arbitrator runs the hearing and decides the dispute in an opinion and award in which one of the two partisan arbitrators joins. Normally, partisan arbitrators do not participate in asking questions at the hearing, although that can vary by workplace.

Subsequent to the hearing, the tripartite board may have an executive session to discuss the dispute, but that is rare. Normally, the neutral arbitrator drafts the opinion and sends it to the partisan arbitrators, who might make suggestions as to changes or corrections. Normally, the partisan arbitrator who represents the side that wins the arbitration simply agrees to join the opinion; the other partisan arbitrator dissents, sometimes with an opinion that is drafted by the advocate for that party.

Sometimes single ad hoc arbitrators issue decisions that neither party likes. The purported advantage of a tripartite board is that the arbitrator issues an award that is at least acceptable to one party. There is also the extremely rare case when a tripartite board issues a unanimous decision, a singular triumph for the neutral.

Tripartite arbitration boards have significant disadvantages, however. The need to have the partisan arbitrators review (and possibly amend) the neutral's award delays the issuance of the award. The arbitrator spends additional time administering the board, which will then add to the cost to the parties of the arbitration. The filing of a dissenting opinion by a partisan arbitrator undermines the acceptability of the award issued by a majority of the tripartite board. Parties that use tripartite board have normally done so for decades. It is difficult to alter, amend, or eliminate a process that has been embodied in the CBA since time immemorial. Parties new to arbitration should avoid using this variation on the process.

3.   *Are arbitrators who are academics, or former academics, not as effective due to their lack of industrial experience?*

It is essential that an arbitrator understand the general ways of the workplace. On the other hand, persons with a long career as a labor relations professional in one industry may not be suitable to hear a case in another industry because their experience has been narrow. Similarly, an arbitrator who comes out of the ranks of labor organizations may lack industrial experience in areas where they did not represent employees.

Similarly, academics who are new to arbitration may be at a disadvantage because of the absence of industrial experience, much like any junior arbitrator. That experience, of course, comes with time and cases. No arbitrator knows exactly how work life and production operate in any given situation; it is the responsibility of the parties to educate the neutral about their circumstances. However, any arbitrator who does not know about arbitrability, seniority, or just cause will not last long in the field.

4.   *How might the parties obtain more information from arbitrators before making a selection of the neutral who will hear the case?*

The problem parties experience in making an informed selection of a neutral is similar to the problems most people experience with regard to hiring professionals. The AAA and FMCS believe that all members of their rosters are qualified and talented—otherwise, they would not place them on their rosters. The agencies select the names of arbitrators at random to distribute to parties seeking to appoint a neutral. That is the fairest system to the arbitrators on the rosters, and the parties will have different perceptions of quality for particular cases. In fact, all arbitrators are not equal, and the parties know that. What they don't necessarily know is the qualities of each neutral on the lists supplied.

The labor arbitrator appointment system suffers from information failure, much like the process of choosing an attorney or a physician. Legal and medical professionals have met minimum qualifications— completing a rigorous educational program, passing the bar examination, or becoming licensed. Arbitrators, by comparison, have no bar to pass and no minimum educational requirements. A few do not even have a college education. Parties need more information than is supplied by the typical biography distributed by the appointing agencies. They contain a lot of relevant information, including the categories of issues arbitrated, their service on permanent panels, membership in professional associations, and any offices they have held. Those biographies, plus a little online searching, should give advocates the objective information they need. The only thing they need beyond that is subjective information from persons who have had personal experience with the neutrals in question.

When selecting a legal or medical professional, we seek personal recommendations and references. Parties should do that as well in selecting an arbitrator, and perhaps arbitrators should facilitate the process. This strategy does not guarantee that the parties will not select a lemon as their neutral, but it will add to the data available in making the selection. Perhaps upon request an arbitrator could supply the parties with a list of references—both union and management advocates.

Seeking information about arbitrators is sensible and already quite common. The current system, although it may be hit or miss, can be made more productive if an advocate finds someone who has personal experience with a neutral. Parties contact people in their field (lawyers, human resource professionals, union representatives) and ask about their experiences with a neutral. If the arbitrator sends advocates a list of references, it is a safe bet they will say good things about the neutral. If the advocates just track down their own sources, they will likely get a wider range of opinions and more honest ones as well.

5.   *In the final analysis, does it really matter who you select as your arbitrator?*

The chances are very good that the arbitrator you select from the rosters of the appointing agencies will perform sufficiently well to meet the needs of the parties. Unless the neutral has reached a state of senility—a risk you cannot ignore, because most arbitrators are quite senior—the arbitrator will preside at the hearing and decide the case. Advocates report that some of the arbitrators they have selected have proven to be just awful. That may be why a small group of neutrals are appointed to hear almost all of the cases. Selecting from among that group of experienced neutrals means the parties will get first-class arbitration for their money. It also means that they may have to wait quite a while to get an available date from these preferred neutrals and pay a bit more for their services.

What are the names of these preferred arbitrators? Most parties have persons they can talk with to find the names of the best arbitrators who will hear cases in their region of the country.

There is good reason, however, for trying to broaden the pool of excellent neutrals. Some of the most experienced arbitrators will be leaving active practice in the coming years. Parties know when they have a case that must be arbitrated, although it does not involve a significant, recurring issue in the plant. For example, if a case involves minor discipline, parties should try out a "rookie" neutral. He or she may turn out to be a future superstar.

For the most important cases, the parties should try to obtain the services of the very best, experienced, talented arbitrators, even if that arbitrator might charge a bit more and have a filled calendar that will cause delays in scheduling a hearing.

Arbitration is final and binding. By appointing someone to decide a critical case, the parties have anointed a neutral with significant power to affect their workplace. Therefore, care in the selection process is critical.

Chapter 3

Prehearing Procedures

I. Overview

Once the parties have selected their arbitrator, they must schedule the hearing at a mutually convenient time. The busiest arbitrators may not have an available date for six months or more. That fact alone may encourage the parties to select more junior arbitrators, who might be able to hold a hearing in a matter of weeks. On the other hand, one or both parties to a dispute might not be ready to have the arbitrator hear a matter that quickly. They also selected the experienced neutral because they wanted that arbitrator, and they are willing to wait for an available date.

Parties claim that arbitrators are the chief culprits in causing delays in the process, and at times that is true. An arbitrator may not have a timely date available for the hearing. Some arbitrators may take too long to write an opinion and award. Although arbitrators can do things to avoid lengthy delays in the issuance of their awards, busy arbitrators are busy because parties think they are very good at what they do.

The representatives of the parties are equally at fault for delays in the process. Especially with busy lawyers representing labor and management, coordinating calendars can be a significant impediment to an expeditious arbitration process.

II. SCHEDULING A HEARING

Once the parties have selected their arbitrator, the process begins by scheduling a hearing date that is convenient for the neutral and the two parties. Sometimes that process can be quick: the arbitrator checks his or her calendar and selects a date, the parties confirm the date, and everything is set. More likely, however, the date offered will work for one party and not the other, and the arbitrator will have to supply an alternative date. This process may take some time to work itself out.

Parties sometimes ask the arbitrator to supply them with three dates, but for busy arbitrators holding three dates might be impossible, especially if the parties do not respond quickly to the offered dates. It is easier for the arbitrator to offer one date and let the parties know that he or she has others available if the first proves inconvenient.

1. *How does the arbitrator handle the scheduling of a hearing?*

The arbitrator should facilitate the scheduling of a hearing date that does not unduly delay the hearing. Under a case administered by the American Arbitration Association (AAA), the arbitrator does not deal directly with the parties in scheduling the hearing date. He or she will supply a few dates, which the tribunal administrator then presents to the parties. If those dates do not work, the AAA administrator will seek additional dates from the arbitrator that may or may not turn out to be convenient. Scheduling can evolve into a very frustrating process for all concerned. At this point, the AAA tribunal administrator should request that both parties submit to the AAA their calendars for the next few months indicating the dates that are available for a hearing. The tribunal administrator will then compare the parties' calendars and contact the arbitrator to ascertain whether he or she is available on any of the dates both parties are available. If so, the date is confirmed, and the tribunal administrator sends out a notice by email to all concerned.

In cases where arbitrators are appointed under the auspices of the Federal Mediation and Conciliation Service (FMCS) or arbitrators are selected by direct appointment of the parties, the arbitrator takes a more active role in scheduling the hearing, and it is most likely handled initially through email. (The FMCS appointment letter includes the email addresses of the representatives of the parties.) If an arbitrator receives no response to his or her email, he or she may directly telephone one party and then the other proposing a date or dates for the hearing. Normally, when the parties hear directly from the arbitrator, it encourages them to accept a relatively prompt hearing date.

Some arbitrators recognize that, even if they are personally involved, this scheduling process can be inefficient and can be particularly stressful for one of the parties, most likely the union that represents the grievant. In general, but not always, the union is seeking a prompt date for the hearing. If direct contact from the arbitrator doesn't result in a date being set, the arbitrator or the parties may request that a conference call be scheduled.

Parties must have their calendars with them for the conference call. Sometimes it is the particular date previously offered by the arbitrator that presents a conflict for one party. Moving the hearing a few days one way or the other might actually work for all concerned. This method of accommodating conflicting schedules cannot be achieved efficiently through email or by the use of an intermediary such as the AAA tribunal administrator. Even after a date is tentatively confirmed by conference call, advocates often have to check with their clients to confirm the availability of necessary witnesses.

Even after a date is set and is confirmed by the arbitrator, there are additional administrative tasks to be completed before a hearing. The parties must inform the AAA tribunal administrator or the arbitrator directly where the hearing will be held. Normally, the arbitrator suggests a time to begin the hearing and the parties concur or suggest an alternative.

2.   Given that arbitration is meant to be expeditious, why would the arbitrator permit one party, over the objection of the other party, to continuously refuse to commit to a relatively prompt hearing date?

There is little an arbitrator can do to compel a party to agree on a relatively prompt hearing date. He or she does not have the power to hold a party or its representative in contempt. On the other hand, the arbitrator must take control of the scheduling process and plainly state that the hearing should be scheduled for the first mutually available date. Even a recalcitrant party will not wish to annoy the arbitrator with groundless objections to a relatively early date.

An arbitrator has power to influence the parties but little power to order them to do things. He or she must use informal methods of persuasion rather than just bang a gavel, as a trial judge would, and order a party to comply. It is a subtle power, but experienced arbitrators know how to exercise it skillfully.

3.   *The parties, not advocates or witnesses, have a right to a prompt hearing. How can an arbitrator let the convenience of an advocate or a witness get in the way of this right?*

It is true that the arbitration case belongs to the parties, not to advocates or witnesses. Although it is not always fully appreciated, it is the union that is a party to the arbitration and not the advocate or any particular witness. In scheduling an arbitration hearing, however, the arbitrator must deal with what is practical. If the arbitrator's calendar is filled for many months, he or she can offer the parties the next available date or, alternatively, offer to withdraw from the case if that date or time frame is not mutually acceptable. Assuming the arbitrator has an early date for a hearing, the issue then becomes reaching agreement with the parties regarding that date. If an attorney advocate has a court appearance scheduled for that date, it would be foolish for the arbitrator to press for its acceptance. Usually after a bit of discussion agreement on a mutually convenient and prompt date can be reached.

There are instances where an advocate's objection to a proposed hearing date may seem to the arbitrator to be querulous and unwarranted. For example, an advocate may claim to be very busy for an entire month or not have a clear date on his or her calendar until spring. Such an advocate has certainly made an unfavorable impression on the arbitrator—something not particularly helpful to his or her case. On the other hand, the arbitrator should not issue an order scheduling a hearing for a time when he or she knows one party will not appear. That approach would make the hearing worthless. An effort at accommodation is the best strategy.

The same considerations apply to the availability of witnesses. Although in some instances a key witness may be ill and thus unavailable to testify, in other instances the objection to an early date may not be based on persuasive reasons. The arbitrator should inquire whether other witnesses can supply the same information. In some instances, however, the testimony of a particular witness may be critical to a party's case, and the arbitrator must attempt to accommodate that party's concerns.

4.   *Don't employers and unions have the responsibility to select another advocate if the attorney of record appears too "inconvenienced" to appear at the hearing in a timely fashion? Is there anything an arbitrator can do in such a situation?*

Parties select their own representatives. They have a responsibility to select someone who will meet their needs in the case at hand. A busy attorney may be a great advocate, but if that person delays the scheduling of a prompt hearing, he or she may be ill-serving his or her client.

The arbitrator should not be involved in any way in the selection of an advocate. The neutral's responsibility is to the process, and he or she should encourage the parties to move forward. It is not part of the arbitrator's job to comment on a party's choice of counsel.

The best approach for the neutral is to use the power of the office to convince a recalcitrant attorney, who must know that displeasing the arbitrator even at an early stage of a proceeding is not a good strategy, to find some time in his or her schedule.

Ultimately, it may be necessary for the party that wants a prompt hearing to go to court seeking such an order. That strategy will take additional time and money. A private resolution to the problem orchestrated by the arbitrator is preferred in this situation.

5.   *How much time should the arbitrator schedule for the hearing?*

Although not all cases can be presented in four hours, most cases can be presented in a day of hearing. That does not mean that the parties should rush through their presentations. It does mean that the arbitrator will not be impressed when a party presents a third witness who says the same things in his or her testimony as the first and the second witness. The more experienced the parties' advocates, the shorter the hearing will be, because they will know what the arbitrator needs to hear.

Parties should discuss between themselves how many days of hearing they think will be necessary in order to present their cases to the arbitrator. Often both parties will plan on calling many of the same witnesses. Once this is discovered, calling witnesses more than once won't be necessary, because the arbitrator will allow a party on cross-examination to ask the questions it would have asked that witness on direct examination.

Upon their first contact with the arbitrator, the parties should inform the arbitrator how many days should be reserved on the arbitrator's calendar. Reserving a single day for the hearing is a waste of time if the case is going to take five days to present. After the first day of the hearing, it may take some time to schedule a convenient second and third day, and, in the interim, the arbitrator is likely to have forgotten what was presented on the first day. It is best to estimate the number of days the hearing would likely take and then reserve all of those days on the arbitrator's calendar in the first instance. It may be necessary to spread a long hearing into two nonconsecutive weeks, but unless it is scheduled early, the case where time needed is underestimated may take a year to hear.

III. Disclosure

It is absolutely essential to the arbitration process that the parties confidently believe that the arbitrator is, in fact, neutral. Although the appointing agencies vet applicants to their panels on issues of competence and neutrality, they do not know whether there is some circumstance present in a particular case that could give rise to concerns about neutrality. It becomes the responsibility of the arbitrator to prove his or her neutrality through disclosing any facts that would not already be known by both parties. Even with full disclosure, there may be situations where an arbitrator just cannot serve. In such situations, the arbitrator must recuse himself or herself from the case.[1]

1. *What types of disclosures by the arbitrator are appropriate to reveal conflict, bias, or predisposition?*

Neutrality does not mean that the arbitrator has an "empty mind," only an "open mind." Arbitrators are not amateurs who arrive at a hearing with no idea what is in store. Remember Justice William O. Douglas' explication in the *Steelworkers Trilogy* of all the wonderful qualities arbitrators have, including a knowledge base about labor relations under collective bargaining regimes.[2] Parties seek as their arbitrator an informed neutral and not an ingenue.

Neutrality is the core precondition for anyone to serve as an arbitrator in a labor or employment dispute. An arbitrator must be neutral

---

[1] *See* Fairweather's Practice and Procedure in Labor Arbitration 106 (Ray J. Schoonhoven, ed., 4th ed. 1999) (discussing the arbitrator's duty to disclose).

[2] See the discussion of Justice Douglas' *Steelworkers Trilogy* analysis in Chapter 1, §V.

with regard to whether the employee (in a nonunion, employment arbitration case) or the union (in a labor arbitration case under a CBA) or management should prevail in the dispute. Of course, after hearing the case, the arbitrator will be anything but neutral, but will not show that predisposition directly to the parties at the close of the hearing. Eventually, the neutral will favor one side or the other on the merits, and the arbitrator's decision should explain in principled terms how the arbitrator reached that conclusion.

It is natural for the losing party to wonder whether the arbitrator had a predisposition toward the prevailing side even before the hearing began. Such a predisposition would corrode the process, undermine its legitimacy, and do grievous damage to the parties' collective relationship. That is why the arbitrator must reveal to both parties any factors that might lead the eventual losing party to think that the case was predetermined.

The Code of Professional Responsibility addresses the issue of disclosure:

> Before accepting an appointment, an arbitrator must disclose directly or through the administrative agency involved, any current or past managerial, representational, or consultative relationship with any company or union involved in a proceeding in which the arbitrator is being considered for appointment or has been tentatively designated to serve. Disclosure must also be made of any pertinent pecuniary interest.[3]

The Code then includes some specific issues:

> When an arbitrator is serving concurrently as an advocate for or representative of other companies or unions in labor relations matters, or has done so in recent years, such activities must be disclosed before accepting appointment as an arbitrator.
>   . . . .
> Prior to acceptance of an appointment, an arbitrator must disclose to the parties or to the administrative agency involved any close personal relationship or other circumstance, in addition to those specifically mentioned earlier in this section, which might reasonably raise a question as to the arbitrator's impartiality.[4]

---

[3] NATIONAL ACADEMY OF ARBITRATORS, AMERICAN ARBITRATION ASSOCIATION, & FEDERAL MEDIATION & CONCILIATION SERVICE, CODE OF PROFESSIONAL RESPONSIBILITY FOR ARBITRATORS OF LABOR-MANAGEMENT DISPUTES §2.B.1 (as amended and in effect Sept. 2007), *available at* http://www.naarb.org/code.html (reproduced in Appendix B).
[4] *Id.* §§2.B.2 and 2.B.3.

The arbitrator is not disqualified by virtue of these disclosures. In fact, if both parties want the arbitrator to serve after the disclosures are made, they can maintain the appointment. Of course, the arbitrator can recuse himself or herself at any time if he or she feels there is a "clear conflict of interest."

Court-made law on arbitrator disclosure provides a broad sweep of information for the neutral to disclose. An arbitrator must inform the parties about any matter that might possibly affect his or her neutrality. The U.S. Supreme Court, in a commercial arbitration case, *Commonwealth Coatings Corp. v. Continental Casualty Corp.*,[5] ruled that arbitrators must disclose to the parties "any dealings that might create an impression of possible bias."[6] The purpose of such wide-ranging disclosure is to avoid even the appearance of bias. Such disclosure, the Supreme Court reasoned, is necessary in order to enhance and protect the legitimacy of the arbitration process.

Experienced arbitrators are likely to know one or both of the representatives of the parties and may even have arbitrated a previous dispute between the parties. None of this demonstrates a bias that would disqualify the arbitrator from hearing a dispute. It also does not seem necessary to disclose this information. But what about disclosing a personal relationship with one of the advocates? It really depends on the nature of the personal relationship. It is not unusual for a longtime neutral to be friendly with members of the community of labor attorneys and representatives, especially because most arbitrators spend their entire careers hearing cases in a particular geographic region. On the other hand, if the arbitrator is the longtime personal friend of one of the advocates, that fact should be disclosed.

The default rule for disclosure should be to disclose. Certainly an arbitrator who once represented one of the parties must disclose this fact. Business relationships with one party or any pecuniary interest of any kind must be disclosed. In many instances, the parties will find the arbitrator's disclosures to be unnecessary. It is better for the process, however, to err on the safe side, because one of the parties eventually will lose the case, and a losing party may look for reasons to set aside an award. One ground that is available in court for setting aside an award is the arbitrator's failure to disclose disqualifying relationships.[7]

---

[5] 393 U.S. 145 (1968).

[6] *Id.* at 149.

[7] Arbitrator disclosure obligations may be more stringent in an employment arbitration case, a matter discussed in detail in Chapter 17.

Arbitrators tend to over-disclose prior relationships with the parties and their representatives. It does no harm to do so. A party that would refuse to allow a carefully selected arbitrator to remain as the decision maker would have been likely to appeal an unfavorable decision to court in any case. The experience of most arbitrators is that parties are somewhat amused by an arbitrator's disclosures, but an arbitrator knows that the parties are ill-served and the process undermined by failing to make appropriate disclosures.

2.   *If an arbitrator relies on one party to a dispute for a considerable amount of arbitration business, how does the arbitrator address that issue with both parties to mitigate any perception of bias?*

Parties must know when they select an experienced arbitrator to hear a dispute that the neutral likely has received numerous appointments from other locals of the same international union and other business operations of the employer. Are these the kind of prior relationships that might create an impression of possible bias? A party might worry that the arbitrator would be inclined in a close case to favor the side that could supply him or her with additional appointments.

The arbitrator should disclose that he or she is a permanent umpire for one of the parties under another CBA unless that information is already included in the biography that the appointing agency sent the parties. On the other hand, no disclosure is required that a busy arbitrator receives numerous ad hoc appointments from an international union or a major national employer. If there is any doubt, the arbitrator should disclose.

It is possible that the arbitrator's disclosures will trigger a request from one party or the other that the neutral recuse himself or herself from the case. It is possible that such a request is simply a ploy designed to put the arbitrator on notice that his or her rulings will be scrutinized to see if they are consistent with any alleged bias. If an arbitrator feels that he or she cannot serve, recusal is in order. On the other hand, the arbitrator should not allow one party to intimidate the neutral who has been duly appointed to hear the case.

3.   *At the hearing, if the arbitrator seems familiar with one side's counsel, does that put the opposing party at a disadvantage?*

It is not unusual for a busy arbitrator to know one or both of the representatives of the parties. Experienced neutrals know the players in their particular geographical region. It might even be unusual if the experienced neutral did not know someone involved in the case.

On the other hand, it can be unsettling to a party for the arbitrator to greet the opposing advocate as if he or she was a long-lost friend. Exchanging stories about old cases and friends in common is simply bad form by the arbitrator. The appearance of neutrality is crucially important.

It is the arbitrator's responsibility to make the parties know through his or her words and conduct that he or she will show no favoritism in the way the hearing is conducted and the dispute decided. Arbitrators must act to enhance the legitimacy of the arbitration process, and that includes avoiding even the appearance of personal favoritism. Experienced arbitrators must play the role of the truly neutral adjudicator in a manner that satisfies both parties as to the fairness of the proceeding.

IV. PREHEARING CONTACT WITH THE ARBITRATOR

After the hearing is scheduled, one party or the other may have reason to contact the arbitrator. Some of this contact will be benign and necessary, for example, to inform the arbitrator exactly where the hearing will be held. Other times, an inexperienced representative may contact the arbitrator to let the neutral know how important the case is to that party. The arbitrator must deal firmly with any such inappropriate contact.

1. Is it ever appropriate to have contact with the arbitrator before the hearing?

It may be appropriate to have contact with the arbitrator before the hearing. The issue is what is discussed during the contact between arbitrator and the representative of a party. When the AAA is the appointing agency, an AAA tribunal administrator handles all contact between the arbitrator and the parties. It is absolutely necessary to have contact with the arbitrator if he or she is directly appointed by the parties or appointed through the FMCS.

It is improper to have any discussion with an arbitrator about the merits of the case in an *ex parte* fashion. The arbitrator may appropriately ask one party or the other by telephone how long the hearing will likely be in order to set aside enough days for the hearing. The parties must inform the arbitrator if there is anything unusual about their arbitration procedure. In general, the parties must tell the arbitrator whether anything out of the ordinary is expected and make sure that the neutral is willing to follow the parties' arrangement. For example, if the arbitrator is required by the CBA to issue a bench award at the conclusion of the hearing, that information must be communicated to the neutral before the appointment is accepted.

If the arbitrator is traveling from out of state for the hearing, it is useful for the parties to offer suggestions as to where the neutral might stay overnight. This is all part of what might be termed "the care and feeding of the neutral." The life of an arbitrator, especially one who works full time, can be arduous. Any assistance would be appreciated.

2.   To what extent is it appropriate to have ex parte *conversations* with the arbitrator on issues such as issuing a subpoena?

Issuing subpoenas is a regular part of the arbitrator's job before the hearing.[8] That can be accomplished by email without a direct conversation between the neutral and an advocate of a party. The advocate should simply request that the arbitrator sign the subpoenas and email them back or fax them to a particular number. It is the party's responsibility to serve the subpoenas.

A direct telephone conversation between the representative of a party and the arbitrator concerning issuing subpoenas is also appropriate as long as the discussion is limited to procedure and not in any way concerning the substance of a witness' testimony or anything further about the hearing.

An arbitrator may be concerned that the party requesting subpoenas understands that a neutral has no power to enforce a subpoena—only a court can do that. The neutral may respond to a party to make sure the party has no misconception about his or her enforcement power.

V. Arbitrator Fees

Although most arbitrators enjoy the practice of alternative dispute resolution, it is also their job. For most experienced arbitrators, it is the sole job by which they earn a living. The parties understand this and likely consider an arbitrator's fee in selecting their neutral.

---

[8] *See* Fairweather's Practice and Procedure in Labor Arbitration 188 (Ray J. Schoonhoven, ed., 4th ed. 1999) (discussing the arbitrator's power to issue subpoenas).

1.   *How do arbitrators charge for their services?*

Arbitrators, like lawyers and other professionals, set their own rates, typically on a per diem or per hour basis. Of course, an arbitrator's decision to charge a certain amount does not mean that anyone will actually appoint the neutral at that rate. The arbitrator's schedule of fees is distributed to the parties by the appointing agency. If the arbitrator is directly appointed by the parties, the arbitrator would be well advised to send the parties a copy of the schedule of fees.

Normally, arbitrators charge parties on a per diem basis, and per diem rates vary. Arbitrators charge for each day of hearing, whether it lasts 10 hours or 10 minutes, although there are some arbitrators who will actually charge "overtime" for a hearing that lasts longer than a stated number of hours a day. Arbitrators will also charge parties a portion of a day for time spent traveling to the hearing when that travel is out of town and takes part of the day prior to the hearing.

In addition, most arbitrators have established cancellation fees for scheduled hearing days that are cancelled or postponed within a set number of days prior to the hearing, normally from 14–28 days. For busy, experienced arbitrators, reserving a date for the parties means the neutral is precluded from scheduling that day for any other parties. The cancellation fees compensates for that lost scheduling opportunity.

The arbitrator will charge the parties for what is commonly called "study time." This is the amount of time it takes to review the parties' briefs; the record and transcript, if any is taken; and to research the issues presented. The arbitrator charges for the time it takes to draft the opinion and award and edit it. Some arbitrators will bill by the hour, a common practice among practicing lawyers, and others will count a normal "day" as six hours of work on a case, thus charging the per diem even though the six hours of the "day" may be accumulated over a number of calendar days.

Although each case is different, normally parties can expect that an arbitrator will charge two to three days of study time for a simple one-day hearing. Practice may vary among arbitrators. An extremely complicated case may require more days of study.

Finally, arbitrators will charge the parties for the reasonable expenses incurred in traveling to the place of the hearing. This includes transportation, room, and meals. Arbitrators will keep receipts for their travel and, on rare occasions, be asked by a party to present those receipts.

With the advent of nonrefundable airplane tickets, arbitrators have differed on how to handle air reservations. It is, of course, less expensive for the parties if the arbitrator flies on a nonrefundable ticket, but what should occur if the hearing is cancelled because the matter is settled? Arbitrators should charge the parties what it would cost to rewrite the ticket, if it is on an airline the arbitrator regularly uses. (Nonrefundable tickets lose all their value after a year.) Some arbitrators will purchase refundable tickets to avoid this problem, but that may end up costing the parties more if the hearing proceeds as scheduled and the arbitrator is not able to switch to a less expensive airfare. Parties should expect to be charged for nonrefundable tickets if their case does not proceed as scheduled.

Arbitrators do attempt to keep total charges for services and expenses reasonable. They understand the financial constraints the parties are under, in particular labor organizations. In their CBA, parties often specify responsibility for paying the arbitrator's bill. Typically, the parties split the arbitrator's charges, but, on occasion, they specify that the losing party is to pay the entire arbitrator's bill. In such a situation, the arbitrator must determine in the award which party is designated the "losing party." If the award is split—for example, the reinstatement of a dischargee but without back pay—the arbitrator will split the bill. In general, the reason for agreeing to a "loser pays all" provision is to deter the union from bringing cases to arbitration that it thinks it will lose. The arbitrator's job in allocating his or her fees is simply to follow the parties' directions.

2.   How much do arbitrators charge per diem?

Arbitrator charges vary from less than $1,000 to more than $2,000 per diem, with the latter customarily charged by the busiest and most acceptable and experienced arbitrators. Parties do consider these charges in making their selection, a criterion that can result in a significant error. The cost of hiring an arbitrator depends only in part on the per diem rate. The actual cost depends on how many days of study time the arbitrator charges. Most experienced and busy arbitrators will take less time to research and write an opinion and award. Thus, two days of study time for an experienced arbitrator who charges $2,000 a day is less than five days charged by a junior arbitrator who charges $1,000 a day.

3.   Is an expensive arbitrator a better arbitrator?

An expensive arbitrator is not necessarily a better arbitrator. In fact, parties may not agree what it means to designate someone a "better arbitrator." Does that mean that one party always wins before that neutral? The opposing side would not agree that that neutral is better.

Because arbitrators can set their own per diem, it would be useful to know how often that arbitrator has been selected to hear grievance disputes, but that information is generally not available. In any case, accumulating appointments is not necessarily a measure of how proficient the neutral is at the task at hand. It may simply be a product of name recognition.

An expensive and busy arbitrator may, in fact, be a better arbitrator, but that really depends on factors not indicated by the prices charged. A busy arbitrator is likely to be a more experienced neutral. A fine, albeit junior, arbitrator starting out in the field is not likely to set a high per diem, which might deter parties from appointing him or her. Thus, price is an uncertain measure of arbitrator quality.

VI. Prehearing Briefs and Conferences

The typical labor arbitration case does not require holding a prehearing conference either by a telephone call or in person.[9] Advocates experienced in civil trials may find that strange, but experienced arbitrators would find common civil practice to be strange. It is rare for an arbitration case to be so complex that it warrants the filing of a prehearing brief, except, perhaps, if a discovery issue must be addressed before the hearing takes place.[10]

1. Should the arbitrator or the parties schedule a prehearing conference?

Prehearing conference calls may be necessary in a grievance arbitration case if the parties are having trouble scheduling the hearing. Once a case is scheduled, prehearing conferences are extremely rare in a labor arbitration case. On occasion, they may be necessary to discuss matters of discovery if there are any contested issues.

It is certainly appropriate for the parties to suggest the possibility of a prehearing conversation with the neutral about the case. That can be accomplished by conference call or, if necessary, in person. The arbitrator, of course, should agree to such a meeting if that is the parties'

---

[9] By comparison, prehearing conferences, either in person or by telephone, are the common practice in employment arbitration, as discussed in Chapter 17.

[10] Once again, the practice in employment arbitration regarding prehearing discovery, filing of motions, and prehearing submissions is quite different, as discussed in Chapter 17.

wish. An in-person prehearing conference would give the advocates for both parties the opportunity to size up the neutral they have selected, but it is an expensive luxury when not warranted by the complexity of the case.

2. Does the arbitrator do anything differently with a really big case—for example, a case with potential exposure of over $1 million?

The arbitrator should treat every case as if it were valuable to the parties, and financial exposure is only one of the factors that determine value. A case may involve an important principle that divides the parties—management operational decisions may have a significant impact not only on employees but also on the employer's bottom line, and a discharged employee loses a considerable amount of money over a work life in addition to the security of a job.

An arbitrator is unlikely to know about the significant financial exposure involved in a case. The appointment letter normally contains only a few words describing the dispute. It is for the parties to inform the neutral of the financial exposure involved in the grievance if they wish.

3. What value do arbitrators place on having parties submit prehearing briefs?

It is common in a civil court proceeding for the parties to submit pretrial memoranda to the court. The opposite is true in labor arbitration. For most labor arbitrations, there is no need for either a prehearing conference or the submission of prehearing briefs. Experienced arbitrators will quickly pick up the essence of the dispute as the hearing begins. In most cases, formal prehearing submissions create an unnecessary expense.

VII. THE SETTING FOR THE HEARING

The arbitration hearing takes place where the parties mutually desire. Although they might request the arbitrator's input on the location, normally they will hold the hearing where they always hold their hearings or have their periodic negotiation sessions. It is critical that both parties feel comfortable in that setting, and the hearing room must meet the needs of the process with adequate light, space, and ventilation.

1. Does it matter to the arbitrator where the hearing is held?

One distinguishing characteristic of labor arbitration is that the adjudicator travels to the parties' location to hear the case. As a matter of general practice, the arbitrator travels to the parties' location because of its convenience for the witnesses. By comparison, the parties come to the courthouse to try their civil suits. That means that experienced arbitrators might be near home on one day and many states away on the next.

Experienced neutrals have held hearings in all kinds of settings. Holiday Inns (or their functional equivalent) seem to receive the most arbitration business because of their ubiquity, but the parties decide where the hearing will be held. If the parties cannot agree on a location, the arbitrator will select a neutral place.[11] Management may have a conference room in its administrative offices, or the union may offer the union hall for the hearing, or the advocates for each side may have space available at their law firms. One party or both may prefer a neutral site, such as a local hotel meeting room. It may cost the parties a small rental charge, but the neutrality is worth the price.[12] Union rank-and-file members may not feel totally comfortable entering a management area, and that may inhibit their testimony.

The arbitrator is interested in a venue that is convenient to reach and will be suitable for an arbitration hearing. The advantage of holding a hearing at the plant is that it would make a visit to the site of an incident that occurred much easier. If the arbitrator has to stay overnight before the hearing, the parties should consider holding the hearing in the arbitrator's hotel. If the hearing is likely to take all day (or many days), the parties should also consider the availability of food for lunch in their choice of a hearing location.

2. How does the arbitrator prefer the hearing room to be set up?

Some arbitrators are very particular about how the arbitration hearing room should be set up. Spatial relationships—what psychologists refer to as "proxemics"—can have an impact on the therapeutic value of the arbitration proceeding as well as the ability of the advocates and the arbitrator to hear the witnesses' testimony. Some arbitrators are

---

[11] *See* ELKOURI & ELKOURI: HOW ARBITRATION WORKS ch. 7 (Kenneth May, ed., 7th ed. 2012).
[12] *See* FAIRWEATHER'S PRACTICE AND PROCEDURE IN LABOR ARBITRATION 200 (Ray J. Schoonhoven, ed., 4th ed. 1999).

satisfied with a large square of tables, but there are problems with that configuration.

There are two factors that should be considered in the arrangement of the hearing room. Where should the witness chair be? How far should the arbitrator be away from the parties? If witnesses will be seated next to the arbitrator, they may not be addressing the arbitrator when questioned by one of the parties. Placing a witness at the far end of the table means that he or she is too far from the arbitrator.

The best configuration of the hearing room is a U-type arrangement, with the witness in front of the neutral and between the parties. The advocates should be within easy reach of the neutral to facilitate the distribution of documents. The arbitrator should be at a separate table that touches the tables of each of the parties.

A hearing room must have sufficient light and ventilation (some hotel meeting rooms are quite deficient in that regard). The room must be large enough to easily accommodate all those who plan to attend.

VIII. Settlements

For most arbitrators, appointment to hear a dispute can seem like just a preliminary round before the parties actually try to settle their case. There is a good reason for that. Neither party can lose anything until an arbitrator hears and decides a case. If the parties settle their dispute during the arbitrator's cancellation period, there may be a charge, but it is often hard to get the opposing side to listen to a proposed resolution until the arbitration hearing is on the horizon.

For arbitrators, it is always best if the parties resolve their disputes as early as possible. It is most annoying to an arbitrator to travel away from home, stay overnight, and arrive at the hearing room only to have the parties announce that they were now going to attempt to settle the matter. It may take them hours to do so, and they may not be successful, and so the hearing, now substantially delayed, must go forth. In any case, the parties own their process and can use it as they wish consistent with ethical and professional constraints.

1.   Are prehearing settlements common?

It is not unusual for parties to resolve their dispute after the arbitrator has been selected and a hearing has been scheduled, before the hearing actually takes place. Settlement rates vary, but for some arbitrators about half of their cases are settled without a hearing.

Parties often settle cases in close proximity to the scheduled hearing date. The arbitrator, in effect, serves in the role of the "courthouse steps," where settlements are often reached in civil cases. The prospect of having to present a party's case to an arbitrator will convince both parties that it is time to resolve the matter themselves.

Parties should be aware of the arbitrator's policies with regard to cancellation periods. Almost all experienced arbitrators will charge their per diem when a case is settled within 14 days of the scheduled hearing. For a full-time neutral, a settlement may be a welcome break from constant travel. The cancelled date will also give the arbitrator time to write opinions in pending cases.

It is, of course, better for the parties' continuing collective relationship to resolve matters privately. An arbitrator will often say that to the representatives of the parties when informed that the case has been settled. Nonetheless, despite good-faith efforts of the parties at resolving their dispute, some cases will have to be presented and decided by a neutral.

2.   Can a case be settled at the hearing or even after the hearing?

At times parties will settle their grievance dispute at the hearing. Some arbitrators have a practice of asking the parties at the start of the hearing or after opening statements whether they have explored the possibility of settlement. The neutral might even offer to mediate the dispute.

The parties can settle their dispute at any time. On some occasions, they actually settle the dispute after the hearing but before the arbitrator issues his or her award. They can even settle the dispute after the award is issued, achieving a resolution other than the one the arbitrator awarded. For example, an arbitrator normally does not have the power to award a dischargee back pay without ordering the reinstatement of the grievant. Parties can agree upon receipt of the arbitrator's award to settle the matter with a payment to the grievant who is then not reinstated.

3.   If the parties request the arbitrator to assist them by mediating their dispute, can the arbitrator later reassume the role of adjudicator?

Before an arbitrator attempts to assist the parties by mediating their dispute, all must agree on the role of the neutral if the mediation proves unsuccessful. During mediation, where the parties are often physically separated by the mediator into different rooms, parties may disclose information that the arbitrator might not otherwise obtain at the arbitration hearing.

Mediation can be far more effective, however, if the neutral retains the power to adjudicate the dispute if mediation fails. He or she then can suggest to one of the parties in mediation that their positions and arguments might not be successful in arbitration and the neutral has the power, if the parties are unsuccessful, to rule on the case. This combination of neutral powers is often referred to as *med-arb,* combining the powers of a mediator and an arbitrator. The proper role of the mediator and how mediation can assist the parties in settling a dispute is discussed in detail in Chapter 18.

With the process clarified, there is no problem with an arbitrator reassuming his or her original role as adjudicator if the effort at settlement proves unsuccessful.

IX. DISCOVERY

Civil litigators know that a case can be won or lost in the discovery phase. A series of depositions, document requests, and interrogatories may seal the fate of the dispute. As a general matter, labor arbitration does not have such an array of prehearing discovery measures, although they are quite commonly used in employment arbitration. Information about the labor case is exchanged throughout the grievance procedure. Although participants do not testify under oath, as in a deposition, they do relate their stories at grievance meetings, and if they change their accounts in the sworn testimony at an arbitration hearing, the opposing party will use that information in cross-examination.

1.   *Does arbitration ever involve prehearing discovery?*

One significant difference between labor arbitration and court litigation is the absence of prehearing discovery. As a general matter, there are no depositions or formal requests for documents in a labor arbitration. In general, parties will have exchanged relevant documents during the course of the grievance procedure.

By comparison, it is not unusual in an arbitration proceeding for one or both parties to request that the arbitrator issue subpoenas to "command" persons to appear at the hearing. An arbitrator certainly has the power to issue a subpoena, but he or she has no power to enforce it. That is why the neutral may inquire of the party requesting the subpoena whether, in fact, this is a willing witness. Subpoenas may be necessary in order to ensure that the witness is paid on the day of his or her testimony or to prove to the opposing party that the witness appeared under compulsion rather than as a matter of free will.

2. What should happen when a party disregards or does not fully comply with an arbitrator's subpoena duces tecum? *Assuming the subpoena is never quashed, how does one party's failure to provide the relevant information impact a case?*

Occasionally, an arbitrator may become involved in ordering the production of documents. A *subpoena duces tecum* requested by one party—normally the union—may order the production of documents, but the arbitrator has no power other than persuasion to enforce the production if management is not willing.

Discovery issues sometimes arise after labor arbitration is invoked, although most information requests are dealt with in the grievance procedure. If the union demands documents to prepare for the hearing and management resists, it is difficult for the labor arbitrator to respond before the hearing. Those discovery disputes are best left for resolution at the hearing—and they often wash away. On the other hand, labor arbitrators should issue subpoenas at the request of a party as long as the party is advised that the neutral has no power to enforce a subpoena, as would a court.

X. POSTPONEMENTS

Arbitrators are accustomed to receiving requests for parties to postpone a scheduled hearing date. The request for a postponement may be based on the fact that the parties are attempting to settle the matter. Alternatively, a party may have a critical witness who has taken ill. Whatever the reason, an arbitrator should grant a request for a postponement. The parties should decide which party is responsible for the arbitrator's bill if the cancellation takes place within the arbitrator's cancellation period or whether they will split the bill.

1. What should an arbitrator do if one party seeks a postponement of the hearing?

Requests for postponement are common in arbitration for a variety of reasons. One party or the other, or even both, may simply not be ready to present their cases; a key witness may be unavailable; a conflict with court litigation may arise for one of the advocates; or perhaps the parties are engaging in an effort to settle the dispute without resorting to arbitration.

In any case, an arbitrator should grant the request of either party to postpone the hearing. Depending on when the request is made, the party requesting the postponement may have to bear the cost of the arbitrator's cancellation fee.

2.   What about a second request for a postponement from the same party?

The arbitrator has the power of his or her influence in ruling on matters such as postponement requests. Delays for other than compelling reasons must be avoided. A case should not proceed to hearing, however, if both parties are not ready to proceed. Postponement should certainly be granted for good reason, for example, if a key witness has taken ill. Alternatives to postponement should be explored, such as taking the testimony of witnesses out of order.

If the union requests a second postponement in a discharge case, the arbitrator might grant the request but inform the parties that the back pay clock shall be tolled, that is, during the period of the second postponement, the grievant would receive no back pay, even if ultimately found to have been wrongfully discharged.

XI. PREHEARING MOTIONS AND OTHER MATTERS

In the typical labor arbitration case, the arbitrator is not asked to rule on prehearing motions—virtually all such motions can be addressed at the start of the hearing.[13] In fact, an experienced labor arbitrator does not spend any time thinking about a case until he or she shows up at the hearing room at the appointed time. There are no pleadings or filings. That is disconcerting to a junior arbitrator, especially one with civil trial experience, but experienced arbitrators quickly pick up on the nature of the dispute when the hearing commences.

1.   How do arbitrators respond to prehearing requests to decide discovery disputes and issues of arbitrability?

Arbitrators would generally prefer if parties would hold discovery issues and arbitrability objections until the hearing. There are times, of

---

[13] The contrary practice is the case in employment arbitration, as explored in Chapter 17.

course, when a party, normally the union, cannot prepare for arbitration in the absence of documents that management possesses. In most instances, the relevant documents are exchanged as part of the grievance procedure, but it is not unusual for labor arbitrators to be involved in discovery disputes before a hearing.

In a case administered through the AAA, the parties should deal with the arbitrator only through the tribunal administrator. In a case administered by the FMCS or by direct appointment, a party seeking documents should email the arbitrator a list of the documents sought and copy the opposing party. The arbitrator will then inquire whether there are any objections to providing the documents requested. The arbitrator's involvement may be sufficient to convince a recalcitrant party to supply the documents. However, if there are significant objections, it is best to have them aired at the arbitration hearing. The arbitrator should inform the parties that if he or she orders the production of the documents, the receiving party will have adequate time to review their contents and, if it requests, the arbitrator will reschedule the hearing.

Issues of arbitrability should be addressed at the hearing, unless there is a provision in the CBA providing for an alternate procedure. As discussed in Chapter 4, resolving such issues often involves an understanding of the factual context, which can only be efficiently explored at a hearing.

2. Should the parties supply arbitrators with the collective bargaining agreement in advance of the hearing? Will the neutral read it?

Parties can mutually agree to submit a copy of the grievance and answers and a copy of the CBA to the arbitrator in advance of the hearing—in effect, submit a set of "pleadings." Most experienced arbitrators do not ask for a copy of the relevant CBA before the hearing. Why don't they do that?

First, half of all scheduled cases are settled after the hearing is scheduled. It is likely that the prospect of having to present or defend a case before a neutral drives the parties toward settlement. Submitting "pleadings" is a waste of time, and if the arbitrator devotes time to preparing for the hearing by reading the parties' submission, the parties should have to pay for his or her study time. Second, the grievance document itself may be poorly drafted or boilerplate and not really reflect the gravamen of the parties' dispute.

Most arbitrators figure out the nature of a case fairly quickly at the hearing. An experienced neutral has likely heard a case like it before. Every case involves a CBA and an assortment of key provisions—like seniority, vacations, holidays, wages, management rights, and others.

XII. Final Checklist

An advocate new to arbitration would find it useful to list the steps to be followed in preparing to present a case in arbitration. It would also be useful—and perhaps essential—to sit in as an observer on other cases to get a feel for the nature of the arbitral process.

1. *Do you have a checklist you might suggest for preparation for an arbitration hearing?*

Every arbitrator wants the parties to be well prepared for the hearing. It makes the process operate more efficiently. The representative of a party in arbitration should take following steps in preparing for a hearing:

1. Develop a theory of your case by reading published arbitration decisions on point and reviewing prior arbitration decisions and grievance settlements involving your client. A quick review of secondary sources such as *How Arbitration Works*[14] would be useful.

2. Study the relevant documents. These would include the grievance and the answer but should also include reviewing the entire CBA. Sometimes there will be provisions other than those cited in the grievance that may be relevant to your case.

3. Determine what facts are essential to your theory of the case. What evidence—both testimonial and documentary—does the arbitrator need in order to decide the case following your theory?

4. Select the witnesses who can present those essential facts. Before the hearing, prepare those witnesses for both direct and cross-examination.

5. Outline the testimony of each witness. Those new to arbitration might find it useful to write out questions, but an experienced representative still needs a list of the issues that should be covered with each witness.

6. Assemble the documents and make sure sufficient copies are made for the witness, the opposing party, the arbitrator, and the stenographer, if any.

---

[14]Elkouri & Elkouri: How Arbitration Works (Kenneth May, ed., 7th ed. 2012).

7. Anticipate opposing witnesses and prepare questions or topics to cover on cross-examination. Remember that you can't make your case effectively from cross-examination. Do not simply ask the opposing witness the same questions that were asked on direct examination—you will get the same answers.

8. Outline your opening statement or, if necessary, write it out. When delivering the opening statement, remember to speak slowly to allow the arbitrator to appreciate the full flavor of the arguments you make.

9. Explore settlement options, and then explore them again.

Chapter 4

Arbitrability: The Jurisdiction of the Arbitrator[1]

---

[1] *See* FAIRWEATHER'S PRACTICE AND PROCEDURE IN LABOR ARBITRATION ch. 5 (Ray J. Schoonhoven, ed., 4th ed. 1999). *See also* ELKOURI & ELKOURI: HOW ARBITRATION WORKS ch. 6 (Kenneth May, ed., 7th ed. 2012).

I. Overview

The power of a labor arbitrator to hear a grievance dispute depends on the provisions of the collective bargaining agreement (CBA) between the parties that appointed him. The issue of arbitral jurisdiction is referred to as *arbitrability.* It adds to the informal arbitration process a very formal initial step normally raised by management to keep an arbitrator from hearing a dispute. That is not to suggest that the employer is doing anything to undermine the arbitration process by raising arbitrability objections, although some employers may have that as their goal. Employers only agree to arbitrate certain matters, and they will raise arbitrability questions at the threshold as a way to uphold the terms of the bargain they made.

An arbitrator's determination that a grievance is arbitrable is not a decision that the grievance has merit. Like jurisdiction, it is only a question of whether the adjudicator has the power to hear the matter. If the case is arbitrable but without merit, the arbitrator will deny the grievance.

Arbitrability is raised by management in about 10 percent of all cases. The threshold objection is more commonly raised in the public sector than in the private sector.[2]

II. ADDRESSING ARBITRABILITY

Arbitrators understand that their appointment to hear a case in arbitration does not give them plenary power to hear and decide the dispute. It is the nature of the arbitration process that the arbitrator's power is limited by the same instrument that gives the arbitrator power—the CBA. It may not be an arbitrator's preference to address legalistic issues like substantive and procedural arbitrability, but that is an essential part of the job when raised in a timely manner by a party to a dispute.

1. *What do arbitrators think about arbitrability objections as a general matter?*

Arbitrators are often quite candid about their feelings about arbitrability. They do not like to hold a matter not arbitrable—they see the central purpose of arbitration as resolving disputes. A finding that a matter is not arbitrable keeps the arbitrator from accomplishing his or her central task. Although it is perfectly understandable for arbitrators to find it distasteful to rule on arbitrability, that disposition is based on a misguided understanding of the arbitration process and the role of arbitrator.

An arbitrator is not, using Judge Cardozo's word, a "knight errant, roaming at will in pursuit of his own ideal of beauty or of goodness."[3] He or she is employed by the parties to resolve disputes, but only those disputes that they agreed could be resolved through arbitration. If the neutral does not have the power to hear a case because a matter is not arbitrable, he or she should tell the parties that, thereby enforcing the provisions of the agreement. To do anything else violates the arbitrator's responsibility to the parties and the arbitration process.

---

[2] *See* Roger I. Abrams, *The Power Issue in Public Sector Grievance Arbitration*, 67 MINN. L. REV. 261 (1982).

[3] BENJAMIN N. CARDOZO, THE NATURE OF THE JUDICIAL PROCESS 141 (1922).

An arbitrator can maintain the legitimacy of the arbitration process only by not usurping power that is not his or hers. Adjudicating cases that the parties did not mutually intend to be resolved through arbitration does injury to the arbitration process. An arbitrator need not be happy about declaring a case inarbitrable, but, when appropriate, that is the neutral's job.

2.   *What is the difference between substantive and procedural arbitrability?*

When management and labor write their CBA and, in particular, design their grievance and arbitration system, they decide what issues can be resolved through arbitration. Typically, parties provide for the arbitration of disputes involving the interpretation or application of the provisions of the agreement. Sometimes they include an even broader clause that covers "any dispute of any kind." Occasionally, they specifically exclude from arbitration certain kinds of disputes, such as those related to pensions or union dues checkoff.

An arbitrator can only hear cases in the categories or classes of disputes that fall within the scope of the arbitration promise. This inquiry into the scope of jurisdiction is referred to as *substantive arbitrability.* This is not an issue of the merits of the claim—the union's grievance may ultimately have no merit at all—it is an issue of the arbitrator's power to hear the case.

Likewise, the arbitrator can only decide the merits of those grievances that have been properly processed through the grievance procedure. This is known as *procedural arbitrability.* Often these cases involve the application of time limits for the initiation and processing of grievances. Both forms of arbitrability are discussed in more detail below.

3.   *Should the arbitrator apply a presumption of arbitrability when this issue is raised?*

A common mistake made by arbitrators in ruling on threshold claims of arbitrability—both substantive and procedural—is to apply the presumption of arbitrability announced by the U.S. Supreme Court in the *Steelworkers Trilogy.*[4] Parties opposing a claim that a matter is not arbitrable often raise this asserted presumption as their central ar-

---

[4]Steelworkers v. American Mfg. Co., 363 U.S. 564 (1960); Steelworkers v. Warrior & Gulf Navig. Co., 363 U.S. 574 (1960); Steelworkers v. Enterprise Wheel & Car Corp., 363 U.S. 593 (1960). See Chapter 1, §V. The *Steelworkers Trilogy* decisions are reproduced in Appendix A.

gument. Arbitrators should decline to apply a presumption, because that is not what the Supreme Court was addressing. There may be other good reasons for holding a matter arbitrable, but relying on a presumption is wrong.

In the *Steelworkers Trilogy,* the Court was asked to determine the appropriate role of a court when faced with a claim that a matter was not arbitrable. The claim is normally raised by management in a suit brought to enjoin the arbitration from proceeding or a suit brought by the union to compel arbitration. The Supreme Court ruled that a trial judge should send the parties to their chosen dispute resolution system—arbitration—unless it could be said with positive assurance that the parties intended cases of this class not to be cognizable in arbitration. This the Court refers to in later cases as the *presumption of arbitrability.*

Justice William O. Douglas explained that arbitration should only be compelled if the parties have agreed to arbitration of cases like the one before the court. That determination is for the court to make. On the other hand, Justice Douglas reasoned that courts are at a strategic disadvantage in ruling on cases involving CBAs because they cannot be as equally informed about workplace issues as an arbitrator. Thus, the Supreme Court gives trial judges a very limited role: they are to see if there is a clear statement in the arbitration provision precluding cases of the sort before the tribunal from arbitration. In its absence, the case goes to the arbitrator.

In later cases, the Supreme Court gave lower courts an even more limited role regarding claims that a matter is not procedurally arbitrable. In such instances, there is no role for the trial court other than to send the parties to arbitration, where the arbitrator will determine threshold procedural issues of arbitrability.

Thus, the Supreme Court never said what an arbitrator should do regarding issues of arbitrability. The terms of the CBA will control those issues. A dispute is either arbitrable or not arbitrable, based on the terms of the agreement; it should not be "presumed" to be arbitrable unless the parties so provided in their agreement.

4. What should an arbitrator do regarding arbitrability if a court has ordered the matter to arbitration?

The arbitrator hearing a case ordered to arbitration by a court still has work to do regarding arbitrability. The court order is not based on a finding that the matter is arbitrable, but only that it is either "arguably arbitrable" (applying the presumption of arbitrability to substantive claims) or that it involves a matter of procedural arbitrability where the court has not even addressed the issue of arbitrability. The arbitrator, therefore, must make the ultimate determination on arbitrability, by taking evidence and hearing argument on the matter.

5.   *Would a union ever raise an arbitrability issue?*

There may be times when a union would raise an argument similar to arbitrability when the CBA provides that a grievance must be considered granted if management does not respond at a grievance step within the time limit set forth in the contract. The union processes the matter to arbitration, because the neutral can read the contract and determine whether management has, in fact, defaulted on the case. The union is really arguing that the arbitrator does not have the power to decide the merits of the case because management must accept and grant the grievance under the terms of the CBA.

III. Process and Waiver

The issue of arbitrability is normally raised at the commencement of the hearing and almost always by management. The employer's advocate may request that the arbitrator limit the hearing only to evidence and arguments that address its arbitrability claim. Only if the arbitrator determines that the matter is arbitrable would the case proceed to a hearing on the merits. This is referred to as *bifurcation*.

The union may respond by expressing surprise at management's claim that the matter is not arbitrable because it had not raised the issue before the hearing. Because it is critical that parties avoid the time and expense of processing a matter through the grievance and arbitration process, the union may argue that management's failure to raise the issue before arbitration should constitute a waiver of its affirmative defense that the matter is not arbitrable.

1.   *How does an arbitrator decide whether to agree to bifurcate a case?*

Some employers will seek to bifurcate the issues in an arbitration case, proposing that the arbitrator resolve only the threshold issue of arbitrability and allow the merits to be addressed only after the arbitrator determines that the matter is arbitrable. If there is no objection to the employer's request, the arbitrator should grant the request to bifurcate and hear and resolve only the arbitrability issue.

It is quite customary, however, for the union to oppose a motion to bifurcate for a number of reasons. First, assuming the arbitrator ultimately determines that the matter is arbitrable, it will substantially increase the cost of the arbitration, especially if the arbitrator must travel from out of town for two hearings. Second, unions also know that, if the arbitrator hears an appealing case on the merits at the same time that he or she hears the threshold issue of arbitrability, the arbitrator may lean toward finding that the case is arbitrable so that the grievance can be upheld on the merits. If there is anything an arbitrator hates more than deciding a case on the "technical" grounds of lack of arbitrability, it is to do so when the underlying case has obvious merit.

In general, arbitrators do not favor bifurcation for practical reasons. Some arbitrability contentions do not require much by way of evidence—either testimonial or documentary. To devote an entire hearing day (consisting of perhaps an hour or two of evidence and argument on arbitrability) is an inefficient use of the arbitrator's time. An even more compelling reason for not favoring bifurcation is that often it is very hard for the arbitrator to rule on arbitrability without hearing more about the facts involved in the dispute. One final reason to avoid bifurcation is that if the grievance is ultimately without merit, the union will at least have afforded the grievant the opportunity to present his or her story to the arbitrator.

Unless the parties' agreement provides for bifurcating issues—and some do—the arbitrator should encourage the parties to present their entire case, including the merits, while making very plain that he or she will not resolve issues on the merits if the matter is not arbitrable. Some arbitrators neither make nor keep that promise—it is so much easier to say that the grievance has no merit, if that is the case, than to say that the grievance is not arbitrable. The arbitrator should take the harder path. If the case is not arbitrable, the neutral should say so and stop without commenting on the merits. One approach the arbitrator should avoid is to state the contentions of the parties on arbitrability and then rule that there is no need to address arbitrability because the grievance must be denied on the merits.

2.   *Should an arbitrator rule that a party waives an arbitrability claim by not raising the issue during the grievance procedure?*

It is not unusual for management to discover belatedly that a grievance is not arbitrable. In fact, this may happen when an outside advocate is brought in to prepare and present the case in arbitration. Then, at the start of the hearing, management raises the argument that the matter is not arbitrable.

If the union does not object to consideration of the arbitrability issue, the arbitrator should proceed to hear the issue as part of the case. Unlike a court, which may raise the issue of jurisdiction on its own motion, an arbitrator should follow the lead of the parties if they agree. But what should the arbitrator do if the union raises its opposition to the arbitrator's consideration of arbitrability?

As with all issues in arbitration, the first thing the arbitrator should do is examine the terms of the parties' CBA to see if it speaks to the issue of delay in raising arbitrability. Some contract provisions state that a party may raise the issue of substantive arbitrability at any time in the grievance and arbitration process. If such a provision is in the parties' agreement, the arbitrator should proceed to hear the argument and any evidence on arbitrability.

In the absence of such a provision, the arbitrator must listen to the parties' arguments and evidence on arbitrability to ascertain whether management raised the issue of arbitrability in the timely fashion during the grievance procedure. Failure to raise the threshold issue of arbitrability at the first available opportunity during the grievance procedure should be considered a waiver of the claim, particularly if management seeks to raise an issue of procedural arbitrability, such as whether the grievance was timely filed.

By the time the parties reach arbitration, many months have likely passed since the grievance was filed. The parties have gone through the effort and expense of processing the matter through the grievance procedure and invoking arbitration. If the claim of untimeliness, for example, had been raised in the first instance when the grievance was filed, all that effort could have been avoided. The employer does not gain any more information about timeliness after the initial filing. This is an appropriate case for applying the waiver doctrine.

Any other approach to procedural arbitrability would allow—and even encourage—management to use the threshold claim as a trap. With the issue in reserve—assuming that it is supported by the facts—management knows it can always prevail by pulling arbitrability out of its back pocket. Such bad faith undermines the efficacy of the grievance and arbitration process and should not be encouraged or countenanced by the arbitrator.

It is more likely in these situations that management simply did not recognize that it had a good claim on arbitrability. If this is the case, at the very least, management was negligent. The grievance process works when the union files a timely grievance. Similarly, it works when management raises its concerns about arbitrability in a timely fashion.

3. Other than waiver, does management's conduct ever extend the time limits within which the employee must initiate a grievance?

Arbitrators will sometimes hear evidence from the union explaining why no grievance was initiated within the contract time period. Occasionally using a word familiar in a court setting—estoppel—an arbitrator will rule that management's action caused the belated filing of a formal grievance. If a management representative had told the grievant or the union that it was open to settling the dispute without a formal grievance, then the strict time limits should not bar the grievance, as long as the grievance was filed in a timely manner once settlement discussions proved unavailing.

IV. DECIDING PROCEDURAL ARBITRABILITY

Procedural arbitrability is a far more common issue in arbitration than substantive arbitrability. Procedural arbitrability objections raise difficult issues of fact and contract interpretation for the arbitrator. Even if the arbitrator would prefer to rule on the merits, the neutral has no power to ignore procedural requirements set forth in the CBA.

The most common situation involving procedural arbitrability deals with a grievance that, according to the employer, was not filed in a timely manner. Grievants also may contend that the employer has not answered a grievance in a timely manner. Parties to a CBA include time limits for filing and answering grievances in their contract in order to foster the expeditious resolution of disputes before memories have begun to fade. Management also wants a deadline after which a managerial decision can no longer be contested. On occasion, a CBA will require a grievant or union to specify those provisions allegedly violated. An arbitrator must make sure that management was made aware of the basis of the union's claim.

1. When does missing the contractual deadlines for filing a grievance or answering one become an issue that will bar review of the merits in arbitration?

Normally, an aggrieved employee must pursue a grievance within the number of days specified in the provisions of a CBA. Similarly, a CBA may impose obligations on management to respond to the grievance at the various steps in a specified number of days. Like every other clause in the CBA, an arbitrator must enforce these time limits if issues regarding them are raised in a timely manner. This may mean that missing the contract deadline will keep an arbitrator from hearing the merits of the case.

2.   But what if management has never enforced the time limits in the past?

As a general matter, an arbitrator will consider evidence of an established past practice that, in effect, constitutes a revision of a contractual time limit provision. This is a hard argument for a union to make, because, in the absence of compelling reasons to the contrary, the arbitrator must read what the parties said in their agreement and apply it to the case at hand. Unless the parties discussed the issue and reached an arrangement, it is difficult to establish that the repeated failure of management to bar consideration of a grievance that is not timely filed should be considered a practice that amends the time limits or constitutes a continuing waiver of some sort.

Arbitrators value the formality of written contract language. To find that the parties did not mean what they said in a time limits provision requires evidence that they, in effect, reached a supplementary agreement that amended their contract. Parties can do that, although it is rarely done orally. If management told the union: "Don't worry about time limits—we will never enforce them," that would be sufficient, but it would also be quite unusual. We will address the issue of contract interpretation in more detail in Chapter 12.

More generally, in cases like these the union argues and witnesses testify that management has never before refused to accept a grievance that was not timely filed. That is not sufficient to constitute a waiver of contractual rights in all future cases, however. The correlative situation would be a union that has never protested a certain management action that is prohibited by the contract but does so now. The failure to protest in the past does not constitute a waiver of contractual rights if a provision on point is contained in the CBA.

3.   What should an arbitrator do if the agreement does not specify a precise time limit for filing a grievance?

Unless the parties' CBA states plainly that an employee or the union can file a grievance whenever it gets around to it—something that is unlikely to occur—an arbitrator should interpret the parties' agreement to allow the filing of a grievance within a reasonable time after the incident occurs. Generally, that time frame is measured in weeks rather than months from the time the grievant or the union knew about the event in question, unless the union has a good explanation for why the grievance was delayed.

4. How does an arbitrator decide issues of timeliness in the filing of a grievance?

Contract grievance procedures normally contain a provision stating that a grievance must be filed within a stated number of days from the incident about which the grievant complains. The provision might also state that an untimely grievance should be denied.

Although it would seem that timeliness issues are easily resolved, it often requires something more than a calendar. A provision may set the time limit at "seven days," but does that mean seven calendar days or seven work days? Obviously, parties should specify one or the other.

One recurring issue is what event triggers the start of the time period. The provision may start the clock running when the incident occurs or when the grievant learns about it or reasonably could learn about it. What if the grievant was away on vacation? Does the clock stop running until he or she returns?

With regard to these issues and many more that have been raised on procedural arbitrability objections, arbitrators may take evidence on prior practice or even bargaining history. Simply because management has not raised a similar issue in the past does not mean that it has waived what the contract says, unless, of course, an understanding was reached between the parties regarding interpreting and applying the contract clause.

5. How does an arbitrator decide when a grievance is actually filed?

This would seem to be the easiest of issues to decide, but it is not. Collective bargaining agreements rarely state who must receive the grievance. First-step grievance procedures may be quite informal, usually involving a discussion between an employee and a supervisor on the floor, a conversation that is rarely recorded.

The problems that can arise with timeliness can be foreseen by the parties in negotiations. All it takes is one arbitration case where the issue is raised to trigger an effort to tighten the rules of the contract. A provision should specify when a grievance "arises," when it must be put into writing, which management office should receive the written grievance, and other such details.

It is not the arbitrator's job to fill in these details for the parties. He or she should use the terms of the grievance and arbitration provision as is, giving the terms a reasonable reading consistent with the parties' mutual intent as evidenced in the contract.

6.   *What if the grievant did not know he or she had the right to file a grievance about a certain management action?*

If the grievant or the union knew about management's action, that will generally trigger the running of the time limit. The fact that the grievant did not check the CBA or consult with the union is not an excuse for not filing a timely grievance.

7.   *What is a continuing grievance?*

Assume that the contract time limit requires an employee to file his or her grievance within 10 days of the occurrence giving rise to the grievance. The employee discovers that he or she was underpaid under the CBA, but only notices it a month after the first time he or she was underpaid. The employee is paid bi-weekly. Is the grievance the employee then files untimely?

The arbitrator could rule that once the time limit passes the grievant cannot complain about the incident—here about being underpaid the first time. On the other hand, the employer pays the employee every two weeks. Each time management pays the employee, it arguably commits another violation of the agreement's wage provisions. This is referred to as a *continuing grievance.* The arbitrator should rule that the late grievance is timely, but only to protest events that occurred within 10 days—the contract time limit in our hypothetical—of the filing of the grievance.

There are limits to the continuing violation approach. For example, assume that management assigns an employee certain work that he or she feels is not covered by the negotiated job description. A late grievance is filed. Should the arbitrator consider the grievance, or is it procedurally inarbitrable? Although the employer expects the grievant to continue to perform the work, it has not made another new assignment. The grievance is therefore untimely.

8.   *Should an arbitrator rule a grievance not arbitrable if it does not cite the contract provisions that were violated?*

Some CBAs require that an employee state in the grievance which provisions of the agreement were allegedly violated. Management will seek such a contractual requirement so it can check the provisions detailed in the grievance to determine whether the grievance has merit. If the grievance does not contain the required contractual references, management will argue before the arbitrator that the grievance is not arbitrable for failure to follow the contractual requirements. Management will also object at the arbitration hearing if the union advocate raises any other provisions in his or her opening statement beyond those originally cited in the grievance.

Unions have learned to deal with contract language that requires the specification of provisions allegedly violated. Shop stewards will know the contract well enough to insert the required allegations. To ensure that the union advocate is not sandbagged at the hearing, the grievance will typically also recite that management's action also violated "all other relevant provisions." The arbitrator should not allow the specification requirement to become a trap for the unwary. Specifying the contract provisions allegedly violated is often just a ministerial task. Management generally knows the CBA as well as the union and generally knows the basis of the union's claim. On the other hand, altering the contractual basis of a grievance at the arbitration hearing does disadvantage management, and the arbitrator must ensure that the process is fair for all concerned.

V. DECIDING SUBSTANTIVE ARBITRABILITY

On some occasions, management may argue that the arbitrator does not have power under the agreement to hear an issue of a certain class or category. The broadest claim might be based on a contract exclusion from arbitration of action taken by management pursuant to its reserved managerial power. More likely the substantive arbitrability claim will be based on an express exclusion from arbitration of a limited class of cases that are expressly noted in the grievance and arbitration provisions.

1. Why would parties exclude certain classes of disputes from arbitration?

Parties will agree to exclude certain classes of disputes from the scope of arbitration when there is an alternative procedure already in place to handle those cases. For example, a multi-employer pension plan in a particular industry may have a separate arbitration system to handle disputes that arise. Those employers and unions covered by the pension plan would not want pension issues to be addressed in the general arbitration procedure. Management may seek to keep certain issues, like subcontracting or pay rates, out of the grievance and arbitration procedure. An employer may be loath to allow an arbitrator to review what it considers inherently managerial concerns.

There is always a tradeoff in eliminating such issues from the internal dispute resolution system. First, all the asserted benefits of arbitration are lost. If the managerial action has an impact on the employees and they have no alternative systems within which to raise their concerns, there might be a work stoppage. Although the Supreme Court has held that a court may grant an injunction when a union strikes over a matter that could have been brought to arbitration, the substantive exclusion may preclude injunctive relief. Second, even if a union is unable or unwilling to strike, the absence of a readily available system to resolve a dispute may have an impact on productivity and morale in the plant.

2.   Should the failure of management to raise the matter of substantive arbitrability early in the grievance procedure constitute a waiver?

Management raises questions of arbitrability on a regular basis in arbitration, but they are mostly claims of a procedural nature. Substantive arbitrability claims are rare. Of course, management should raise substantive arbitrability claims in the first instance in the grievance procedure and not leave them for airing in arbitration. All the reasons offered above for finding waiver based on the failure to raise procedural claims before arbitration are applicable with regard to substantive arbitrability. Yet, the arbitrator should take a different approach.

In the absence of evidence that management purposefully held back a claim of lack of substantive arbitrability—evidence that is most unlikely to be produced—an arbitrator should be reluctant to find waiver of a substantive arbitrability claim. Admittedly, this is a difficult issue, and parties can make it easier—as some parties have done—by specifying in their agreement whether substantive arbitrability claims can be raised for the first time in arbitration.

Substantive arbitrability raises the question of whether the parties intended that their private tribunal have the power to address certain kinds or classes of issues. Procedural arbitrability, on the other hand, addresses matters that involve the process followed in pursuing a claim—whether the grievance was filed in a timely manner, whether the grievance included the contract provisions allegedly violated, or whether the grievance was on the correct form or was signed. Hearing a dispute based on a grievance that was filed a day too late when that defect was not raised by management until the arbitration hearing matches two defaults: the union's failure to timely file and management's failure to raise the objection in the first instance. A substantive arbitrability claim, however, goes to the power of the tribunal to adjudicate certain classes of issues. Management's failure to raise this issue—a failure, admittedly—should not bestow on an arbitration process a power it never had—to hear a dispute of a certain kind.

Chapter 5

Preparing for Arbitration

I. Overview

Arbitrators can easily tell whether a party is prepared to present its case in arbitration. The advocate will have notes (or even a full draft) for an opening statement; the exhibits are copied and ready to be offered into evidence either as joint exhibits or as exhibits offered by that party; the advocate has a list of questions or topics to cover with each of his or her witnesses and issues to raise on cross-examination of opposing witnesses; and, most importantly, the advocate understands the case and what it will take to prevail before the arbitrator. A party that is ready for arbitration has a much better chance of winning its case than a party that is not prepared.[1]

Why does this matter to the arbitrator? In fact, it is crucial: An arbitrator benefits when both sides are fully prepared to present their cases. The hearing moves along more smoothly, and even if the dispute is not easily resolved, it is easier to decide because of the preparation of the parties.

II. THE THEORY OF THE CASE

1.   What is the "theory of the case?"

As a dispute progresses through the various steps of a grievance procedure, each side refines its explanation of why it should prevail. Although management can simply deny a grievance at each step, it often explains to the union at a grievance meeting why it will not grant the request. Similarly, the union refines its argument as the case progresses. As a dispute moves through the grievance procedure, different people will become involved—top human resource management officials for the employer, and representatives from the international for the union. In some labor relations systems, lawyers may get involved at the final step. At any point, of course, management can grant the grievance and, alternatively, the union can decide to drop its protest. A case that makes it all the way to arbitration, however, must be important to the parties, with each side having good reasons to think that it will prevail once a neutral arrives on the scene.

The arguments and evidence brought to bear at the higher steps of the grievance procedure set the foundation for the *theory of the case,* that is, the reasons why each party thinks it should succeed in the resolution of the dispute. This theory becomes the basis for preparing evidence for the arbitration hearing and ultimately in writing a post-hearing brief in support of a party's position.

---

[1] *See* MARVIN HILL, ANTHONY SINICROPI, & AMY EVENSON, WINNING ARBITRATION ADVOCACY (1997) (discussing useful ideas on preparing and presenting a case in arbitration); LABOR ARBITRATION: A PRACTICAL GUIDE FOR ADVOCATES pt. IV (Max Zimny, William Dolson, & Christopher Barreca, eds., 1990) (practical and thoughtful discussions on preparing for arbitration).

Determining a theory of the case is the most important step in preparation for the arbitration hearing. Yet, it is surprising that so few parties seem to think in those terms. They certainly know that the case involves a discharge or is a contract interpretation dispute. They know they must prove just cause or compliance with, or violation of, the contract, but within the grievance procedure they may pose their arguments in their most adversarial stance. This may be useful in terms of the internal politics of management and the union, but it is misguided when it comes to prevailing in arbitration.

In every case—whether meritorious or meretricious—each party has some basis for its claim. It is critical that the arbitrator understand each party's theory. Every experienced advocate should know how the neutral can decide the case for its side—an arbitrator is not going to base a decision on a principle at the extreme, for example, that management can do whatever it wishes in all instances notwithstanding contract restrictions or that a clear contract eligibility requirement is unfair to the workers and thus should be set aside. If either extreme approach is the basic theory of a party's case, it should be reconsidered. Only a myopic partisan could actually believe that an experienced arbitrator would ignore contract requirements—it simply will not happen.

2.   How does one use the theory of the case?

Once a party has determined the theory of its case, everything that happens before, during, and after the hearing then has a direction. A party's theory of the case, if carefully thought through prior to the hearing, will be reflected in the opening statement, in the selection of the witnesses who will testify, and in the documents that will be presented. After the hearing, the post-hearing brief will follow the guideposts established in the theory of the case.

There are times, of course, when parties are surprised by what happens at a hearing. The testimony and documents offered by the opposing party may alter the factual basis of the dispute. If that occurs, a party must have the flexibility to change course. With a mature grievance procedure, however, documents have already been exchanged and the arguments of the parties have already been fully explored. In order to avoid a surprise at the hearing, parties sometimes provide in their collective bargaining agreement (CBA) that a document not supplied to the opposing side during the grievance procedure cannot be offered into evidence at the hearing. Arbitrators should enforce such provisions to avoid surprises and to encourage settlement prior to the hearing, if that is possible.

3.   What kinds of cases are brought to arbitration?

There are three basic types of cases that are brought to arbitration: discharge and discipline cases, which we will discuss in Chapter 10; management operational cases, which we will discuss in Chapter 11; and benefit cases, which either involve contract interpretation (covered in Chapter 12) or are based on evidence of past practice (discussed in Chapter 13).

With regard to discharge and discipline cases, the parties normally supply the arbitrator with little by way of contractual guidance. Management will normally have the right to discipline or discharge employees for "just cause."[2] As we shall see, that standard recognizes the legitimate interests of both management and the union, and it requires the neutral to determine what happened and whether what happened warranted the discipline or discharge meted out by the employer.

With regard to operational decisions, including, for example, work assignments and staffing, management action based on legitimate and substantial business reasons must be considered to be presumptively permissible in the absence of restricting contract language. In contesting a management operational decision, a union must be able to show a significant negative impact on the bargaining unit. Management must then demonstrate why it acted. The union can rebut the claim by showing that the purported business reason is a pretext.

Finally, with regard to matters of employee benefits, an arbitrator will apply a presumption against forfeiture of the benefit, such as paid vacations, paid holidays, insurance, or leaves. Management should not be allowed to unilaterally create qualification requirements limiting such benefits that are not set forth in the terms of the CBA.

4.   Should an advocate do research into reported arbitration decisions before the hearing?[3]

Unlike court adjudication, decision making in labor arbitration is not controlled by precedent[4]—a neutral need not follow the reasoning used by some other arbitrator. When the previous case was between the same parties, however, the arbitrator should show deference, an

---

[2] Some parties use "proper cause" or simply "cause" in their CBAs. In the public sector, a common reference is that discipline or discharge is warranted "for the good of the service." Arbitrators treat all these terms as synonyms for "just cause."

[3] *See* Charles S. Loughran, How to Prepare and Present a Labor Arbitration Case ch. 6 (2d ed. 2006) (explaining the value of researching authorities).

[4] The Latin phrase that parties and arbitrators use to describe this is *stare decisis*.

issue discussed in more depth in Chapter 14. Although not controlled by precedent, arbitral decision making normally proceeds within the boundaries set by what might be called "the common law of the labor agreement." Arbitrators are likely to follow established norms in reading and applying CBAs.

Therefore, it is useful when a party designs the theory for the case to find support in reported arbitration cases. These are available in law libraries and online. Starting research with a secondary source, such as *How Arbitration Works*,[5] can save time, but an advocate should read some of the more recent cases cited in the footnotes of such a source. Each party must determine whether its theory of the case is viable or, at least, defensible.

None of this research work is wasted effort even if it is never mentioned at the hearing. It becomes the basis for preparing witnesses, assembling documents, and, eventually, for drafting a post-hearing brief. If the opposing party argues at the hearing that no arbitrator would ever support such a position, a prepared advocate has at hand the reported decisions that rebut the claim. Some parties will submit to the arbitrator at the hearing copies of some well-reasoned arbitration decisions in support of its theory of the case as part of its closing argument.

Not all reported arbitration decisions are created equal. Experienced advocates understand the value of the decisions of Arbitrator Harry Shulman, whose formative work as the permanent umpire at Ford Motor Co. in the 1940s laid the groundwork for modern labor arbitration. Citing a decision by any member of the National Academy of Arbitrators (NAA) has more value than citing decisions issued by a less experienced neutral.

5. Do parties ever bring a case to arbitration for reasons other than the merits of the dispute?

At times, the union and management must stick to a position on a grievance even when it recognizes that its argument is not compelling. A grievance filed by or on behalf of a long-time, dues-paying union employee protesting his or her discharge will often be brought to arbitration because the employee's job is on the line, even if the case is not likely to succeed—the worker has been loyal to the union for a long time and finally obtains the union's representation in the most important case of his or her work life. In another case, the union might be concerned that its failure to process a dispute to arbitration might result

---

[5] ELKOURI & ELKOURI: HOW ARBITRATION WORKS (Kenneth May, ed., 7th ed. 2012).

in a lawsuit claiming that it breached its duty of fair representation. Even though those claims are very hard to prove, union leaders may be sufficiently concerned about the political implications of such litigation that they will process a grievance to the ultimate step of arbitration even if they don't think it will succeed.

Similarly, management may feel it necessary to deny a grievance throughout the grievance process as a way to show support to its front-line supervisors. These men and women represent the employer on the work floor, and they must have the confidence that management will have their backs. It may be easier for the organization to have an arbitrator to blame for overruling the actions of a supervisor.

Although every experienced arbitrator hears his or her share of such cases, the neutral knows that by doing so he or she plays an important role in serving the needs of the parties. In the case of the dischargee who will never win his or her case, the arbitrator offers the grievant the opportunity to tell his or her story to someone who will listen. In the case of a shop foreman whose action is rightfully contested by the union, the arbitrator likewise gives the supervisor a chance to explain. On cross-examination, the union should be able to develop facts that will show why what the foreman did violated the agreement, an explanation that might later be the basis of the arbitrator's decision.

III. Disparity in Resources

Union representatives bemoan the fact that they might not have the financial resources that management might have to fully prepare for arbitration, or at least to prepare as well as management can. If one party is not represented by an attorney at an arbitration hearing, that party is likely to be the union. Union advocates express concern that this disparity in resources means that the union will not prevail in its case. It is the arbitrator's job to make sure that the case is decided on the merits rather than on the resources of the parties.

1. Does the disparity between deep-pocket parties and parties with insufficient funds for legal expertise make a difference in an arbitration?

As a general matter (but not always), an employer has the advantage of "deeper pockets" in preparing for a hearing and in presenting the case. That means that it may be able to afford more attorney time in prehearing research and witness preparation. Most labor arbitration cases, however, do not require the extensive work that law firms can give to a case in civil litigation. Experienced union-side advocates, however, can effectively prepare for a case by meeting with their witnesses and focusing on the development of a theory of the case that will prevail before the arbitrator.

2.　*Do arbitrators recognize that monetary pressures exist, i.e., that employers will often use their financial advantage to impose on unions certain obligations beyond their resources?*

Arbitrators understand that in any given case management may try to take advantage of a union based on its own likely advantage regarding financial resources. For example, that factor might play a role in management requests to bifurcate a hearing, dividing threshold issues of arbitrability from the hearing on the merits. Such a move may encourage a union to drop a grievance or reach an unfavorable settlement. Management may unduly extend a hearing by calling unnecessary witnesses and repeatedly raising objections. Management will often be the party that requests a transcript, while a union probably could not afford to pay for a stenographic record. Unions may seek to avoid filing post-hearing briefs and prefer to close a case through oral argument at the hearing, whereas management may prefer to write a long, detailed brief.

Experienced arbitrators realize that one party may be playing strategic games to disadvantage its opponent. There is no evidence that this has an impact on the way experienced arbitrators actually decide cases on the merits. The arbitrator must make sure that the parties receive a hearing that provides due process to both parties. At the hearing, there must a level playing field.

The way the arbitrator accomplishes his or her assigned task is to keep focusing on the merits of the dispute. A union should not be disadvantaged by not filing a brief if its arguments are solid on the merits and it presents evidence in support of those arguments. An arbitrator should not bifurcate a hearing just because one party demands it. Fairness should be the arbitrator's lodestar.

IV. Prehearing Submissions

Normally, before the hearing the labor arbitrator receives a single email from an appointing agency that includes a word or two describing the dispute to which the neutral has been appointed to serve. Alternately, the parties will contact the arbitrator directly but not provide any additional information about the nature of the dispute. This is a far cry from the stacks of papers a civil trial judge might receive before a trial begins, including a complaint and answer, depositions, and other submissions. It also differs substantially from employment arbitration cases, where prehearing motions and submissions are common.

1.   Would the arbitrator benefit from receiving a prehearing brief?

In some very rare cases, the parties agree to submit to the labor arbitrator prior to the hearing memoranda explaining their side of the case and offering in summary form the arguments they intend to make. That is the norm in employment arbitration, as discussed in Chapter 17. There is no question this practice could help the labor arbitrator understand the case he or she is about to hear, but there are good practical reasons why parties and labor arbitrators do not favor this practice.

A significant portion—perhaps half—of all cases in which arbitration has been invoked and arbitrators are selected are settled prior to the hearing. Although some of these settlements are the result of the judgment by one party or the other that it cannot prevail in arbitration, they are also motivated by a practical assessment. Balancing the financial cost of pursuing the matter against the benefits of prevailing and discounted by the risk of losing, parties often decide to address the dispute themselves. Spending money to produce a prehearing brief may therefore be a wasted expenditure.

From the point of view of the experienced arbitrator, although prehearing briefs would be helpful in understanding the most complicated cases, for run-of-the-mill grievance disputes they are quite unnecessary. Moreover, if the arbitrator spends time reading the submissions—as he or she should—that adds to the parties' eventual bill. If the case settles after the arbitrator has read the prehearing submissions, it is difficult for the arbitrator to justify charging the parties for the study time spent.

2.   Is there any other way an arbitrator prepares for a hearing?

Junior arbitrators can prepare for a hearing by making a list of all the matters that must be covered when meeting with the parties at the arbitration hearing. There is a customary order of events that must be followed. For example, the arbitrator must remember to help formulate a stipulated issue. There are many tasks, and the new arbitrator needs a system to make sure all are covered.

It can be disconcerting to a new arbitrator to realize that he or she shows up at the hearing with only the names of the parties and the general category of the dispute. Some junior arbitrators will request a copy of the grievance and the CBA but after a while will find that they don't have time to read those documents before a hearing.

V. Witnesses[6]

The arbitration hearing offers the parties the opportunity to present their arguments and evidence to the neutral they have selected to resolve their dispute. Almost universally, evidence in a party's case is presented through witnesses who are sworn to tell the truth and who will be subject to both direct and cross-examination at the hearing.

1.   What witnesses should a party plan to call in arbitration?

With the theory of the case in hand, a party must identify those witnesses who will provide the facts at the hearing. After first carefully examining the grievance, the answer, and, of course, the contract, the advocate must meet with those who have firsthand knowledge of the events involved. The theory of the case provides the roadmap—the advocate needs to determine what facts are essential to make out the case and should select the best witnesses with personal knowledge to present each part of the case.

It is not unusual for each side to have one major witness and a series of secondary witnesses. As a general matter, however, parties present too many witnesses at a hearing. Perhaps they are concerned that the arbitrator might not be listening the first time a fact is explained and feel that a second and third iteration by another witness will be needed; maybe they think that the arbitrator decides a case based on counting the number of witnesses who testified; maybe they think that the party with more witnesses wins.

In fact, the opposite may be true. An arbitrator should be able to learn what happened from the first or second run-through—there is no need to present the dozens of persons who witnessed an event. By the third or fourth witness, the arbitrator should speak up and tell the advocate that he or she has heard the testimony and that it has become repetitive. If the party insists on presenting all of its witnesses, the arbitrator should allow the redundancy

An advocate should select the best witnesses to explain what occurred. Testifying is not fun, and for some people it can be a very stressful experience that may affect how well they can tell the story. Some are inarticulate or quick to anger, especially on cross-examination. After they have been prepared to testify, witnesses should be confident but not arrogant.

---

[6] *See* Loughran, *supra* note 3, at 167–205 (detailing the process of selecting and preparing witnesses); *See also* Labor Arbitration: A Practical Guide for Advocates pt. V (Max Zimny, William Dolson, & Christopher Barreca, eds., 1990) (offering suggestions on preparing and presenting witnesses as well as delivering opening statements).

2. How should an advocate prepare a witness for a hearing?

Direct testimony should flow into the record without need for leading questions or undue prompting. Some witnesses appear to arbitrators as if they met counsel representing their side only moments before testifying. An arbitrator can tell when a witness has not been prepared to testify. An unprepared witness may ramble, and in the process bury key evidence in a torrent of testimony. An arbitrator has to evaluate whether a witness' testimony is probative and truthful. Preparation can make a difference in this regard.

Preparing a witness for a typical arbitration case does not mean months of practice. Except for a key witness, a brief talk before the hearing about what the witness knows that is relevant to the case is all that is required. For many witnesses, this will be their introduction to the adjudicatory process, and the advocate should explain what will occur. The advocate should practice asking questions of the witness.

It is not the advocate's job to tell the witness what to say, although witnesses are very good at picking up hints of their preferred script. It is best to start with questions to the potential witness like those to be asked at the hearing. There is a significant risk if a witness embellishes his or her testimony at the arbitration hearing. An advocate should advise a witness to stick to the relevant facts. A short answer is preferable to a long one.

At the very least, the advocate should outline the testimony of each witness. For someone new to arbitration, it is often useful to actually write out the questions and share the list with the witness so that he or she knows what is to come on direct examination. Advocates should ensure that witnesses know that they will likely be sworn in by the arbitrator. An advocate should not be surprised if a witness is nervous when involved in the arbitration process, even in the preparation stage.

3. How should an advocate prepare a witness for cross-examination?

Preparing a witness for cross-examination is more of a challenge—obviously because an advocate does not know exactly what questions will be asked. A good cross-examiner will ask leading questions—questions that contain their own answer and often start with, "Isn't it true that . . . ."

An advocate should make clear to witnesses that it is not their responsibility to help the other side. Witnesses should tell the truth in as short and concise a manner as possible and should not volunteer information. If the cross-examiner demands a "yes" or "no" answer and the witness is unable to do so, the advocate should object to the question, and the arbitrator should interrupt and tell the witness to answer "yes" or "no" only if he or she can. If he or she cannot, the arbitrator should allow the witness to elaborate on his or her answer.

4.   How should an advocate prepare for cross-examination of the opponent's witnesses?

The worst cross-examination of a witness simply repeats the questions asked of the witness on direct examination, as if the advocate thinks he or she will get a different and better answer the next time around. However, if the arbitrator just happened to miss the point made on direct examination—something that happens during a long hearing—upon hearing the testimony for a second time, it is sure to make an impact.

The advocate should prepare for cross-examination by referring again to the theory of the case. What information can this witness provide that can help the opposing party make its case? That may or may not involve going back over some of the areas touched on in direct examination, but when an advocate ventures back into territory already covered, he or she should use the tools of cross-examination. On cross-examination, an advocate should never ask non-leading or open-ended questions. An advocate should always ask a question on cross-examination that contains its own answer, for example, "Isn't it true that . . . ." Finally, an advocate should not badger the witness—the arbitrator will take notice even if there is no objection. Cross-examination, as a general matter, should be short and not repetitive.

5.   Will the arbitrator notice if a key witness does not testify?

An experienced arbitrator will certainly notice when a key witness does not testify. If the fight on the work floor involved two employees, there was one witness to the incident, and that witness does not testify, the arbitrator will draw the negative inference that the witness would not support the position of the party that does not call him or her. If this is obvious, an advocate might explain to the arbitrator (if there is an explanation) why the witness is unavailable.

A more difficult case is presented when the person disciplined or discharged does not testify. Drawing a negative inference from such a failure to testify would likely doom the union's case. Although constitutional principles do not apply, arbitrators do recognize an individual right not to be compelled to testify against oneself. As a practical matter, however, the arbitrator will expect to hear from the grievant.

6.   Should a party subpoena witnesses?

As discussed further in the next chapter, an arbitrator will sign subpoenas at the request of a party. However, arbitrators do not have the power to force people to attend and testify—only a court can do that.

If a witness feels compelled to testify against his or her will, the party should not expect a great deal of cooperation—it is not likely there will be an opportunity to prepare that witness for the hearing. However, a subpoena may be useful as a "cover" when management seeks to have a fellow employee testify against the grievant. The witness should be able to return to the workplace and explain that he or she did not have a choice but to testify—the subpoena compelled the appearance.

Another situation where a subpoena might be useful is when a worker will only be paid when he or she appears at a hearing under a subpoena. This is a common situation and should not cause problems for a party.

VI. Documents

An arbitrator normally leaves the arbitration hearing room with a pile of documents presented by the parties either as joint or partisan exhibits. Many of these documents are only tangentially related to the merits of the case, but parties like to be comprehensive in their presentations. No party should ever present into evidence a document that its advocate has not read—the document as a whole may not support the party's case.

1.   How should a party prepare documents for a hearing?

Each party needs a system for organizing documents so they can be easily retrieved at the hearing. By placing them in clearly marked folders, the advocate will appear organized; by scattering them across the table or on the floor, the advocate makes an unfavorable impression on the arbitrator. Copies should be made for the opposing party, the witnesses, the arbitrator, and the court reporter if one is retained. An advocate should not pre-mark exhibits with numbers.

A recent practice in arbitration is for an advocate to place pre-marked exhibits into a tabbed loose-leaf binder for the opposing party, the witness, the arbitrator, and the court reporter. This is a very bad idea. Although it may be convenient, it should be avoided, because this approach assumes that every document in the binder will be admitted into evidence in the order the party predetermines. On the other hand, an advocate might keep his or her own copies of the unnumbered exhibits in a loose-leaf notebook with tabs.

Hearings can be orderly, but they don't proceed on script. Some arbitrators will refuse to accept the binder and instead tell the party to offer documents one by one so they can be identified, marked, objected to, and then accepted into evidence.

The arbitrator may have his or her own system for marking exhibits or might allow the court reporter to mark the exhibits. In either case, as discussed in Chapter 6, the introduction of documents one at a time will allow the arbitrator the opportunity to examine the exhibit and understand how it fits into the case.

2. What kind of documents will an arbitrator find useful?

The kind and amount of documentation assembled for an arbitration hearing depends on the nature of the case. If the dispute involves contract interpretation, documents about bargaining history, including notes and proposals, should be assembled. Records that demonstrate how the contract provision has been applied in the past are also commonly presented. Cases involving an incident in the plant may be documented by written witness statements that were prepared as part of management's investigation.

Some cases are so document-intensive that each party should think about summarizing the contents of large stacks of paper. Simply handing the arbitrator a pile of documents is worthless. A witness should testify about the portions of the document the party wants the arbitrator to read.

3. What will an arbitrator do with an exhibit created just for purposes of the arbitration hearing?

Documents created for a hearing can be very helpful to an arbitrator but will certainly generate an objection from the opposing side. That is why a party should share such an exhibit with the opposing party prior to the hearing or at least inform the opposing party that the exhibit is being prepared. This will give the opposing party an opportunity to check the underlying facts.

Summary documents may be particular useful to the arbitrator when they present a chronology of events; it is sometimes a challenge for the neutral to follow the course of events in a complicated case.

4.   *How do arbitrators feel about demonstrative evidence?*

Everyone in the hearing room except the arbitrator may know what a certain machine part looks like, or how the plant is arranged, or the appearance of a certain place where an incident occurred. Although parties should certainly consider taking the arbitrator on a visit to the plant, it may be useful to prepare demonstrative evidence that the arbitrator can take with him or her. Photographs, videos, charts, and graphs are common forms of demonstrative evidence and can be very useful;[7] blueprints of the shop floor can also help. Although the arbitrator is not going to take home a machine tool, he or she would mostly likely want to see it at the hearing.

VII. Exploring Settlement

As a general matter, it is much better for parties to settle their dispute privately than to have an arbitrator issue an award in a case. Sometimes, of course, that is not possible because a significant principle is involved or the parties need an arbitrator's order to blame for a particular result.

Arbitrators know that they play numerous roles in the procedure they are selected to administer. At times they serve the role of the "courthouse steps." In addition, there is always a risk in adjudication—once an arbitrator is selected and a hearing date is scheduled, each party is presented with the possibility of losing. Settlement discussions may then prove more fruitful, much like those that are said to occur on the courthouse steps before a civil case is tried.

Arbitrators also know that they play the role of scapegoat. If the grievant is returned to work, management can blame the labor arbitrator even if reinstatement was clearly indicated. If management's operational decision such as reducing the staffing on a machine is upheld, the union can blame the neutral. Arbitrators know that this is simply part of the service they provide to the parties, even when they decide cases correctly on the merits.

---

[7]*See* Loughran, *supra* note 3, at ch. 5 (comprehensive discussion on assembling evidence).

1.   When should the parties explore settlement options?

Parties should explore the possibility of settling the dispute early and often.[8] In practice, however, parties sometimes will not explore settlement until right before a scheduled hearing—that may be the time when each party finally appreciates the weakness of its case. Other parties wait until the actual hearing begins to discuss settlement. It is annoying to the arbitrator to sit for hours in the hearing room while the parties explore the possibility of resolving the dispute, but at least he or she is getting paid to sit and wait.

2.   Why aren't all cases settled?

Some cases simply cannot be settled. If management simply will not allow a dischargee to return to work in the plant—something the union insists on—settlement will be difficult. On the other hand, if a dischargee is working at another job, it may be possible to settle a discharge grievance with a cash payment and a promise not to inform future employers of the reasons for his or her termination.

Other cases are not settled because one party or the other recognizes the political implications of a settlement. Management must stand steadfast behind its supervisors, and a union must not allow management to get its way. Those cases will have to be tried.

3.   Are there ways to settle a case that will not have future implications?

Parties can settle a dispute on the basis that their arrangement to resolve the case is nonprecedential—in other words, they agree that the settlement should not be raised in the future by either party. If the issue remains important, it can be negotiated when the current CBA expires.

VIII. DISCOVERY

Parties create a dispute resolution procedure in an effort to resolve disputes in an expeditious manner without the expense normally involved in civil litigation. A significant portion of that expense is normally involved in pretrial discovery. Depositions, interrogatories, requests for documents, and the like take time and money. As a result, however, parties can discover where their claim stands. Pretrial

---

[8] *See id.* ch. 3 (suggestions on how to explore settlement).

discovery is essential in court, but it is rarely, if ever, used in labor arbitration. By comparison, extensive discovery is normally involved in employment arbitration cases, as discussed in Chapter 17.

1.   *Is there a role for discovery in arbitration?*

The labor arbitration hearing is the final step of the grievance procedure set forth in the parties' CBA. One important component of the grievance procedure is to allow the parties to exchange information. Normally, management will have documents that the union does not have. If it relies on those documents in responding to the grievance, it certainly must present those documents to the union. Parties may be mandated by their CBA to share information before the hearing. They should disclose those documents as part of the grievance procedure.

A union will normally make a request for documents, for example, the entire personnel file of a terminated employee. This exchange of documents takes place generally without the involvement of the neutral, who is yet to be selected. An arbitrator will get involved, however, if after appointment the union seeks documents that management has not supplied. There may be issues of privilege or some other basis for the reluctance of management to supply the information requested. In such an instance, the arbitrator will have work to do.

If management refuses to provide documents because it determines that they are not relevant, the arbitrator should ask management to comply with the union's request. If management declines to supply information because it claims it is unavailable, then there is nothing an arbitrator can or should do.

Unlike civil litigation, in labor arbitration there are no prehearing depositions or interrogatories. The information normally obtained through those procedures in a civil trial should be exchanged through the grievance procedure. Of course, in the absence of a deposition it will be difficult to impeach a witness, but the informality and comparative expeditiousness of labor arbitration should not be sacrificed.[9]

2.   *Should a party seek from the arbitrator a* **subpoena duces tecum** *to obtain documents?*

The arbitrator will sign a subpoena seeking documents *(subpoena duces tecum),* but it will take a court order to enforce the subpoena if

---

[9]*See* FAIRWEATHER'S PRACTICE AND PROCEDURE IN LABOR ARBITRATION ch. 6 (Ray J. Schoonhoven, ed., 4th ed. 1999) (discussion on obtaining evidence, including how parties can use subpoenas in arbitration).

the opposing party remains recalcitrant. At times the arbitrator's signature on a formal document will jar loose documents that have not been supplied. In any case, it will trigger a discussion with the arbitrator about one party's asserted need for the documents and the reasons why the opposing party will not supply them.

IX. *EX PARTE* HEARINGS

In some rare cases, management will inform the union that it will not participate in the arbitration hearing based on some claim that it is not required to do so. If the union knows that management does not intend to show up for the hearing, it will likely inform the arbitrator. Arbitrators should be prepared to address this issue even if it does not happen frequently.[10]

1. Does the arbitrator have the power to proceed to hear a case if one party does not participate?

There is no question that an arbitrator can hear a case *ex parte* as long as certain conditions have been met. Under the Rules of the American Arbitration Association (AAA)[11] and the Code of Professional Responsibility,[12] for example, as long as the absent party has received adequate notice,[13] the arbitrator can hear the case and decide the dispute based on the evidence presented by the party that participated.

A more difficult situation is presented when management has not participated in the selection of the arbitrator. If the CBA provides for joint selection of the arbitrator and that has not occurred, the arbitrator

---

[10] *See id.* ch. 3 (discussing bringing suit to compel or to stay arbitration, a matter in which the arbitrator is not involved).

[11] *See* AMERICAN ARBITRATION ASSOCIATION, LABOR ARBITRATION RULES (amended and effective July 1, 2013), *available at* http://www.adr.org/aaa/faces/rules/searchrules/rulesdetail?doc=ADRSTG_012406&_afrLoop=422248314580768&_afrWindowMode=0&_afrWindowId=7og4tr6be_1#%40%3F_afrWindowId%3D7og4tr6be_1%26_afrLoop%3D422248314580768%26doc%3DADRSTG_012406%26_afrWindowMode%3D0%26_adf.ctrl-state%3D7og4tr6be_57 (reproduced in Appendix D).

[12] *See* NATIONAL ACADEMY OF ARBITRATORS, AMERICAN ARBITRATION ASSOCIATION, & FEDERAL MEDIATION & CONCILIATION SERVICE, CODE OF PROFESSIONAL RESPONSIBILITY FOR ARBITRATORS OF LABOR-MANAGEMENT DISPUTES (as amended and in effect Sept. 2007), *available at* http://www.naarb.org/code.html (reproduced in Appendix B).

[13] The AAA Rules use the term "due notice." *See* AMERICAN ARBITRATION ASSOCIATION, *supra* note 11, at Rule 27.

does not have the power to proceed in the absence of a court ruling that orders arbitration.

2. *Should the arbitrator proceed to hear a case* ex **parte?**

There is a difference between whether the arbitrator *can* proceed and whether the arbitrator *should* proceed. Although the power to proceed is certain, discretion suggests an alternative course. Assuming that the arbitrator is satisfied that the absent party received notice of the hearing or even directly informed the arbitrator that it did not intend to attend the hearing, the arbitrator might delay or reschedule the hearing, offering the absent party an opportunity to change its mind.

Advocates in arbitration know that only courts, not arbitrators, can compel an absent party to participate in a hearing. The arbitrator can inform the participating party that, although the hearing can proceed, any resulting award might be worthless without court enforcement. If the participating party wants to proceed with the *ex parte* hearing in any case, the arbitrator should do so.

Chapter 6

Hearing Process and Procedures

I. OVERVIEW

The hearing is the critical phase of the labor arbitration process.[1] During the hearing, the arbitrator will receive relevant documents and oral testimony about the events that gave rise to the grievance. He or she will hear arguments from the representatives of the parties as to why their side should prevail. By the end of the hearing, most experienced arbitrators have a very good idea how the case will eventually be decided, although they normally afford the parties the opportunity to submit post-hearing briefs to summarize the facts and further argue their positions in the dispute.

Although some cases are so one-sided that the outcome cannot be altered by what happens at the hearing, most cases involve contestable issues that can be won or lost based on the evidence and arguments presented at the hearing.[2] That means that good advocacy can make a

---

[1] *See* John Kagel, *Practice and Procedure,* in NATIONAL ACADEMY OF ARBITRATORS, THE COMMON LAW OF THE WORKPLACE: THE VIEWS OF ARBITRATORS ch. 1 (Theodore J. St. Antoine, ed., 2d ed. 2005) (extensive and first-rate commentary on arbitration practice and procedure).

[2] *See* CHARLES S. LOUGHRAN, HOW TO PREPARE AND PRESENT A LABOR ARBITRATION CASE (2d ed. 2006) [hereinafter LOUGHRAN]; MARVIN F. HILL, JR., ANTHONY V. SINICROPI, & AMY L. EVENSON, WINNING ARBITRATION ADVOCACY (1997).

difference and affect the arbitrator's determination. Well-thought-out arguments and the professional presentation of the evidence have an impact. In addition, even if a grievance is totally frivolous, the conduct of the hearing itself can have a positive or negative effect on the workplace. Each case is an important event in the history of a collective relationship.

II. THE THERAPEUTIC EFFECT[3]

A labor arbitration hearing is an important event in the labor relationship between management and the union. Men and women who normally see each other only on the shop floor come together for a very different purpose. The union and the employer have selected an outside neutral to decide a dispute they could not resolve themselves. This arbitrator, who likely has never met the parties before, will be entrusted to carry out the mutual intent of the parties in resolving the questions at hand. One thing the parties know for sure: the arbitrator will resolve the issue. The dispute can be of crucial importance in the workplace or can simply involve one employee's complaint on a matter that rarely arises.

The arbitration hearing can be a very interesting event, although it will not likely be fun. It will look something like a court proceeding some may have seen on television, but the arbitrator does not wear a black robe or sit on a raised bench. The arbitrator takes charge, but without a gavel or a bailiff at hand. At first, some will confuse the hearing with a grievance meeting that normally takes place between management and labor. Some will want to speak up and make sure they can tell the arbitrator their story. The arbitrator will remind them that only each side's advocate will talk for their side. There might be a court reporter present to take a transcript, but that only happens on occasion.

For many who participate, a labor arbitration hearing is memorable, even if their position does not prevail. Although some parties arbitrate regularly, even once a week or more, for other parties an arbitration hearing is a very rare event. For workers, the event is noteworthy because for the first time a neutral person will be listening to and learning about their grievance. Through the grievance procedure, management had the right simply to deny the claim without giving much by

---

[3] Roger Abrams, Frances Abrams, & Dennis Nolan, *Arbitral Therapy*, 46 RUT-GERS L. REV. 1751 (1994) (comparing labor arbitration with psychological counseling and concluding that Justice Douglas was correct about the therapeutic and cathartic values of the labor arbitration process).

way of reasons for its action. Now the arbitrator will listen without a personal interest or preexisting bias.

1.   Does an arbitration hearing really have a "therapeutic" effect?

Justice William O. Douglas recognized the value of the arbitration hearing in *American Manufacturing,*[4] the first case of the *Steelworkers Trilogy,*[5] where the U.S. Supreme Court decided that even frivolous grievances should be ordered to arbitration in order to stabilize the workplace. But what value could there be in arbitrating a frivolous grievance? Justice Douglas posited that the arbitration hearing itself could have a cathartic or therapeutic effect—a grievant can feel a sense of relief in being able to tell his story to a neutral party, even if his or her discharge is ultimately upheld, and both parties benefit from a neutral hearing the evidence and listening to their arguments.

How does an arbitrator provide the "arbitral therapy" that Justice Douglas promised? Through *active listening.* It is important to the therapeutic value of arbitration that the parties present their own cases and that the arbitrator not serve as some form of investigator.

Every arbitrator has his or her own way of conducting a hearing, but arbitrators are not all equal in the eyes (and ears) of advocates. Some arbitrators just sit back and take notes, unless, of course, the hearing is transcribed, in which case the arbitrator might simply observe the hearing. This kind of docile and almost somnambulant neutral ill-serves the parties.

Other more aggressive arbitrators usurp the advocates' role—they not only decide the case, they try it as well. They may also interrogate the witnesses. It may be that these arbitrators are so skilled that they can ask witnesses better questions than the representatives of the parties, and they know the information they need to decide the case.

Both the arbitrator who usurps the roles of the advocates and the arbitrator who remains dormant throughout the hearing ill-serve the parties. It is critical that the arbitrator participate in, but not dominate, the hearing. The "therapy" that Justice Douglas talks about comes from the parties being able to present their own stories to the neutral they helped to select and see that the arbitrator is interested in their dispute. The process belongs to the parties, however, and it is not the role of the arbitrator to take over the hearing from the advocates. The parties own the arbitration—they just "rent" the arbitrator.

---

[4] Steelworkers v. American Mfg. Co., 363 U.S. 564 (1960).

[5] *Id.;* Steelworkers v. Warrior & Gulf Navig. Co., 363 U.S. 574 (1960); Steelworkers v. Enterprise Wheel & Car Corp., 363 U.S. 593 (1960). See Chapter 1, §V, and Appendix A.

2.   *Should an arbitrator intervene to clarify information?*

Sitting back as if judging a moot court contest may not be the most appropriate or effective role for the neutral with regard to therapeutic value. The arbitrator should "engage" in the hearing. When warranted, an arbitrator should participate in the exchanges between advocates and witnesses and ask questions of the advocates to clarify matters about which he or she may be confused. There are bound to be instances during a long day of hearing when the neutral does not fully understand certain testimony, and the parties will not always appreciate when the neutral loses track of what is going on during the hearing, especially if the arbitrator fails to communicate with the advocates. An arbitrator must speak up, if only for clarification purposes. This assures the parties that the arbitrator is listening and is following the presentation of evidence.

3.   *Should an arbitrator actively request missing information?*

From the moment the hearing begins, the arbitrator starts to learn about the nature of the case. Based on experience, an arbitrator knows generally what critical facts will be important. For example, in a subcontracting case where the CBA is silent on the issue, the arbitrator will listen for evidence of past practice and the impact of the contracting out on the bargaining unit. The arbitrator needs to learn management's business reasons for its action.

If the parties do not supply vital information, a well-timed question by the arbitrator could elicit that information from a witness, but that is not the arbitrator's role. The arbitrator should not make out a party's case. The absence of important evidence can be telling, and the arbitrator should assume that the parties know the common law of the labor agreement just as he or she does and not attempt to elicit evidence that one party or the other has either neglected or not chosen to present.

4.   *Should an arbitrator maintain control over the proceedings?*

It is the arbitrator's responsibility to make sure that the hearing offers a fair opportunity to both parties to present their cases. That may mean ruling on objections to the admission of evidence, or protecting a witness against belligerent badgering. It certainly means leaving the hearing with a good grasp of the key issues and the evidence presented.

This is all part of due process, and that is what the parties bargained for when they agreed to include arbitration in their CBA.

Although arbitration has the potential of being beneficial for the parties' relationship, a poorly run hearing disrupted by disputatious representatives can have a destructive impact on a labor relations system. Lawyers who confuse arbitration with an adversarial fistfight can seriously harm their clients in the long run. Some have referred to an arbitration hearing as a "family meeting," although, at times, the family appears to be quite dysfunctional. Nonetheless, the comparison may be apt in terms of the need to avoid permanently alienating individuals who one must "live with." If the arbitrator does not maintain control over the proceedings, the arbitration experience can exacerbate workplace wounds, affect productivity and morale, and provide none of the therapeutic value that Justice Douglas promised.

III. ATTENDANCE AT THE HEARING

Although the arbitration hearing can be an important event in the history of the labor relationship, it is not daytime entertainment. More to the point, it is not a public court hearing. It is a special-purpose meeting of the leadership of an enterprise—both company and union—and is designed to supply the neutral decision maker with the data needed to resolve a dispute.[6]

1.   Who can be present at a hearing?

An arbitration proceeding is private. Normally, in addition to the grievant and the representatives of the parties, each party comes to the arbitration with its witnesses and other directly interested persons. Other persons not involved in the case should not be allowed to attend unless both parties agree.

On some occasions a private arbitration becomes a matter of public importance. For example, when all the drivers for a city's bus company go on strike and management terminates them, the grievance of the dischargees becomes a matter of public concern. It might be that the local media will want to cover the hearing. (In states with

---

[6]*See* FAIRWEATHER'S PRACTICE AND PROCEDURE IN LABOR ARBITRATION ch. 7 (Ray J. Schoonhoven, ed., 4th ed. 1999) (discussing the hearing).

government-in-the-sunshine laws, the press likely has the right to attend a public sector arbitration hearing.) The arbitrator must be ready to
deal with the media in a way that makes the arbitration process meaningful to the public. At the same time, the process belongs to the parties, and therefore the arbitrator must work with the parties and other
stakeholders to maintain privacy as much as possible.

**2.   What should the parties and the arbitrator do when the
      grievant shows up with his or her own attorney?**

If a dispute arises under the terms of a CBA, the grievant has no
right to separate representation. The arbitration is between the signatories to the CBA, that is, the employer and the union. The presence of an
outside attorney, however, raises a practical problem.

It is apparent that a grievant who appears with separate representation wants to make sure his or her rights are being protected. He or
she may feel that the union is not adequately protecting those rights.
Excluding the outside attorney from the hearing room ensures that the
arbitration will not be the last word on the matter if the grievant does
not obtain all the relief he or she seeks. The arbitrator certainly wants
the hearing to be meaningful and not simply a prelude to a lawsuit
based on an alleged violation of the duty of fair representation.[7]

The arbitrator should talk privately with the representatives of the
parties and urge them to allow the third-party attorney to remain at the
hearing.[8] The arbitrator may even suggest that an outside attorney be
allowed to ask questions, but only after the parties have completed their
questioning of a witness. The third-party attorney should not be offered
the opportunity to argue before the neutral.

Parties may object strenuously to any outsider involvement, especially the union, which may rightfully be concerned that the outsider's
presence undermines its status as the exclusive bargaining representative. In the final analysis, the proceeding belongs to the parties, not to
the arbitrator. The arbitrator must follow the directives of the parties
even if he or she finds them unwise, as long as the directives are not
unethical. If one party continues to object, the arbitrator should exclude
the outsider from the hearing.

---

[7] *See* WILLIAM OSBORNE, LABOR UNION LAW AND REGULATION (2003).

[8] One informed commentator suggests that arbitrators might even warn the
union of its potential liability under the duty of fair representation if the grievant
seeks, but is denied, separate representation. DENNIS R. NOLAN, LABOR AND EMPLOY-
MENT ARBITRATION IN A NUTSHELL ch. 7 (2d ed. 2006).

IV. TRANSCRIPTS, NOTES, AND RECORDINGS

The purpose of the hearing is to allow the arbitrator to gather enough information to resolve the dispute. Even if the neutral were to simply engage in a conversation with the parties, he or she would still need to take notes. In fact, the arbitration proceeding almost always takes the form of a hearing, albeit informal, and for the arbitrator taking good notes is absolutely essential. A transcript might also be helpful.

1.   *Are transcripts worth the time and expense? Does the arbitrator prefer an official transcript?*[9]

Some arbitrators insist that the parties arrange for taking a transcript. With a transcript being taken, they can focus directly on the witnesses and their testimony without worrying about scribing notes. Other arbitrators actually prefer that there not be a transcript, although they rarely learn that the parties intend to have the proceeding transcribed until the hearing. Arbitrators will not object to the presence of a court reporter. Unless otherwise specified in the CBA, the official record of the hearing, even if the transcript is taken, is the arbitrator's notes.

Transcripts provide certain benefits. For the most part, they provide an accurate record of what was said at the hearing if some later controversy arises about the testimony. The transcript can be vital in helping advocates to prepare post-hearing briefs because it may be difficult for advocates to take notes during a hearing. However, transcripts are quite expensive for the parties—the cost often exceeds that of the arbitrator's fees. Also, waiting for the transcription to arrive may cause additional delays in the post-hearing phase of the arbitration proceeding.

It is not unusual for management to arrange that a transcript be taken without informing the union. The union may object to the taking of the transcript unless it has access to it without, of course, sharing in its cost. Under the Code of Professional Responsibility,[10] the arbitrator may make sure that the union has access to the transcript, an effort that commonly creates a conflict with management, which is paying for it. When a transcript is taken, the arbitrator receives a copy, and the neu-

---

[9]FAIRWEATHER'S PRACTICE AND PROCEDURE IN LABOR ARBITRATION, *supra* note 6, at ch. 7, §VI (strongly advocating the taking of a transcript).

[10]NATIONAL ACADEMY OF ARBITRATORS, AMERICAN ARBITRATION ASSOCIATION, & FEDERAL MEDIATION & CONCILIATION SERVICE, CODE OF PROFESSIONAL RESPONSIBILITY FOR ARBITRATORS OF LABOR-MANAGEMENT DISPUTES §5.B.1.c (as amended and in effect Sept. 2007), *available at* http://www.naarb.org/code.html (reproduced in Appendix B). *See* ELKOURI & ELKOURI: HOW ARBITRATION WORKS ch. 7 (Kenneth May, ed., 7th ed. 2012).

tral should offer to share that copy with the union. That will often prove a sufficient compromise for management and the union. If management objects to such an arrangement, and if the arbitrator cannot obtain resolution on this issue, the arbitrator should remind the parties that it is his or her notes that constitute the official record, not the transcript. In effect, this converts the court reporter into a stenographer taking notes for the employer, much as the union could have members of the grievance committee present at the hearing to take notes.

2. Does an arbitrator always read the transcript?

Most neutrals are used to taking their own notes and will look at the transcript only if there is a conflict between their notes and the facts stated in the parties' post-hearing briefs. Reading a transcript only adds to the time an arbitrator spends on a case, which, in turn, increases the costs to the parties. However, if there is a particularly critical section of testimony, the arbitrator may quote it from the transcript in his or her decision.

3. Should arbitrators use computers to take notes?

As arbitrators have become more comfortable using computers, more have begun to employ the devices in lieu of legal pads and pens to take notes. Some parties have problems with this trend, although they will not tell their arbitrator about their concerns during a hearing. The reason for this concern is that, when arbitrators take notes by longhand, they also follow the proceeding and watch the witnesses. The opposite occurs when the arbitrator is hidden behind a computer screen. The neutrals seem to become stenographers, and that is unfortunate.

Mindful of the therapeutic aspects of arbitration, it is better for the arbitrator to stick with pen and paper until technology allows the arbitrator to electronically transcribe notes based solely on the spoken word of witnesses.

4. If the arbitrator records the arbitration hearing, does he or she go back and listen to the recording?

Some arbitrators continue their longstanding practice of tape recording hearings. Under a few CBAs, the arbitrator is required to tape each hearing and maintain the tapes. There are two instances where an arbitrator will listen to the tape of a hearing: (1) if the arbitrator has not taken notes at the proceeding; or (2) if there is a conflict between the arbitrator's notes and the facts as included in the parties' post-hearing briefs. It may be very risky for an arbitrator to rely on his or her techno-logical prowess and not take handwritten notes. In very rare cases, an arbitrator will listen to the recording if he or she has already taken copi-ous notes of the proceeding when there is confusion as to what actually occurred at the hearing. As a general matter, however, listening to the tape recording of a hearing is a waste of time and the parties' money.

V. A Typical Hearing

1.   *What is the normal order of presentation at the hearing?*

There is no required order of events at an arbitration hearing,[11] although there are established practices that the parties can antici-pate. Parties can design their own procedures, but they normally ac-cept the practices that are most common, following the lead set by the arbitrator.[12]

A hearing normally begins with the labor arbitrator introducing himself or herself to those present. Some arbitrators spend a few mo-ments explaining that they are not a judge, but rather have been ap-pointed by the parties to hear and resolve the dispute at hand. The arbi-trator will then ask the parties if there are any joint exhibits. Once the exhibits are marked and entered into the record, the arbitrator will ask for opening statements. The established practice in a labor arbitration case is that management proceeds first in a discharge or discipline case and the union proceeds first in a contract interpretation case. After the opening statements, the arbitrator will work with the parties to set a precise statement of the issues to be resolved.

The parties then present their cases in turn. Once again, manage-ment proceeds first in discharge and discipline cases, the union in all other cases. Witnesses called to testify are normally sworn in by the ar-bitrator or the stenographer. After the direct examination of a witness, the opposing party has the right to cross-examine.

---

[11]In fact, in their CBA the parties can determine how they want their hear-ing to proceed. *See* Federal Mediation and Conciliation Service, Arbitration Policies and Procedures Part 1404, Subpart C, http://www.fmcs.gov/internet/itemDetail.asp?categoryID=197&itemID=16959. The FMCS Arbitration Policies and Procedures are reproduced in Appendix C.

[12]The parties should seek a process that achieves accurate results in an efficient manner that is fully acceptable to the parties. *See* Roger Abrams, *The Integrity of the Arbitral Process*, 76 Mich. L. Rev. 231 (1977).

After both parties present their direct cases, the party that proceeded first will be offered the opportunity to present further testimony and documents in rebuttal. Most arbitrators will caution parties that rebuttal should be limited to matters raised for the first time in the opposing party's case—it is not a second chance to present the evidence that could have been presented earlier. The opposing party might then have the right to present testimony and documents on surrebuttal, once again limited to matters raised for the first time in the rebuttal case.

The arbitrator will call periodic breaks during the course of the day and normally break for lunch if the hearing will not be concluded by early afternoon. At the end of the hearing, the parties may request the opportunity to file post-hearing briefs or close orally at the hearing.

Arbitration proceeds with an ordered informality. The process described here is the default procedure normally followed in labor arbitration, but parties can design their own process. As long as the arbitrator agrees—and he or she should—parties can design a court-like proceeding or even an informal "chat" with the neutral about the facts of the case. In any case, the purpose of the hearing is to make sure that the arbitrator receives enough information about the dispute to render an informed decision.

VI. Interpersonal Factors

Much like judges, arbitrators are affected by the behavior of advocates who appear before them. That may not mean that a disputatious advocate will lose a case he or she should win, but it could mean that, in a close case, the arbitrator might subconsciously consider that factor. Although the arbitrator must guard against such influences, to deny that it is a possibility is to ignore the fact that arbitrators are human.

1.   How important is an advocate's personal interaction with the arbitrator?

An advocate should address the arbitrator with the same respect he or she would (or should) give a judge, but not make the common mistake of referring to the arbitrator as "your Honor." Advocates should simply call him or her "Mr. Arbitrator" or "Ms. Arbitrator." An advocate need not accept everything an arbitrator does at a hearing without objection, but objections should be made pleasantly.

Advocates should keep an eye on the arbitrator during the hearing. During the opening statement, for example, they should make sure that the arbitrator is paying attention and writing notes. An advocate should remember to speak slowly. The advocate has the arbitrator's full attention and should use it to his or her advantage. When an advocate refers to a provision in the CBA, the advocate should tell the arbitrator what page it is on and give him or her time to find and read it.

An arbitration was once described as a play staged before an audience of one—the arbitrator. Advocates should know their audience and continue to learn about their audience during the hearing. Arbitration is not a mechanical process—it is a very human process, and arbitrators cannot help but be affected by the people who present the cases before them and the quality of their presentations.

Advocates should be careful with showing extreme displeasure when an arbitrator rules against them on an evidentiary matter during the hearing. Advocates who scowl have one strike against them. Arbitrators, in general, do attempt to be fair, but conducting a hearing is not easy work. Be kind and generous, and it will pay off. This also applies to arbitrators. If an arbitrator is grumpy and dismissive, he or she will not serve the parties well.

2.   *How is an arbitrator affected by the interaction of opposing advocates?*

Arbitration is not a pleasant day at the beach—it is work for the arbitrator and the parties. Representatives of the parties, however, may see the hearing as more than that—as, for example, another battlefield. As champions of their parties, they come to do battle with the enemy. Otherwise perfectly professional lawyers can become piranha at an arbitration hearing.

On one hand, it is the responsibility of the arbitrator to keep control of the hearing and not allow such unprofessional behavior. On the other hand, labor and management may simply not get along, and the arbitrator cannot expect them to hold hands. The neutral should allow some venting at the hearing. (After all, the representatives have to show their clients they are earning their fee.) After a brief explosion, the arbitrator should speak with the representatives together, outside the hearing room, and "read them the riot act." The arbitrator should tell them to cease sniping because it interferes with the arbitrator doing his or her job. Nasty venting at the hearing keeps the arbitrator from learning about the case, and it must be stopped.

VII. Joint Exhibits

Although the parties will prepare and present their own cases to the arbitrator, the hearing normally begins with a demonstration of bipartisanship. The arbitrator needs the basic documents in the case. Traditionally, those are supplied by the parties as joint exhibits.

1. What should be included in the joint exhibits?

Most arbitrators will start a hearing by asking the parties whether they have any joint exhibits. Normally, the CBA will be offered as the first joint exhibit, followed by a grievance package, which consists of the actual grievance and management's answers at various steps of the grievance procedure. The parties may agree that company rules or prior disciplinary letters should be part of the record as joint exhibits.

Parties new to arbitration may worry that allowing documents to be entered into evidence as joint exhibits might be considered some form of an admission against a party's interest. The norm in arbitration is the contrary. For example, accepting work rules as a joint exhibit does not mean the union accepts the rules as binding—it simply means that this document is what it says it is: the company's rules. Unless the rules are negotiated between the parties—a rare circumstance—only the terms of the negotiated CBA control. Marking a document as a joint exhibit should not in any way be considered an admission.

VIII. Other Preliminary Matters

The parties have work to do before the actual hearing begins. They must set forth the arbitrator's job, that is, what issues he or she is charged with deciding. They should decide whether to take the time and effort to stipulate that certain facts are true and uncontested. Finally, they must decide whether witnesses who will testify should be excluded from the hearing room while other witnesses are testifying. The arbitrator will want to get some sense from the parties how long the hearing will take. While no one can promise an exact time frame, parties generally know if the case will take all day or will be done by lunch. That is important information for the neutral because he or she will pace the hearing accordingly.

Before the hearing begins, arbitrators will ask the parties to sign an appearance sheet indicating the names of the persons in attendance and who will be testifying. The arbitrator also needs to know who should receive a copy of the opinion and award and who should receive the arbitrator's bill. The arbitrator may also use the appearance sheet to ask the parties whether they have any objection to the ultimate submission of the opinion for publication.

1.   What is the importance of the "statement of the issues?"

Parties must agree on what questions they want the arbitrator to answer. Sometimes prior to the hearing the parties agree on a statement of the issues that the arbitrator is to resolve,[13] although that practice is rare. A provision in the CBA's arbitration clause might even require that a joint submission of the issues be presented at the hearing. More likely, although each side may spend some time thinking about how it would want an issue to be formulated, the actual drafting of the issue is left to the hearing.

An arbitrator can learn about the nature of a dispute by hearing the parties' conflicting statements of the issues to be resolved. Extended discussion of the formulation of the issues, however, is counterproductive. Some issues are self-evident: a discharge case normally presents the issue of whether the employer had just cause to terminate the grievant, with the subsidiary question on remedy if just cause were not established. Some arbitrators will formulate the issue themselves and ask the parties whether this would be an appropriate statement of the submission. The parties normally agree and stipulate to the issues. At times, if the parties cannot reach agreement on the statement of the issues presented, they will authorize the arbitrator to formulate the statement of the issue in his or her decision.

The submission has possible legal implications. That statement defines the jurisdiction of the arbitrator. If an arbitrator ignores the stipulated issue in rendering the award, it constitutes sufficient grounds to set aside the award.

---

[13] *See* LOUGHRAN, *supra* note 2, at ch. 5, §III.A. Rule 25 of the AAA Rules states that the parties are to give the arbitrator "the demand and answer, if any, or the submission" at the opening of the hearing. In fact, this never happens. *See* AMERICAN ARBITRATION ASSOCIATION, LABOR ARBITRATION RULES (amended and effective July 1, 2013), at Rule 25, *available at* http://www.adr.org/aaa/faces/rules/searchrules/rulesdetail? doc=ADRSTG_012406&_afrLoop=422248314580768&_afrWindowMode=0&_ afrWindowId=7og4tr6be_1#%40%3F_afrWindowId%3D7og4tr6be_1%26_afrLoop% 3D422248314580768%26doc%3DADRSTG_012406%26_afrWindowMode%3D0%26_ adf.ctrl-state%3D7og4tr6be_57 (reproduced in Appendix D) [hereinafter AAA LABOR ARBITRATION RULES].

2. *Should the parties make the effort to reach stipulations of fact?*

Sometimes parties will seek to streamline a hearing by reaching stipulations of fact that they jointly submit to the neutral.[14] Of course, if parties reach those stipulations before the hearing, the arbitrator should receive them. It is not likely, however, that these stipulations will cover any matters in real controversy.

Alternatively, one party may suggest at the commencement of the hearing that the parties should now attempt to reach stipulations in an effort to make the arbitrator's work easier. In fact, attempting to stipulate to facts is not worth the time. It is much easier for parties to simply call witnesses who will testify to one fact or another. If the testimony is not controverted on cross-examination or by other witnesses, it becomes, in effect, the equivalent of a stipulated fact.

3. *Should witnesses be sequestered?*

In cases that depend on the factual recollections of witnesses rather than on documents, it is common for one or both parties to request that the witnesses be sequestered, that is, excluded from the hearing room.[15] This motion is generally referred to as "invoking the rule" and is often made even before opening statements are offered. The arbitrator will grant such a request. As a matter of practice, the grievant stays throughout the hearing, even if he or she is going to testify. Each party has the right to keep one person to help its representative in the presentation of the case. Any person in attendance who will not testify can stay throughout the entire proceeding.

Why should witnesses be sequestered? It is a practice firmly based on human nature. Witnesses can be affected by hearing the testimony of other witnesses, and sequestering allows the arbitrator a fresh hearing of each person's story. Before ordering witnesses to leave the hearing room, the arbitrator should explain to those excluded why they are being sent out of the room. They probably already knew about the

---

[14] *See* LOUGHRAN, *supra* note 2, at ch. 5, §IV.

[15] Earlier versions of the AAA Rules referred to this as the "retirement" of the witness or witnesses, a term the parties and arbitrators never use. The current Rules simply state that the arbitrator has the power to order the "exclusion" of any witness "other than a party" during the testimony of other witnesses. *See* AAA LABOR ARBITRATION RULES, *supra* note 13, at Rule 21. This reference also is in error; although the grievant does stay throughout the hearing, the grievant is not a "party"; the union is the party in a labor arbitration.

likelihood of sequestration, and each party has likely identified a place where the witnesses can wait to be called for their testimony. The arbitrator should also advise the sequestered witnesses that after they testify they are not to talk to one another about what happened during their testimony, because that would undermine the reason for their sequestration.

IX. OPENING STATEMENTS

With the preliminary matters completed, the hearing is ready to begin. It starts with opening statements.[16] Who goes first? It depends on the subject matter of the hearing. In discharge and discipline cases, management makes its opening statement first, followed by the union. In contract interpretation cases, the union proceeds first, with management to follow. The opening statements set the stage for the testimony to come.

1. What do arbitrators want to hear in opening statements? What is the impact of opening statements?

Parties must remember that the labor arbitrator knows nothing about the case and likely knows nothing about the parties. The first time the arbitrator learns about the nature of the parties' dispute is through opening statements. These generally brief recitations of the essential facts and positions of the parties are vitally important. They should explain to the arbitrator what each party's case is all about. An opening statement should be orderly but brief.

Most experienced arbitrators have previously heard a dispute like the one to be presented. From the moment the opening statement begins, the arbitrator begins to formulate a mental list of the kinds of evidence needed to establish a contract violation. The opening statement is also when the arbitrator begins to size up the arguments of the parties and the qualities of the representatives of the parties. It is a critical step in the hearing. Although opening statements are not evidence, arbitrators will note the asserted facts as presented in the arguments. Advocates must not overpromise. The opening statements will provide the arbitrator a roadmap for the hearing.

---

[16] *See* LOUGHRAN, *supra* note 2, at ch. 9.

2.   Should an advocate use an opening statement to rebut what he or she knows the opposing party will argue?

By the time parties come to arbitration they know (or should know) the opposing side's arguments. The first party to proceed with its opening—the union in a contract interpretation case or management in a discharge or discipline case—should use a part of its opening to rebut what it knows the other party will be arguing. It requires skill to do this well. After hearing what the case is about, an experienced arbitrator will likely know what arguments the opposing side will make. It is best then to address those arguments early and often. After the other party's opening, if the opposing party in its opening raises an argument not heard before, the arbitrator may allow the surprised party time to respond to matters raised in the opponent's opening.

It is not unusual that one side will find some parts of the opposing party's opening statement to be objectionable, false, or even outrageous, but advocates cannot object during an opening argument. The second opening party may use part of its opening argument to respond to factual mistakes in the opposing side's opening, but the advocate should only aim for the major errors and not confuse the arbitrator by focusing on minutiae.

3.   Are there circumstances where an advocate should refrain from making an opening statement or should provide an abbreviated opening statement? How do arbitrators react to this?

Although some advocates generally believe that an opening statement is essential to capture the attention of an arbitrator, it is not unusual for the union in a discipline or discharge case to "reserve" its opening statement.[17] Because management bears the burden of proof, it proceeds first with its opening statement and with the presentation of its direct case. Union representatives sometimes prefer hearing management's evidence before even offering an opening statement of its position. This common practice may be a significant error and, although arbitrators understand the union's strategy, they would much prefer to hear the union's position in the case up front. Arbitrators may also think there is some gamesmanship in the union's request to reserve its opening argument.

---

[17] *Id.* (suggesting this possibility in a discharge case that involves allegations of criminal misconduct).

The labor arbitrator uses opening statements to understand what a case is about. It alerts the arbitrator to factual controversies that he or she may have to resolve and the conflicting arguments that will determine the outcome of the case based on the evidence that is presented. A union should not reserve or waive an opening statement. It should alert the arbitrator, if only in a summary fashion, to what the union intends to show.

The opening statement need not detail a party's argument. Generalizations are appropriate, as are conclusory remarks, such as "the union will show management simply did not have just cause to discipline the grievant." By the time a case reaches arbitration, the union generally knows what the employer's witnesses will say. If management's opening statement offers no surprises, the union suffers no disadvantage by joining the issue at the threshold, and the arbitrator knows where the case is headed.

4.   *What is the impact on an arbitrator's thinking when an advocate offers either a lengthy opening statement in the nature of a summation or a detailed last-step grievance answer that is akin to a prehearing brief?*

An advocate who delivers a detailed, fact-oriented opening statement risks losing the arbitrator's attention at the very start of the hearing. Every case has different layers to it—the critical facts, the subsidiary evidence, and the tertiary matters that can clutter the proceeding and really have no impact on the outcome. An advocate who includes every fact in an opening loses the opportunity to present the most important evidence to the arbitrator in narrative form.

A very lengthy opening statement is not as effective as a summary of "coming attractions"—what the arbitrator will hear from witnesses at the hearing and how that testimony fits into a party's theory of the case.[18] The last-step grievance answer will likely become part of the joint exhibits, and the arbitrator should read it after the hearing if it is lengthy.

X. Witnesses

At the arbitration hearing, each party will call witnesses to testify about the facts that underlie the dispute. This may not be the most efficient way to present the facts. Advocates could simply relate to the arbitrator their version of events. Testimony of witnesses, however, may

---

[18]*Id.* ch. 9, §IV.C.

give the arbitrator a less perfect but more complete version of events. Cross-examination of witnesses offers the potential to reveal inconsistencies or other deficiencies that would convince an arbitrator not to credit the testimony presented on direct examination. Throughout the testimony, an arbitrator reaches judgments about what actually occurred.

1. Should the arbitrator swear in the witnesses?

As a matter of practice, arbitrators ask the parties what their "pleasure" is regarding swearing witnesses. Normally they want witnesses sworn. An arbitrator might do so at one time at the beginning of the hearing to get a better idea as to the number of witnesses who will testify. Others will swear in witnesses as they are called to testify to emphasize to the witnesses the solemn nature of sworn testimony. In a hearing that is being transcribed, an arbitrator may have the stenographer swear in the witnesses as they are called. It is better, however, for the arbitrator himself or herself to look the witness in the eye as he or she asks them to tell the truth.

Members of some religious sects will not "swear" to tell the truth, but rather "affirm" that they will do so. The arbitrator should be mindful of the conscientious objection of some witnesses. Whether they "swear" or "affirm," witnesses generally take their promise to tell the truth quite seriously. This cannot be out of fear that false testimony will lead to a perjury action, a most unlikely event even in court. It must be that people generally do take oaths seriously.

This does not mean that witnesses won't lie in their testimony. Some will fabricate testimony in an effort to assist their side of the case. More likely, witnesses may stick with the story they have told since the grievance arose, even if it was not totally truthful at that time. Finally, different people see and remember different things. That doesn't mean their testimony is intentionally false; it only means that testimony and memory can be faulty.

2. How does the arbitrator view the presentation of a party's direct case?

Arbitrators expect that a party's direct case will be prepared, organized, and smoothly presented.[19] There is no excuse for it not to be. Leading questions—where the question contains the answer the

---

[19] *Id.* ch. 10.

questioner seeks—should be avoided on direct examination, and they are unnecessary if a witness is well prepared. Some advocates seem incapable of asking non-leading questions. If the opposing party does not object, the arbitrator should allow the questions to be asked. However, if there is an objection, the arbitrator should explain to the offending representative that the question is argument and not evidence and that it is preferable if the arbitrator hears the facts directly from the witness.

As part of the direct case, witnesses should fill in the facts needed to make out the party's theory of the case so that by the end of the direct testimony of the key witnesses the arbitrator could (but won't) say "you win." Of course, there is cross-examination of witnesses and then the opposing party's direct case that leaves the ultimate question open and unanswered.

3.   Will an arbitrator accept direct examination witness testimony in writing?

One purpose of a hearing with live witnesses is for the arbitrator to hear and observe the witnesses in person. Although direct testimony can and should be prepared so that it is delivered as the party desires, it is always fascinating how the oral recitation under oath at the hearing may modify even the most practiced testimony.

On occasion, a party may seek to offer into evidence an affidavit from a witness who is not available for the hearing. The use of affidavits is common in employment arbitration cases, but not in labor arbitration cases. This "testimony" by affidavit may be absolutely accurate, but it is also not subject to cross-examination. Unless the proposed affidavit has been discussed and agreed to by the opposing side prior to the hearing or is not objected to at the hearing, the arbitrator should not allow it into evidence.[20]

4.   When might a party use an expert witness, and how does it affect the arbitrator?

Some cases lend themselves to the use of expert testimony, and the arbitrator may be called on to rule on the qualifications of a proposed expert witness. The advantage in presenting expert testimony is that an expert will be allowed to express an opinion regarding certain matters

---

[20] Although Rule 28 of the AAA Rules allows the arbitrator to "receive and consider the evidence of witnesses by affidavit," it should not be a favored practice. *See* AAA LABOR ARBITRATION RULES, *supra* note 13, at Rule 28.

that may be disputed.[21] In a case involving medical testimony, for example, both parties likely will have expert testimony. The arbitrator may even request permission of the parties to appoint his or her own expert to help decipher the testimony that is presented.

5. *Is aggressive cross-examination an effective technique?*

Cross-examination performed well can win a case;[22] cross-examination done poorly can lose a case. A belligerent, demeaning cross-examination of a witness will annoy the arbitrator and may push him or her to protect (and credit) the witness. It will certainly encourage nasty cross-examination of witnesses by the opposing party. It is far more effective to show respect to hostile witnesses and then skillfully carve up their testimony on cross-examination.

Parties must appreciate the limitations of cross-examination. It is almost impossible to make out a case through cross-examination of opposing witnesses—advocates should not expect to do that. An advocate should understand his or her party's case well enough to know what (if any) part of the direct examination of a witness has been harmful and should punch holes in that testimony. That may be the most effective accomplishment on cross-examination.

There may also be a few matters that can be elicited from a witness on cross-examination that were not raised on direct. Arbitrators do not apply the court rule that limits cross-examination to matters raised on direct examination. Advocates should ask leading questions on cross-examination that procure testimony that helps their case.

Advocates should never ask open-ended questions—why, what, when, where, or who—on cross examination. Advocates should also never ask the witness questions already asked on direct examination. A witness' second time answering the same question likely won't result in a different answer. If an advocate doesn't like a witness' answer, he or she shouldn't ask the question a second time. The witness will just say the unfavorable testimony one more time, and the arbitrator will write it down again.

Some of the most effective cross-examination is very short. In fact, there are times when a witness' direct examination has destroyed the opposing party's case. The most effective cross-examination is for an advocate to say to the arbitrator with a smile that he or she has no questions. It is possible that the arbitrator missed the import of the devastating direct examination.

---

[21] *See* LOUGHRAN, *supra* note 2, at ch. 10, §VI.
[22] *Id.* ch. 13.

6.   Can a party ask the arbitrator to direct a witness to answer a proper question?

If a witness refuses to answer a proper question, a party can ask the arbitrator to direct the witness to answer. The arbitrator cannot order the witness to answer and hold him or her in contempt for not answering, as would a trial judge. If the witness still refuses to answer, the arbitrator properly presumes that the testimony would not have been favorable to the party who called the person as a witness.

7.   Can an advocate ask a witness the same question over and over?

In court a common objection heard when an advocate, typically on cross-examination, asks a witness the same question again and again, is that the question has been "asked and answered." Judges will uphold the objection and tell the questioner to "move on." A different practice is preferred in labor arbitration. An arbitrator will likely allow an advocate to repeat a question on cross-examination, offering greater leeway. The advocate might think that the witness did not understand the question the first time; more likely, however, the advocate is just trying to obtain a better answer for his or her side.

The practice of trying to get a witness to change his or her testimony by repeating questions may be misguided, but it should not be the basis for sustaining an objection to the question. At some point, of course, the arbitrator will suggest to the misguided advocate that he or she "move on."

8.   Will an arbitrator allow a party to present witnesses and evidence in a rebuttal case?

Arbitrators vary in their practice regarding a rebuttal case, which is presented after both parties have offered their testimony and documents. Rebuttal should not be seen as another opportunity for the moving party—management in a discharge or discipline case and the union in all other cases—to again present the same evidence it offered in its direct case.

It is certainly understandable that the moving party would like the last word just in case the arbitrator forgot what it thinks it proved hours earlier. Under that theory, the case would go on forever, because both sides would want the last word. This is an abuse of the process that the arbitrator should not allow.

A rebuttal should be just that—a response to matters raised by the opposing party in its case that have not been addressed in the moving party's direct case. The better practice for an arbitrator is to limit rebuttal to those matters of evidence raised for the first time in the opponent's case. It is not an opportunity to present another direct case.

XI. Exhibits

In addition to testimony, parties to an arbitration hearing almost always present the arbitrator with documents as exhibits. In the near future, these documents might all be presented in electronic form, but for now the arbitrator leaves the hearing room encumbered by paper. It is remarkable to even the most experienced neutral to discover that the parties have saved and stored a piece of paper that is many decades old. It is even more remarkable that they are able to retrieve the document from their filing system.

1. How do arbitrators prefer exhibits to be marked and offered into evidence?

Arbitrators want a party to present them with an unmarked document, with copies to the opposing side and the witness. The arbitrator will then mark the document for identification. The party's representative should ask the witness if he or she can identify the document: "What is this?" Once the document is identified, the arbitrator should ask the opposing party whether there is any objection to the document. If there is none, it should be admitted into the record.

The opposing party may have questions about the document that should be held until cross-examination of the witness. If the questions address the authenticity of the document or its origins, then questions can be raised immediately on *voir dire*. However, most documents presented at an arbitration hearing have been seen by the opposing party during the grievance procedure. In those very rare cases where there is a genuine issue as to the authenticity of a document, the arbitrator may inquire about the evidence and, if warranted, exclude the document from the record if there is a significant risk that it is fabricated.

2. Can a party introduce exhibits that are specifically prepared for the arbitration?

Parties may object to the admission of documents prepared just for the arbitration, but the arbitrator may find these summary documents to be very helpful. When there is a large stack of papers involving events over a period of time, a party should create a summary of the materials for the convenience of the arbitrator. The best practice is to inform the opposing party before the hearing that a summary is being made. If the opposing party is surprised at the hearing by the summary, the

arbitrator must assure that party that it will have plenty of time to review the primary documents even if the hearing has to be continued to
a later date. Although arbitration is adversarial, arbitrators know that
it is rare for parties to create intentionally fraudulent exhibits for the
hearing, if only because the downside risk of discovery is too great.

XII. RULES OF EVIDENCE

Shortly after testimony begins, a party may raise an evidentiary
objection, claiming, for example, that the question asked by the opposing advocate calls for an answer that would constitute hearsay. Trial
lawyers are well trained in the often arcane rules and exceptions that
apply in court. They will make the same objections in labor arbitration,
hoping for the same response they would receive from a trial judge. An
arbitrator will likely disappoint them.

1.   What effect do rules of evidence have on arbitration?

Arbitration is normally informal. Strict adherence to court rules
of evidence can distort this practice, although the reasoning underlying
the rules of evidence may have some role in arbitration.[23]

The AAA's rule regarding the admission of evidence states that the
"arbitrator shall determine the admissibility, the relevance, and materiality of the evidence offered and may exclude evidence deemed by the
arbitrator to be cumulative or irrelevant and conformity to legal rules
of evidence shall not be necessary."[24] The universal practice is not to
conduct an arbitration hearing in accordance with court rules, although
parties can, if they wish, design their own system and procedure.

Some CBAs prohibit the presentation of documents for the first
time during arbitration when they were not disclosed during the grievance procedure. When an arbitrator faces such a surprise document and
the opposing party objects, he or she must follow the terms of the CBA
and keep the document out of the record.

---

[23] *Id.* chs. 11 and 12 (setting forth rules of evidence in case the parties might have
chosen as a neutral an arbitrator who thinks he or she is a judge). *See* FAIRWEATHER'S
PRACTICE AND PROCEDURE IN LABOR ARBITRATION ch. 12 (Ray J. Schoonhoven, ed., 4th
ed. 1999) (lengthy discussion of the rules of evidence). *See also* ELKOURI & ELKOURI:
HOW ARBITRATION WORKS ch. 8 (Kenneth May, ed., 7th ed. 2012).

[24] *See* AAA LABOR ARBITRATION RULES, *supra* note 13, at Rule 27.

2.   *What evidentiary standard should an arbitrator apply?*
Arbitrators work across state lines, and rules of evidence differ
from state to state, but is there any uniformity for arbitration
hearings? Do arbitrators even acknowledge different state
rules of evidence? Or do they rely on the Federal Rules?

Arbitrators do not apply rules of evidence—state or federal—at labor arbitration hearings. Many arbitrators who are lawyers know the rules of evidence, but unless both parties direct the neutral to apply those rules, they simply interfere with the presentation of the case. Many parties are represented in arbitration by non-lawyers, both human resource managers and union representatives. Applying court-designed rules would not be generally what the parties intended when they provided for arbitration as the alternative dispute resolution (ADR) method in their CBA.

3.   *To what extent should an arbitrator serve as a gatekeeper*
during an arbitration hearing regarding exclusion of evidence
in response to objections?

Although everyone knows that rules of evidence do not apply in arbitration, there are instances when, in fact, an arbitrator should keep evidence out of the record. *Gatekeeping* sounds like too harsh a characterization of the role of the arbitrator because it suggests that the norm should be to exclude testimony. In fact, the opposing default position should guide the neutral.

Rules of evidence keep testimony and documents of questionable reliability out of a court record. The purposes of a typical labor arbitration, however, are not well served by a strict application of those rules. The greatest risk is that an arbitrator will not learn enough about the dispute to resolve it accurately in a manner consistent with the terms of the parties' CBA.

4.   *Why don't arbitrators bar documents that were not produced*
in response to a subpoena? How should an arbitrator rule
when the parties have a multistep grievance process but one
side waits until the arbitration filing and appointment of the
arbitrator to engage in "discovery?" Should the arbitrator
manage the situation where one side or another uses the
grievance procedure to "hide the ball," and if so, how?

In the absence of express guidance in the provisions of the CBA, an arbitrator is loath to exclude documents from the record. But parties should follow agreed-to procedures in their ADR process, including their grievance procedure. At the hearing, however, the arbitrator's primary goal must be to learn enough about the dispute to decide it correctly in accordance with the parties' contract.

What then should the arbitrator do about noncompliance with a subpoena or belated discovery or any one of a thousand ways a party can abuse its own system of adjudication? Although most arbitrators would hope that ancillary matters just go away, that is wishful thinking and will not always happen. The best move for the arbitrator is to direct that a party fully comply with a subpoena and continue the hearing to a later date to allow the opposing party time to review the relevant documents.

Counsel familiar with the tactics of court adjudication may fight on every front in an arbitration, even on tertiary matters. An arbitrator just wants to get to the heart of the dispute. This difference in perspective may make a hearing a rocky adventure.

5.   Should an advocate raise evidentiary and testimonial objections?

Objections raised by either party at the hearing can be disruptive, but at times they seem unavoidable.[25] Consider an objection based on the relevance of certain testimony. How can an arbitrator possibly know whether testimony is relevant when there are no pleadings? The arbitrator may patiently explain to the objector that he or she has no basis for determining relevance, adding that if the arbitrator later determines that the testimony is not relevant, he or she will not consider it in reaching an award. If the party raises another objection based on relevance despite the arbitrator's admonition, the objection may be purposely designed to disrupt the flow of testimony. The arbitrator might then ask the person asking the allegedly "irrelevant" question to explain to the arbitrator how the testimony is relevant, in effect giving that party another opportunity to make his or her case to the arbitrator. That usually is enough to end spurious objections based on relevance.

6.   How do arbitrators react to an advocate who remains convinced that evidence should be excluded from the record even though the arbitrator has ruled that it is admissible?

Advocates should be respectful of the arbitrator even if the arbitrator has ruled against them during the hearing. Similarly, arbitrators must treat both advocates with respect. Arbitrators are people (as well

---

[25] *See* LOUGHRAN, *supra* note 2, at chs. 11 and 12.

as adjudicators) and cannot help but feel offended by offensive advocates. Arbitrators also are capable of making mistakes, and arguing further after an arbitrator has ruled against a party may give the arbitrator an opportunity to correct a mistake. On the other hand, at some point the arbitrator will say simply "I note your objection. Please proceed."

7.   What does it mean when an arbitrator takes a document into evidence "for what it is worth?" What is it "worth?"

Parties are rightfully outraged when arbitrators simply state that they will take an offered document into evidence "for what it is worth." Unless the arbitrator explains what he or she means, the party that offered the document might think he or she has won the case and the party that opposed the document might think that all is lost. Neither may be true, but the arbitrator is the person at fault. An arbitrator should explain what a document is, or may be, "worth." If it is relevant to the merits of the dispute, it may be worth quite a lot.

8.   Given that arbitration is meant to be informal and expeditious, why should an arbitrator attempt to resolve complex and confusing hearsay objections as if this were judicial litigation? Doesn't this only encourage the advocate to pile on needless objections and prolong the hearing?

The arbitrator must assure the parties that he or she understands the rules of evidence, including, mostly importantly, the hearsay rules. However, the arbitrator should not exclude testimony that is hearsay. The arbitrator should explain to the parties that he or she understands why hearsay is often excluded in court. The arbitrator should note if the testimony offered was double or triple hearsay and therefore of questionable reliability and value. However, it is important that parties and witnesses in an arbitration feel that they can testify freely about what they think they know. People rely on hearsay in their everyday lives—it should be no different in arbitration.

9.   Should an arbitrator apply evidentiary standards and exclude evidence or, alternatively, take proposed evidence into the record and evaluate the evidence later in light of the entire record?

There are times when an objection to the admission of evidence raises a genuine issue that the arbitrator will want to study before either admitting or excluding the evidence. For example, what should an arbitrator do when the basis of the grievant's discharge was evidence obtained in an illegal police search? The evidence would prove the grievant stole material from the employer. If the arbitrator excludes the evidence, as it likely was excluded from the grievant's criminal trial for theft, the discharge must be set aside.

The arbitrator should take the evidence and the testimony connected with it and reserve judgment on its admissibility. This allows the parties to argue the issue in their briefs. In fact, referring to this hypothetical, arbitrators should not exclude evidence obtained in violation of the Fourth Amendment. The arbitration is a collateral proceeding, and the U.S. Supreme Court has ruled that the exclusionary rule does not apply to such processes.

10. Are evidentiary objections an effective technique?

Lawyers who come to arbitration to represent parties find it difficult to leave their civil trial practice experience behind. They will object when the opposing side asks a question of a witness that calls for an answer that would be inadmissible in court. Is that proper? Should an advocate object when someone offers hearsay? What should the arbitrator do?

The rules of evidence do not apply in arbitration, because they were designed to keep certain types of evidence away from an untutored jury. An experienced arbitrator should know the value of evidence and discount unreliable testimony as not very useful. Parties can, if they wish, mutually decide that their labor arbitration hearing should be conducted in accordance with the rules of evidence, but that is extremely rare. It may be more common in employment arbitration, a process described in Chapter 17.

It might be useful to raise an evidentiary objection to test how the arbitrator addresses these issues, assuming that the advocate is not familiar through prior experience with the person selected to hear and resolve the dispute. In this way an advocate can learn how the arbitrator thinks about evidentiary matters.

Labor arbitrators are not judges in jury trial cases. They should err on the side of learning too much about a case as opposed to too little. Legalisms should, for the most part, be put aside. The labor arbitration hearing should be a safe place for people to present their best recollections without having to confront the cold formalism of a courtroom.

11. *Should a party raise an objection when the opposing party seeks testimony that may violate, for example, the attorney-client privilege? Should an arbitrator exclude such testimony?*

An arbitrator should exclude matters that would violate a privilege recognized by law. Communications between lawyers and their clients and between doctors and their patients should be respected in arbitration.[26] Offers made in an attempt to settle the dispute should not be allowed into evidence as a concession.[27] Arbitrators should not do anything that would discourage parties from settling their disputes.

12. *Is there any other evidence that an arbitrator should refuse to receive into the record?*

The results of an unemployment compensation hearing should be excluded from the record. Unemployment compensation operates under its own system, with different burdens of proof and statutes under which decisions are made. Of course, the arbitrator knows exactly what happened at the hearing based on who offers the evidence on the issue. If management attempts to offer the testimony, that means that the grievant's request for unemployment compensation was denied. If the union attempts to offer the testimony, it is apparent that the request for unemployment compensation was granted. In either case, the evidence is sufficiently prejudicial that it should be excluded from the record.

13. *Should testimony by telephone be allowed?*

When a party has an out-of-town witness, it is perfectly appropriate to request that the arbitrator take the testimony by telephone. It may also be possible now (or in the near future) to hear testimony live online through a service like Skype. One problem with telephone testimony is that the witness cannot see the advocate who is asking questions. At times, a witness' telephone testimony can really hurt that party's case. If the witness were at the hearing, he or she could see the advocate's facial expressions and, as a result, think more carefully about his or her testimony. This risk may be avoided when witnesses can appear online and can see the advocate who is asking the questions.

---

[26] *Id.* ch. 11, §IV.E.103.
[27] *Id.* ch. 11, §IV.F.1–3.

14. What is the impact on a case of a missing witness or even a missing grievant?

Experienced arbitrators know that at times parties will not present a witness because the value of that witness' testimony is counterbalanced by the risks presented by other parts of that witness' testimony. If the missing witness appears to the arbitrator to have played a critical role in the events raised in the grievance, the neutral will draw a negative inference that the missing witness would not have testified in support of the claim.

A missing grievant is more unusual, but an arbitrator can likely surmise that the dischargee is unavailable because he or she is incarcerated. That fact should be irrelevant, much like a grievant's failure to take the stand on his or her own behalf. Obviously, the absence of testimony by a grievant that supports his or her case cannot help the case, but even a missing grievant wins a case now and then.

15. Should an arbitrator ask questions of a witness?

The arbitrator is supposed to decide cases presented to him or her, rather than being an active participant in eliciting evidence. This means that the arbitrator should not make the case for either side through his or her questions at the hearing. But an arbitrator may be confused or uncertain as to a factual matter. An arbitrator's question posed after the parties have questioned and cross-questioned a witness is certainly appropriate. There are times when a question from an arbitrator in the middle of a witness' testimony is necessary in order to clarify matters, but it should not be a substitute for the parties' questions.

16. Should the arbitrator subpoena a missing witness or missing documents?

The AAA Rules provide that an arbitrator may subpoena both witnesses and documents "independently."[28] This is a terrible idea. It runs directly contrary to the basic nature of labor arbitration as "owned" by the parties. It suggests that the arbitrator is there as an expert to investigate the dispute rather than resolve it as the alter ego of the parties.

---

[28] *See* AAA LABOR ARBITRATION RULES, *supra* note 13, at Rule 27.

XIII. Housekeeping Matters

Arbitration hearings can drag on for days. It is the arbitrator's responsibility to make sure the hearing lasts only as long as necessary to develop the record needed to decide the dispute. Some arbitrators will just sit back and let the parties take control of the pace of the process, which is a significant error.

1. What can the arbitrator do to ensure the promptness of the parties and that the hearing moves forward at a reasonable pace?

Cases scheduled to begin at a certain hour should begin when scheduled. There may be exceptional situations—normally traffic—that may cause a delay, but it is the responsibility of both the arbitrator and the representatives of the parties to be there on time. The arbitrator must control the pace of the hearing to make sure it moves forward without undue delay.

One practice that can frustrate the arbitrator's effort to keep the arbitration moving forward is the repeated requests of one party for time to caucus at length before cross-examining a witness. This allows other witnesses to counsel their representative on every matter that should be raised on cross-examination. As a general matter, a witness' direct testimony at an arbitration hearing should be foreseeable. Parties should be prepared to cross-examine immediately. An arbitrator will be annoyed by the delay. Parties certainly do not want to incur the displeasure of the arbitrator when it comes to abiding by the arbitrator's rule limiting caucus time.

It is important for the arbitrator to realize that the representatives of the parties and others in the room need regular breaks to deal with personal issues such as using the bathroom. Certainly, when one party asks for a break, the arbitrator should grant the request. However, it is important to keep the hearing moving along. Most arbitrators will call for a 5- or 10-minute break and round up participants sitting in the lobby of the hotel after that time limit passes.

Some arbitrators will conduct the hearing without a break for lunch. For other arbitrators, that break in the day is necessary and useful in processing the material that has been presented. Of course, when the parties break for lunch the arbitrator should not sit with either party. The appearance of impartiality is critical.

2. Are arbitration hearings too long? What can the arbitrator do to keep the parties focused?

It is likely that only a few salient factual matters presented during the course of a long hearing will ultimately be considered critical in making the determination in a case. Although arbitrators hope that the parties understand this fact, they often do not. They will claim that they never know for sure what an arbitrator will find to be determinative. Perhaps half or more of the evidence presented, including the testimony, will be unnecessary or repetitive.

There are times when the parties present the arbitrator with cumulative evidence. The arbitrator should let the presenting party know that he or she has already heard that information and that there is no need to repeat it. Parties may be willing to stipulate that, if additional witnesses were called to address a particular matter, they would offer the same information as the witnesses who have already testified.

3.   Can a case ever be submitted without a hearing?

The hearing is not the only place where an arbitrator can discover the facts that underlie the dispute. There are times when the parties agree on the facts and differ only on the proper interpretation of a contract provision in question. Here the case might be submitted on a set of stipulated facts, with briefs filed by both parties. For the arbitrator such a submitted case is a very sterile exercise, much like answering a take-home examination. Nonetheless, the proceeding belongs to the parties, and if the arbitrator is willing to take the "exam," it is perfectly appropriate for the parties to suggest it.

Of course, a submitted case may leave the arbitrator with some questions. Arbitrators may agree to resolve such a dispute with the caveat that the representatives of the parties be willing to hold a conference call to answer the arbitrator's questions after he or she has reviewed the submitted materials.

4.   Should the advocates take the arbitrator on a plant visit?

Arbitrators generally find plant visits to be useful exercises.[29] Testimony about what gave rise to the grievance can be put into context by a quick visit to the plant. In carrying out the visit, the arbitrator must be concerned about the appearance of impartiality. The arbitrator should always be accompanied by one management and one union representative.

Should the conversations that take place on the workplace visit be considered part of the record? It is hard to handle the mechanics of bringing a court reporter along for the walk. The conversation is not evidence, but more in the way of argument.

---

[29] AAA Rule 30 refers to this not as a "visit" but as an "inspection," a term no one uses. *See* AAA Labor Arbitration Rules, *supra* note 13, at Rule 29.

It is best for the plant visits to take place during or after the hearing rather than before it commences. In this way the arbitrator can reflect on the testimony he or she is hearing or has already heard and place it into a physical context.

5. Any advice on the "care and feeding" of arbitrators?

Common courtesies are much appreciated by arbitrators. Unless the arbitrator is hearing a case in or near his or her home city, travel, and normally an overnight stay, are involved. The parties should make hotel suggestions that are convenient to the hearing. They should offer to drive the neutral to the airport after the hearing. (The opposing side will be unlikely to object.) Of course, no mention of the case should ever be made *ex parte* on the way to the airport (or anywhere else).

The Code of Professional Responsibility cautions arbitrators about "personal relationships with the parties"; the arbitrator should have "no contact of consequences with representatives of either party while handling a case without the other party's presence or consent."[30] That means, for example, when there is a break in the hearing for lunch, the arbitrator must eat alone (or perhaps with the court reporter). The reason for this well-established practice is not that the arbitrator would be influenced by sharing a sandwich with an advocate, but that it might give rise to a concern by the other side. The appearance of impartiality is absolutely essential.

XIV. At the Close of the Hearing

At some point every arbitration hearing ends. There are then strategic decisions to make, both by the advocates and the arbitrator. Should an advocate waive closing arguments and rely on a brief? What should an advocate do if one advocate wants to file a brief and one does not? The arbitrator must set a briefing schedule if post-hearing submissions will be filed.

---

[30] National Academy of Arbitrators, American Arbitration Association, & Federal Mediation & Conciliation Service, Code of Professional Responsibility for Arbitrators of Labor-Management Disputes §2.D.1.a (as amended and in effect Sept. 2007), *available at* http://www.naarb.org/code.html.

1.   Should an advocate waive closing arguments?

After a long day of hearing (or many days in some cases), the arbitrator likely has a pretty good idea about the parties' arguments and what he or she has heard about their cases. If the parties are going to file post-hearing briefs, there is no need for closing arguments. Even if there will be no briefs, closing arguments should be summary in fashion, wrapping the case together with the evidence the arbitrator has heard.[31]

2.   In a noncomplex case, should the arbitrator encourage the parties to make closing statements in lieu of full briefings? Why should the arbitrator insist that both parties agree on whether briefs or oral closings will be used?

The arbitrator should not insist on any particular procedure at the close of the hearing. If one party (typically management) requests permission to file a brief, the arbitrator should grant the request. If the other party (typically the union) requests permission to make a closing statement, the arbitrator should agree and grant the request. If management is going to file a brief, the arbitrator should always give the union the opportunity to file a brief, which need not be lengthy, in addition to offering a closing statement. The arbitrator should not make it appear as if the union is at a disadvantage in not filing a brief, and, in fact, because briefs may not make much of a difference in the outcome of a case, the union is not at a disadvantage.

The employer's advocate may object if the union is offered the opportunity to both write a brief and offer a closing statement. The arbitrator should then offer management the same opportunity. If management declines, it has nothing to complain about. The arbitrator should never refuse a request of a party to make a final statement orally.

Some arbitrators allow the union to make its closing argument to the neutral in private, that is, after banishing management from the hearing room. The idea apparently is that if management can hear the union's closing argument, it will have an advantage in writing its brief. Excluding management is a bad option. There will be no surprises in the union's closing. Management likely knows the union's arguments already from its opening statement—or even from the positions it took in the grievance procedure. If the union feels it is at a disadvantage, it should take the opportunity to write a short brief—sometimes called a "letter brief"—for the arbitrator.

---

[31] *See* LOUGHRAN, *supra* note 2, at ch. 15.

3. Does an arbitrator prefer closing oral arguments by advocates, or should such closing arguments be made in the form of post-hearing briefs, which will have the benefit of the transcript of the proceedings and additional legal research if necessary?

An arbitrator appreciates a good closing argument and a good brief. As between the two forms of argument, an arbitrator would likely prefer a brief. He or she has already heard the parties' argument as part of the opening statements. The brief may give a party the opportunity to reshape and rethink some parts of its presentation, and that may assist the arbitrator in formulating his or her opinion and award.

There is a substantial cost difference to a party in pursuing one strategy or the other. An oral closing statement does not increase the cost to a party, but a brief normally does. For management, the cost may simply be seen as part of "the cost of doing business"; for a union on a tight budget, however, a closing statement might make more sense.

4. When and how should an arbitrator retain jurisdiction in a case?

After the arbitrator issues the award, he or she no longer has any power to address issues in the dispute. In particular, as discussed in Chapter 7, the arbitrator is considered *functus officio*, the task as neutral having been performed. In a discharge case, however, it is not unusual for the union to request that the arbitrator retain jurisdiction in the matter if he or she upholds the grievance in order to address any issues that may arise concerning the implementation of the remedy, in particular with regard to the calculation of back pay.[32] As discussed in Chapter 10, parties normally do not encumber hearings on discharge or discipline with evidence about back pay and mitigation efforts on the part of the grievant.

Arbitrators normally will agree to retain jurisdiction for a limited period of time—generally 60 days—to address particular issues, such as the calculation of back pay. During that 60-day period either party can request that the arbitrator address the matter in question. In fact, it is rare that the parties will need the arbitrator's assistance after the award is issued.

5. How long should the parties have to submit a brief?

It is customary to grant the parties 30 days in which to submit their post-hearing briefs. If a transcript has been taken, that 30-day period runs from the date the parties receive the transcript. It is not unusual for

---

[32]LOUGHRAN, *supra* note 2, at ch. 17, §VIII.B.5.

the parties to agree between themselves to extend this period, although an arbitrator should be reluctant to allow multiple extensions that delay resolution of the dispute.

In cases administered by the AAA, the parties simultaneously file their briefs electronically with the AAA administrator of the case. The tribunal administrator then forwards both briefs electronically to the arbitrator when they are received. In cases administered by the FMCS or by direct appointment, the arbitrator must set the procedures for the submission and exchange of briefs. Some arbitrators have now moved toward electronic filing of briefs attached to emails to the arbitrator, with hard copy briefs to follow to the opposing party and to the arbitrator if there are attachments to the briefs.

It is important to make sure that one party does not have the advantage of seeing the opposing party's brief before submitting its own, although, presumably, parties can agree on a different system that allows for the filing of one brief, then a reply brief, and even another brief in further reply. That approach, which is not unusual in court proceedings, should be disfavored in labor arbitration because, once again, it delays the resolution of the matter in dispute.

6. *Is there any truth to the lore among parties that arbitrators always already know their decision by the end of the hearing?*

Experienced arbitrators generally know how a case will come out by the end of the hearing. It is not a myth; it is a fact. As explained earlier, during the course of the hearing the arbitrator makes interim judgments about the state of each party's case. What elements are necessary in order to make out a case on this claim? Does the contract language say what a party claims it says? Was a witness credible? How does the testimony from various witnesses fit together? Evidence will trickle in to the arbitrator through documents and testimony about these matters. With each point taken, the arbitrator makes tentative judgments within the framework of the established common law.

This reality does not mean that the arbitrator is making a purely subjective judgment. In order to reach certain interim conclusions, an arbitrator must be schooled in the common law of labor arbitration[33]—those principles that traditionally have been applied by neutrals in deciding cases like the one the arbitrator has been appointed to resolve. We have explored some of those principles and will continue to do so throughout the remainder of this text.

---

[33] *See* NATIONAL ACADEMY OF ARBITRATORS, THE COMMON LAW OF THE WORKPLACE: THE VIEWS OF ARBITRATORS (Theodore J. St. Antoine, ed., 2d ed. 2006).

7. *Should the arbitrator issue a bench decision?*

Under some arbitration provisions, the arbitrator must issue a decision immediately upon the close of the hearing; this is referred to as a *bench decision*. Under the Code of Professional Responsibility, an arbitrator should fulfill this obligation or not accept the appointment if he or she does not intend to issue a bench ruling. In addition, with the permission of the parties, an arbitrator can offer to issue a bench decision at the close of the hearing even if the agreement does not require it. As a general matter, however, arbitrators rarely offer to issue bench awards.

If, as discussed earlier, arbitrators generally know how the case will come out by the end of the hearing, why would neutrals be reluctant to let the parties know? In part, the reason is based on telling the losing party in person that it has lost. Although an arbitrator must have courage to carry out the functions of the office, telling an advocate face-to-face that he or she failed to prevail is uncomfortable at the very least.

Even if an arbitrator knows how the case will come out, the neutral may also find it useful to think further on the matter before issuing a decision. The process of writing an opinion may clarify the arbitrator's reasoning. The parties' briefs can also affect the ultimate judgment. Indeed, for outside advocates, writing a brief may be one way to demonstrate to their clients the contribution they made to the case—whether they prevail or do not.

Chapter 7

Post-Hearing Procedures

I. OVERVIEW

With the completion of the arbitration hearing, the parties have created a record on which the arbitrator will base his or her decisions regarding the submitted issues. On occasion a party will request permission to supplement the record with, for example, a deposition taken later of a witness who for good reason could not appear, or additional documents that were unavailable at the time of the hearing. In general, however, the case is closed when the hearing is over.

After the hearing there is obviously more work to be done both by the advocates for the parties and the arbitrator. As a matter of general practice, parties will file post-hearing briefs that summarize the important facts contained in the record and reiterate the arguments made at the hearing. The arbitrator will review the record and his or her notes, read portions of the transcript if any has been taken, and assemble the data into an opinion and award that resolves the dispute. The decision must explain to the parties the reasoning behind the arbitrator's award.

II. Briefs

The arbitrator will normally ask the parties at the close of the hearing whether they wish to submit briefs. If the parties have prepared for arbitration by developing their theory of the case and then presented witnesses and documents in support of that theory at the hearing, preparing a brief is not that difficult.[1]

1. *To what extent do briefs make a difference in the arbitrator's decision?*

Briefs can make a difference in the decision of the arbitrator, but normally they do not. That may astound some lawyers who are sure that their court filings determine judicial outcomes, but it is true both in labor and employment arbitration and in court that briefs might not make a difference in the case. Although labor arbitrators generally make up their minds on cases by the end of a hearing, there are exceptional cases where briefs can be of significant importance. Some cases are extremely difficult; others are too confusing to understand in the absence of careful study of the record. In such instances, a clarifying and persuasive brief can be critical.

The problem for advocates in labor arbitration is that at the close of the hearing they do not know into which category their case falls. Is this one of those "slam-dunk" cases where a brief is mere surplusage? Or is it a really tough case where the arbitrator needs the help that a brief can offer? Almost always, extreme partisans tend to think that

---

[1] *See* CHARLES S. LOUGHRAN, HOW TO PREPARE AND PRESENT A LABOR ARBITRATION CASE ch. 16 (2d ed. 2006) (discussing post-hearing briefs).

their cases are in better shape than they actually are, which would make a brief unnecessary. In the absence of any information as to whether the arbitrator has made a decision in the case when the hearing has ended, the advocate should write a good brief based on the assumption that it might make a difference.

2. Has a party's brief ever persuaded an arbitrator to reach a different conclusion after the hearing itself has concluded? If so, what are some of the persuasive factors?

Some arbitrators say that post-hearing briefs are worthless, although they rarely admit that publicly. Why then do parties file them in virtually every case? There are both practical and strategic reasons to file a brief. For an outside attorney retained for a particular case, a written brief offers the opportunity to further demonstrate to his or her client that the attorney has made a genuine contribution to the case. Put more bluntly, writing a brief is another way for the advocate to earn his or her fee.

On some occasions, however, briefs can make a substantial difference in the outcome of a case. The arbitrator may have misunderstood a party's argument made at the hearing. On occasion, an argument is much better made in writing than orally. Facts and arguments that become hazy in the jumble of evidence at a hearing can be clarified in a well-crafted brief.

With regard to cases that are truly difficult to resolve, a brief might determine the outcome. Some cases offer a significant challenge to both the advocates and the arbitrator. Although parties may think that their cases are easily resolved in their favor, there are some that are a major test of the arbitrator's reasoning and writing skills. In a very few cases, an arbitrator may actually write two opinions with two different outcomes before deciding which way to go on a case. In those situations, a terrific brief will make a real difference.

3. What makes a good brief?

A brief is a written piece of advocacy. An arbitrator will find a brief helpful if it summarizes the facts objectively and presents a party's arguments clearly and fairly. With regard to the facts, an advocate should cite page references if there was a transcript taken. The party's arguments should explain once again the contentions it made at the hearing, setting them forth in a clear fashion. A good brief also responds to the significant arguments made by the opposing party, explaining why the arbitrator should not accept them.

Parties must be careful not to engage in hyperbole either at the hearing or in their briefs. It is critical to maintain the trust of the arbitrator. Name-calling may be a way of life for attorneys practicing in some state courts, but it can really be annoying to an arbitrator. If a brief misstates a fact (or includes facts that were not presented at the hearing), an arbitrator will lose faith in that advocate and discount the value of other parts of his or her presentation.

4. Should the parties always file briefs?

Although arbitrators have differing views regarding the value of post-hearing briefs, they are not likely to refuse a party's request to submit its views in writing. The ultimate value of a brief, of course, depends on its quality. Arbitrators can always use good briefs, whereas poor briefs seem like a waste of time. However, no one sets out to write a poor brief, although, for many parties going through the process of composing a brief, it may seem like cruel and unusual punishment. Most would rather just argue the case orally at the close of the hearing.

As explained in Chapter 14, by the close of the hearing arbitrators normally have decided the outcome of a case and generally have determined what the reasoning will be. If that is the case, what good can come from filing a brief? In some instances, a good brief will cause an arbitrator to change his or her mind about a case. In all instances, briefs give the parties one last chance to state their case in a cogent fashion. Issues, arguments, and facts that were confusing to the arbitrator at the hearing may be clarified in a brief even if it does not alter the ultimate outcome of the case.

5. Are there types of cases where a brief is particularly helpful?

The general rule should be that the more complex the case, the more help a brief may provide to the arbitrator. Complexity can be the result of a multi-day hearing that produced stacks of documents. The brief will explicate intricate arguments that weave together the common law of the labor agreement, the provisions of the collective bargaining agreement (CBA), and the facts. If a hearing is filed with jargon that is specific to a particular workplace, a brief is certainly useful in explaining what occurred as long as it does more than simply repeat the confusing jargon.

By comparison, in a simple case where the parties agree on what occurred but differ on its implications under the CBA, a brief might be less useful. Nonetheless, even in the simplest of cases, arbitrators may find something in a brief that will be helpful in constructing the opinion and award.[2]

6. Do arbitrators actually read post-hearing briefs, and, if so, is it better to keep them shorter rather than longer?

Although a party that does not prevail in the arbitration might think otherwise, arbitrators actually do read post-hearing briefs. It is true that a long, tedious brief will not delight an arbitrator, but sometimes a very complex case warrants such extensive treatment.

The default rule in writing briefs should be that "less is more." The advocate should know by the end of the hearing whether the arbitrator had been paying attention. If the neutral has followed the testimony, there is no need for the brief to recite every bit of what every witness said. If the arbitrator was engaged during the hearing, he or she already knows each party's basic arguments. The brief should repeat those arguments in a clear and straightforward fashion.

7. What use does the arbitrator make of a party's brief?

Arbitrators will read the parties' briefs even if they do not turn out to be particularly helpful, let alone determine the outcome. Presented with a brief of a party that will lose the case, the arbitrator has the opportunity to respond in the opinion to each and every argument made in that brief. That is a critical part of the arbitrator's job, and, although the losing party might not be pleased with the ultimate outcome, responding to every argument in the brief enhances the legitimacy of the arbitration process. It is essential that both parties appreciate that the arbitrator has listened to their arguments and digested their proof.

When the arbitrator responds to every argument made by the party that does not prevail in the arbitration, he or she demonstrates respect for that party and for the positions it proffered at the proceeding. A careful response explaining why each argument does not alter the outcome is the arbitrator's final contribution to the therapeutic value of arbitration.

Arbitrators rarely ask the parties to submit briefs, although they will raise the issue at the close of the hearing and seek input from the

---

[2] Although standing alone it would not justify writing a brief, an arbitrator often finds a brief useful because of the inclusion of names spelled correctly and of places discussed at the hearing.

parties as to their desires. As a matter of practice, outside counsel will normally want to submit a brief, especially if counsel represents management. It is more likely that a union representative, either an international representative or an attorney, would prefer to argue the matter orally. Oral presentations at the end of the hearing, however, may come at a time when an arbitrator is tired after a long day of hearing testimony. Effective closing arguments may summarize the case, but the arbitrator should always give the party an opportunity to submit something in writing as well.[3]

8.   *What should a brief contain?*

The contents of a brief should reflect its purpose, which is to convince an arbitrator of the merits of a party's case. It should contain a recitation of the evidence already presented and a reiteration of the arguments already made, and it must do so in a manner that allows the arbitrator to decide the case in favor of that party.

Advocates who are not used to the ways of labor arbitration might suggest incorrectly in their briefs that the arbitrator must decide a dispute a certain way—either because precedent "commands" such an outcome or the evidence in the record is so compelling for that party. Arbitrators do not respond well to arguments that they do not retain discretion in deciding the case.

An arbitration brief is part of the adversarial process. It is not a neutral memorandum or a short law review article that contains the best arguments made by both parties. It is a continuation of the hearing, restating and refining the arguments already made. Raising new arguments for the first time in a brief is bad form because, as explained below, briefs are normally filed simultaneously. An argument raised for the first time in a brief may result in a justified request by the opposing party to respond to that argument by filing a reply brief.

A brief should contain a summary of the facts presented at the hearing through documents and witness testimony. Occasionally, a party might forget to ask a witness a particular question at the hearing but will insert the missing information in its brief. Once again, such

---

[3]Some commentators have suggested that if the union offers to make a closing argument orally and management indicates that it will file a brief, the arbitrator should exclude management's representatives from the hearing room while the union delivers its closing. That would be an absurd practice. The union's closing likely reiterates arguments it made in its opening statement. The parties have presented evidence through testimony and documents, and it is unlikely that management will learn any secrets by being present during the union's closing argument.

a practice is bad form and may lead to a request for a reply brief. The brief should only contain a discussion of the actual evidence that was presented at the hearing.

A brief should also restate a party's arguments. As discussed above regarding the theory of the case, these arguments should provide the arbitrator with a road map that he or she can actually follow in reaching a destination favorable to one side or the other. The arguments should not present extreme partisan positions that an arbitrator could not possibly adopt, such as management's right to do whatever it wishes in the interest of profitability or the union's desire for "fairness" in the face of an express contract clause that does not support its interests.

9.   How long should a brief be?

Normally, a party can summarize the facts and its arguments in 10 to 15 pages. This means that a 20-page brief would be much better than a 50-page brief. Some advocates seem incapable of writing a 20-page brief and think that longer is better, which is not necessarily so. It depends on what is said in the longer brief.

At some hearings, especially those that last for many days, the parties may raise the issue of whether there is a page limit on the briefs they will submit. The arbitrator should suggest to the party that a brief of modest length would be sufficient. Setting an upper limit—something that is quite common under local practice rules in civil court litigation—seems unwarranted.

III. Using Legal Research in a Brief

In preparing for the arbitration hearing, parties should research related arbitration cases to learn the types of arguments that arbitrators have used in resolving disputes like theirs. Although these published opinions might not be raised at the hearing, they will be useful in writing a party's brief. Although lawyers are more familiar with using legal precedent, nonlawyers who present cases in arbitration are well qualified to read and use published arbitration decisions in their briefs.

1.   Should a brief cite and discuss arbitration awards?

Whether a brief should discuss published arbitration decisions depends on the practice of the arbitrator who hears the case. Arbitrators vary regarding their use of published awards in their opinions. Some believe that the parties have selected them as their neutral in order to obtain just his or her opinion regarding the issues at hand. To such an arbitrator, citing in a brief what some other arbitrators have said about similar issues in cases involving different employers and unions would not make sense. Writing a brief for such a neutral, an advocate need not cite or discuss other reported arbitration cases.

Other arbitrators recognize the value in citing arbitration decisions both in terms of how that arbitrator's opinion and award is received by the parties and in terms of placing the arbitrator's views in the mainstream of arbitral reasoning. Parties should appreciate that their arbitrator's decision falls within the established order, that the outcome is consistent with the way all (or at least many) other arbitrators would decide the case, and that their arbitrator provided what they wanted— regular, standard arbitration. This affords the ultimate opinion and award greater legitimacy with the parties, in particular with the party that does not prevail.

How do advocates know whether their arbitrator wants to receive a brief that cites and discusses published arbitration decisions? Most experienced arbitrators have published arbitration awards. Reviewing those awards will inform the advocates whether their arbitrator regularly cites other arbitration decisions. Some published arbitration decisions cite no other awards, and that is indicative of how an advocate should design his or her brief. In the absence of such data, the advocates can certainly ask the arbitrator at the close of the hearing about his or her preference on citing and discussing other arbitration decisions in their briefs.

Of course, prior arbitrations between the parties to the case that are discussed at the arbitration hearing should be covered in a post-hearing brief. Normally, these prior cases have been submitted into evidence, and the arbitrator will have to address them in his or her opinion. The briefs must explain how the parties see the impact of these prior decisions on the case at hand.

2. How compelling are other arbitrators' decisions to an arbitrator?

Assume, as in most instances, that at the close of the hearing the arbitrator has a very well-defined view as to how the case should come out. Can the arbitrator be convinced by other arbitrators' decisions to reverse direction? An experienced neutral likely has heard and decided cases like the one the parties have presented for resolution. Finding that some other arbitrator has ruled the other way in some unrelated case not involving these parties will not likely change the outcome he or she has already reached.

In a case where the arbitrator is really at equipoise, however, other arbitrators' decisions can be very persuasive —"compelling" may be too strong a characterization. Who these other arbitrators are can make a difference. Experienced arbitrators who are members of the NAA know many of the other members, and their assessment of the other arbitrators' abilities may color the impact that the other arbitrators' decisions will have.

3.   How do arbitrators feel about a party citing secondary sources as a rationale for the arbitrator's decision?

Some arbitrators rely on secondary sources, such as the definitive work originally written by Frank and Edna Elkouri, *How Arbitration Works.*[4] These arbitrators would not mind if parties simply point them to the section of the tome that covers the issue at hand. In any case, it is certainly a good place to start researching an issue. Other arbitrators would much prefer if the parties would read and, where appropriate, cite and discuss the cases included in the copious footnotes of the Elkouri text.

How Arbitration Works does a good job of summarizing what arbitrators say they are doing in resolving particular issues. It does not analyze those issues or express an opinion on what the preferred approach is when arbitrators differ. Thus, unlike the work on restatements of the law by the American Law Institute, *How Arbitration Works* does not take sides. By comparison, *The Common Law of the Workplace: The Views of Arbitrators*, edited by distinguished academic and arbitrator Ted St. Antoine,[5] is a better source to cite simply because NAA arbitrators wrote the chapters, and they do analyze issues and reach reasoned judgments on matters about which arbitrators differ.

IV. THE MECHANICS OF FILING A BRIEF AND ISSUING AN AWARD

Parties ought to know what to expect regarding the filing of their briefs and the arbitrator's issuance of the decision and award. It is the arbitrator's responsibility to plainly explain how this is to be accomplished.

1.   When are the briefs due?

At the close of the hearing, the arbitrator should work with the advocates to formulate the briefing schedule. The parties' CBA may

---

[4] ELKOURI & ELKOURI: HOW ARBITRATION WORKS (Kenneth May, ed., 7th ed. 2012).
[5] NATIONAL ACADEMY OF ARBITRATORS, THE COMMON LAW OF THE WORKPLACE: THE VIEWS OF ARBITRATORS (Theodore J. St. Antoine, ed., 2d ed. 2005).

include a provision on point. In the absence of such a provision, it is most common to give parties 30 days to file a brief, or 30 days from receipt of the transcript if one is taken at the hearing. In some instances, the parties or the arbitrator will propose an even shorter schedule, especially if the case involves a discharge and the grievant is not working.

It is not unusual for parties subsequently to seek an extension of time in which to file a brief because of the press of business. Normally, the advocates will consult with one another. Upon reaching an agreement, they will inform the arbitrator and seek his or her agreement to the extension. The arbitrator will normally agree to one extension, but may not be very agreeable to a second extension request from the same party.

In a case administered by the AAA, the arbitrator will inform the tribunal administrator when the parties will file their briefs. Today this is normally accomplished electronically. The tribunal administrator will then forward both parties' briefs to the arbitrator and will forward a copy of the other party's brief to each party.

2. *Why do parties file briefs simultaneously in arbitration?*

The norm in labor arbitration is the simultaneous filing of briefs, with no reply briefs allowed. (In court, by comparison, reply briefs may be the normal local practice, and it may also be the practice followed by some employment arbitrators.) The thinking behind this is that the parties in arbitration have heard each other's arguments, both at the hearing and throughout the grievance procedure, and it is time for the case to be resolved. The simultaneous filing of briefs accomplishes that goal.

Each arbitrator may have his or her own method for filing briefs. As noted, in a case administered by the AAA, the parties transmit their briefs to the tribunal administrator, who, in turn, sends them on to the arbitrator and sends each party a copy of the other party's brief. In all other instances, the arbitrator explains to the parties at the hearing how briefs are to be filed. One common way is to transmit the brief to the arbitrator attached to an email on the date established for filing. The arbitrator might then ask each party to send by regular mail a hard copy of its brief to the arbitrator and a hard copy to the other party. In this way, the parties do not see the other parties' brief before they file their own. The hard copy transmission to the arbitrator also allows an advocate to attach copies of reported cases and other such material to the brief—something that might be more difficult to accomplish electronically.

If one party includes in its brief matters that were never raised at the hearing or arguments that are proffered for the first time, the arbitrator will normally grant a request by the opposing party to respond in writing to those new arguments.

3.   *Is it necessary to attach all cases and statutes cited in a brief?*

Most arbitrators have access to reported cases and statutes, but it is certainly more convenient for the arbitrator to have an advocate attach the important cases and statutes to the brief. Full-time arbitrators may be traveling when the opportunity to work on a pending case arises. It may be somewhat harder to get access to reported cases and statutes when on an airplane.

Sometimes cases involve materials that are not easily accessible by arbitrators. In a particular employment setting, such as federal public sector cases where decisions of federal personnel agencies might be important and might not be easily accessible, parties should attach copies of the relevant materials to their briefs.

4.   *How does an arbitrator issue his or her opinion and award?*

The arbitrator issues his or her opinion and award through the AAA tribunal administrator in a case administered by the AAA and directly to the parties in a case administered by the Federal Mediation and Conciliation Service or by direct appointment. Arbitrators are increasingly issuing their awards electronically, attached to an email to the advocates along with the arbitrator's bill.

V. INVOKING RESERVED JURISDICTION

Most issues of remedy are addressed by the parties themselves without the need for further intervention by the arbitrator. Calculation of back pay is not easily accomplished if the parties intend to come up with a precise figure exactly equivalent to lost wages and benefit. It is more likely they will reach a reasonable estimate of the amount lost by the grievant. There will be occasions, however, when the arbitrator will have further work to do in implementing the award.

1.   *In some cases, with the permission of the parties, an arbitrator reserves jurisdiction in a case to address any problems that may arise concerning implementation of the award. How does a party invoke that reserved jurisdiction?*

The arbitrator normally reserves jurisdiction for a stated period of time, usually 60 days, to respond to any problems that may arise concerning the implementation of the award or the calculation of back pay. Within that 60-day period, either party can contact the arbitrator, normally done now by email, to seek his or her assistance. The party should briefly explain what issues remain to be resolved.

Upon receiving such notification, the arbitrator will contact the opposing party to seek its input. It is rare that a further hearing would have to be held, but it may be necessary to schedule a conference call to allow the parties to argue their positions to the arbitrator. The arbitrator can then issue a supplementary ruling on the matter.

VI. ATTORNEYS' FEES

In some instances, under the provisions of a CBA or by statute, the party that prevails in arbitration can seek an award of attorneys' fees by petitioning the arbitrator. However, arbitrators may not be familiar with this practice, and the prevailing party will have to educate the neutral on the process and procedure.

1. *Can a prevailing party seek legal fees?*

The norm in labor arbitration, as in civil court, is that both parties are responsible for their own legal fees. In the federal sector under the Back Pay Act, prevailing parties can receive legal fees. They must set forth the information required by the federal statute, indicating the hours spent on the matter and providing information about the prevailing rate for attorneys in the region where the case took place.

In rare cases, the arbitrator may determine that one party has acted willfully in bad faith, for example, by unduly delaying or obstructing a proceeding. In such instances, the arbitrator will consider a request to award attorneys' fees even in the absence of a statutory basis.

2. *Why are legal fee applications sometimes denied despite clear contractual and/or statutory language providing for them?*

There is no good explanation for arbitral error. Although arbitrators may be unfamiliar with the statutory language, the applying party's submission should certainly make that information available.

VII. POST-AWARD CONTACT WITH THE ARBITRATOR

Parties that are new to arbitration may attempt to contact the arbitrator after he or she issues the decision, either with questions or complaints. Once again, the informal nature of the process may confuse the representatives of inexperienced parties.

1.   Can a party contact the arbitrator to ask questions about the opinion and award?

After an arbitrator issues an award, he or she no longer has jurisdiction over the dispute. It is not unusual, however, for a party unfamiliar with the law and practice of arbitration to seek a "clarification" as to the meaning of an award. If both parties do so as a joint request, the arbitrator should answer the inquiry. Otherwise, the case is over.

2.   Do parties ever contact the arbitrator to complain or to thank an arbitrator for his or her service?

On rare occasions, an inexperienced party or advocate or even the grievant will contact the arbitrator after the opinion and award has been issued. The person generally calls to complain about the outcome and perhaps even to attempt to reargue the case. A successful grievant, on occasion, may call to thank the arbitrator.

The arbitrator should handle these contacts diplomatically and inform the caller that he or she can no longer discuss the case but wishes the caller well in the future.

3.   How often do parties select the same arbitrator to hear another dispute?

It may be surprising to some how often parties select an arbitrator a second or third time, regardless of the outcome of the first case. A party that loses a case may think that the arbitrator owes that party the next case. That party will be rudely awakened if he or she brings a loser case to the same arbitrator a second time. More likely, however, is that, although a party did not prevail in the first case, the party liked the way the arbitrator conducted the hearing and responded to the arguments it made in its brief and that this time it will do a better job and hopefully prevail.

Selecting an arbitrator a number of times addresses the information failure involved in the selection of *ad hoc* arbitrators. At least the parties know what they will get if they select an arbitrator who has heard a case before them in the past. That may not be perfect—arbitrators can be good or bad, but rarely perfect—but they are a known quantity.

Chapter 8

Remedies

I. Overview

If an arbitrator decides that a grievance should be granted on the merits of a claim, the issue remains as to what is the appropriate remedy.[1] At times, the arbitration clauses of collective bargaining agreements (CBAs) address the issue directly. For example, they might instruct the arbitrator who finds a discharge grievance meritorious to order the reinstatement of the grievant with full back pay. A contract provision may limit the calculation of back pay to the time the grievance was filed rather than to the time of the discharge. In most instances, however, an arbitrator is left to design a remedy consistent with his or her findings regarding the case and the prevailing common-law principles of the labor agreement as to what constitutes a reasonable remedy.

Remedies in grievance arbitration often have an impact on non-grieving employees as well. If the arbitrator orders management to change work assignments back to the way they were, employees other than the grievant are likely to be affected. If the grievant should have received the promotion, but the junior employee received it instead, promoting the grievant may have an effect on that junior employee. In none of these instances is the arbitrator responsible for telling management how to implement the award, unless the parties bring that issue back to the arbitrator. Even then, management should be able to choose from among reasonable options regarding how to proceed. For example, management need not reassign the junior employee to his or her prior position if it determines that it needs another person at the promoted job level and there are no other more senior employees who want the position.

The late Jean McKelvey of the Cornell University School of Industrial and Labor Relations and one of the first nationally recognized female labor arbitrators used to tell an apocryphal story about remedies. The parties appointed a local minister to serve as their neutral. He heard the case and found the employee to have been correctly terminated. He then issued the following award: "The grievance is denied and the grievant shall burn in hell." This remedy would appear to be beyond the neutral's jurisdiction.

---

[1] *See* Marvin F. Hill, Jr., *Remedies in Arbitration,* in National Academy of Arbitrators, The Common Law of the Workplace: The Views of Arbitrators ch. 10 (Theodore J. St. Antoine, ed., 2d ed. 2005); Fairweather's Practice and Procedure in Labor Arbitration ch. 15 (Ray J. Schoonhoven, ed., 4th ed. 1999). *See also* Elkouri & Elkouri: How Arbitration Works ch. 18 (Kenneth May, ed., 7th ed. 2012).

II. Deciding on a Remedy

If the arbitrator decides that the grievance has merit, he or she normally has to determine the appropriate remedy for the contract violation. Sometimes the remedy is clear. If the grievant did not receive a particular benefit, the arbitrator should order the employer to give the grievant that benefit and make him or her "whole." Sometimes the relief is not clear, such as the appropriate remedy when an employee does not receive an opportunity to work overtime to which he or she was entitled under the agreement. Should the grievant receive the next overtime opportunity when, under the contract, that should be assigned to the most senior employee or to the employee with the least amount of overtime during a certain time period?

Remedy issues can be challenging to the arbitrator, and parties should be clear at the hearing and in their briefs as to exactly what remedy they seek. For management, the issue should not arise as a general matter, because its position is that the grievance is without merit and thus no remedy is warranted. For the union, fashioning the remedy may be critical, because it can have an effect on other members of the bargaining unit it represents.

1. How does the arbitrator determine what the appropriate remedy is?

The typical statement of the issues to be resolved to which the parties stipulate at the hearing includes the question of the appropriate remedy. If a grievance is denied, the arbitrator should so rule and say nothing more. The arbitrator should avoid offering gratuitous advice to the parties—this can only cause more problems.

The default remedy in a wrongful discharge case is the reinstatement of the grievant with full back pay—known as the *make-whole remedy*. However, there may be very good reasons based on the facts of the case to order reinstatement without back pay or with partial back pay—in effect converting the discharge to a suspension. The default remedy in a meritorious contract interpretation case is to order the company not to do what has been found to be in violation of the agreement or to order the company to do what the agreement mandates. If management's action has affected employees' wages or benefits, the employees should be made whole.

A longstanding conundrum in discipline cases is whether it is the arbitrator's prerogative or responsibility to determine whether the suspension that management imposed was too long and, if so, how long of a suspension would have been warranted. One way to address this issue is not to face it at all, as some arbitrators do. They simply conclude that, as long as some suspension was warranted, management can decide the length of the suspension. This approach, although certainly easier for the arbitrator, ignores the fact that the parties have agreed to a "just cause" provision that allows for review of management's action, which includes the length of any suspension. This issue is examined in more detail in Chapter 10.

2.   When do arbitrators address the discharged employee's obligation to mitigate?

A discharged employee has a duty to mitigate his or her damages by seeking other employment after being discharged. Typically, the issue arises in arbitration only if raised by management—it is not the arbitrator's responsibility to inquire about mitigation.

Mitigation issues are best left until after the arbitrator determines the grievance on the merits. If a dischargee is returned to work with full back pay, management may claim in its discussions with the union that the grievant failed to adequately seek employment while off work. If the arbitrator has reserved jurisdiction to address any issues that might arise under the award, management might invoke that jurisdiction if the parties are unable to resolve questions involved in the calculation of back pay, such as mitigation. The employer bears the burden of proving that the employee has not adequately mitigated his or her damages. As a practical matter, in a period of high unemployment, it might be impossible for a discharged employee to have found alternate work, especially because he or she has just been discharged.

A discharged employee should be advised by his or her union to periodically seek other employment while off work and, most important, to keep good records of that effort. If the issue is raised, those records should be sufficient to prove that reasonable efforts were made to mitigate.

3.   Outside of the disciplinary context, where most remedies are determined by the positions of the parties, how do arbitrators remedy contract violations?

An arbitrator should respond to the questions posed by the parties in their stipulation of the issues to be resolved. When the case involves the interpretation of the provisions of the CBA, the appropriate remedy might be simply to inform the parties what their contract provision means and order the employer not to violate the provision in the future.

In some cases, however, a contract violation has injured employees monetarily through, for example, loss of work. An employee who was laid off in violation of the seniority provisions should be made whole through back pay as well as returned to his or her job. Contract violations that injure the bargaining unit as a whole should also be remedied with a monetary award that constitutes a reasonable estimate of the total amount of money lost. If it is not clear exactly who in the bargaining unit lost money and what that amount should be, the arbitrator can order that the union divide the back pay equally among those affected.

There may be some cases where the arbitrator is reluctant to order a return to the previous status quo. It is unlikely that an arbitrator will order a company that closed a plant in violation of the agreement to reopen the operation. However, if the CBA contained an express provision in which management promised to keep a plant open, the arbitrator should certainly consider such a remedy upon proof of the contract violation. In lieu thereof, the arbitrator might simply order management to make the employees whole for their lost wages. Although unscrambling the egg by returning the operation to its previous condition is difficult for the arbitrator to administer, arbitrators should order management to offer employees displaced by a wrongful plant closure the opportunity to follow their work by relocating and paying their moving costs.

Arbitrators should remedy contractual violations in contracting out work by ordering management to return the work that was improperly subcontracted to the workplace and make the employees who were affected by the contract violation whole for their monetary loss. The arbitrator should order the employer to rehire employees wrongfully laid off. Similar orders should be issued in contract-based cases where management has moved bargaining unit work to nonbargaining unit employees or shifted work to nonunion facilities in violation of contract promises.

4. *Are any cases of such a trifling nature as not to warrant a remedy?*

Some observers may wonder why a union would go to the effort and expense of arbitrating a dispute where only a few dollars are at stake, but cases cannot be measured in money alone. Often a principle worth protecting through arbitration is involved. The promises contained in a CBA are only valuable when a union is willing to defend the gains it made in negotiations. That does not mean, of course, that the union must or should take every case to arbitration. In fact, a case without much at stake financially might not be worth the effort and expense. Those are decisions for the union to make. An arbitrator may wonder why the union has brought a particular case to arbitration, but he or she should treat every case as if there were a million dollars in dispute.

III. CALCULATING BACK PAY

Normally, the arbitration hearing on a discharge grievance does not include evidence on calculating back pay. If the arbitrator orders the reinstatement of the grievant with full back pay, the parties will generally be able to calculate the amount of back pay that the grievant should receive. On occasion, the parties are not able to reach agreement on calculating back pay, and they will call on the arbitrator for further assistance.

1. What does the arbitrator mean when he or she orders that the grievant be "made whole?"

The default remedy in a wrongful discharge case is the reinstatement of the grievant to his or her previous position with full back pay, including benefits, and with no loss of seniority. The back pay amount should make the employee whole for the loss of earnings incurred by reason of the employer's contract violation. The payment generally covers the period from the date of actual separation from employment to the date of the employee's return to the payroll or the employee's rejection of an unconditional offer to resume employment. This amount would include any bonuses, overtime, and salary increases the employee would have received during the back-pay period.

In sculpting the remedy, the arbitrator may also take into consideration the actions of the parties. For example, if a union has requested more than one postponement of the hearing, the arbitrator might inform the union that granting a second postponement may mean that "the back pay clock stops." The same approach might be followed if the union unduly delays in filing its brief. If the union prevails and the grievant is reinstated with back pay, the amount that would have been earned during the period of time occasioned by the union's delays should be deducted from the amount owed.

2. Why should the grievant receive any back pay for work not performed?

Employees are normally paid only for the work they perform. But when the employer wrongfully denies the employee the opportunity to earn during the period of discharge, arbitrators rarely question the appropriateness of the default remedy, which includes back pay. If the evidence in the record establishes that management wrongfully terminated the grievant, the arbitrator should not see the make-whole remedy as a windfall for the employee. A wrongfully discharged employee without alternative sources of income suffers a serious financial and psychological penalty even if later made whole as a result of the arbitrator's award.

3. Should the parties present evidence about back pay during the hearing on the merits?

Normally, during the case on the merits, the arbitrator does not want to receive evidence about calculating back pay. Requiring the parties to present evidence on back pay is also awkward. The fact that the grievant has been employed or did not seek employment in the interim is irrelevant to whether the discharge was for just cause. The same is true regarding details of how much the discharged employee would have earned from the company, including projected overtime and promotions. Presenting those facts at the arbitration hearing encumbers the record and is not needed by the arbitrator in order to issue an award on the merits.

4. What if the parties cannot reach agreement on back pay amounts or on other issues that arise from the implementation of the arbitrator's award?

At the close of the arbitration hearing, the arbitrator should ask the parties if he or she should retain jurisdiction in the case after issuance of the award. In doing so, the arbitrator should make sure that the parties do not think that the decision has already been made to grant the grievance. The request to retain jurisdiction is important, however, because normally after the award is issued the arbitrator no longer has power with regard to the dispute.

It is preferable for the arbitrator to retain jurisdiction, generally for a limited period of time—60 days is a common period—in the event the parties have difficulty in reaching agreement with regard to implementing the award or calculating back pay. In some cases, the issue might arise as to whether the employer has complied with the award when it does not offer the grievant his or her exact prior position. The employer may have abolished the job after the discharge. By reserving jurisdiction, the arbitrator is available to resolve questions that could be raised concerning compliance with the award.

Reservation of jurisdiction also comes into play with regard to the calculation of back pay. Again, either party can invoke the continuing jurisdiction of the arbitrator to rule on matters left unresolved. Sometimes, although not often, parties will ask the arbitrator to hold a hearing to receive evidence on contested matters of calculation. The arbitrator likely will be able to handle any outstanding matters through a conference call or by written submissions by the parties.

Although management bears the burden of proving a grievant's failure to mitigate, arbitrators will look to the union for evidence of the reasonable efforts taken by the dischargee to mitigate his or her losses while off work. The union can establish mitigation by presenting documents that memorialize efforts taken by the grievant to seek alternative employment.

5.   *How do the parties, or the arbitrator, if needed, calculate back pay?*

If the arbitrator issues a remedy order including the award of back pay, the parties can normally calculate the lost wages on their own. They must determine with "reasonable certainty" what earnings the employee would have received during the back pay period. Any amounts the dischargee earned during the back pay period should be deducted from back pay, because he or she would not have been able to earn those amounts if prior employment had been continued. In addition, the parties should not count any period of time the dischargee would have been on strike, laid off for a seasonal slack period or for lack of work, or for periods of time the dischargee would have been unable to work because of illness and other incapacity, such as time incarcerated.

In additional to regular pay lost, the back pay award should also include amounts the grievant would likely have earned working overtime. That can be projected based on the grievant's prior experience in accepting overtime (assuming it was voluntary) and how much overtime was worked by other employees during the back pay period. The back pay award should also include any other benefits the dischargee would have received during the back pay period, including normal raises and earned vacation pay.

6.   *Should the amount of unemployment compensation the grievant received while out of work be deducted from back pay?*

On occasion, parties ask the arbitrator whether unemployment compensation payments that the grievant received while off work because of the discharge should be deducted from back pay. The arbitrator should order the amount deducted from back pay if under state law the state will not seek recoupment of payments made. This is consistent with the practice of the National Labor Relations Board (NLRB) in unlawful discharge cases. Other states will allow recoupment of unemployment compensation paid, and therefore this amount should not be deducted from back pay.

IV. Awarding Interest

When an arbitrator orders the reinstatement of a wrongfully discharged grievant with full back pay, that award does not really make the grievant whole. He or she may have been out of work for a year or more without a regular paycheck. One way the arbitrator can make up for the grievant's loss is by ordering management to pay interest on the back pay amount.

1. Should the arbitrator award interest on back pay amounts?

The issue of whether an arbitrator should award interest on back pay for a wrongly discharged employee continues to divide experienced arbitrators. The long-established practice was for the arbitrator to award interest only in those situations where the arbitrator determined that management acted in bad faith and that its discharge of the grievant was based on frivolous grounds. In effect, the award of interest was punitive in nature.

Some arbitrators, however, regularly awarded interest, adopting the practice followed by the NLRB in wrongful discharge cases. The logic behind awarding interest is that management had the use of the grievant's wage money for the period he or she was off work, and during that period the grievant's money earned interest. Why should management, which violated the agreement, be able to keep that interest?

The question of whether back pay should include payment of interest is best left to the parties to address in their agreement. They can agree that an employee who is reinstated with back pay shall or shall not receive interest on the amount of the back pay. Interest rates have been low enough in recent years that the amount in question is not very significant. This is a foreseeable issue, and it should be negotiated by the parties.

2. Should the arbitrator raise the question at the arbitration hearing of whether his or her back pay award should include the payment of interest?

It is the responsibility of the union to request the relief it seeks through its grievance. Normally, the union will seek reinstatement of the grievant with no loss of seniority and full back pay. It is not the responsibility of the arbitrator to tell the union what it should ask for. That includes the matter of interest on back pay amounts. Enough arbitrators have ordered back pay with interest in reported cases for the union to know that it could (and should) raise that issue in arbitration.

V. REINSTATEMENT

When the union processes a discharge case to arbitration, its primary goal is to get the arbitrator to order the grievant reinstated to his or her prior position. That remedy fulfills the union's interest in protecting job security for members of the bargaining unit in the face of wrongful management action. At the same time, management's primary goal may be to avoid the reinstatement of the grievant. It terminated the employee because it determined that he or she could not fulfill the obligations of the job in the future; therefore it seeks to avoid having to return the grievant to that job. The parties' conflicting interests on reinstatement is the motivating force behind the settlement of discharge cases. Management may be willing to pay the grievant a sum of money in exchange for the union dropping the case. In this way, the employer avoids having to reinstate the grievant. The union and the grievant may be willing to accept this settlement if the grievant has obtained other employment or does not wish to return to work for the employer.

1. Does an arbitrator ever order back pay without reinstatement of the grievant?

In some rare cases, an arbitrator might consider issuing a remedy that does not require the reinstatement of the grievant. For example, the plant may have closed in the interim or the company's business may have changed in a way that makes the work functions previously performed by the grievant no longer necessary. If the operation has ceased and the employer has no other operations where the grievant could work, back pay without reinstatement might be in order. On the other hand, if the grievant's job has been abolished but there are other similar jobs still being performed, reinstatement should be ordered.

There may be cases where the grievant's post-discharge behavior is so destructive of the employment relationship that an arbitrator will not order reinstatement. For example, if after his or her discharge the former employee threatens a supervisor at a local bar, returning that employee to the workplace might be dangerous. In other cases, even if the grievant was not discharged for just cause, intervening events, such as deterioration in the grievant's mental or physical health, might make the dischargee unsuitable for reemployment. The default remedy, however, includes reinstatement.

2. *What should the arbitrator order if the grievant's job has been abolished?*

If a wrongfully discharged employee's job has been abolished, he or she is entitled to reemployment with comparable work at the same pay and benefits. An employer should not be able to avoid reinstating a wrongly discharged grievant simply by reorganizing its operation or deciding that the grievant's work is no longer needed.

Assuming that the arbitrator has retained jurisdiction in the dispute with the permission of the parties, the parties may return to the neutral with the question of whether the grievant has been offered comparable work. If management questions whether the grievant is capable of performing the available work, the arbitrator can order that the grievant be given a trial period to determine whether he or she is capable of performing the available work.

3. *What if the grievant's job has been filled by another employee in the interim period?*

It is not the arbitrator's responsibility to tell the employer to reassign (or even layoff) an employee who is filling the grievant's previous job. The remedy in the case before the arbitrator should include reinstatement of the grievant to the prior position. How that is accomplished is up to the employer. It can increase the number of jobs or reassign the incumbent employee in the exercise of its managerial powers.

4. *What is the appropriate remedy when the grievant is also at fault, at least in part?*

A more difficult case involves an employee who was partially at fault regarding the events that led to his or her discharge. For example, the grievant may have continued to experience serious problems with absenteeism, but had demonstrated prior to the discharge an ability to substantially improve attendance. Another discharged employee may have been provoked into a shouting match with his or her supervisor, including the use of vile language inappropriate to that workplace. A similar situation is presented when the arbitrator determines that discharge simply was too severe a penalty under the circumstances. The arbitrator certainly has the power to modify the penalty imposed by management.

In addressing cases such as these, the arbitrator can, in effect, convert the discharge into a substantial suspension. The arbitrator can also order the grievant reinstated to his or her prior position but without back pay. Some parties may see this remedy as "cutting the baby in half," but that would be a mischaracterization. Management has a legitimate interest in deterring absenteeism, for example, and keeping employees from cursing out a supervisor. Neither interest necessarily warrants termination, however; both the grievant and other employees should be deterred from such misconduct, but the employee in such cases has not shown such a fundamental breach of the employment understanding sufficient to allow management to discharge. This is not a compromise, but a clear reflection of the competing interests of the parties in the context of the case.

5.   Can an arbitrator issue a "final warning" to the grievant?

In fashioning an appropriate remedy, an arbitrator may give a final warning to a reinstated grievant, in effect converting the discharge into a *last chance agreement*. What the arbitrator cannot do, however, is take away a grievant's right to protest any subsequent discipline under the grievance procedure of the parties' CBA, something only the parties may do when they reach a genuine last chance agreement. The arbitrator's warning to the grievant, however, will likely have an enormous impact if any later case arises.

6.   Can the arbitrator impose conditions on a grievant's reinstatement?

In the absence of any contract limitations, and assuming that the neutral has found the grievant's discharge not to have been for just cause, an arbitrator is free to sculpt a remedy consistent with the resolution of the dispute and the facts of the case. For example, a dischargee who was terminated because alcoholism made it difficult to meet reasonable attendance requirements might be reinstated with the condition that he or she join Alcoholic Anonymous and attend its meetings. Another employee who experienced psychiatric problems might be reinstated only after cleared to return to work by a psychiatrist. In designing these conditional remedies, the arbitrator uses a full measure of common sense. Returning a troubled worker to the workplace without any conditions may create more problems for the employee, fellow employees, and management.

Reinstatement might be conditioned on the grievant taking a particular action, such as apologizing to a supervisor who was rightfully offended by his or her conduct or agreeing to lose weight to meet service requirements. A grievant may be required to accept counseling or submit to random drug testing. In a case where an employee was wrongfully discharged for not being fit for work, an arbitrator can require that the grievant submit a medical note vouching for his or her physical or psychological fitness. In some rare cases, an arbitrator may even order that a grievant be reinstated to a different job to avoid continued conflict with his or her former supervisor.

7. *Are punitive damages ever warranted?*

There will be some cases where the neutral finds management's actions to be shocking. For example, consider a case where management decided to lay off certain employees instead of others because, as it explained at the arbitration hearing, it found the seniority provisions of the CBA to be too cumbersome and inefficient. Such a conscious and deliberate violation of the contract is unconscionable. However, an arbitrator does not have the power to award exemplary damages in the absence of a contract provision to that effect.

It is not the arbitrator's job to do "justice" in some free-floating way. The neutral's responsibility is to determine whether there has been a contract violation and to remedy that contract violation. An arbitrator's patience may be further tried if management's pattern of flagrant conduct continues at the arbitration hearing. Although an award of punitive damages by the arbitrator would be upheld in court, given the broad deference extended to the arbitration process under the *Steelworkers Trilogy*,[2] the arbitrator does not have free reign to do whatever he or she may want.

How then is a union able to seek redress for egregious misconduct on the part of management? Enforcing an arbitrator's award in court—something fairly easy to accomplish—can give the court jurisdiction to use its contempt power to penalize any future similar actions by management. This is a power that an arbitrator does not have. The union could even seek in negotiations a provision that would expressly allow an arbitrator to award punitive damages.

An arbitrator is not a labor relations physician brought in to heal a labor relationship. If the parties do not enjoy a harmonious relationship, there is little the arbitrator can (or should) do about it. Although the arbitrator should not allow a hearing to become just another venue for belligerence, there are limits to what an arbitrator can accomplish that would improve a dysfunctional labor relations situation in the long run.

---

[2] See the discussion of the *Steelworkers Trilogy* in Chapter 1, §V. The *Steelworkers Trilogy* decisions are reproduced in Appendix A.

8.   *Is an award of attorneys' fees ever appropriate?*

In the absence of a contract provision or a statute that addresses the issue, an arbitrator does not have power to award attorneys' fees to the prevailing party.

9.   *How should the arbitrator remedy the wrongful distribution of overtime opportunities?*

Challenging remedy issues can also arise in non-discharge contract interpretation cases. For example, what should an arbitrator order when a grievant was wrongfully passed over for an overtime assignment? Many CBAs provide for the equalization of overtime opportunities.

In situations where a clerical error results in the grievant not receiving the opportunity he or she deserved under the parties' contractual system, many arbitrators have simply ordered that the grievant should receive the next overtime opportunity that is available, but that is not the appropriate remedy. An order that the grievant should receive the next overtime opportunity takes that opportunity from some other employee who was entitled to it under the agreement. The better remedy is to order management to pay the grievant the amount of overtime pay he or she lost. Alternatively, the arbitrator could order that management pay the grievant at overtime rates for regular hours worked equal to the hours that would have been worked on the missed overtime opportunity.

10.   *What remedies are available for other contract violations?*

The default remedy in a contract violation case is an order directing the employer to do what it should have done under the agreement or to stop doing what it is wrongfully doing in violation of the contract. That may be a sufficient remedy, unless employees lost money as a result of the employer's error. In that case, the arbitrator should issue a make-whole monetary remedy.

It may be difficult to determine exactly which employees were disadvantaged financially by an employer's violation of the agreement. In that case, the arbitrator may order that the union share a lump sum equally among all employees who could have been disadvantaged.

There may be cases where it is unclear exactly how much money employees lost as a result of management's violation of the agreement. In that situation the arbitrator should order the parties to make a "reasonable estimate" of the amount involved.

A union may request an extraordinary remedy from the arbitrator in a situation where management has repeatedly violated the agreement. It may request that the arbitrator supervise the employer's compliance with the agreement or ask the arbitrator to order management to file periodic reports with the arbitrator demonstrating compliance. The arbitrator should avoid such continued involvement in the parties' ongoing relationship. If the union is concerned about future management violations, it should seek court enforcement of the arbitrator's award. Future violations would then constitute contempt of the court's order. Alternatively, the union may bring the matter to the attention of the NLRB, which could find the employer in violation of the National Labor Relations Act and exercise continuing supervision.

Chapter 9

Finding Facts

I. OVERVIEW

Arbitrators decide real cases, not hypothetical ones. Parties initiate cases to be resolved through the procedures they have created. Although arbitrators use well-established principles to decide grievance disputes, the relative uniformity of these principles is meaningless until the arbitrator has accurately determined what actually gave rise to the dispute.

How does a neutral know what actually happened? In many cases, the neutral never really knows, although he or she will generally write an opinion that shows no doubt regarding the facts. When parties differ on the critical facts, the arbitrator has work to do. Parties may make a good-faith effort to narrow the facts to the dispute at hand, but a workplace dispute is always part of a seamless web of events stretching back in time and covering many more people than those who appear at the hearing. Even if all the witnesses to an event testify, an arbitrator will not be surprised if they remember different things in their testimony. Some witnesses consciously lie, but sometimes inconsistent testimony is simply the result of differences in perception and recollection.

There are other reasons why an arbitrator never learns everything that is going on. The parties interact on a variety of issues and disputes at the same time. They do not want the arbitrator to be confused by (or, alternatively, to even consider) other matters. For example, in the background there may be a political situation involving a union election or a management shake-up, neither of which should cloud the arbitrator's thinking.

It is best for a neutral to start with certain basic assumptions about how people normally behave in certain work situations. The unusual is not impossible but is presumptively unlikely. Arbitrators use a series of tools to "find facts," none of which is foolproof.

II. Finding Facts Based on the Record

During the course of a hearing, an arbitrator hears the testimony of many witnesses and receives numerous documents. The parties' arguments and their questions to the witnesses will point out where there are conflicts as to what occurred. The arbitrator enters a case knowing very little about the parties, but by the time the hearing has concluded, he or she has a fairly good idea what went on. Reviewing the record, the arbitrator will be able to make a credibility determination and ultimately find the facts as proven by the evidence.

1. How does an arbitrator "find facts?"

Perhaps the most challenging part of an arbitrator's job is to determine what actually happened that gave rise to the grievance. Normally there will be plenty of witnesses who have firsthand knowledge. After determining what occurred, the neutral must apply the appropriate principles in order to resolve the case. But, first and foremost, the arbitrator must determine what happened. Arbitrators have used a variety of approaches, with varying success, in determining what happened.

The arbitrator must avoid the tendency to be cynical about the testimony presented at the hearing. For the most part, witnesses who are sworn to tell the truth actually try to do so. It is inevitable that the stories that the arbitrator hears will not match perfectly. Witnesses to the same event see different things from different physical perspectives, and people remember different things. Even if it is understandable for witnesses to offer stories that aid their side of the case, the oath can have a real impact at the hearing. Arbitrators should presume that witnesses are telling the truth rather than lying. That does not mean the witnesses will all agree what occurred—it is more likely that they will disagree.

During the course of a hearing, events may give the arbitrator pause regarding any presumption of truthfulness. Witnesses may have talked among themselves and reached a consensus as to what the story will be. The arbitrator will hear conflicting versions of the same events witnessed by different people and from this collection of recollections attempt to construct a version of what most likely did occur.

2. Is there value in the arbitrator sequestering the witnesses?

It is not the prerogative of the arbitrator to decide to sequester the witnesses. The parties have the right to request that the witnesses be excluded from the hearing room. If one party makes the request to "invoke the rule," as it is often called, the arbitrator should inquire whether the opposing party has any objection, and even if the opposing party does, the arbitrator should grant the request. Witnesses who have not yet testified are then excluded from the hearing room. Each party can keep, in addition to their representatives, one person to help in the presentation of the case. Also, the grievant always stays to hear his or her case. If neither party raises the request, the hearing should proceed with all in attendance.

The testimony of sequestered witnesses rarely aligns perfectly unless witnesses have prepared their stories together. That does not mean that the arbitrator should automatically discredit stories simply because they are consistent, but it does and should raise questions. Deciding credibility issues can certainly be helped by sequestration, but there are downsides as well. Excluding people from the hearing room undermines the therapeutic value of the proceeding. The hearing itself is an important event in the ongoing collective relationship, and it is often useful for all to witness what goes on.

Without sequestration it is possible that an initial witness' testimony about an event may color the testimony of later witnesses. However, the parties may be perfectly satisfied with having all witnesses in attendance; it is their proceeding, not the arbitrator's.

3.   *If there are many witnesses to an incident, should the arbitrator credit the person who was closest to the event and had the best view of what occurred?*

An arbitrator can employ numerous useful methods to make a credibility determination. None of these rules should be considered absolute and determinative, but they are helpful. An arbitrator should examine who was in the best position to see or hear what occurred. Perception may vary from person to person, but someone closer to an event with an unobstructed view might be credited over someone who was much farther from the scene and only witnessed part of the action.

4.   *Can an arbitrator determine who is telling the truth and who is lying by watching the witness' behavior on the stand?*

There is no magic formula for credibility resolution. Although popular culture suggests that liars perspire profusely on the witness stand and fidget in their chairs, some liars are perfectly comfortable weaving their false tales. Other witnesses, intimidated by the arbitration proceeding, may fumble and fidget—and then tell the truth. Demeanor is a weak reed on which to rely, and no arbitrator should rest a decision and award solely on such a determination.

5.   *Can the arbitrator discern anything valid about testimony from the way the witness testifies?*

There are elements of the science of body language that may be useful in arbitration fact finding, but few arbitrators, if any, are formally trained in that science or are willing to rely on its principles in resolving a grievance dispute.

6.   *Can the arbitrator assess who is lying by determining who has a motive to lie?*

There are several approaches to determining credibility, and some are more helpful than others. Arbitrators often say that they first examine who has a motive to fabricate in deciding whether to credit or discredit a witness' testimony about what happened. Although this may be useful, the "motive" issue has been twisted into knots by some neutrals. Some labor arbitrators actually say that they cannot credit the testimony of a person who is discharged because the grievant is just trying to save his or her job. The grievant, therefore, always has a motive to lie! That is an absolutely absurd presumption—the arbitration case is about management proving just cause. Applying that presumption means necessarily that the grievant's version of what occurred will not be credited. This reverses the accepted burden of proof on management to support the just cause of its discipline. The presumption also has no empirical basis. Some grievants lie because they have to; others tell the truth because it is true.

The "grievant lies" presumption is often accompanied by another baseless maxim: that supervisors never have a motive to lie, and therefore they should always be credited. But supervisors are people—some lie, and some don't. This approach to resolving credibility once again is outcome-determinative, empirically unsupported, and totally worthless. Always crediting a supervisor in a situation where the case depends on believing what a supervisor said occurred necessarily means that management's discipline is upheld. Management's discipline may have been for just cause, but that cannot be established based simply on the bald assertion that supervisors never lie.

These shortcuts to fact-finding are widespread and dangerous to arbitration. A grievant lies when forced to, but he or she may simply be telling the truth. Supervisors sometimes tell the truth and sometimes fabricate; every plant is filled with age-old antipathies and jealousies; participants in an arbitration hearing also have a life outside of the plant gates that may affect their testimony at a hearing; ill will may color recollections; union folks may just stick together and tell a good story, and the same is true of management. How is the arbitrator to know which is happening in the case before him or her?

7. Does it help an arbitrator to hear other witnesses' corroborating testimony?

A helpful tool in determining whether to credit testimony is whether it is corroborated by other witnesses, especially if those witnesses appear to be disinterested. There is risk involved, of course. Despite taking the oath, witnesses may fabricate or adjust their testimony to help their friends and allies. But it may be difficult for an arbitrator to credit a story from the grievant that is not corroborated by any of the other witnesses to an incident.

8. If a case comes down to believing the grievant or the supervisor involved in the incident, should the union always prevail?

Although union advocates may believe that, based on management's burden of proof, the union will always prevail in what is sometimes called a "one-on-one truth-telling contest," that is not the case.

The arbitrator can credit one party or the other—not because the witness is an employee or a supervisor, but because of the consistency of the testimony over time, whether the witness immediately told others what had occurred, or whether the witness presented the story in such detail that it has a ring of truth.

9.   Will cross-examination help the arbitrator decide who to credit?

Cross-examination is a most valuable tool in assessing credibility. Cross-examination does not mean badgering—a good arbitrator will not allow that—but it does mean testing the testimony presented on direct examination: Does the witness tell the same story on direct and cross-examination?

One useful approach an advocate might use on cross-examination is to ask questions that do not follow the entire sequence of events that was related on direct examination. Does the witness recall what happened, or does he or she only recall the story already told on direct examination?

10.   Should the arbitrator consider the reputation or prior conduct of a witness?

Arbitrators also examine evidence about the participants' prior conduct. It may be hard to accept a story that someone behaved in a certain way if he or she had never done anything like that before. Of course, this does not mean that it could not happen. But prior conduct can be a useful tool in determining what happened in the case before the arbitrator.

A person's reputation is based on actual and imagined events over time. An arbitrator should be cautious in crediting such characterizations. A workplace is alive with rumors that are worthless in the fact-finding business.

11.   Can an arbitrator rely on assumptions about how people would normally behave in determining how a grievant behaved?

Arbitrators use their general understanding of how people normally behave in determining what happened in a case. The default of normal behavior, although not foolproof, is useful. Is it likely that someone could behave as was claimed in the testimony? Is it possible? How would one expect people to behave in the same or similar circumstances?

Consider these examples. An employee is disciplined because he allegedly screamed that he would cut someone's throat. Only one of many witnesses testified to that effect. An arbitrator can rightfully assume that this is not the kind of statement someone would forget. Similarly, the grievant was fired when he allegedly pulled a large machete out of his car to threaten his supervisor. It is hard to assume that direct witnesses would make up a story involving a large machete.

12. What if the witness has changed his or her story over time?

Another way to evaluate testimony is to examine whether the witness has stuck to the same story since the event occurred. A written record made shortly after an event is extremely valuable. (Timing may be critical. That is why the first thing that should be done after an incident is to have witnesses write down their recollections.) Examining those statements and comparing them to subsequent versions of the incident is also useful. Did the witness stick to the story? It is very hard for a witness to tell a consistent lie, especially one that is filled with details.

13. Does the detail included in a witness' testimony suggest that he or she is telling the truth?

A person who is making up a story rarely presents a fully comprehensive and complex picture of the facts. Although it is neither the arbitrator's job nor his or her prerogative to cross-examine a witness, parties should certainly seek details in attempting to discredit testimony. Similarly, truly unusual facts are hard to believe. Although on cross-examination an advocate might be able to get a witness to admit that an alternate version was "possible," the arbitrator shouldn't confuse possibility with likelihood.

14. Are the results of a lie detector test significant?

There are times when an arbitrator wishes he or she had some foolproof way to determining who is telling the truth. Polygraph results[1] are generally not admissible in court, but what should an arbitrator do when the results are offered into evidence?[2]

---

[1] *See* FAIRWEATHER'S PRACTICE AND PROCEDURE IN LABOR ARBITRATION ch. 14 (Ray J. Schoonhoven, ed., 4th ed. 1999).

[2] The Polygraph Protection Act of 1988 prohibits an employer from discharging an employee solely on the basis of the results of a lie detector test. *See* 29 U.S.C. §2001.

Some arbitrators apply an absolute rule prohibiting the admission of polygraph evidence on the grounds that the evidence is unreliable—that seems short-sighted. Because the rules of evidence do not apply in arbitration as a general matter, one would think that the results of a lie detector test should be admitted but should not be determinative.

15. Is it relevant that a grievant does not take the stand in his or her own defense? What about missing witnesses? Expert witnesses?

In virtually every case, the discharged employee will take the stand, normally as the last witness in the union's case. There is no obligation that the grievant testify, but the arbitrator would find it strange if he or she does not. One reason a grievant might not take the stand is another pending proceeding—even a criminal matter—where the grievant's arbitration testimony might somehow affect his or her prospects.

Regarding missing witnesses, arbitrators know that there often are good reasons for someone not attending a hearing. A witness may have relocated or may be in jail. A key witness may decide that it is better as a matter of discretion not to testify in a particular case. Although an arbitrator can certainly draw an inference from the failure to present testimony about the case, unexplained circumstances of an absence do not necessarily mean that a case is over.

Expert witnesses can be helpful at times in resolving disputes. Once qualified, they can offer their opinions. Other than cases involving medical evidence, however, they are rarely used in arbitration.

16. How much weight does an arbitrator give to bargaining notes written and maintained by one party and unverified or not agreed to by the other party?

Cases sometimes come down to what happened in negotiations, and the arbitrator must make that determination when the parties cannot agree on what occurred at their joint bargaining session. Parties will offer witnesses who will testify, often with great certainty, as to what occurred at the session, and it is foreseeable that each side's version will differ from its opponent's version.

There may be cases where the provisions of the parties' collective bargaining agreement will be sufficiently clear that the arbitrator will not have to resolve these types of factual disputes. If the contract on its face can reasonably be read only one way, bargaining history is irrelevant. A party who claims not to have understood what the contract meant is bound by what he or she signed.

Resolving many disputes may require the arbitrator to make factual determinations as to what actually occurred in bargaining, and bargaining minutes may be useful in this regard. Bargaining minutes are not transcripts—they are scribed by each side and thus likely partisan in nature. The arbitrator should look for points of agreement between the two versions of what happened at negotiations and credit those points.

If one party has notes and the other has none, there is a temptation to credit the side that has a written version. Those notes are contemporaneous, but admittedly are hearsay, much like any recollections in the testimony as to what was said at the bargaining table. In sum, they become part of the mix of evidence, including testimony to the contrary. No part of that testimony becomes determinative except that admissions against interest carry greater weight.

III. Unique Problems in Understanding Witnesses

Today's workplace is multilingual, and that is reflected in arbitration. The parties and the arbitrator may have to address the issue of non-English-speaking witnesses. In addition, parties who spend their work lives in a specialist environment often internalize the jargon of that workplace. The only person in the hearing room who does not understand what the witness is saying is the arbitrator—the only person who must understand the testimony. Parties have to prepare for both situations long before the hearing commences.

1. What should the parties do if the witnesses are non-English speakers?

It is increasingly common for the arbitrator to conduct a hearing where most, if not all, of the witnesses speak a foreign language. The parties should prepare for that by securing a translator. With a unionized workforce that is increasingly Spanish speaking, it certainly would be useful for an arbitrator to speak that language, but few arbitrators are fluent in that skill.

In an arbitration where the advocates can foresee the need for translation, they should both have a translator available—one to translate the testimony for the arbitrator and the second to confirm for the opposing party that the translation is correct.

2. Does the jargon of the workplace have significance?

In many workplaces, jargon has replaced plain English. Parties are so used to referring to a form by its number or certain functions by their specialized names that they do not even realize that the arbitrator has no idea what's going on. It is essential for the neutral to raise issues about jargon the first time a word is used that he or she does not understand. Otherwise the case may go on for hours while the arbitrator is left in the dark.

IV. THE APPLICABILITY OF JUDICIAL RULES

The arbitrator's responsibility regarding the admission of testimony and documents is discussed in Chapter 6. Arbitrators inform the parties (sometimes in a cavalier fashion) that he or she will take the evidence "for what it is worth." The question remains, however, what use the arbitrator should make of those parts of the record.

1. Should an arbitrator rely on hearsay testimony in making a finding of fact?

Hearsay evidence is admissible in arbitration, but the question remains as to the value of this type of evidence, in particular in determining what happened that gave rise to the grievance. *Hearsay* is any statement made outside of court (or, in our case, outside of the arbitration hearing) that is offered for the truth of the matter asserted.

The rules of evidence allow for numerous exceptions to the exclusionary hearsay rule, and if any of those exceptions apply to an arbitration witness' testimony, the evidence should be valued and used. For example, if a witness testified that the grievant told him that he had punched his supervisor and would do it again if he had the opportunity, that would constitute an admission against interest and thus be admissible in court. In addition to being admissible in arbitration, it is quite useful for the arbitrator in the process of finding fact if, and only if, the arbitrator credits the testimony of the witness.

What then should the arbitrator do with hearsay evidence that would not be admissible in court but is admissible in arbitration because the rules of evidence do not apply? The arbitrator should consider the nature of the statement. If the witness is relating a story he heard in the plant that had gone through three layers of persons before it reached his ears, this triple hearsay has lost much of its probative value. Is it possibly true? Of course, but the arbitrator must recognize that there are good reasons behind the age-old rules of evidence, and triple-hearsay testimony lacks reliability.

2. Is the "best evidence" rule applicable?

It is common in court to raise objections to a copied document based on the assertion that it is not "the best evidence." If an objection is raised to a document on that basis in arbitration, the arbitrator should inquire of the proponent as to the whereabouts of the original. Although the arbitrator will not exclude documents on that basis, it is certainly best for an advocate to have the original document available, especially if there might be some question raised as to its authenticity.

Similarly, it is better to see a document than to have to someone recall what it included. Documents that disappear are suspect. Business records will come into evidence in the hearing as a matter of course, and the opposing party should be able to *voir dire*—that is, ask the witness questions about the origin of the document—before a document is admitted into evidence.

3. Is demonstrative or real evidence useful in finding facts?

Sometimes the main challenge that advocates face is teaching the arbitrator about the plant operations that gave rise to the grievance. Demonstrative evidence can be very helpful to an arbitrator in this regard. This issue is not one of choosing one version of the facts over another, but rather in understanding the uncontested facts. Describing a piece of equipment is not as effective as showing the arbitrator the equipment and describing it in front of him or her. Photographs, videos, and blueprints can also make dry testimony come alive.

4. How useful are plant visits?

A plant visit may be the most effective demonstrative evidence of all. Each party should consider the possible advantages of taking the neutral to see where an event took place or the operation occurs. Even the best schematic of the plant floor will not convey a full sense of the place. Describing how fast a machine runs is good evidence, but showing the arbitrator the machine while it is running is great evidence.

Chapter 10

Just Cause Decision Making

I. Overview

A 1945 text published by the Cornell University School of Industrial and Labor Relations warned management not to agree to a provision that would limit its right to discipline employees only to situations where it could prove just cause. Despite this early "warning," management regularly agreed to such a clause. Job security has always been a significant goal of union negotiators. In fact, management rarely discharges employees for no reason. Although discharge and discipline arbitration cases do not always uphold management's action, an employer simply does not want to dismiss an employee unless it is necessary. It costs money to find and train a replacement who may not turn out to be the best worker.

A plurality of arbitration cases involves the discipline and discharge of employees. Almost all collective bargaining agreements (CBAs) include a provision regarding discipline and discharge, but those provisions rarely say more than that management has the right to act "for just cause." Occasionally, parties use the synonymous phrase "proper cause," "sufficient cause," or some variation thereof. Thus, much more than in contract interpretation cases, the arbitrator is left without much guidance from the parties.

Exactly what constitutes just cause for discharge has troubled (and, at times, confused) arbitrators for more than 70 years.[1] Regrettably, many arbitrators tend to decide cases by relying on conclusory statements rather than by explaining the reasons for their decisions. Others apply a facile "seven-part test," first formulated by arbitrator Carroll Daugherty in an arbitration case in 1966,[2] which only begins to address the issues that the arbitrator must face.[3]

When the arbitrator's opinion arrives, the parties are left at sea: what could it possibly mean when an arbitrator rules that management's action was "reasonable" and not "arbitrary and capricious?" These clichés do not explain anything.

Unions have had the greatest impact on the workplace in terms of job security. Management must provide reasons for its actions. It cannot act simply based on subjectivity. Management must be consistent in its application of discipline, something akin to "equal protection." Management must be fair both in its investigation and in the procedures it uses to impose discipline. Does this mean that unions have made it substantially more difficult for management to remove a bad actor from the workplace? In fact, he or she may not be bad, and might not have done anything wrong. The union through negotiating a just cause provision has made management prove its case.

---

[1] NORMAN BRAND & MELISSA BIREN, DISCIPLINE AND DISCHARGE IN ARBITRATION (2d ed. 2008) (best text on "just cause" and application of the standard in discharge and discipline cases; addressing most kinds of such cases that parties will bring to arbitration). *See also* ELKOURI & ELKOURI: HOW ARBITRATION WORKS ch. 15 (Kenneth May, ed., 7th ed. 2012); Gladys Gershenfeld (chapter ed.), *Discipline and Discharge,* in NATIONAL ACADEMY OF ARBITRATORS, THE COMMON LAW OF THE WORKPLACE: THE VIEWS OF ARBITRATORS ch. 6 (Theodore J. St. Antoine, ed., 2d ed. 2005).
[2] Enterprise Wire Co., 46 LA 359 (1966).
[3] *See* ADOLPH KOVEN & SUSAN SMITH, JUST CAUSE: THE SEVEN TESTS (Kenneth May, rev., 3d ed. 2006) (best explication of Daugherty's seven tests).

II. THE UNDERLYING ASSUMPTIONS OF JUST CAUSE

It is best to examine the discharge and discipline cases that arbitrators face by examining the basic interests of management and unions that underlie these cases. That starts with the establishment of the employment relationship, which is based on the fundamental understanding between management and an employee when he or she is hired. That agreement between an employee and the employer creates mutual obligations: When a worker is hired, he or she makes certain implicit promises to his or her employer, which may be considered part of the employment bargain. The employee will provide a reasonable amount and quality of work. In exchange for this satisfactory work, the employer will provide a safe workplace, appropriate tools and raw materials, competent supervision, and relevant training, as well as compensation as provided in the CBA.

During the course of employment, an employee may breach his or her side of that bargain by, for example, providing substandard work or by experiencing problems with absenteeism. An employer need not accept these deficiencies but can institute discipline to rehabilitate the worker. (There are also times when an employer fails to meet its side of the bargain, and the union can invoke the grievance and arbitration system to obtain the correct emoluments.) Ultimately, an employee might not be rehabilitated and might demonstrate that he or she will not be able to fulfill the reasonable obligations of the job in the future. The employer might terminate the employment relationship, and the union might bring a grievance to arbitration under the parties' just cause standard.

1.   Are arbitrators permitted to review the underlying assumptions of discipline cases?

Parties can, if they wish, review the underlying assumptions in discipline cases as part of the negotiating process. The common law of the labor agreement belongs to the parties, and the arbitrator must fulfill their mutual expectations. An arbitrator, however, must be careful not to create new "law" on his or her own. For example, if an arbitrator decides that the union should proceed first or bear the burden of proof in a discipline or discharge case, he or she would be overstepping the bounds of the appointment.

This recognition of the limited authority and proper role of an arbitrator does not mean that the neutral cannot help clarify principles and explain their underlying rationale. It also does not mean that an arbitrator cannot favor one approach to decision making over another where arbitrators differ, for example, in reviewing the extent of discipline imposed by management. There are limits to this arbitral discretion, however. Unlike a court (or, more likely, the highest appellate court), an arbitrator should not create new "rights" or "prerogatives" that are not based on the parties' agreement and relationship.

This may mean, at times, that the arbitrator does not do "justice," if the parties' CBA is not "just" in some natural law kind of way. The arbitrator's decision in discharge and discipline cases must reflect the parties' values and interests, not the arbitrator's personal conception of how the workplace should be run. Of course, the parties do not always agree on some fundamentals and may use formulations like just cause to embody what they do agree on under the terms of their contract. Admittedly, this gives an arbitrator some wiggle room, but there are constraints imposed by the general way arbitrators have interpreted just cause over the years.

The CBA rarely gives the arbitrator much guidance besides two words—just cause. Most arbitrators describe just cause using fairly general terms: management must exercise a fair and reasonable judgment; an action will not be upheld if it is arbitrary, capricious, unreasonable, or discriminatory; an arbitrator will uphold management's action if it is not an abuse of discretion. The problem with these commonly expressed principles is that they are undefined and without boundaries. What is it that makes management's judgment reasonable? How come it is not arbitrary or capricious? There must be a better way to resolve these ubiquitous cases.

Some agreements include a list of dischargeable or disciplinable offenses, but more likely the list is included in a management handbook distributed to employees. Even the existence of a list does not make discipline or discharge automatic. The listed items must be interpreted and applied to the facts at hand once the arbitrator has determined what actually happened. Such a list does constitute notice to employees that certain classes of behavior will lead to discipline and discharge. The labor arbitrator must still determine whether what the employee did gave the employer just cause to terminate the employment relationship.

2. *Is discipline punishment?*

It is a common error for arbitrators to view discipline as a punishment for employee misconduct of one kind or another. An employer is not the equivalent of the state, empowered to punish wrongdoers in the workplace. Management has but a single, valid purpose: to enhance productivity. It disciplines an employee in an effort to rehabilitate that employee so that the misconduct does not reoccur. The focus is always on the future, not the past.

An employee is required to provide his or her employer with satisfactory work. This means that an employee must meet regular attendance requirements, obey reasonable work rules, provide a reasonable quality and quantity of work, and avoid any conduct that interferes with the activities of production within the workplace. When an employee does not provide satisfactory work, he or she is subject to discipline. Repeated failure to fulfill this primary obligation can result in termination.

Management also disciplines an employee in order to deter that worker from repeating the misconduct in the future. A suspension from work without pay, for example, may teach a lesson. Similarly, discipline also acts as a general deterrent. Other employees learn what happens if they were to follow the same path.

Therefore, the arbitrator should avoid talking about "the punishment fitting the crime." The employee did not commit a crime, and if he or she did, punishment would be meted out by the public authorities. The discipline must be proportionate to the employee's offense, because under the just cause standard excessive discipline is more than is necessary to achieve the employer's goals of rehabilitation and deterrence. The result is the industrial rule of law, which is different from criminal or civil law. Individuals relinquish certain rights when they become employees—for example, the right to control their freedom of action during working time. A plant, as a special purpose community, has its own internal "law" embodied in the just cause standard and applied in arbitration.

3.   Isn't discharge "industrial capital punishment?"

A discharge is not easy on an employee, especially during times of high unemployment and few available jobs. Even if the arbitrator returns the employee to work, there will have been months without income, and a back pay award can never really make a grievant whole. Yet a person discharged is not led into the gas chamber or charged with bolts of electricity. "Industrial capital punishment" is hyperbole that can be harmful to the decision-making process.

If the arbitrator actually thinks he or she has been asked to rule in a life-or-death situation, those alleged stakes influence the decisional process. If the employer was warranted in separating an employee from his or her employment, then the arbitrator should find that there was just cause. If management successfully convinces the arbitrator what the employee actually did and if that conduct indicates that he or she cannot fulfill the obligations of the job in the future, there was just cause.

Junior arbitrators forget that they are not responsible for the grievant. Management, not the arbitrator, discharges the employee. The arbitrator's task is to carefully review the process followed by management and the substance of the alleged misconduct. The arbitrator reviews management's decision and does not sentence the grievant to oblivion.

4. Can a former employee bring a claim to arbitration if he or she quits a job?

Occasionally an employee quits a job, and the threshold issue in arbitration is whether this was a voluntary act by the worker. If he or she was forced to quit because of the actions of management, the termination should be cognizable in arbitration under the just cause standard. For example, a company might tell an employee he or she will be fired if the employee does not resign based on allegations of theft. If the employee voluntarily resigns, he or she should be able to contest the termination of employment under the contract procedure. However, an employee who quits employment for a reason unrelated to any management action and then thinks better of it cannot bring his or her case to arbitration.

III. DAUGHERTY'S SEVEN TESTS

Perhaps because they are so deceptively simple, the "seven tests" of just cause posed in 1964 by Arbitrator Carroll Daugherty in *Grief Brothers Cooperage Corp.*[4] have attracted much following in the arbitration community. Many advocates and junior arbitrators cite them frequently. Determining just cause, however, is not as mechanical as Arbitrator Daugherty made it out to be: if any of his questions are answered in the negative, he would have the arbitrator conclude that the employer did not have just cause for the discipline or discharge.

Because the seven tests are engrained in arbitral jurisprudence, it is worthwhile to explain why they are at best only a partial answer to the puzzle of what the parties intended by their just cause standard.

---

[4]42 LA 555 (1964).

1.   What are Daugherty's seven tests?

Carroll Daugherty pronounced these seven tests for just cause:

1. Did the company give the employee forewarning or foreknowledge of the possible or probable disciplinary consequences of the employee's conduct?
2. Was the company's rule or managerial order reasonably related to (a) the orderly, efficient, and safe operation of the company's business and (b) the performance that the company might properly expect of the employee?
3. Did the company, before administering discipline to an employee, make an effort to discover whether the employee did in fact violate or disobey a rule or order of management?
4. Was the company's investigation conducted fairly and objectively?
5. At the investigation, did the "judge" obtain substantial evidence or proof that the employee was guilty as charged?
6. Has the company applied its rules, orders, and penalties evenhandedly and without discrimination to all employees?
7. Was the degree of discipline administered by the company in a particular case reasonably related to (a) the seriousness of the employee's proven offense and (b) the record of the employee in his service with the company?

2.   What criticisms have commentators made of the seven tests?

There are serious problems with some of Daugherty's simplistic tests.[5] First, they suggest that the role of the arbitrator is not to find the facts, but to review the facts as found by some "judge," apparently a person within management who was not involved in the incident leading to the imposition of discipline. Second, the tests make no mention of progressive discipline, very much an essential element in just cause determinations. Third, the tests are redundant, focusing repeatedly on the investigation conducted by management before it determines whether to discharge or discipline an employee. Fourth, and most important, the tests do not explain why these questions should be asked.

---

[5]*See* ADOLPH KOVEN & SUSAN SMITH, JUST CAUSE: THE SEVEN TESTS (Kenneth May, rev., 3d ed. 2006) (thoughtful explication of Daugherty's tests, recognizing and responding to criticisms that have been raised and defending limited goals Daugherty intended to achieve when he first presented the seven tests).

3. Why not simply ask the arbitrator to decide whether management's disciplinary action was "reasonable?"

Arbitrators certainly consider whether discipline or discharge was "reasonable," but relying only on that single word as the basis for judgment does not explain to the parties why the arbitrator upheld or denied the grievance. Why was it reasonable? Why was it not reasonable? Similarly, using other words, such as "arbitrary" and "capricious," simply expresses a conclusion and not a reason.

IV. Proving Just Cause

Disciplinary cases make up a significant portion of an arbitrator's caseload. Therefore, it is vitally important to understand the parties' competing interests that led to inclusion of the just cause standard in their CBA. These interests will explain what the standard means from the perspective of the parties.

When management acts to discipline or discharge an employee, it knows it may ultimately have to support its action in arbitration. When the discipline or discharge is accomplished fairly, an arbitrator will uphold management's action if there is strong proof that the incident warranted the discipline imposed, that the employee was given an opportunity to explain his or her side of the story, that the employer considered all mitigating factors that might benefit the employee, and that the employer's action was consistent with how previous cases of the same kind were treated.

1. Why does management bear the burden of proof in a discharge or discipline case?

The established arbitral practice in a discharge and discipline case is for management to present its evidence first and then to bear the burden of proof in resolving the dispute. In all other cases—those that involve contract interpretation—the union proceeds first and bears the burden of proof. The only explanation for the origin of this practice is that Arbitrator Harry Shulman first did it as the permanent umpire at the Ford Motor Company in the 1940s. Perhaps he was mirroring the practice in a criminal case where the prosecution proceeds first and bears the burden of proof.

In any case, the practice with regard to management putting on its proof first makes sense. It knows why it acted. It investigated the incident that led to discipline and discharge. It concluded that it had a legitimate and substantial business reason for the grievant's discipline or termination. Because job security is the most important right secured by the CBA, management should bear the burden of explaining why the employment relationship should be severed temporarily (with regard to a suspension) or permanently (as in a discharge).

None of these reasons explains why the union bears the burden of proof in all other cases. Perhaps this follows the practice in a civil trial, where the complainant or plaintiff presents its proof first and must carry the burden of proving its case by at least a preponderance of the evidence. The union normally does not know why management acted the way it did. It can explain the impact of management's actions on the employees, but beyond that it is often reaching in the dark. For efficiency's sake alone, an arbitrator would be better served by having management put on its proof first, but the established practice is so engrained in arbitration that the parties would not even think of changing the norm.

2.   *Assuming that management must bear the burden of proof, what quantum of proof is appropriate and why is there continuing confusion about the proper standard of proof in a discharge or discipline case? Why do arbitrators differ on this issue?*

The confusion regarding the appropriate quantum of proof in a discharge or discipline case is the product of importing concepts from criminal and civil law into labor arbitration. In a criminal case, the prosecution must prove guilt "beyond a reasonable doubt." We do that because as a society we feel that, before we take away one's liberty through incarceration (or even one's life in a death penalty case), we must be as certain as possible as to what happened, the accused's responsibility for it, and the accused's mental state evidencing intent. In other words, it is better to let 10 guilty defendants escape penalty than convict one innocent person.

None of these concepts has anything to do with what goes on in a labor arbitration. A discharged employee does not face incarceration or death—he or she faces life without a job at the employer's place of business. Although the arbitrator does want to be sure that the grievant did what management says he or she did and that the conduct warrants separation from employment, that does not support an onerous burden of proof for management.

The arbitrator needs to determine what happened, although he or she knows that an outsider can never be positive "beyond a reasonable doubt." There are always doubts and differences in recollection as a result of the informal processes followed in arbitration. If arbitrators actually followed the "beyond a reasonable doubt standard," no discharges would be upheld. Many of the arbitration cases that employ the standard of the criminal law are from the early days of arbitration, but the confusion lingers. The reported decisions demonstrate, however, that discharges are regularly upheld even when the arbitrator states that the requisite quantum of proof is beyond a reasonable doubt.

The same problems occur with the less onerous burden, adopted from civil law, of proof by a "preponderance of the evidence." Arbitrators have yet to figure out how to "weigh" evidence. If the test is whose version is more likely to have occurred, there is an assumption that a discharge could be upheld even if the union has presented substantial proof that the incident did not occur.

This leaves some middle formulation of the burden of proof— "clear and convincing evidence"—the quantum of proof that most arbitrators say they apply. This certainly requires more compelling evidence than a mere "preponderance," but is this any different from "beyond a reasonable doubt?" If an arbitrator is convinced, can he or she still have reasonable doubt?

There is continuing controversy about burden of proof because it remains a legal fixture shoehorned into a private adjudicatory system. More to the point, arbitrators tend to use burden of proof as a make-weight to justify their conclusions. In any arbitration case, the neutral makes a decision based on the competing arguments and evidence. He or she will explain why one reading of the contract is preferable while pointing out the faults in the opposing reading. That is called decision making. The same goes on in discharge and discipline cases, although couched in burden of proof terms. Many arbitration decisions discuss the issue of quantum of proof, but that issue is camouflage. It is easier for an arbitrator to set aside a discipline or discharge on the asserted grounds that management failed to meet its burden of proof rather than by stating that management witnesses were lying. It is true, however, that the employer must convince the arbitrator what occurred. If it does, its discipline will likely be upheld.

3. What must management actually prove in the arbitration of a discharge or discipline case?

There are two separate and identifiable steps in every discharge and discipline case. First, management must prove what the grievant did. This may involve contested issues of fact based on witness recollection. It might be documented in company records. It might be based on the company's investigation. Unless management can prove what happened, its case will fail.

Even if management proves what the grievant did, management must then convince the arbitrator that the proven conduct constitutes sufficient grounds to support the discipline or discharge imposed. That can be more difficult. Relying on the fundamental understanding of the employment relationship, management will attempt to show that the employee, by virtue of the proven conduct, defaulted on his or her side of the bargain.

Just cause for discipline must be evaluated on the basis of the grounds asserted by management for its action at the time it took action. It cannot change its grounds later. It cannot investigate further after the discharge to add more charges to bolster its case. Due process requires a fair procedure for administering discipline. Although management can certainly suspend an employee pending investigation, once it acts and explains to the employee the basis for the termination, that basis must be proven to the arbitrator.

4.   Can management call the grievant as its witness in a discharge or discipline case?

It is not unusual for management to call the grievant as its first witness in a discharge or discipline case. If there is no objection from the union, the arbitrator should proceed to hear the testimony. If there is an objection, however, the arbitrator should first inquire whether the union intends to call the grievant as part of its case. If the union indicates, as it likely will, that it intends to call the grievant, the arbitrator should inform management that it will have the opportunity to cross-examine the grievant at that time. As is the case generally in arbitration, cross-examination will not be limited to matters raised on direct examination (see Chapter 6).

Management has the responsibility to make its case based on the information it received that was the basis for its decision to discharge the grievant. This information might include statements made by the grievant during the course of the investigation leading to his or her discharge, as well as other information management assembled. Management will have an opportunity during the hearing to ask the grievant to confirm the essential facts that led to management's ultimate conclusion. Shortcutting this process by getting the grievant to admit to certain facts at the start of the hearing tends to deny the grievant and the union the fair process of hearing what management knew when it acted. That is the critical information as far as just cause is concerned—not what management can get the grievant to admit at the arbitration hearing, but what management knew before it acted to terminate the employee.

5. Can management rely on evidence of a grievant's prior misconduct or reputation? What about the use of such evidence in progressive discipline cases?

It is common in a discipline or discharge case for management to present evidence of the grievant's prior misconduct. That evidence has two purposes: to demonstrate that the grievant had previously misbehaved in the same manner as is alleged in the current case or to show that the grievant is just a bad actor. The arbitrator will likely admit such testimony but will be cautious regarding how it is used.

In a case involving progressive or corrective discipline—for example, a discharge for excess absenteeism—management will have to show that the grievant has been disciplined in the past and received the opportunity to change his or her ways. Prior discipline is obviously admissible and directly relevant.

Prior discipline is also relevant as a way to rebut any claim the union might make as to mitigation. The union will certainly make sure that the arbitrator appreciates the fact that the employee has served the employer for a long period of time. Management will then want to show that the employee has received discipline over the course of that long employment.

Evidence presented by either party concerning the grievant's "reputation" is much more problematic. The fact that the grievant is a deacon at his church does not mean that he or she reports for work on time.

6. Why is there so much reliance on due process? If the employee behaved badly, why does it matter whether there was a proper investigation?

A cynical observer might suggest that what the union seeks in a just cause provision is lifetime job security for its members. The same cynic might suggest that management seeks an unlimited right to discharge or discipline an employee at any time for any reason with no review in arbitration. Although parties can embody either extreme version in their CBA, that does not happen.

The union's primary focus in negotiating a just cause provision is in obtaining fair treatment for employees. The union knows that some persons who are hired just won't work out. It also knows that management will treat some employees harshly for reasons other than their performance. The union's job is to make sure that only the "true positives," the employees who warrant discipline, are disciplined and that the "false positives" are not.

The union might seek to negotiate procedural protections in the CBA. For example, a company might be required to give the union immediate notice of any discipline. This will allow the union to initiate a grievance in a timely manner. Some contracts require that employees be suspended prior to the imposition of discipline. In some cases corrective or progressive discipline must be followed under the terms of the agreement.

Management agrees with labor that only "true positives" should be disciplined or discharged, although it might also prefer to make that determination itself rather than leaving it to an arbitrator. That is why management decides to thoroughly investigate incidents before acting and why it offers an accused employee the opportunity to give his or her side of the story.

Both parties seek the same goal of accuracy. That is why the concept of "due process" is inherent in the just cause provision. A fair outcome is one that is accurate, even if the union would like an arbitrator to cut the grievant some slack and management would like the arbitrator to recognize an employer's right to promote the interests of the enterprise through the exercise of its discipline and discharge prerogative.

There is no precise delineation of what a proper investigation requires, but arbitrators prefer seeing evidence that management took written statements from all concerned—employees and supervisors alike—early on while memories were fresh and offered the accused employee the opportunity to contribute before the investigation hardened into a decision. A discharge followed by an investigation obviously puts the cart before the horse. An employer need not keep an employee at work, but there is no obvious reason why it cannot suspend the employee pending investigation.

7.   Is it important to the arbitrator that management have a well-established procedure for dealing with discipline and discharge cases?

When management has an established process to be followed in discharge and discipline cases, it demonstrates to the arbitrator that the employer has thought about its own responsibilities as well as the obligations of its employees. It also demonstrates that management at least attempts to treat like cases similarly, at least with regard to procedure.

However, simply because management attempts to afford employees due process does not mean that it has accomplished this goal.

8.   *How important is it to an arbitrator that an employee has received notice that certain conduct will result in discipline or discharge?*

Employees must be told what is expected of them in terms of work and conduct, unless the behavior in question is inherently unacceptable, like striking a supervisor. An employer must prove to the arbitrator that the employee has received adequate notice. For example, if management has a certain procedure that employees must follow when clocking in, the employer must inform the workers of that procedure. If employees must call a particular supervisor if they are going to be tardy, notice of that obligation is essential.

Management can impose reasonable work rules, but they must be announced. Normally, management will have a training session for employees who must sign in. The sign-in sheet with the grievant's signature is often offered into evidence at the arbitration hearing.

9.   *Why do arbitrators uphold discharges when employees commit so-called "cardinal sins" even if they have a long work record with no previous discipline?*

With regard to the most serious workplace transgressions—striking a supervisor, theft, and sabotage, for example—the arbitrator's focus is not on the rehabilitation of the employee or his or her future productivity. Once management has established what the grievant did, the propensity of the disciplined employee to repeat the misconduct is not the issue. The discharge must be for just cause, and the focus should be on whether the discharge of the offending employee is warranted in order to deter other employees from such misconduct in the future.

Management cannot fit every bit of employee misconduct into the cardinal sin category, which is limited to those truly outrageous acts that are totally unacceptable in the workplace. It is not simple negligence; it is intentional and intolerable.

10.   *Why do arbitrators require employers to follow progressive discipline with most discharges?*

Arbitrators actually do not require employers to do anything; they merely apply the parties' standard embodied in their CBA. Under the contract standard, employers normally can terminate employees only for just cause. Inherent in the concept of just cause is management's obligation to establish that the employee has breached the fundamental understanding of the employment relationship. For simple (and not "cardinal") matters, such as poor work performance, absenteeism, and the like, the employer can only demonstrate just cause if it shows the arbitrator that the grievant will be unable to fulfill the essential obligations of his or her job in the future. To do that, management must show it tried without success to correct the employee's mistakes. Because the employee cannot be rehabilitated, discharge is the only option available.

Some parties negotiate a contract provision that requires progressive discipline and, in other situations, management's own rules require progressive discipline. The essence of progressive discipline is that employees who commit violations of company rules should be warned not to repeat their transgression or more serious discipline will follow and be counseled and trained as to how to fulfill their obligations. When a violation is repeated, management might impose a brief suspension of a few days off from work without pay. Finally, if the employee has not changed his or her ways, termination might be warranted.

There is no particular version of progressive discipline that is required under just cause; a worker must only be offered a genuine opportunity to turn things around. It makes sense for management to try to salvage an employee it has trained, and that is why employers follow progressive discipline even in nonunionized operations. An arbitrator, however, is not interested in what does or does not make sense, but rather what the parties mutually intended when they provided for just cause.

11. Can management discipline or discharge an employee for something that occurs away from the workplace?

Arbitrators refer to off-duty misconduct that has an impact on the employment relationship as the "nexus" to management's legitimate business interests. If an employee gets into a fight with his or her supervisor at a local bar after work, the connection to the workplace is obvious. An employee who disparages the company's products to the local newspaper also is subject to discipline or discharge.

The more difficult cases of off-duty misconduct involve employees' activities that can have an impact on a business' goodwill in the public mind. For example, if the employee is accused of a serious crime off-duty that makes headlines in the local newspaper, potential customers may see that event as reflecting on the business for which the employee works. Arbitrators will examine these cases carefully to make sure that management has demonstrated more than a suspicion of harm to the interests of the business.

12. Some arbitrators have ruled that an arbitrator does not have the authority to review the extent of discipline imposed by management. Does that make any sense?

From the earliest days of modern labor arbitration a minority of arbitrators have avoided the difficult task of determining whether management had just cause to impose discipline in a particular case. As long as some discipline was warranted, the choice of the extent of discipline would be left up to the employer. Although it is understandable why some neutrals would like to avoid the heavy lifting of examining the extent of discipline, it is the arbitrator's responsibility to do so under the just cause standard.

Assume that an employee has been warned about performing shoddy work in fabricating widgets. Management needs its employees to perform their work obligations reasonably well. Otherwise, the widget company will go out of business. When the employee once again makes a bad batch of widgets, management suspends the employee for 30 days. The CBA simply states that management may discipline for just cause.

At the arbitration, the company proves that the employee made bad widgets. Must the 30-day suspension stand? The discipline seems way too harsh, beyond the norms of industry, and far more punitive than is required to rehabilitate the employee. Under the minority view, however, management could impose whatever penalty it wishes, and the arbitrator has no power to review the extent of discipline. That is not what the parties intended when they mutually agreed on the just cause standard for discipline.

Assuming that the arbitrator has the power to review the extent of discipline where there was just cause, what should be the remedy in this case? The arbitrator should change the discipline to the longest suspension an arbitrator could find passes muster under just cause—perhaps a week or less.

V. Specific Issues in Discipline and Discharge Cases

Cases involving the termination and discipline of employees break down into three major categories. An employee has an obligation to provide good work in exchange for the compensation mandated by the CBA. Work performance and conduct at work make up a significant portion of discipline and discharge cases. An employee's misbehavior in the plant can be disruptive and undermine the power of supervision.

Thus, in-plant misconduct cases make up a second major category. Although not as common, out-of-plant misconduct, the third category, may give rise to a discipline or discharge.

1.   How does an arbitrator react in a discharge case when the grievant does not take the stand and testify?

Arbitrators understand that there is no obligation for a dischargee (or any grievant for that matter) to testify. As a practical matter, however, arbitrators will generally draw an adverse inference from the fact that the grievant does not offer his or her side of the story directly to the arbitrator. That does not mean that management must prevail if the grievant does not testify. It means, rather, that an arbitrator expects to hear from the accused party.

There may be a variety of good reasons supporting a union decision not to call the grievant. The grievant may be a particularly bad witness in his or her own behalf. He or she may seem confused on direct examination or be quick to anger on cross-examination. Yet, without question, it is best to call the grievant.

2.   How much weight does an arbitrator place on last chance warnings that are not violated for 10 or more years?

When an employee is given a "last chance" by management to improve his or her ways or be discharged, that does not allow the employer to sidestep the just cause provision when many years later the employee engages in misconduct. Formal "last chance agreements" normally come with a time limit. If the employee commits another offense within a year or 18 months, the agreement may preclude the union from grieving the discharge. General warnings that an employee is now given one last chance should be understood to be similarly bounded.

A last chance warning focuses on a pattern of behavior by an employee. If the employee is able to break that pattern, although his or her prior discipline may be relevant in determining just cause, it might not be determinative. The issue is whether the grievant has resumed the prior pattern of behavior. If he or she has, there might be just cause for discharge.

3.   Do arbitrators take into consideration "mercy of the court" arguments in discipline and termination cases?

Arbitrators certainly consider facts about the grievant in ruling on just cause. Mitigating factors, such as the length of service of the grievant and the prior disciplinary record, are relevant in making a just cause determination. However, these are not pleas for "mercy," something the arbitrator is not empowered to give. It is not the arbitrator's job to excuse certain conduct if the employer has proven that the worker's actions justified the discipline imposed. It is the arbitrator's job to return an employee to the job if the employer has not made out its case.

The parties have set the standard in their CBA. Just cause does not involve a benevolent outsider giving a wrongdoer another chance. The grievant's conduct may warrant a second chance based on just cause, not the arbitrator feeling sorry for him or her. The fact that the grievant has three young children and a sick mother at home may be considered in a criminal sentencing hearing, but, once again, arbitration is not a criminal trial. It is a private internal dispute resolution system involving, in this instance, the discipline or discharge of a worker for something the worker has done or failed to do.

An employer is not a social service agency and need not keep an employee at work no matter what the employee has done. It is a business and need only keep employed workers who will fulfill their side of the employment bargain by providing a reasonable amount and quality of work. Similarly, an arbitrator is not a social worker brought in to mete out justice and mercy.

4.   *What are the views of arbitrators on "zero tolerance" policies?*

In an effort to rid the workplace of certain behaviors it considers intolerable, management creates certain policies that it says show "zero tolerance" for the misconduct. An example would be possession of alcohol or drugs in the workplace or coming to work drunk or high on drugs. In order to show that it is serious, management must then apply the rules on a no-exception basis.

Does that mean that arbitrators must uphold all discharges imposed under zero tolerance rules? Consider a poor attendance case. Can management impose a zero tolerance rule for absenteeism? One absence does not support the prediction that the employee will be unable to meet the legitimate expectation of an employer that he or she will meet reasonable attendance requirements.

Assuming that the parties have not embodied these rules in their agreement, the arbitrator's task remains unchanged. Just cause still applies even if management has promulgated a zero tolerance rule. Otherwise, management could just announce that all its rules fit into that category and vitiate the just cause standard. There might be viable explanations and excuses for violating the rules. For example, an employee may be taking prescription drugs for an illness and needs to have them at work. Zero tolerance would mandate discharge, but just cause might not.

5. Do arbitrators give weight to recent news events that may have affected a company decision regarding level of discipline (e.g., a workplace violence issue following a string of well-publicized violent acts)?

Arbitrators preside over arbitrations in context, which includes current events outside of the workplace. If management imposes a higher level of discipline on employees because of a growing societal recognition of the danger of certain misconduct, that should certainly be factored into the just cause determination. However, management cannot bootstrap imagined fears into just cause discharges. For example, firing a good employee because he or she is a Muslim will not pass muster under the just cause standard even if extreme jihadists have become an international threat.

6. Why does an arbitrator consider mitigating circumstances in determining whether there is just cause for termination?

When an employer decides to discharge an employee, it believes that the employee can no longer serve. That judgment is not final, however. When the parties have provided for the just cause standard for discharge and for arbitral review, the arbitrator's responsibility is to determine whether management has proven just cause. For an employee who has served for many years without work problems but suddenly fails to meet the obligations of his or her job, the prior work record is relevant, because it shows that the employee was able to meet the requirements of the job at one time. Length of service, however, is not always determinative.

Mitigating circumstances play an uncertain role in discipline cases, although they may be useful at the extreme. An employee with many years of adequate service before the events that gave rise to the discipline or discharge has demonstrated the ability to meet the requirements of the job, suggesting that recent events may be an aberration. On the other hand, a good employee can go bad, and, as a result, be unable to fulfill the obligations of his or her job in the future.

7. ***Does the employer appear callous by acknowledging the employee's sad story but holding to the fact that the incident occurred and that the company should therefore be permitted to enforce its rules?***

An arbitrator is likely affected by the way management approaches a discharge case. Everyone knows that the grievant has lost his or her job, and the termination will impose a cost on the former employee. Nonetheless, an employer need not make excuses for its actions or its rules if they are generally what management would do in the same or similar situation. Every workplace needs rules and has rules, regardless of whether they are written down. Rules that are "reasonable," that is, promote management's interest in productivity balanced against the union's interest in fairness, are acceptable.

Management need not express any sorrow for the discharged employee. In most discharge cases, the employee has made a wrong choice—or a number of wrong choices. Blame is not part of the process, but responsibility is. Management should not be callous toward the dischargee but need not apologize for doing what management is supposed to do.

8. ***Is an arbitrator more likely to issue a decision denying the grievance when the grievant has a difficult personality?***

Arbitrators are human. The process of deciding discharge and discipline cases in arbitration inherently involves an evaluation of the people involved. A disputatious dischargee does not help his or her case if the reason for the termination was insubordination. Basically, the grievant has proven that what the supervisor says was certainly a possibility.

The arbitrator, however, knows that the grievant may not be in the best frame of mind at the arbitration hearing, even if well prepared by the union. That is why the neutral's focus must be on the evidence in determining what occurred. Even the most irascible worker can be wrongly accused.

9. ***In cases involving customer complaints, how critical is it for a company to provide the customer as a witness?***

The question about bringing in an outside witness to an event that gives rise to a discipline or discharge case is not unusual. Whether it is a customer who complains about the grievant's conduct in a retail setting or the person whose car was hit by the grievant while driving the company's truck, having that person at the hearing certainly is helpful to the arbitrator. It may not be possible to accomplish that in every case, and the arbitrator appreciates that fact.

Management needs evidence as to what occurred to prove its case. Having the complaining customer or the outsider involved in the incident at the hearing may be the only way to rebut a grievant's claim that the incident never occurred or that someone else was at fault. There may have been other witnesses, and the arbitrator will listen to their stories if the key person is unavailable.

10. Why should a wrongfully discharged grievant be reinstated with full back pay when he or she has not provided the employer with any services?

In discharge cases, the default remedy where just cause is not proven is reinstatement of the wrongfully discharged employee to his or her prior position with full back pay. Why should that be the case? The employer has received no services from the discharged employee since his or her separation from employment. Providing no services generally means receiving no pay.

Arbitrators understand that the wrongfully discharged employee has suffered an extended period out of work. He or she was not allowed to provide those services as a result of the wrongful decision of management.

If the dischargee was partially at fault, but the misconduct was not sufficient to warrant separation from employment, reinstatement without back pay would seem appropriate. This is not a compromise, but a remedy reflecting the comparative fault of the parties (see Chapter 8).

11. In a theft case, some arbitrators consider the value of what the grievant stole in determining just cause. Is that correct?

Theft cases should not turn on the amount an employee steals as long as the theft is proven. Some arbitrators wrongly hold that an employee who steals an item worth very little should be allowed to resume his or her job. That is a fundamental misunderstanding of what is involved in a theft case.

The employment relationship requires an employee to respect management's property and not take any of it. Employers cannot supervise employees so closely as to catch every theft every time. The employee's intention is at question in a discharge case for theft. Theft implicates a substantial and legitimate business interest of management.

12. Do arbitrators consider the context of an employee's job, for example, if he or she is entrusted with the safety of others?

An arbitrator is mindful of the context of the employee's work. Someone who deals with retail customers represents the employer to the public. Less concern about interacting with others outside the workplace is involved when an employee works in production and maintenance and does not deal with the public on a regular basis. In cases involving employees who are entrusted with the safety of others, such as bus drivers, management may terminate an employee in order to try to avoid (or to decrease) the potential for tort liability for any accident that occurred. Concern about safety is essential in the workplace for every employee and for the employer. An arbitrator cannot uphold the discharge of an employee, however, whose conduct did not warrant termination even if a tort suit is filed.

The union will often argue in a discharge case that management does not have a rule prohibiting the conduct alleged to have been the basis of the grievant's discharge. Rules are certainly important in the workplace, but in many instances their absence makes no difference. For example, management may not have a rule that prohibits harming a supervisor, but such action would be wrong. Also, management's rule may itself be unreasonable and simply because the employee violated the rule does not mean that discipline was warranted.

13. Should arbitrators enforce last chance agreements?

It is not uncommon for management to agree with a union request that it not discharge an employee for certain misconduct, but to give him or her one last chance. This understanding is typically embodied in a document that sets forth the terms of the parties' understanding and is normally signed by the dischargee as well as the union and management.

A last chance agreement generally provides that if the employee commits another offense within a certain period of time, he or she shall be subject to discharge. This type of agreement normally provides that the employee will not have access to the grievance and arbitration system to contest the extent of the discipline imposed—in this case, discharge.

Arbitrators should and do enforce last chance agreements as long as the facts support the claim that the employee engaged in further misconduct covered by the agreement. These agreements offer to management and the employee an opportunity to salvage an employee and demonstrate a positive benefit the union brings to the workforce. They may not always work, however.

Chapter 11

Management Rights

I. Overview

Every case that comes to labor arbitration involves an issue of management rights to one degree or another. The union protests certain actions by management as in violation of the collective bargaining agreement (CBA). Management responds that it had the right to act as it did either under the particular provisions of the CBA raised by the union or based on management's rights expressed in the agreement. Alternatively, management may argue that because the contract is silent on the issue, management has an implied reserved right to act as it did. The arbitrator must read and interpret the agreement in light of the context of the work relationship in order to determine the extent of management's right to act.

Some employers view management's rights as basic and unlimited, except as specifically limited by a clear contractual provision. Management can fire employees at will, except if the CBA provides otherwise, and can certainly decide without limitation how much discipline is warranted for an employee's bad acts. Management can take any operational decision it wishes, whatever the impact on employees. There is in this absolutist view a sense of entitlement that management insists an arbitrator cannot invade.

By comparison, a union sees management's rights as limited by provisions of the CBA that say nothing about reserved prerogatives. Management has negotiated a recognition clause, wage provisions, and various benefits provisions. If management were not limited in what it could do, these promises would be worthless. Thus, a union might argue that the arbitrator must limit management's rights to purely operational decisions or even prohibit the employer from acting at all where there is some economic disadvantage to the employees.

Arbitrators come out somewhere in the middle. They recognize that there are both express and implied limits to the exercise of management's rights. Management may have the right to act to achieve business efficiencies and organizational flexibility, but that prerogative must be balanced against express promises to employees made in the CBA and in established past practices that may bind the employer. Even if a CBA is silent on an issue, such as subcontracting or just cause, arbitrators will read the contract as a whole to imply some limitation on management's discretion. The primary implied limitation is that management must act for legitimate and substantial business reasons and not in an effort to negate contract promises or undermine the union it has recognized as the exclusive bargaining representative of the employees.

It is not an arbitrator's job to determine whether management made a wise or foolish decision. If the arbitrator determines that the employer had the right to act as it did considering the impact on the employees and the promises contained in their CBA, then the arbitrator's role has ended. The union may have a much better way to run the business, but its insight is not relevant in arbitration. Management is allowed to decide whether and how it wants to make widgets or aircraft, and the arbitrator is not to second-guess the choice it made.[1]

II. THE THEORY OF RESERVED RIGHTS

Before the employees formed their union, management had the right to operate its business in pursuit of productivity and profit. Those rights were never unrestricted, however. An employer always had to operate within the limitations imposed by law. With the coming of the union, management and the union bargain collectively over wages, hours, terms, and conditions of employment. The CBA imposes significant restrictions on managerial discretion, but in arbitration management often maintains that any matter not specifically addressed in the agreement is left to its unlimited discretion.

---

[1] *See* MARVIN HILL, JR. & ANTHONY SINICROPI, MANAGEMENT RIGHTS: A LEGAL AND ARBITRAL ANALYSIS (1986) (definitive text on the rights of employers). *See also* Carlton J. Snow, *Contract Interpretation,* in NATIONAL ACADEMY OF ARBITRATORS, THE COMMON LAW OF THE WORKPLACE: THE VIEWS OF ARBITRATORS ch. 2 (Theodore J. St. Antoine, ed., 2d ed. 2005) (summarizing principles arbitrators will apply in cases involving both management and union rights).

1.   Does management have "reserved" or "residual" rights?

The basic theory of reserved or residual rights provides that management's rights are inherent and, in the absence of specific contract restriction, unlimited. The employer runs the business and provides the capital. It decides what to make and how to produce what it makes. It can act at will.

This pristine version of management's rights, however, does not reflect the reality of the CBA. In the absence of a union, management had the right to act at will, but was always limited by statutory law. For example, management may have wanted to pay employees a subsistence wage rate, but the minimum wage laws limited its actions. Management must also provide a safe working environment under the provisions of the Occupational Health and Safety Act. Although the "at will" doctrine regarding employee job security remains alive in nonunion settings, management's decision to terminate an employee may be cognizable under a host of statutes, including laws that prohibit discrimination on the basis of race, gender, age, and national origin. If the reserved rights doctrine is based on the concept that management's prerogatives in the absence of a union were unrestricted, that is a fallacious concept. Management's rights were and are limited.

Even arbitrators who are inclined to adopt and espouse the theory of residual management rights always condition the exercise of those rights on a finding that the exercise of these rights must be "reasonable." The neutrals do not explain what "reasonable" means other than to offer conclusory opposites: an action is reasonable if it is not arbitrary, capricious, or taken in bad faith.

Actually, what these arbitrators mean, but do not say, is that management may act when (in the absence of contract restrictions) it is acting for managerial reasons, that is, with a substantial business justification. This limitation is not very onerous. Management normally acts only for business reasons. If it cannot explain why it acted and the employees suffer a significant negative effect, management's action is not reasonable, but is rather arbitrary, capricious, or taken in bad faith.

2.   What kind of actions can management take under the aegis of management rights?

The extent of management's discretion depends, on course, on the terms of the parties' CBA. A union can always attempt to negotiate for a limitation on those rights, even if management might not have to bargain about issues that lie at the core of entrepreneurial control under the National Labor Relations Act (NLRA).[2]

In general, management rights clauses will reserve to the employer the right to determine the fundamental nature of the business, including what products are made or what services are provided, and how the business will be conducted. Management normally retains the right to establish reasonable work rules and determine working conditions not otherwise limited by the CBA.

3.   *Can management rights be limited by past practice?*

Evidence of an established past practice is commonly used in arbitration as an interpretive gloss on ambiguous contract language. It is also used as the basis for a quasi-contractual right to an employee benefit.

Management can always decide before a series of actions has ripened into a past practice that it will apply an ambiguous contract clause in a different manner. If, for example, the employer has allowed employees to schedule their own vacations for a few years and then decides to allow supervisors to reject an employee's choice for operational reasons, the scheduling practice is not controlling in interpreting a contract vacation clause that does not speak to scheduling. After a practice has reached a level of consistency over time, however, management cannot use its implied management rights to alter the practice unilaterally. See Chapter 13 for a discussion as to how management can abolish an established past practice.

If management has the express right under the contract's management rights clause or in the vacations provision to "schedule employee vacations," then, in the absence of evidence of a mutual agreement by the parties to amend their contract, management may use the discretion it has reserved, even if it has not done so in the past. In the absence of express mention in a management rights clause or a vacation provision, however, an established past practice that is a benefit to the employees, such as the right to schedule earned vacation, will be a binding limitation on management's discretion.

4.   *If management has the right to take a particular action, how does the arbitrator have any power to hear the dispute?*

It is important to distinguish between arbitrability and the merits of a case. Regarding arbitrability, parties can exclude from an arbitrator's

---

[2]Fibreboard Paper Prods. Corp. v. NLRB, 379 U.S. 203 (1964).

jurisdiction any issue they wish. For example, if management does not want an arbitrator to hear matters involving subcontracting, it can attempt to get the union to agree to the exclusion in the provisions of the grievance and arbitration clause. In the absence of such an express exclusion, the arbitrator typically has the power to hear disputes over the interpretation of the terms of the agreement.

On the merits of the case, however, the arbitrator might decide that management has the reserved right it claims. As a result, it will deny the grievance on its merits.

III. Duty to Bargain

Lawyers and arbitrators trained in federal labor law sometimes confuse the role played by arbitration with requirements under the NLRA. It is true that an employer's violation of the terms of a CBA may constitute an unfair labor practice under Section 8(a)(5) of the NLRA. In arbitration, however, an employer does not violate Section 8(a)(5). It violates the CBA, and the arbitrator should issue a remedy.

A union grievance may claim that management had a duty to bargain before instituting a unilateral change in the terms of the agreement. If the parties wish, an arbitrator can make that determination, yet it is better to think of management's action as an alleged breach of the agreement, which includes implied limitations and past practices. The union can bring its claim under the NLRA to the National Labor Relations Board (NLRB), which will likely defer the matter to arbitration in any case.

1. How can arbitrators rule that management had an obligation to bargain in good faith with the union before taking a certain action?

An arbitrator serves the parties by responding to the stipulated issues. He or she has the power they bestow. If the parties' stipulated issue asks the arbitrator to determine whether management met its duty to bargain, the arbitrator's award could order management to bargain with the union, although determining whether it constituted "good faith" bargaining is a difficult job. Although an arbitrator normally would not think in terms of an NLRB remedy, such as posting a notice of an NLRA violation in the plant, there is no particular reason why the arbitrator could not include that in his or her award, but it is not the arbitrator's traditional job.

An arbitration award that orders the parties to bargain does not end the dispute and thus it fails at the arbitrator's primary task—to resolve the dispute. It is much better for the arbitrator to be given a traditional contract interpretation issue to resolve rather than an issue better addressed by a federal agency.

IV. THE SCOPE OF MANAGERIAL DISCRETION

Management rights are essential in every workplace. Someone must decide what the operation does, who will be hired to perform the work, and who performs what tasks in the workplace, among other innumerable decisions. As Justice William O. Douglas wrote in the *Steelworkers Trilogy*,[3] "[m]anagement hires and fires, pays and promotes, supervises and plans."[4] In effect, "management manages." Management certainly has the right to direct and control the operations and property; to determine the methods, products, services of the enterprise, as well as the composition and direction of jobs and employees; to determine the type of product it will produce; and to establish production methods and the equipment that will be used.

It is not the arbitrator's job to second-guess management. All managerial decisions have an effect on employees. If management decides to make a product that does not have a market, the company will go out of business, and everyone will lose their jobs. If management makes unwise decisions on how the plant should operate, the same unhappy result could occur. Even if management makes correct decisions to redirect the operations of the enterprise or to invest in technological improvements, some employees will be affected.

These decisions are undoubtedly reserved to management in the absence of express limitations in the CBA, and if the union protests these decisions in arbitration, their grievances will be denied. It is important to emphasize that it is not the arbitrator's role to review the wisdom of management's decisions taken pursuant to its reserved rights.

---

[3] Steelworkers v. American Mfg. Co., 363 U.S. 564 (1960); Steelworkers v. Warrior & Gulf Navig. Co., 363 U.S. 574 (1960); Steelworkers v. Enterprise Wheel & Car Corp., 363 U.S. 593 (1960). See Chapter 1, §V. The *Steelworkers Trilogy* decisions are reproduced in Appendix A.

[4] *Warrior & Gulf Navigation,* 363 U.S. at 583.

1. Does management have a greater scope of discretion when it comes to operational decisions?

Management manages, and when it does so and the union protests, the arbitrator is asked to determine the scope of managerial rights. The arbitrator should first examine the provisions of the CBA to see if they speak to the issue. An express clause allowing management to take the action it did will end the matter. More likely, the management rights clause will reserve to the employer the right to make a whole series of decisions essential to the operation of the business. Here the arbitrator may have to interpret the clause as it relates to management's decisions.

As a general matter, management has a broad scope of discretion when it comes to making operational decisions. As explained above, those decisions can have a deleterious effect on the workers, but in the absence of exceptions expressed in the CBA, management manages. In fact, although arbitrators rarely state this, there may be a presumption in favor of management when it comes to making operational decisions. The union will offer the union security clause, the wage and seniority clause, and other provisions as implying a limitation on management's right to make the operational decisions it has made. The union may also explain to the neutral how wrong-headed management's action was. These arguments will rarely be sufficient to overcome management's right to make operational decisions.

In some situations, arbitrators follow a theory of implied restrictions on the exercise of management's decision based on the express obligations contained in the CBA. However, as a general matter, when the decisions contested are traditionally those for management to make, in the absence of express limitations in the contract, management's action should be upheld as long as it is based on substantial and legitimate business justifications, even if it affects employee rights protected by the agreement. The arbitrator must balance management rights and employee benefits. If management could not make any decisions that affected employees, it would have lost control of the business. Unless they say so, the parties' agreement should not be so interpreted or applied.

2. What about management's decision to subcontract work?[5]

Contracting out work has always been of major concern to unions that represent employees who see their job security heading out the

---

[5] *See* ELKOURI & ELKOURI: HOW ARBITRATION WORKS ch. 13 (Kenneth May, ed., 7th ed. 2012).

door with the work they have traditionally performed. Thus, it is not surprising that grievances are filed when management subcontracts work that the union believes could have been performed by bargaining unit employees. That is especially troubling to unions when employees have been laid off.

As with every contract case (as opposed to a discipline and discharge case where the contract likely only says that management is limited by the standard of just cause), the parties must draw the arbitrator's attention to any relevant language in the CBA. Provisions on subcontracting come in all shapes and sizes and are the product of negotiations between the parties. If management seeks broad discretion to contract out, it will likely have to "pay for it" somewhere else in the agreement. If a provision allows management to subcontract work without limitation, the arbitrator must follow the contractual edict even if existing employees could have performed the work.

Subcontracting clauses may allow management discretion to contract out in certain situations, for example, where the current employees do not have the skills and abilities needed to perform the work in question, or where management does not own the equipment needed to perform the work. At the arbitration hearing, each party will attempt to prove that the conditions were or were not met.

It is not unusual for management to seek to have the right to contract out included in the list of reserved rights embodied in the management rights clause. Those rights normally come with the proviso "except as expressly limited by the terms of this collective bargaining agreement." A union may argue that this right to subcontract is subject to limitation by the wage clause. If employees are to be paid a certain amount per hour, how can they obtain this benefit if their work has been subcontracted? The answer is that the wage provision simply determines what the employees will be paid if they work. It is not a promise that work will be available.

The union is in much better shape in arbitration if the CBA contains a bargaining unit work provision that protects work traditionally performed by employees. Management violates such a provision by reassigning the work to nonbargaining unit salaried employees or contracting out the work. Once again, these provisions do not promise employees that there will be work, but only that, if there is work, it will be performed by bargaining unit employees and not others.

The most difficult subcontracting cases that arbitrators address occurs when the CBA is silent on the issue of contracting out. Management will argue that, in the absence of any restriction contained in the

CBA, its right to contract out work is unlimited. This is where an arbitrator must read the CBA as a whole, including the wage, seniority, and recognition clauses. If management could contract out work without any limitation, these provisions would be rendered meaningless. However, there are situations when management simply does not have the employees to perform the work in question. The company may not have the correct machinery and it may not be possible to acquire the equipment, or the company's employees may not have the skills to perform the work in question. All the employees may be already working a full week plus overtime, and thus retaining the work would jeopardize time limits on delivery. All of these are good reasons, if supported by the evidence, as opposed to mere conjecture.

When the contract is silent on the issue, arbitrators should uphold management's right to make "reasonable" decisions regarding subcontracting. That means management must have a genuine and substantial business justification for its actions. The existence of those reasons negates the possible inference that management was acting to undermine the promises made to the union in the CBA. In the absence of such reasons, the arbitrator should uphold the union's grievance, but it is most likely that management will attempt to present some neutral reason for contracting out the work.

3. What should the arbitrator do in cases where management has assigned work outside of the bargaining unit?

Management makes decisions all the time as to who should perform certain work in the workplace. Moving work from one bargaining unit employee to another is common. Even if an employee thinks otherwise, a particular employee does not "own" his or her work. The amount and type of work an employee performs may have an effect on that worker's job classification and wage rate, but management will still be able to reassign the work.

However, when management moves work outside of the bargaining unit to be performed by salaried employees, different considerations apply. This is a loss of work to the bargaining unit, which will likely result in a union grievance. The presence or absence of a clause that protects bargaining unit work will be very important to the arbitrator, as will a clause in the management rights provision that grants the employer the right to move work in this fashion. In the absence of any mention in the CBA, once again an arbitrator will review the reasons offered by management for its actions and assess whether they were based on substantial business considerations. One consideration—that the nonbargaining unit employee can perform the work at a lower rate of pay—will not be considered reasonable by the arbitrator. It is a direct affront to the wage provision in the CBA.

V. Work Rules

Management will normally create a set of work rules to be followed in the workplace. The rules might specify attendance and reporting requirements, explain how management will address issues of workplace safety, include information on how management will allocate overtime, list offenses for which management will impose discipline, specify a dress code, and cover a variety of other issues. By publishing and distributing work rules, management attempts to create uniform policies known to both employees and their supervisors. Typically, employees must acknowledge receipt of the work rules.

Simply because management creates work rules does not mean an arbitrator must enforce them. A union might grieve any and all of the rules as unreasonable and in conflict with the provisions of the CBA. The fact that an employee has violated a work rule does not mean that any resulting discipline or discharge was for just cause. It simply establishes that management has given the employee notice of the rules it expects the employee to follow.

1.   *Can a union challenge the reasonableness of management's work rules?*

Under the typical arbitration provision, a union can protest management's work rules. While a grievance is pending, however, employees are obliged to follow the rules unless they present a significant safety hazard to the workers or require the employees to do something illegal. The basic rule is "work and grieve."

The arbitrator will review management work rules to determine whether they are reasonable. This means that the rules generally enhance employee productivity and management's other operational goals without an undue negative impact on the workers. The arbitrator will also entertain arguments from the union about how the work rules affect rights and benefits expressly protected in the agreement or binding and well-established past practices.

2. What about management work rules that result in employee discipline or termination?

Arbitrators would generally prefer to review work rules in the specific factual context of a discipline or a discharge. But reviewing work rules that can lead to discipline or discharge "on their face" is perfectly appropriate. The arbitrator should determine whether discipline imposed under the work rule could pass muster under the just cause standard. If, for example, a management rule states that an employee will be discharged for one instance of tardiness of any length, administration of that rule could not result in a just cause discharge. Employees should not have to suffer a long period of unemployment simply to test the reasonableness of that rule.

The reasonableness of many management work rules does depend on the context. Some work rules could result in discipline for just cause depending on the circumstances. It does seem reasonable, for example, for management to require that employees punch in at a particular time clock. If the circumstances of a particular case were later to show that there was no substantial business justification for imposing such an attendance requirement, and it was arduous for employees to comply, the arbitrator would overturn management's discipline.

VI. A VARIETY OF MANAGEMENT DECISIONS

1. Can management decide to combine jobs and establish the rates of new jobs?

Management must make operational decisions or the enterprise will not function. Who does what in the workplace is at the heart of management's function. However, every time management makes such an operational decision, it has an effect on employees. Management acts, and the union reacts by filing a grievance.

The decision to combine job classifications may result in more work and more training for the persons holding the combined job. As a result, the union might file a grievance claiming that management did not have the discretion to combine the jobs and, if it did, the new job should be paid at a higher wage rate. Unless the CBA freezes job classifications and work assignments, the union is likely to lose on its claim of an abuse of management discretion in combining jobs. The pay claim, however, may have merit, especially if the operation has a wage system that compares job functions to benchmark jobs.

Establishing the pay rates for new jobs, and the procedure that management must follow, is normally addressed in the CBA. In the absence of such a provision, the union can grieve the rate management sets on a new job. The parties likely have a schedule of wage rates by job classification, and the arbitrator will be asked to determine which job is most like the new job that management has created.

Some arbitrators will send the parties to the bargaining table to resolve their differences on the wage rate for the new job. That is not very helpful, because the parties have likely discussed the issue throughout the grievance procedure. The arbitrator should resolve the issue, leaving it to the parties to negotiate further, if they wish.

2.   How does an arbitrator address those grievances involving work assignments?

Management normally decides who does what work. Employees, in turn, understandably feel a sense of "ownership" in the work they have always performed. Unless the CBA contains some express restrictions or there exists powerful evidence of a mutual, albeit oral, agreement, management has the discretion to assign work. We discuss the establishment of past practices in Chapter 13.

3.   Will an arbitrator let management decide to reduce staffing on a certain operation in order to save money?

Management does not need the arbitrator's permission to reduce crew size. The issue is brought to arbitration by the union if it is not satisfied with management's explanation for its action offered in the grievance procedure. The arbitrator's job is then to read any relevant language in the contract. Reducing staffing may create a legitimate concern about the safety of the employees, and a contract provision on safety and health might prove useful to the union's case. The management rights clause, however, may expressly reserve to management the right to determine the staffing on an operation. Both provisions must be read together. Management cannot risk the safety of employees in an effort to save money, but the union must present evidence that the risk is real and not imagined.

The union may have an alternate approach. Reducing crew size may change the nature of the employees' duties to a sufficient degree as to warrant a change in the rate of pay. Although employees may want a return to the status quo ante, that might not be possible in the absence of a "hook" in contract language. They may have to settle for more pay.

Chapter 12

Interpreting the Contract

I. Overview

In the *Steelworkers Trilogy*,[1] Justice William O. Douglas extolled the skills and abilities of labor arbitrators. These skilled neutrals, Justice Douglas said, know how to read and interpret the provisions of a collective bargaining agreement (CBA), the "generalized code" of the workplace negotiated by the parties that inevitably contains "gaps."[2] Douglas said that arbitrators are able to fill these lacunae. Parties select their arbitrators based on their expectation that their neutrals can perform this essential function.

---

[1] Steelworkers v. American Mfg. Co., 363 U.S. 564 (1960); Steelworkers v. Warrior & Gulf Navig. Co., 363 U.S. 574 (1960); Steelworkers v. Enterprise Wheel & Car Corp., 363 U.S. 593 (1960). See the discussion of Justice Douglas' *Steelworkers Trilogy* analysis in Chapter 1, §V. The *Steelworkers Trilogy* decisions are reproduced in Appendix A.

[2] *Warrior & Gulf Navigation,* 363 U.S. at 578, 580.

Douglas also said that the parties trust the neutral's "personal judgment" and knowledge of the workplace context.[3] The neutral can bring to bear knowledge of the effects of a decision on productivity and the morale of the shop and whether tensions will be heightened or diminished by a particular result in arbitration. In this way, the arbitrator provides stability to the workplace.

There are two phases of an arbitration proceeding where the neutral can attempt to accomplish what Douglas saw in the process. The first occasion is the arbitration hearing where the arbitrator, through skilled administration of the proceeding, can offer to the parties a fair opportunity to make their case. The second occasion is in writing the decision, which includes a recitation of the facts, the reasoning employed by the neutral, and ultimately the award that resolves the dispute.

It is comforting as an arbitrator to know that Justice Douglas thought that labor and management have so much confidence in the corps of labor arbitrators. Although every arbitrator certainly attempts to decide every dispute correctly, the most important thing the neutral does is bring the dispute to a definitive conclusion.

II. INTERPRETING THE CONTRACT[4]

When parties reach agreement in the form of a CBA, they think they understand what the terms of their contract mean. Negotiating is hard work and normally involves significant compromises and skilled use of language to bridge differences in interests and views. Some provisions may appear to be crystal clear, but, as disputes arise during the term of the CBA, this seeming clarity turns opaque. As Owen Fairweather wrote: "No amount of care can eliminate potential ambiguity."[5] Language that can reasonably be read to have more than one meaning is ambiguous. It is inevitable that disputes will arise on the margins of a contract provision. Thus, the parties provide an internal system for

---

[3] *Id.* at 582.

[4] *See* Carlton J. Snow, *Contract Interpretation,* in NATIONAL ACADEMY OF ARBITRATORS, THE COMMON LAW OF THE WORKPLACE: THE VIEWS OF ARBITRATORS ch. 2 (Theodore J. St. Antoine, ed., 2d ed. 2005) (thoughtful and comprehensive discussion of contract interpretation); FAIRWEATHER'S PRACTICE & PROCEDURE IN LABOR ARBITRATION ch. 9 (Ray J. Schoonhoven, ed., 4th ed.) (excellent discussion of the principles of contract interpretation). *See also* ELKOURI & ELKOURI: HOW ARBITRATION WORKS ch. 9 (Kenneth May, ed., 7th ed. 2012).

[5] FAIRWEATHER'S PRACTICE & PROCEDURE IN LABOR ARBITRATION, *supra* note 4, at 163.

resolving those disputes—the grievance and arbitration system. If the parties cannot reach agreement, they can appoint an arbitrator to interpret what they agreed to.

1. *Why do the parties need an arbitrator to read, interpret, and apply their agreement?*

Every workplace allocates operational prerogatives, work opportunities, and matters of compensation according to a system. In the unionized workplace, the process of collective bargaining is the system. How much vacation should an employee receive? Who should be awarded an available promotion? Who should be laid off when there is a lack of work? Many employers, both unionized and nonunionized, use some form of seniority to make a number of these determinations. Although seniority is certainly "the coin of the industrial realm," questions often arise concerning contract interpretation and application.

Where parties intend that a certain approach be taken to a foreseeable workplace issue, such as the assignment of work or the promotion of an employee, they try to be as definitive as they can in the CBA. However, parties simply cannot foresee every aspect of every issue that might arise. How could they when their negotiators often reach agreement after midnight, when they are too tired to resist (or insist) any further? How could they when there are myriad issues and the agreement must be of manageable size to make it usable?

Collective bargaining agreements are not clear documents. Every agreement contains holes and vague terms that need extrapolation in the case at hand. The parties did not intend to leave holes; they intended to reach an agreement. They employed vague terms like "reasonable" in order to reach that agreement. They also know that the gaps could be filled in and the vague terms interpreted by labor arbitrators who would do so by applying what they say is the "intent of the parties." Often that intent is anything but evident.

Arbitrators employ many presumptions and maxims in reading, interpreting, and applying contract provisions to resolve pending disputes. At base, these are simply commonsense principles. Arbitrators also employ post-hoc rationales to justify the decisions they have made.

2. *How can there be any real controversy as to what the contract language means?*

If the parties have actually reached an agreement expressed in clear language, they are bound by their deal. The arbitrator will gladly recite the "plain meaning" rule that requires the neutral to apply the words of the contract as written. The arbitrator can correctly presume that the parties knew what they were doing when they reached their agreement.

It is not unusual, however, for advocates for both parties to insist before the arbitrator that the applicable contract language is "clear." Clear language should be applied according to its plain and ordinary meaning, but the same language cannot be "clear" and point in two different directions. Clarity, like beauty, apparently is in the eye of the beholder. If the agreement was, in fact, clear, it is not likely that the parties would have made it all the way through the grievance procedure to arbitration.

At times, the parties' opaque language can drive an arbitrator crazy. He or she would like to send the dispute back to management and the union with the direction that they clean up their "intentions" by clarifying their language. That should never actually happen, however, in part because it is unlikely that the parties would be any more successful at such a project than the arbitrator would be and in part because the primary goal of the arbitrator must be to resolve the dispute. If the end result is sufficiently unsettling to one party (or both), they can address the issue at any time, upon receipt of the arbitrator's award or when their next set of negotiations to reset the bargain occurs. The arbitrator's word is final only so long as the parties want it to be final.

The parties' negotiated CBA controls the workplace, and the arbitrator's responsibility is to apply the parties' deal to the facts of the disputes he or she is appointed to resolve. This may sound like a fairly easy task, but the parties have not made it that easy for their neutral. The parties agreed to certain words, but they cannot agree what those words mean as applied to the current dispute.

It is understandable why agreements are not always easy to comprehend and enforce. Collective bargaining can be an arduous process, and agreements are often reached at the last minute before parties resort to economic weapons in an effort to obtain a more favorable deal. Therefore, contract language tends to be imperfect and not self-applying. However, it is the primary evidence the arbitrator has regarding the parties' intent.

What then is the arbitrator to do when presented with a provision that is more cloudy than clear? The guiding principle must be for the arbitrator to determine the intentions of the parties by relying on objective, rather than subjective, evidence. Each CBA is unique, but an experienced arbitrator has likely interpreted similar provisions before. There are generally understood rules of interpretation available to the neutral and known to the parties that will assist the arbitrator in the interpretive process.

3.   *Does an arbitrator look for whether the parties had a "meeting of the minds?"*

Basic common law contract principles require that the parties reach a "meeting of the minds" in order for there to be a binding arrangement. If at the time the agreement was reached the two sides have different views as to the meaning and extent of the bargain, there is no contract. Arbitrators, most of whom are trained in the law, often use the phrase in their opinions without realizing that the distinctive nature of CBAs makes the "meeting of the minds" rationale inapplicable.

It would be preferable, of course, for parties to reach a mutually shared understanding of their arrangement, and they often agree on their shared intention regarding much of the contract. There are other clauses, however, that are intentionally left ambiguous in order to wrap up the arrangement and avoid a strike or lockout.

For example, the union may seek a clause requiring management to schedule employee vacations based on seniority. Senior employees would choose first, and junior employees would select from what was left of available vacation weeks. Management, however, may be concerned that using strict seniority would leave vital operational functions understaffed during critical times of the year. If the union obtains a clause that makes seniority the only, and thus controlling, variable in scheduling vacations, an arbitrator must follow that guidepost, even if management has good and compelling business reasons for not granting the senior employees scheduling preferences. In another instance, the parties might reach a compromise formulation that requires management to use "reasonable efforts" to meet employee preferences based on seniority. This formulation offers room for management to deny a particular request based on proven operational needs. It does not allow management to convert the clause into one that gives it total discretion in scheduling vacations even if it would have good business reasons for wanting to do so.

Was there a "meeting of the minds" between the parties on the scope of management's discretion and employee rights when a compromise formulation is adopted? The term *reasonable efforts* is intentionally ambiguous, a phrase used without evident boundaries. There was mutual agreement on something other than total seniority or total discretion, but the contours of that deal will need to be fleshed out in arbitration if management denies the vacation request of a senior employee.

4. If the neutral fills in the gaps in the contract, doesn't that mean the arbitrator writes the contract?

Justice Douglas in the *Steelworkers Trilogy* plainly stated that it was the arbitrator's job to fill in the inevitable gaps in the provisions of a CBA. There are limits to this power, of course. For example, an arbitrator cannot construct an entire seniority system. When the parties have reached an impasse in bargaining a new contract, they might employ *interest arbitration* as a viable alternative to a work stoppage. Rarely used in the private sector, interest arbitration is much more common in the public sector where strikes and lockouts are likely illegal.

The more common grievance arbitration cases will require the arbitrator to finish the bargain that the parties have reached by filling in the gaps they have left. In effect, arbitration continues the collective bargaining process. Interpreting an ambiguous term will turn a provision in one direction or another. The arbitrator will rationalize his or her decision as consistent with the parties' intention, but he or she is certainly writing part of the deal. The alternative is unacceptable—to remand the case back to the parties to finish bargaining. If they could have reached agreement on the dispute, they would have done so in the grievance procedure, and the case would not have been submitted to arbitration in the first place. Although the arbitrator's ruling is final and binding, the parties always have the opportunity to rewrite their agreement after the arbitrator has ruled.

5. When the arbitrator fills in the gaps in the parties' contract, does that violate the typical contract provision that prohibits the arbitrator from adding to, subtracting from, or otherwise modifying the terms of the collective bargaining agreement?

Few arbitrators ever consciously violate this typical contract restriction. They know, however, that they have to interpret the language of the CBA consistent with the available evidence of the parties' intent. At the arbitration hearing and in its brief, management usually reminds the arbitrator of these limitations on his or her power. An arbitrator may not overstep that boundary, but it is unclear where the boundary lies.

These common limitations on an arbitrator's power in interpreting the contract are as ambiguous as most contract provisions. When an arbitrator interprets a contract clause consistent with the longstanding, mutually understood and accepted past practice, is he or she adding to the contract? Or is the arbitrator simply interpreting the written contract consistent with the parties' intent?

There are instances where these typical contract admonitions will have an impact. Arbitrators will find that past practices that provide employees with a benefit of value are binding. Few would contest that well-established principle. Yet an arbitrator should pause before issuing an award recognizing that benefit and make sure that the evidence persuasively supports the unexpressed benefit. This does not mean that the practice can be ignored, but it does mean that the proof must be solid.

6.   Should the arbitrator ever remand a dispute to the parties to be resolved through further negotiations?

Since the earliest days of arbitration, neutrals have, on occasion, concluded that the parties have not reached an agreement on the matter at hand and remanded the case to the parties for further negotiations. That is the worst option available to an arbitrator and should be avoided at all costs. The one thing the parties seek through arbitration is the arbitrator's reading of their CBA. If that text and practice is unclear, the arbitrator must do his or her best.

Silence in an agreement on an issue speaks loudly. If there is no mention of a typical limitation on an employee benefit, such as qualification for holiday pay, the arbitrator should rule that none exists. If management's right to take a particular operational action is unlimited, the arbitrator can seek guidance in the terms of the management rights clause. There is always an answer, even if the arbitrator is left without the clear guidance he or she might prefer.

A remand to the parties leaves them without guidance or direction. It likely will exacerbate the relationship and may result in a disruption of work. It will certainly undermine the parties' trust in the labor arbitration process.

7.   How does the arbitrator ever know enough about the parties and the workplace to determine their actual intent?

The arbitrator's job is to determine what the parties intended, or, more likely, what they would have said they intended had they been asked when they were negotiating the relevant provisions. The arbitrator cannot ask them now, because if they agreed on their mutual intent, there would be no dispute to resolve. How does the arbitrator go about his or her job of reconstructing (or even constructing) the parties' mutual intent?

The arbitrator starts with the words the parties used. Although not self-applying, they are tools in the hands (or mind) of the arbitrator. The neutral understands, or can learn about, the context of the shop, which may help to give meaning to the parties' choice of terms. The parties negotiated an entire agreement, not just one troublesome clause, and so there may be some help elsewhere in the agreement. The parties do not help, however, by simply insisting that the language is clear—and clearly supports their position.

It is not unusual for witnesses at the arbitration to be asked what their intent was in proposing or agreeing to a particular provision. That question will likely trigger an objection from the opposing party's advocate. Subjective intent not communicated to the other party cannot pierce the veil of ambiguity in drafting. Yet an arbitrator should allow the question. If the witness responds with a statement of intent that is totally at odds with the language adopted in the agreement, that raises real questions as to the witness' credibility and reliability. On the other hand, an alternate response may indicate to the arbitrator that the parties may not be that far apart as to the meaning of their contract. In either case, the question solicits information that may be useful to the arbitrator.

The arbitrator never knows as much about the parties as they know about themselves. Intent, of course, is a "will o' the wisp," a conclusion more than a finding. Yet the arbitrator generally knows how businesses operate. The arbitrator may not know how to make glass or run schools, but he or she knows how seniority systems operate and why management insists on reasonable attendance. The arbitrator knows a lot in general, if not specifically, about these parties.

The parties in arbitration select their neutral with the confidence that the arbitrator will bring this knowledge to the proceeding. Their obligation during the hearing is to inform their neutral about anything that distinguishes their workplace from the norm. In the absence of such information, the arbitrator must assume that the default information about the common, ordinary, and regular workplace applies.

III. Addressing Ambiguity

When a contract interpretation case comes to arbitration, both parties believe that the terms of the CBA can be read in their favor. The union will have a proposed reading of the contract terms that supports granting the grievance, and management will have an alternate reading that mandates denying the grievance. It is possible that both readings are reasonable, in the sense that they are reasonably possible interpretations. The arbitrator's job is to determine which one is the more reasonable interpretation.

1. How does an arbitrator deal with ambiguity in contract language?

Every word of a CBA has some measure of ambiguity. The ubiquitous term *reasonable* is a paradigmatic example, a term without boundaries except as understood in context. At the other extreme, numbers used to count things, such as the staffing of a machine, generally mean what they say, although even in such situations there may be room for interpretation. For example, if the contract mandates that a certain work operation must have "five" people per machine, does that include the supervisor?

Once it is accepted that ambiguity is a fact of life, the role of the arbitrator becomes clearer, albeit not easy. The arbitrator must use the intent of the parties as the lodestar, with the primary evidence being the words they used to express their bargain. Words must be given their most likely meaning in the context of the particular workplace. The arbitrator may entertain evidence about prior practice with regard to the matter left ambiguous in the terms of the provisions. To return to the prior example, if the work operation has always been staffed with four employees and a supervisor, then the contract requirement for five per machine most likely includes the supervisor.

The arbitrator may also find recourse in the parties' bargaining history, if it is available. Who at the bargaining table proposed the language about staffing? Arbitrators often say that any ambiguity in contract language should be held against the party that proposed the language, although such a hard-and-fast rule ignores the reality of the give-and-take during negotiations. Both sides had the opportunity to clarify language if that was a concern.

2. Does an arbitrator ever use a dictionary to understand the meaning of the parties' contractual terms?

The ordinary meaning of the words used in a contract provision should be the default position in interpretation. It is perfectly appropriate for an arbitrator to look to the dictionary for a definition. That reading may favor one party's case. It would then be incumbent on the other party to present evidence and argument that a different reading was intended, perhaps a technical meaning common in the industry.

3. Is contract language ever so ambiguous as to be unenforceable?

There are times when contract language is so difficult to interpret that an arbitrator would like to throw up his or her hands and send the whole mess back to the parties. That should be avoided at all costs. If the parties mutually agree that the reading the arbitrator gives their language does not meet their expectations or their needs, they can change the provision. Any contract can be interpreted, although admittedly with different degrees of confidence in the reading given by the neutral.

Consider a case where the parties agree that management will take certain action "where possible." That formulation is certainly vague and ambiguous, but it does offer the arbitrator some guidance. For the union to prevail, it must show how the action in question was "possible." Management will explain why it acted (or failed to act) as it did. The arbitrator will decide the case in accordance with the evidence presented pursuant to the language the parties adopted in their CBA.

4. What is the plain meaning rule?

One party may attempt to justify a reading of contract language based on what is commonly called the *plain meaning rule*. In this situation, the arbitrator would then read the language and tell the parties what it says. Of course, what one party sees as the "plain meaning" the other party sees as a patent distortion of the parties' intent. The rule seems to be a conclusion reached after analysis of the context rather than a useful guide to contract interpretation. The arbitrator's decision, however, will state with confidence the arbitrator's conclusion that one party's interpretation is preferable because it gives the words their "plain meaning." Because arbitrators employ the plain meaning rule in expressing their conclusion, parties will make that argument in arbitration. Much like the common protestation that the language is "clear," the plain meaning of contract language is a mirage.

In fact, the application of the plain meaning rule offers a perfect example of what goes on in the arbitrator's mind before he or she drafts the opinion. Although the ultimate decision will not likely explicate this decisional process, an arbitrator may be in equipoise regarding the correct interpretation, at least for a while. It is rare, however, for this balance to remain very long in the arbitrator's mind. At some point in the process, he or she will reach a conclusion on meaning, perhaps realizing that, without exercising some judgment, the case cannot be decided. At that moment, one meaning seems to be more reasonable than another. Once that point is reached, the arbitrator's initial quandary disappears. He or she writes with certainty about something that may not have been certain at all.

The arbitrator's alternative, of course, is to rely on the burden of proof that the union bears in contract interpretation cases. If two meanings are equally balanced, the arbitrator can always say that the union has failed to meet its burden of proof and deny the grievance. The same ploy, although with an opposite result, can be used in discharge and discipline cases, where management bears the burden. These are makeweights rather than decisional guides. See Chapter 15 for a discussion of burdens of proof.

IV. Using Past Practice

An arbitrator will use all the help he or she can get in interpreting contract language. Past practice and bargaining history are often the most helpful tools when the contract language is ambiguous, because they demonstrate how the parties have applied their contract language and how it was created. However, the arbitrator must focus first on the words the parties used. If a reasonable reading of those words is possible, that should control.[6]

1. How does an arbitrator use evidence of past practice in interpreting the provisions of a collective bargaining agreement?

If the parties to the collective relationship have operated under the terms of the CBA for some period of time, they have likely developed practices as to how certain provisions should be applied. These practices do not nullify the contract language; they simply demonstrate the parties' understanding through their conduct as to how the contract is applied. They are valuable guides to the arbitrator, who has been asked to read, interpret, and apply the contract language.

The parties, after all, reached agreement on the words of the contract. Words are rarely self-applying, and the parties knew that administration of the agreement was going to be necessary. How they applied their contract is the clearest indication of what they intended when they agreed to the words in the agreement.

Usually it is management that "creates" a practice. Applying the bare bones of the agreement requires certain unwritten protocols based on the needs of the operation. If the union is aware of these events over a period of time, they have become established practices that act as a gloss on the contract language in question.

---

[6]*See* Elkouri & Elkouri: How Arbitration Works ch. 12 (Kenneth May, ed., 7th ed. 2012).

2. What evidence is sufficient to establish a past practice?

The essence of a past practice is that it is demonstrated to be mutual—that is, both management and the union, by their conduct, have reached some implied understanding regarding certain matters. The list of topics that can be covered by a past practice is almost limitless.

In 1961, at the National Academy of Arbitrators (NAA) annual meeting, Arbitrator Richard Mittenthal presented his famous and much-cited paper on past practices that has served as a template for parties and arbitrators for more than a half century.[7] Mittenthal emphasized that the core characteristic of a practice is that it must be mutual—there is no such thing as a binding unilateral past practice. A practice must also be clear and consistent over time.

3. How does the arbitrator respond to evidence of past practice?

Past practice plays a vital role in defining the parties' intent. An arbitrator expects to hear evidence about past practice at a hearing, even if both parties insist that the contract language is absolutely clear. The quality of the evidence that the arbitrator receives on past practice varies tremendously.

Sometimes a party may attempt to prove past practice based on mere recollection that something like the present case arose many years ago and then explain how the parties dealt with the situation. Such evidence, even if well-meaning, is worthless to the arbitrator. It may be the best a party has to offer, but it will not sustain the finding of a past practice.

In order to be given weight by the neutral, proof of past practice must explain the factual situations previously presented and how management addressed them to the satisfaction (or at least to the knowledge) of the union. When did these events happen? How often did they occur? Were these cases ever handled differently? Even if an arbitrator would like to ask these questions, he or she should not—it is for the parties to make out their cases. The arbitrator should listen to what is presented and then conclude whether it presents a consistent pattern of similar conduct in the administration and operation of the contract provision in question.

Not every provision in the CBA is applied and reapplied on a sufficiently regular basis to generate a past practice. That is fine—the

---

[7]Richard Mittenthal, *Past Practice and the Administration of Collective Bargaining Agreements*, in ARBITRATION AND PUBLIC POLICY: PROCEEDINGS OF THE 14TH ANNUAL MEETING, NATIONAL ACADEMY OF ARBITRATORS 30 (Spencer D. Pollard, ed., 1961).

arbitrator will take what he or she has and make the best of it. An event that only happened once previously is not a past practice. It is evidence, however, and should be admitted and considered.

Can the arbitrator ignore a past practice? Assuming the evidence shows that the parties have regularly addressed a certain issue of interpretation in a certain way, the arbitrator cannot ignore it. The practice, in effect, has become a binding gloss on the contract.

4.   Can past practice negate a contract provision?

A much more difficult case involving the use of established past practice requires the arbitrator to consider whether the parties, by their conduct, have negated a contract clause. Parties can certainly amend their CBA—they do so periodically through their scheduled negotiations. But can they revise a contract provision by practice?

First, if a course of conduct does not meet the standard of a mutually understood and acceptable way of doing things over a considerable period of time, it is not a past practice. Second, a past practice does not require a writing, but in order to negate a written contract clause, the practice must be proven with compelling evidence. A promise created through formal negotiations can only be modified by a conscious and deliberate interchange, albeit oral, between the parties.

V. Bargaining History

Parties periodically renegotiate the terms of their CBA. Most agreements expire after three years, and the parties may start the renegotiation process a few months before the expiration date. Typically, parties will privately review every provision of their agreement and examine grievances that have arisen under each provision and any arbitration decisions. Then, after seeking input from stakeholders in the organization, a party will prepare proposals for the negotiation process. Once the parties meet and exchange general ideas and concepts, bargaining will begin, often accomplished in bilateral subcommittees with a complete and finished bargain only made at the main negotiating table. Generally, each party will take notes of what is discussed and agreed to.

1.   Does an arbitrator find bargaining history useful?

Parties will often present bargaining history concerning the provision in question in an attempt to clarify the parties' intent. Each side will assemble the bargaining notes it took during negotiations. At times, the notes may show the neutral that the parties did not even agree at the time of negotiations what certain words meant!

Oral recollections as to what was said across the negotiation table are harder to credit than written notes. Unless an issue was particularly salient in negotiations when dozens of provisions are discussed, one wonders how any discussions could be remembered years later. That does not mean that the witnesses are lying, only that the arbitrator must recognize the limitations of such testimony.

Better evidence of bargaining history would come in the form of proposals and counterproposals. The arbitrator can learn how negotiations progressed, but he or she must be cautious in using this information. The contract language still controls, not the bargaining history.

2.   What should an arbitrator do with evidence that a party, during negotiations, proposed certain contract language that was not accepted by the opposing party?

It is not unusual for a party's proposal to be rejected during negotiations—that is one way bargaining commonly proceeds. Does that mean that the approach proposed in the rejected clause is not part of the parties' agreement? The party that rejected the proposal in negotiations will argue that its opponent should not be able to obtain in arbitration what it could not obtain in negotiations. That truism is, of course, correct, but it assumes that the agreement and past practice did not already embody such an approach.

One situation involving bargaining history offers the arbitrator some clear guidance. If the previous CBA contained an obligation and the rejected proposal would have negated that obligation, the arbitrator can conclude with some confidence that the continuing contract provision should be read to contain the obligation.

In another situation, a party may offer a proposal in negotiations to embody in clear contract language what the parties' practice had been for years. The opposing party will argue in a later arbitration that, because the proposal was not accepted, the contract cannot be read to give the proposing party what it was unable to win in negotiations. That is not necessarily the case. A failed proposal to embody a practice in contract language does not mean that the established practice has disappeared—it still may be the basis for an independent claim or for an interpretive gloss on ambiguous contract language. A failed proposal may simply have been an effort to substitute clear contract language for poorly drafted previous language or for contractual silence on the issue. Although some arbitrators are quick to find that the practice somehow vanished, the failure of the proposal does not necessarily mean that the essence of the proposal was not already part of the parties' mutual and binding arrangement.

The ultimate question presented to the arbitrator is the nature of the parties' deal. Their understanding includes both matters expressed in the agreement and those left to an unwritten rule through past practice. One party may wish to embody the established past practice in the terms of the agreement to make it easier to enforce in the future. Its failure to achieve that goal should not mean that the past practice is gone.

On the other hand, evidence of the failure to reach agreement on a matter that the parties had not addressed in the past through their practice does indicate that no agreement has been reached on that matter. If rejected when presented in negotiations for the first time, it is difficult for the neutral to find other than a lack of mutual acceptance of the proposal.

3.   Does consideration of bargaining history violate the parol evidence rule?

The *parol evidence rule*, applied for centuries by common law courts as a limitation on the evidence that can be considered in determining the meaning of contract language, has no role in labor arbitration. The rule assumes that the final contract language clearly and plainly represents the parties' agreement. Yet language in a CBA is always ambiguous to some degree. Parol evidence has always been admissible in court to show the meaning of the language that was agreed to. Evidence of the exchange of proposals and the discussions at the bargaining table can enlighten the arbitrator as to what the parties intended.

VI. OTHER INTERPRETIVE TOOLS

The arbitrator's primary job is to determine the "intent" of the parties as evidenced in their CBA and prior practice. It is possible that an arbitrator can make use of a variety of tools in interpreting contract language—tools that courts have used for centuries in determining what parties to a contract intended. The arbitrator must be cautious, however, to make sure that the interpretive tools fit the collective bargaining context. Another problem with court-created "maxims" of interpretation is that they often appear in matching pairs. For example, a contract "should be read as a whole" balances against "each provision must be given meaning and effect." Which is correct? Determining that is the arbitrator's job.

1.   What general maxims will an arbitrator use in interpreting contract language?

There are some presumptive approaches to interpretation that may prove useful in understanding and applying language in a CBA. They reflect the reality of collective bargaining. For example, it is the normal practice in negotiations that tentative agreement on one provision is not binding until the entire contract is agreed to. Thus, the maxim that the arbitrator must "consider the contract as a whole" rings true in the collective bargaining context, because there is no agreement until the entire agreement is reached. The arbitrator should attempt to give effect to every contract provision.

It is also useful for the arbitrator not to focus solely on an isolated word or phrase. Those particular words might only be understandable when considered in the context of an entire provision, or even the entire contract. If two or more clauses in the agreement might be read to refer to the same issue, the more specific clause should take precedent over the general reference. A provision negotiated more recently takes precedent over an earlier formulation of that subject matter that has been continued in the current CBA.

At times, a party in arbitration may claim that the agreement does not really reflect what it intended during bargaining. However, if they signed the contract, they have purchased its contents. Parties are presumed to have meant what they said and are bound by what they signed.

Arbitrators also should read contract language so that it has a reasonable meaning, and avoid harsh, absurd or nonsensical results. Examining the contract language, which party's reading has the better of it? The more reasonable version should control, as long as the arbitrator can explain why it is more reasonable in this context.

These and other maxims regarding contract interpretation may prove useful to the arbitrator in interpreting contract language, because the parties would likely have known about them when they negotiated their CBA. The particular formulation of a maxim is not critical; there are just commonsense rules and applied logic. Thus, as default rules for contract interpretation, they reflect what negotiators intended would be used to read and to understand their agreement.

2.   Are there other maxims that arbitrators can use in understanding and applying bargaining history?

There are contract interpretation maxims that are used based on bargaining history. For example, which party offered the language in question during negotiations? Language is normally interpreted against the party that proposed it in negotiations if it is ambiguous in the final agreement.

Language that was included in a previous CBA and was interpreted in a prior arbitration should be considered as retaining the same meaning that the previous arbitration gave that language. The parties had the opportunity to alter the contract during negotiations and did not.

3.   How does an arbitrator determine the meaning of the special terms used by the parties in their collective bargaining agreement?

Many, perhaps most, workplaces have technical terms or jargon to describe particular situations. It is foreseeable, then, that the parties would use those terms in their contracts to describe specific events and circumstances. Although an arbitrator should normally attempt to apply the ordinary and generally recognized meaning to contract terms, in the context of a workplace those terms may take on a special meaning. Advocates for the parties must inform the arbitrator of their special usage; if they do not, the arbitrator must inquire.

4.   Do the maxims that arbitrators use in interpreting contract language really mean anything in the end?

The maxims commonly used by arbitrators are only helpful if they reflect simple logic consistent with the collective bargaining context in which CBAs are negotiated. Arbitrators also use these maxims as a way to rationalize their decisions. There is always a maxim available for any purpose, because they tend to arrive in matching pairs. For example, one maxim is that an arbitrator must give each and every provision in the contract a meaning while reading the contract as a whole. Reading the contract "as a whole" may mean ignoring what is said in one provision or another. Specific language should be preferred over general language, but that means ignoring the general language.

At best, these maxims are useful if understood and applied not as controlling edicts (they are not embodied in the agreement itself) but as logical approaches to reading a contract: look at every provision; look at the agreement as a whole; determine using both perspectives what it was that the parties intended to achieve.

One helpful and regularly used maxim is applicable when parties list a series of circumstances where a rule or principle will be applied.

The maxim tells the arbitrator that "the expression of one means the exclusion of another." (Arbitrators show off their erudition by announcing this maxim in Latin: *expressio unius est exclusio alterius*. It is better expressed in English.) In a contract that contains a list of seven items, but not listing others, an arbitrator can conclude that the parties intended to exclude the others if they arise. Of course, the parties may have simply intended the list of seven as examples of the kinds of things the parties intended to cover. If another event similar to those listed occurs, perhaps the parties would have wanted to include it. Here bargaining history can help. If one side or the other proposed including an eighth item and the other party refused, the arbitrator has the evidence to conclude that the eighth was not intended to be included on the list. Parties can easily avoid this outcome in bargaining, if that is their intention, by adding the phrase "including, but not limited to" before the list. Thus, the list becomes illustrative, not limiting.

VII. Presumptions in Contract Interpretation

Arbitrators explain that their assigned task is to apply the terms of the parties' CBA to the dispute at hand. They express their conclusions in definitive terms as if they had no trouble reaching the outcome. That is simply not true in many cases. Yet, in order to enhance its acceptability and legitimacy, the arbitrator's decision must be definitive and unambiguous, even if the contract language is opaque and uncertain.

The arbitrator must follow the guidance set forth by the parties in their CBA, however imperfect that instrument may be. Cognizant of the differing interests of management and labor, an arbitrator may be able to apply presumptions in his or her reading of the contract language. Arbitrators will rarely, if ever, state that they are employing a presumption, but examining reported decisions confirms that the neutrals think differently about contract language depending on whether the provision addresses an operational matter or involves an employee benefit.

1. Might the arbitrator use presumptions in reading contract language?

When the arbitrator interprets the terms of the CBA, he or she approaches the task with certain presumptions. Contract language that addresses operational discretion should be read as affording management leeway. On the other hand, the arbitrator should not read an ambiguous provision in a way that results in a forfeiture of an employee benefit. Thus, the specific topic the grievance addresses may be determinative in any given dispute involving the interpretation of the contract language.

If a provision covers an employee benefit, such as vacations, holiday pay, and any other matter of compensation, arbitrators should hesitate before concluding that the benefit is forfeited. This, in effect, is a presumption in favor of the union when it comes to benefits. Doubts should be resolved against forfeiture. The presumption can be rebutted, of course, by evidence to the contrary, but in the absence of such contrary evidence, the grievance should be granted. Such a presumption runs counter to the customarily stated burden on the union to prove a violation of the contract in an interpretation case. As explained below, those "burdens" are really decisional makeweights employed by arbitrators to decide hard cases when little else compels a conclusion.

On the other hand, if the matter involves an operational decision, such as the assignment of work, management should enjoy the benefit of the doubt created by ambiguous contract language, in the absence of evidence to the contrary. As Justice Douglas wrote in the *Steelworkers Trilogy,* "[m]anagement hires and fires, pays and promotes, supervises and plans."[8] In other words, "management manages." That does not mean, however, that managerial decisions about operational matters are not important to the employees or to their union. They are important, yet management should be given the benefit of the doubt on how to operate the workplace.

2.   What does the "burden of bargaining" mean, and is it useful in interpreting contract language?

One tool that an arbitrator can use in order to resolve a contract interpretation issue is determining which party—management or labor—had the obligation to bargain for a particular provision in the CBA to clarify a matter. For example, the parties may have a long-standing past practice that conveys a benefit to the employees. If management wants to eliminate the practice, it bears the "burden of bargaining" for a provision on the issue. If the union wants to reverse an unfavorable arbitration decision that interprets contract language, it bears the "burden of bargaining" for that change.

In general, there are default decisional rules that an arbitrator applies in resolving grievance disputes. Any party that wants to ensure that an arbitrator does not follow one of those default rules in ruling on

---

[8] Steelworkers v. Warrior & Gulf Navig. Co., 363 U.S. 574, 583 (1960).

a future grievance must obtain contract language in negotiations negating the default rule in question. That party has the "burden of bargaining." If it fails to achieve such a clarification, the default rules apply. Thus, it is useful for the arbitrator to determine which party had the "burden of bargaining" for express contract language. If that language does not appear in the CBA, the party that did not meet its burden is unlikely to prevail in arbitration.

VIII. PRIOR ARBITRATIONS AND GRIEVANCE SETTLEMENTS

An arbitration is an event in the history of a collective relationship. It would not be unusual for the arbitrator to be told that the parties have addressed a similar issue previously, either in an arbitration case or in the settlement of a grievance. Does that mean that the issue has been decided and should not be revisited by the arbitrator? What if the previous arbitrator was wrong in his or her decision?

1. *How should the arbitrator deal with prior arbitration decisions involving the parties?*

One of the parties to an arbitration will certainly present the arbitrator with prior arbitrations between the parties if it considers them relevant (and helpful to its position) in the case at hand. Is the arbitrator bound to follow the ruling of the predecessor neutral? First, it depends on whether the prior case or cases involves similar facts under similar (or the same) contract language. Although the judicial principle of precedent does not operate in arbitration, there is good reason to maintain stability in the workplace by following established arbitral precedent.

What if the previous arbitration was under a prior CBA? That suggests that there is even more reason to follow the arbitral precedent. If the case involved a reading of the contract language that remains in the CBA, the parties had the opportunity to respond to the prior arbitrator's reading and change the language in negotiations. If they did not do so, that suggest to the subsequent arbitrator that the parties have adopted the prior arbitrator's reading as part of their agreement. The party that lost that previous arbitration may not be happy with that result, but it was unable to modify the contract language in the subsequent negotiations.

There is one important caveat to this approach. If the prior arbitrator's decision was completely wrong and beyond anything a typical arbitrator would render, it should carry no weight with a subsequent arbitrator. The first arbitrator's decision may have been "crazy," perhaps not literally, but sufficiently out of the mainstream so as to undermine the value of the prior award. It is more difficult to ignore the prior decision, however, even if "crazy," if it was based on contract interpretation and the parties have negotiated a new agreement in the interim without addressing the prior award.

2.   *Would the same rules apply to previous grievance settlements?*

Parties settle grievances for all kinds of reasons and not necessarily because they wish to give a definitive reading to the terms of their CBA. Cases are settled to make them go away. Cases are traded in the grievance procedure—some for management; some for the union. Grievances may be granted for senior employees who have years of loyal service to the employer and denied for junior employees who have yet to prove their value in the workplace. Sometimes the parties will expressly provide that a grievance settlement shall not be considered precedential for future cases.

The arbitrator should certainly admit prior grievance settlements into evidence, but those settlements should not be given the weight of a prior arbitration decision unless they were embodied in a formal memorandum of agreement that constituted an addition to the contract.

IX. Statutory Law

A contract provision may have implications in arbitration and in other forums, such as courts or administrative agencies. Similarly, statutory law outside the CBA may be useful to an arbitrator when asked to interpret what the parties intended by their contract language. When is it appropriate for an arbitrator to use that law in determining the parties' intent as evidenced by the provisions of their agreement?[9]

1.   *Should the arbitrator use statutory law external to the agreement in interpreting a contract?*

Federal and state laws that address the employment relationship continue to multiply. It was inevitable that the law external to the CBA would become a major controversy in arbitration. What is the proper role, if any, that statutory law not embodied in the CBA should play in interpreting contract language? If there is a conflict, should the law or

---

[9]*See* Elkouri & Elkouri: How Arbitration Works ch. 10 (Kenneth May, ed., 7th ed. 2012).

the contract control? Can an arbitrator ignore the law of the land, such as the nondiscrimination provisions of Title VII, the Americans with Disabilities Act, or the Family and Medical Leave Act?

As a general rule, labor arbitrators should limit their focus to the contract language. They have not been appointed to dispense justice, but to read and interpret the provisions of the CBA. If a dispute can be resolved without resort to law outside the four corners of the agreement, that is precisely what the arbitrator should do, unless that reading of the contract would be illegal under the external law.

The issue of external law has a different significance in the public sector. The term itself is a misnomer in that context because in the public sector, the CBA itself is enacted into law, for example, as a city ordinance. Once again, the arbitrator's primary responsibility is to interpret and apply the provisions of the CBA. However, that agreement, by its terms, is likely to incorporate law outside of its provisions, and the arbitrator must follow the parties' directions and use external law as an interpretive guide.

Generally, labor arbitrators are selected based on their knowledge of the common law of the labor agreement, and not necessarily the law of the land. Some arbitrators are certainly as capable as any judge in reading and applying statutes and ordinances, but the question really is one of the intent of the parties. Did they intend that their arbitration procedure would use statutory references in interpreting contract provisions?

These issues are easier to decide when the CBA language tracks the terms of statutory law. Then the arbitrator will look to the external law for guidance because the parties have, in effect, made the statutory reference part of their agreement. Similarly, if the parties specifically request that the arbitrator address statutory law, the arbitrator should follow the parties' direction. The arbitrator's job is to resolve the dispute in the manner consistent with the parties' legitimate needs and expectations. The neutral should certainly presume that the parties sought to reach an agreement that was legal. If a contract provision has two possible readings, the arbitrator should read it in a way that is consistent with the external law.

X. Examples of Contract Interpretation Issues

There are hundreds of different topics covered in a CBA. The more complex the organization, the more issues need to be addressed in negotiations. Each provision can give rise to disputes during the term of the CBA. But the first thing an arbitrator should always do is read carefully the contract provision at issue.

1.   *How can there be ambiguity when it comes to seniority?*[10]

Although at times employees tend to think of seniority as some sort of inherent right, it is not. Seniority rights are strictly a matter of contract, created by the parties through negotiations. Their contract language typically establishes relatively priority among the employees for certain benefits and jobs. Seniority is based on length of service within a particular unit at the workplace, or, depending on the particular benefit involved, it may be the total length of employment with the employer. The benefit of using seniority as a measuring tool is that it eliminates the potential unfairness associated with subjective evaluations by management.

Contract interpretation issues arise regarding when seniority "attaches"—that is, when an employee starts to accrue seniority. Does that happen when an employee is hired? Does it occur after an employee's completion of the probationary period? What happens when two or more employees are hired on the same day? When must an employee question his or her seniority date? Add to these issues of contract interpretation all the potential disputes involving seniority that arise when an employee experiences an interruption in employment or joins the bargaining unit after working for the company in a nonbargaining unit position. When companies merge, do their seniority lists merge? All of these issues are easily resolvable by the parties in their CBA, but an arbitrator may have work to do if the agreement is silent or ambiguous.

2.   *How should an arbitrator address a dispute over premium pay?*

When a worker accepts a job at an established rate of pay, he or she promises to provide work during a certain period of time, normally eight hours a day, five days a week. The rest of the employee's life should be considered his or her leisure time. Management may have the right to purchase some of the employees' leisure time at premium rates. Overtime or premium pay is normally at time and a half for all hours above eight in a day or above 40 in a week.

---

[10]*See* Calvin William Sharpe, *Seniority,* in NATIONAL ACADEMY OF ARBITRATORS, THE COMMON LAW OF THE WORKPLACE: THE VIEWS OF ARBITRATORS ch. 5 (Theodore J. St. Antoine, ed., 2d ed. 2005) (perceptive chapter on seniority). *See also* Roger Abrams & Dennis Nolan, *Seniority Rights Under the Collective Agreement,* 2 LAB. LAW. 99 (1986).

An arbitrator presented with a dispute over premium pay may have to determine how hours are to be counted. If an employee normally works from 6:00 p.m. to 2:00 a.m. and is asked to work an additional hour, is that hour paid at premium rates? It depends on how the contract "counts" hours. Does the contract use a calendar day? If so, overtime will depend on whether the employee was scheduled and did work his or her normal shift the following evening. What if the contract does not specify how time should be counted? What if the employee was asked to work the extra time and accepted, and later was told he or she was not needed? Should time not worked, but paid, on a holiday count toward the 40 hours a week over which overtime is due?

Other premium pay provisions may provide for call-in pay and pay guarantees when an employee is told to report to work at other than his or her normal shift.[11] Related issues involve the question as to which employee should receive an overtime opportunity. Some employees would prefer not to work overtime, but for others it is a way to enhance their earnings. Allocating overtime can present enormous difficulties. An arbitrator always finds an express contract clause on the issue, but the clause may omit certain essential directions. The arbitrator must read, interpret, and apply the contract the parties have made, filing in the gaps with evidence of established past practice and presumed intent from the generally accepted notions of the common law of the labor agreement.

3. Is the arbitrator's approach different when the contract issue involves matters of compensation?

The typical CBA includes various provisions that address the ways employees are compensated—straight wages, salaries, premium pay, vacation and holiday pay, pensions, insurance coverage, and numerous others, including length of service increments, attendance awards, retirement gifts, wedding gifts, and suggestion awards. Each topic covered contains the seeds of foreseeable disputes. It is exceedingly difficult for labor and management to write an agreement that covers all the particulars needed to resolve those disputes. Each time they return to the bargaining table, they may supply more of the needed details, but there will always be work for arbitrators to do in filling in the gaps in the interim.

The arbitrator's obligation is to read the clauses in question and then, applying the facts as the arbitrator finds them, to apply the contract. Hearing evidence about how the provision has been applied in the

---

[11] Roger Abrams & Dennis Nolan, *Buying Employees' Time: Guaranteed Pay Under Collective Agreements*, 35 Syracuse L. Rev. 867 (1984).

past is often useful. These forms of contractual benefits should not be easily held to be forfeited.

Perhaps the most difficult arbitration cases involve job evaluation systems. In a large plant, there may be hundreds of different job classifications, each with its own job descriptions of qualifications and job duties. Parties will use a job evaluation system to determine compensation for the employees who fill each of those jobs. A job is described using a variety of negotiated categories and a points system. The parties will also negotiate benchmark jobs. Duties for jobs other than benchmark jobs are assigned values based on skills needed, measuring the input, for example, for education, experience, initiative and ingenuity, physical demand, and mental and visual demand; and responsibility for equipment, material, products, safety, the work of others, and working conditions and hazards. Under a job evaluation system, these factors are all considered in determining a job's labor grade. A dispute arises when the parties disagree as to the value that should be attached to one or more of the input factors. An arbitrator should apply the "best description" principle to determine whether a job has been placed in the right slot under the job evaluation system.

4. *What contractual interpretation issues arise regarding safety matters?*

A workplace can be a dangerous place. Even in a plant that is in compliance with the federal Occupational Safety and Health Act, accidents happen. Unions seek to reduce such events by negotiating provisions on plant safety and other conditions of employment that affect employee health. There are clauses that address the need of employees for clean toilets and fresh drinking water as well as for rest periods and lunch breaks. All of these provisions give rise to disputes that may need to be arbitrated.

The arbitrator's job in a safety dispute starts with the contract language. The words the parties employed may sufficiently evidence their intent. There may be prior practice that is relevant, as well as bargaining history. The arbitrator can assume that the parties sought to make the workplace safe, but recognized that every workplace—even the safest—has some risks.

Management benefits from a safe work environment. Lost time disrupts productivity and increases health benefit costs. It is not uncommon for the parties' agreement to provide for the establishment of joint health and safety committees to provide an ongoing forum for dialogue on these issues.

5. **What union rights addressed in collective bargaining agreements may present issues of contract interpretation for an arbitrator?**

The union may negotiate provisions in the CBA that are intended to support its status and recognition as the exclusive bargaining representative of the employees. Depending on the law of the state, union security provisions requiring employees to join the union after they are employed and pay union dues for the services the union provides are also common. Of vital importance to the union is a dues checkoff clause.

Some CBAs provide that issues involving the checkoff of union dues are excluded from the scope of the arbitration procedure. The arbitrator must respect these limitations on his or her jurisdiction.

Union privileges, such as use of a bulletin board and office space, are often included as well in CBAs. In order for a union to carry out its function as exclusive representative, it must have access to information that management maintains. Normally this information will be provided during a grievance procedure, but the contract may require management to provide it earlier so as to avoid unnecessary grievances.

Chapter 13

Custom and Past Practice

I. Overview

Justice William O. Douglas reasoned in the *Steelworkers Trilogy*[1] that arbitrators know the workplace better than generalist judges ever could and therefore courts should defer to these private neutrals. He was specifically addressing the arbitrators' appreciation of the importance of the customs of the shop. Labor and management formally order the workplace through periodic collective bargaining and the interim resolution of grievance disputes. They also interact informally on a variety of issues of importance to employees and management that may never be embodied in a written agreement. These customary ways of addressing issues may ripen into past practices that will prove critical to an arbitrator appointed to resolve a later-arising grievance. Justice Douglas expressly recognized the importance of customs and practice in *Steelworkers v. Warrior & Gulf Navigation Co.*:

> The labor arbitrator's source of law is not confined to the express provisions of the contract, as the industrial common law—the practices of the industry and the shop—is equally a part of the collective bargaining agreement although not expressed in it.[2]

In many, perhaps most, arbitration cases that involve interpretation of contract provisions, the parties will present evidence concerning how the provisions in question have been applied in the past. By combining this evidence with evidence of the bargaining history of the provisions, the arbitrator will be able to determine the meaning of an ambiguous contract clause.

---

[1] Steelworkers v. American Mfg. Co., 363 U.S. 564 (1960); Steelworkers v. Warrior & Gulf Navig. Co., 363 U.S. 574 (1960); Steelworkers v. Enterprise Wheel & Car Corp., 363 U.S. 593 (1960). See the discussion of Justice Douglas' *Steelworkers Trilogy* analysis in Chapter 1, §V. The *Steelworkers Trilogy* decisions are reproduced in Appendix A.
[2] *Warrior & Gulf Navigation,* 363 U.S. at 581–82.

Past practice can be an extremely valuable aid in interpreting contract language. What the parties intended by a contract formulation may be best evidenced by how they administered the provision in question over time. If the contract is clear—something both parties often argue but is unlikely to be the case in most instances—there is no need for evidence of practice because "the contract speaks for itself."

In some arbitration cases, the union will argue that the consistent past practice has ripened into a binding financial obligation that management must continue until nullified in negotiations. An established past practice on a matter not addressed in the collective bargaining agreement (CBA)—for example, the Christmas turkey that management has annually given each employee—may be the basis for a binding understanding, much like an express contract provision.

An established past practice may even constitute an amendment by conduct of the written language of the CBA. In rare cases, one of the parties may even argue that past practice nullifies express contract language. These practices should be much more difficult to establish because the primary evidence of the parties' intent is the collection of words they have used to express their bargain—the words contained in their CBA.

II. Finding Custom and Practice[3]

Parties to a collective relationship appreciate the fact that their workplace is tied together by customs, i.e., generally understood ways of doing things that help productivity and enhance worker morale and benefits. The parties never sit down to catalog all the practices that have evolved, because they are too busy making things or providing services and handling the next set of disputes that have arisen. Some of these practices have been followed since the beginning days of the collective relationship; others are new practices devised to address technological innovations and other changes in the workplace. Both parties would agree that past practices and customs exist. The question is how one party or the other proves to the arbitrator the existence and scope of these implied understandings.

---

[3] *See* Richard Mittenthal, *Past Practice and the Administration of Collective Bargaining Agreements*, in Arbitration and Public Policy: Proceedings of the 14th Annual Meeting, National Academy of Arbitrators 30 (Spencer D. Pollard, ed., 1961) (definitive work on the establishment and proof of past practices). *See also* Elkouri & Elkouri: How Arbitration Works ch. 12 (Kenneth May, ed., 7th ed. 2012).

1. How does an arbitrator know the customs of the workplace?

Justice Douglas' opinion in the *Steelworkers Trilogy* seems to suggest that an arbitrator is better equipped to resolve industrial disputes because he or she knows the "law of the shop." Although Douglas' praise is flattering to neutrals, it is generally not the case that an ad hoc arbitrator knows anything about the "law" of the shop where he or she has been appointed to resolve a dispute.

An arbitrator arrives at the hearing knowing nothing about the parties except their names and the general nature of the dispute they have appointed him or her to resolve. If the neutral has served the parties before, if he or she is a member of their panel of arbitrators, or if he or she serves as the parties' permanent umpire, the arbitrator likely knows much more about them. The arbitrator will know what the business does and what work the employees perform. But the arbitrator still does not know much about the parties' customs and practices, unless they arose in the context of a prior case.

What an arbitrator does know, however, is the kinds of customs and practices that generally do arise in the workplace. The neutral knows that management directs the workforce and establishes methods of operation, that employees often receive certain benefits not enumerated in the terms of a CBA, and that practices arise in parts of a large operation but may be unknown to upper management. Every workplace is a special-purpose community with established ways of doing things. The arbitrator only needs to find out what particular customs and practices have evolved at the workplace in question. Justice Douglas was correct that arbitrators know the "law of the shop"—they just don't know the law of this particular shop.

It is the responsibility of the parties in their arguments, testimony, and documents to teach the arbitrator about the relevant customs and practices of their workplace. Of course, the parties likely do not agree on the existence, scope, or applicability of those customs and practices, so making findings of fact about custom and practice is another task assigned to the neutral.

2. What evidence does an arbitrator look for in determining whether there is a past practice?

Arbitrators often state that, in order to establish a past practice, behavior must be "clear, consistent, long-standing and frequent." They rarely explain why these criteria are used, however. In fact, these criteria demonstrate that parties by their mutual conduct have added an interpretive gloss to a provision of their CBA or have even added a new substantive term to their contract. The arbitrator will want to know based on the evidence presented whether the workplace behavior demonstrates a tacit agreement. The neutral will look for evidence that every time (or almost every time) a certain kind of situation arises, the parties react in a certain way and that both parties were cognizant of that fact. Assuming that an arbitrator could ask an employee and a front-line supervisor what happens when a certain circumstance arises, they would both independently say, "Oh, we do this." If the "this" is the same from both sides, there is "mutuality." Of course, the arbitrator does not have that luxury, nor is it his or her role to ask that question. The arbitrator must examine the testimony that the parties present to determine whether it would meet this test.

Mutuality can be rebutted by evidence of inconsistency. If the union complained when management acted a certain way, management might still have the contractual right to act as it did, and there would be insufficient grounds on which to make a claim of past practice.

3.   Can a practice arise when one party does not know that the other party is acting in a certain way?

The establishment of a practice requires both parties to be aware of the behavior in question. Neither party needs to expressly acknowledge that they are creating a practice, but to establish mutuality the conduct must be open and known. Simply acting in a certain manner unilaterally does not constitute a practice if it remains unknown to the other party.

A party that opposes a claim of practice cannot deny the obvious, that a reasonable party in the same or similar circumstances would know that the practice is taking place. Management is normally the initiator of behavior that can ripen into a practice. Its witnesses can explain how management officials acted and, equally important, how union officials became aware of the behavior.

4.   Does management's or the union's failure to enforce a right it has under the terms of the collective bargaining agreement constitute a binding practice?

The failure to enforce a contract provision is not a practice. Merely declining to enforce a contract provision or failing to grieve a certain class of contract violations does not constitute a practice or a waiver of contract rights. Of course, parties can agree to modify their agreement during its term, but arbitrators normally require compelling evidence where the modification of a written agreement is accomplished by an oral understanding.

The issue of waiver arises most often in terms of enforcement of time limits on the filing of grievances. If management raises the issue of procedural arbitrability, the arbitrator should apply the terms of the written CBA even if management has never enforced them in the past.

III. Applying Past Practice

Once an arbitrator has determined that a past practice exists, he or she must apply that practice to the case at hand. How that should be done depends on the use the moving party wishes to make of the practice. Does the party want to use the evidence of practice to limit an operational decision by management? Does the party want to use the evidence of practice to assist in interpreting ambiguous contract language? Does the party want to use practice as the basis for an employee benefit not mentioned in the CBA?

1. How does past practice operate as an interpretive gloss on ambiguous contract language?

Past practice is most commonly used in the arbitration process as a tool to try to understand what the parties meant by certain contract language. The arbitrator's central focus is to determine what the parties intended by a contract provision. What better evidence could there be of their intent than how they have applied that language over the years?

Consider contract language that says that an employee who wants to be considered for a posted promotion must submit an application form to a supervisor. In the dispute that arose between the parties, the facts show that the grievant told the supervisor of his or her interest in the promotion, but did not submit the form until the expiration date of the posting had passed. The contract provision did not indicate when the form needed to be filed, but did state that a promotion opportunity would only be posted for two weeks. The evidence in the record, however, showed that management had always allowed timely oral indications of interest when it was followed by a written application. The past practice explains the parties' intent, and the arbitrator should grant the grievance.

2. Under what circumstances will an arbitrator find that a past practice has created a limitation on management's methods of operation?

The most common use of evidence of a past practice is for help in interpreting ambiguous contract language. However, there are two other circumstances where the union will allege that evidence of a past practice is strong enough to constitute a binding obligation. One is a past practice as the source of an employee benefit that has monetary value. Another is evidence of a past practice that demonstrates that management must follow certain methods of operation, including, for example, the ways it directs the workforce. It is true that negotiated provisions of a CBA can restrict management's right to change work schedules, assign work, and otherwise operate the plant; in the absence of such contract limitations, however, management will not be held to have bound itself to a past practice by exercising its rights in a certain manner in a consistent fashion over many years.

Consider, for example, a case involving the staffing of a certain operation. Management may have assigned five employees to work on a particular machine since the plant opened. The union files a grievance when management reduces the staffing to four persons, claiming that there was a five-person past practice. The arbitrator will deny the grievance in the absence of any evidence that the parties discussed the staffing and agreed it would remain at five. This evidence would be of an oral agreement, not a past practice. Oral agreements can be binding in the absence of a contract clause that limits binding obligations to written agreements.

However, the union's grievance about the change in staffing may have merit if it is phrased in a different manner. If the reduction in staffing creates a safety hazard, management's action may have violated the typical contract clause that requires the maintenance of a safe workplace. Also, if the reduction in staffing required the remaining employees to develop different skills, that may have implications under a job rating system and result in increased compensation for those jobs. If the main thrust of the union's grievance is that management cannot change staffing because it had always provided staffing at a certain level, it will fail.

3. **If management does not use a prerogative embodied in the collective bargaining agreement, can that repeated non-use establish a practice?**

A union may argue that management has developed a "practice" of not using a right reserved in the CBA. For example, management may have the express right to subcontract work, but always declined to do so after informing the union of its plan. When management decides to actually subcontract, the union grieves based on the "practice." In the absence of evidence that management and the union agreed to modify their agreement, management has the right to use its contract prerogative. It is not a practice—it is an operational decision. Similarly, the failure of management or the union to enforce time limits on the filing or processing of grievances does not mean that they have created a practice or modified the agreement. This behavior might be used to interpret what the parties intended, but should not constitute a binding waiver of contract restrictions.

4.   Under what circumstances will an arbitrator find that a past practice has created a benefit for employees?

An arbitrator can read in the parties' CBA about the variety of ways employees are compensated for the work they perform. In addition to wages and overtime, employees commonly receive insurance, pensions, various awards of monetary value, paid work breaks, and a variety of other benefits. In some cases, some emoluments are not mentioned in the agreement, but management has consistently given the workers these benefits over the years. Can those benefits "ripen" over time into binding past practices?

Custom and practices can ripen into binding obligations of personal value to employees. Some might involve monetary awards or bonuses for good attendance or excellent productivity. Others could involve discounts on the company's product. Still others might be prerogatives of special value to employees, such as a parking space close to the plant entrance. The list, although not endless, is broad.

Management might stop a benefit because it says it costs too much, and that is perfectly understandable. In fact, management may think the compensation provisions in the CBA cost too much. That is not a defense to a grievance complaining about the termination of a contract benefit; it also is not a defense to a grievance complaining about the termination of an otherwise binding past practice. The way to end a binding practice that provides a benefit of personal value to employees is through collective bargaining.

The evidence an arbitrator looks at to determine whether there is such a binding past practice on an employee benefit is fairly simple. Did management compensate employees in this manner over a period of time? Was the practice consistent? If both questions are answered in the affirmative, the practice is established.

Management may argue with regard to certain practices that the employees have abused the benefit. For example, assume management has provided coffee machines. Over the years, employees had been allowed to leave their workstations to get coffee and return to continue their work. The employees then extended their time at the machines into informal work breaks, and management warned them that this was an abuse of the practice. If management locked up the machines during work time and the union grieved, the arbitrator should deny the griev-ance. Management can limit the amount of time employees spend away from their workstations. The employees abused the practice.

5.   Can a past practice negate contract language?

The parties can modify their CBA whenever they wish. Even though a contract states that it is effective for three years, parties can mutually tear it up (or revise parts of it) whenever they wish and start anew. The question is whether they can do so by practice rather than through direct negotiations. The answer requires a better understand-ing of the nature of a practice and how it arrives on the arbitrator's desk in different shapes and sizes.

A practice that is not fully formed can be modified unilaterally. For example, assume that management considers employees' length of service in determining ability for a promotion for the three times there was a promotional opportunity under the CBA. The contract, however, provided that management can select the best-qualified applicant for a promotion. That practice, albeit short in length, might constitute an interpretive gloss on what constituted "best qualified." If management decided on the next promotion not to consider length of service, it could unilaterally change the "practice," relying on the express language of the agreement.

The more difficult issue for arbitrators is when an established practice—clear, consistent, and fixed over time—can negate a contract provision or, in effect, amend the contract. With strong evidence of mutuality analogous to a conscious amendment to the agreement, the practice could be considered a contract revision.

A CBA is a living document, formally negotiated but revised, amended, and elaborated on during its term. When arbitrators fill in the inevitable "gaps" in the agreement, they are continuing the ongoing process of making the contract consistent with how the parties would do it themselves. Practice under the agreement should work in the same way.

IV. PROVING A PRACTICE

Some customs of the workplace recur daily or monthly. Others only arise rarely. They are not recorded in any master log of practices. Often they are simply the way things are done, and no one thinks any more of them than as generally understood customs. By their very nature, they are difficult to prove, but their importance in arbitration is evident.

1.   What are the common errors arbitrators see in parties trying to establish a past practice?

No workplace keeps a list of current practices. They just happen, and if they happen again and again in a manner that evidences mutuality, they may ripen into binding practices that may be used to interpret contract language, or they may constitute a continuing, stand-alone benefit to employees. The problem before the arbitrator is one of proof.

In order to prove a practice, a party must reconstruct events for the neutral. Management would have records of when it gave employees something of value, such as a Christmas turkey, and the union should be able to get a copy of those records. An arbitrator will not be impressed, however, by general witness testimony to the effect that "the company always does this or that." An advocate has to tie down a practice with dates and events, not simple recollections.

V. Ending a Practice

Starting a practice is rarely a conscious and carefully considered action. An issue arises on the work floor, and the supervisor suggests it be handled in a certain manner. The shop steward responds that that seems fine to him or her. Whenever the issue arises again, the supervisor follows the same course of conduct.

Ending a practice may be more difficult. If it is an established past practice, it must be ended with formality—perhaps in collective bargaining.

1.   Under what circumstances will an arbitrator rule that management has ended a practice?

Practices are not forever. Specific practices can be ended through collective bargaining. They can also be ended by the mutual agreement of the parties during the term of the CBA.

Management cannot unilaterally announce during the term of a CBA that an established practice that afforded employees a benefit will no longer be followed. Parties can do that together through interim bargaining. Otherwise, the practice stands until modified in bargaining. At the commencement of bargaining, management can announce that it will no longer follow a particular practice but is willing to negotiate with the union about it. If the practice is not then embodied in the agreement, management has effectively abolished it.

Arbitrators are sometimes asked to determine the fate of an established practice when the parties agree to a *zipper clause* in their contract, which typically states that only conditions of employment embodied in the terms of the CBA are maintained. Arbitrators will take the parties at their word with regard to employee benefits that have been established practices but are abolished by the zipper clause. Even with a zipper clause, however, arbitrators should consider evidence of past practice in interpreting the meaning of ambiguous contract language, if that language is continued in the current agreement. The zipper clause ends employee benefits not embodied in the agreement—it does not end the use of evidence of past practice to interpret contract language.

On the other extreme, parties might include in their agreement a past practices clause that preserves all existing practices for the term of the agreement. This is a broad promise not easily obtained by a union, because neither party likely knows the extent and number of those practices. The arbitrator should once again take the parties at their word. In a case raising the issue of established practices, the union must still demonstrate that the benefit had ripened into a practice. The preservation of practices clause does not give the union the right to claim a practice that the parties have not mutually established by their conduct over time.

Chapter 14

Deciding the Case

I. Overview

Deciding an arbitration case requires the arbitrator to use all the qualities Justice William O. Douglas, in the *Steelworkers Trilogy*,[1] said that an arbitrator possesses—knowledge of the common law of the labor agreement and the ways of the workplace, the ability to find facts

---

[1] Steelworkers v. American Mfg. Co., 363 U.S. 564 (1960); Steelworkers v. Warrior & Gulf Navig. Co., 363 U.S. 574 (1960); Steelworkers v. Enterprise Wheel & Car Corp., 363 U.S. 593 (1960). See the discussion of Justice Douglas' *Steelworkers Trilogy* analysis in Chapter 1, §V. The *Steelworkers Trilogy* decisions are reproduced in Appendix A.

and evaluate arguments, and, most important, the skill to understand and apply data about the context within which labor arbitration plays its vital role. It is not easy work, and it is important for the parties to understand how an experienced arbitrator goes about that job.[2]

II. DECIDING AN ARBITRATION CASE

An experienced arbitrator has heard it all before. The employee is discharged for poor work performance or misconduct on the job site. The employer refuses to pay holiday pay because an employee came in to work tardy on the day before or after the scheduled holiday. Management moves work traditionally performed by bargaining unit employees to salaried employees who are not represented for purposes of collective bargaining. There are a hundreds of different factual scenarios, plus innumerable variations, but an experienced arbitrator has heard it all before. He or she has thought through what it takes to make out a case of the particular class or kind that the parties will present. The question before the arbitrator is: What does the record establish in the case at hand?[3]

1. Does an arbitrator ever decide which party should win before deciding which arguments are convincing?

The essence of neutrality for a labor arbitrator is to have an open mind before entering any case. Certainly, and without exception among experienced arbitrators, a neutral enters a dispute without a favorite in the race. That neutrality shifts as the parties begin to present their cases at the arbitration hearing. From the opening statements to the conclusion of the hearing, the arbitrator makes interim decisions about witness credibility and the meaning of the parties' contract. He or she gradually learns where the turning points are in the case and recognizes what questions must be answered in order to resolve the dispute.

---

[2] *See* William P. Murphy, *The Role of the Collective Bargaining Agreement;* Eva Robins, *The Law of the Shop;* Eric J. Schmertz, *The Uniqueness of the American Labor-Management Arbitration Process and Its Role as a Stabilizing Influence in Labor-Management Relations;* and Nancy J. Sedmak, *Value of Published Awards;* in LABOR ARBITRATION: A PRACTICAL GUIDE FOR ADVOCATES 215–54 (Max Zimny, William F. Dolson, & Christopher A. Barreca, eds., 1990) (thoughts from experienced arbitrators on the decisional process).

[3] Roger Abrams, *The Nature of the Arbitral Process: Substantive Decision-Making in Labor Arbitration*, 14 U.C. DAVIS L. REV. 551 (1981).

2.   *How does the arbitrator go about making a decision?*

The most important thing to understand about how arbitrators actually make decisions is that, by the time opening statements have been completed, the arbitrator generally knows what questions he or she will need answered at the hearing in order to decide the dispute. In most cases involving operational decisions by management, for example, the arbitrator needs to know why the employer acted the way it did. Although management likely will claim a reserved right to make a particular kind of decision—and there may be some general language in the management rights clause that supports management's claim—the arbitrator still wants to know why management decided to exercise that right in the particular case. Management always has a reason—certain employees did not have the requisite skills, the plant did not have particular equipment, the job needed to be reorganized in order to achieve productive efficiency. Management must support its purported reasons with evidence, either testimonial or documentary. If it fails to do so, the arbitrator will wonder whether there was some ulterior motive involved, such as undermining the union or avoiding paying union rates.

The union in an operational case must present the arbitrator with evidence of the capabilities of the workforce and the impact of management's action on members of the bargaining unit. The arbitrator will be expecting to hear such evidence. Are there laid-off employees? Did the employees actually have the skills and experience to perform certain work? Have employees performed that work in the past? A broad complaint that management made a stupid business decision will not hold sway with the arbitrator. In the absence of an express contract restriction and in the presence of evidence explaining why it acted as it did, management is allowed to make decisions, even if they don't turn out as well as planned.

Discharge and discipline cases present their own set of questions because the parties rarely give the arbitrator more guidance than two words—"just cause." We explore those issues at length in Chapter 10. The arbitrator must find out what the grievant did. It will take the arbitrator most of the hearing—including listening to the testimony of the grievant—to reach a conclusion on this factual matter. The arbitrator also will have to determine whether what the grievant did warranted the discipline or discharge meted out by management. The more egregious the grievant's alleged conduct, the more likely the second issue is proven, but the more egregious the grievant's alleged misconduct, the harder it is for management to convince the arbitrator that the grievant actually did what the employer claimed he or she did.

Consider the broad array of employee deficiencies in performance and conduct. If an employee was discharged because he or she was unable to perform the job, either as a result of physical limitations or pure negligence in completing the required tasks, it should not be difficult for management to prove the first part of its case, that is, what actually occurred. Much the same follows with absenteeism issues. Companies keep records and evaluations. Did they follow progressive discipline? The failure to have any such evidence or a system of progressive discipline dooms management's case. If management's allegation is that the dischargee committed a serious transgression—insubordination, fighting, sabotage, and theft, among others—it is harder for management to make out its factual case, but easier to sustain terminations once this class of misconduct is proven. The arbitrator focuses on the factual disputes, and the result follows accordingly.

An arbitrator's decision-making process is thus a matter of filling in the blanks—answering the questions—based on the nature of the claim. The experienced neutral knows what has to be proven—based on either the provisions of the CBA or the common law of just cause. Success or failure in answering an experienced arbitrator's questions will determine the outcome in the case.

3.   *What should the arbitrator do if his or her questions are not answered during the hearing?*

The arbitrator must decide the case correctly, but must not inject himself or herself into the parties' cases. This may put the arbitrator into a difficult position. The arbitrator knows he or she needs an answer to a particular question—for example, did management give the dischargee an opportunity to offer his or her side of the story before discharging the employee? If neither advocate has raised this issue, but the arbitrator knows it is important, what should he or she do?

The best advice is that the arbitrator should do nothing. Advocates know the common law of the labor agreement as applied to just cause. The arbitrator must assume that if the dischargee was not given an opportunity to explain his or her side of the story, the union would offer that information in its case. If the dischargee was given that opportunity, management would offer that evidence as part of its case.

There are times when the arbitrator believes that the parties are missing a very important part of the case, and it is almost impossible to resist inquiring. Yet the parties might be intentionally avoiding that issue. There may be reasons for their reluctance to get into a particular area of inquiry, and the arbitrator must let the parties be.

4. Can an arbitrator seek advice and suggestions about a pending case from other arbitrators?

Although in a simple case an experienced arbitrator will have little difficulty reaching a result, at times he or she might find it useful to consult with another arbitrator about a pending matter. The Code of Professional Responsibility for Arbitrators of Labor-Management Disputes[4] expressly allows this type of private discussion. Such consultation may be particularly useful in a case involving an industry where an arbitrator has not had much experience but another neutral has. In any case, the Code emphasizes that the arbitrator appointed to resolve the dispute retains "sole responsibility for the decision."[5]

Consulting with another arbitrator might be particularly useful for a neutral who has less experience. Issues often arise during a hearing, and the junior arbitrator should seek guidance from a more experienced neutral.

III. Examples of the Decisional Process at Work

Arbitration cases fall into predictable categories, but there are almost endless variations of facts and context. When the arbitrator hears the opening statements, he or she thinks, "It's one of those cases." As the hearing progresses, however, this categorization becomes more refined: "It's one of those cases with this twist and turn to it." Although the arbitrator has most of his or her questions answered by the end of the hearing, the post-hearing briefs may raise new questions.

One difference between an experienced arbitrator and a novice is that the experienced neutral likely already knows the questions that must be answered at the hearing. This is the true basis of the distinction between an arbitrator and a judge. The judge is a generalist and cannot possibly know all the questions that must be answered in a jury-waived trial in order to make a decision. As a specialist, an experienced arbitrator does know those questions. The novice, by comparison, will treat the hearing as a platform to collect data that he or she will later convert into a problem to be researched. This decisional process is much more like what a civil trial court judge does.

---

[4]National Academy of Arbitrators, American Arbitration Association, & Federal Mediation & Conciliation Service, Code of Professional Responsibility for Arbitrators of Labor-Management Disputes (as amended and in effect Sept. 2007), *available at* http://www.naarb.org/code.html (reproduced in Appendix B).

[5]*Id.* at 2.C.

The next sections explore a few typical categories of cases—vacations, overtime, and subcontracting—to demonstrate how the decisional process actually operates. Although not every type of case is explained in this chapter, an advocate can unearth questions that the arbitrator will need answered through research into reported decisions and the use of secondary sources.

1. What questions would an arbitrator have in a vacation case?[6]

As soon as an arbitrator hears that the grievance addresses the issue of vacations, he or she knows that the application of the precise terms the parties used in their CBA will be vitally important. The arbitrator knows that paid vacations are a matter of contract, that employees typically earn their vacations during an *accounting period or base year*, and that they receive their paid vacations during a later period, often referred to as the *vacation year*. The arbitrator knows that paid vacations are deferred compensation, not gratuities. Two major issues normally arise: eligibility and calculation.

If eligibility is the issue, the arbitrator knows that the primary question is: Did the grievant meet the contractual eligibility requirement during the specified accounting period or base year? There are two subqueries that accompany this question: Does the case involve a threshold minimum service requirement? Does the case involve whether the employee fulfilled the contractual work requirement during the accounting period? The parties in their opening statements should point the arbitrator in the right direction.

Why wouldn't the employee have met these requirements? The arbitrator is aware of many common reasons. For example, the grievant might have been laid off right before he or she completed the required amount of minimum service. Or perhaps the grievant was absent for some time during the threshold minimum service period. The experienced arbitrator knows that, with regard to matters of compensation, there has to be a very good reason to rule that the employee benefit was forfeited.

The vacation clause might not specify eligibility requirements. The experienced arbitrator knows that he or she is not going to create any eligibility requirements that the parties did not specify. The arbitrator also knows that generally an employee must earn his or her vacation, and, if the grievant did not meet the contractual requirements, the arbitrator is not going to uphold the grievance even if some other vacation system would be more "fair" to the worker.

---

[6]*See* Roger Abrams & Dennis Nolan, *The Common Law of the Labor Agreement: Vacations*, 5 INDUS. REL. L.J. 603 (1983).

One recurring scenario in vacation disputes involves an employee who has met the eligibility requirements but is no longer on the active payroll at the time of the vacation period. Why is the employee no longer employed? Does the contract clause specify what happens in that case? The arbitrator knows the general purpose of the "active employee" requirement. It is designed to encourage employees to remain in their jobs after fulfilling the contractual work requirements. Thus, once the arbitrator has learned why the employee was no longer employed, he or she can reason through the case. If the worker left on his or her own volition, the contract requirement is not met and the grievance seeking vacation pay will be denied. If the worker is no longer employed because of management's decision, for example, to close a plant and terminate all employees, vacation pay is due. The employees earned the vacation pay, and their failure to meet the "active employee" requirement was a result of management's actions.

Of course, there are other issues that arise in a vacation cases involving, for example, the calculation of the amount of paid vacation and the scheduling of vacations. If these are the issues raised in the opening statement, the arbitrator will have a whole series of other questions that need to be answered by the evidence presented at the hearing.

2.   What questions will an arbitrator need to have answered in an overtime and premium pay dispute?[7]

Most CBAs include provisions for premium pay for performing overtime work and for work performed outside of the normal shifts of work. These cases also often involve difficult questions as to the appropriate remedy.

Once again, the arbitrator starts with the relevant provisions of the CBA. The contract should delineate when premium pay is due, although it is foreseeable that disputes would still arise. From the opening statements, the arbitrator learns the category of overtime and premium pay dispute the parties have submitted for his or her determination. The first question is whether the grievant actually worked in an overtime or premium pay situation as specified in the CBA. These contract provisions can be very complicated, detailing precisely how hours of work are counted in a "day," or specifying, for example, that call-in pay does not attach when an employee is required to report to work early but without a break in time before the beginning of the shift, or designating

---

[7]Roger Abrams & Dennis Nolan, *Time at a Premium: The Arbitration of Overtime and Premium Pay Disputes*, 45 Ohio St. L.J. 837 (1984).

what activity constitutes actual "work" within the meaning of the parties' overtime provision.

Alternatively, the parties' opening statements may direct the arbitrator down other avenues of inquiry. For example, who is entitled to work a particular overtime opportunity? Are the employees required to work overtime? Does the assignment of overtime have to be equalized? Each question evokes a series of subqueries that the arbitrator will need to have answered during the hearing.

The remedy question in overtime and premium pay case also raises problems but will not likely be addressed at the arbitration hearing. Ordering that the grievant be given the opportunity to "make up" for the lost overtime will mean some other employee will be denied that opportunity when he or she did nothing wrong. The alternate approach is to award the grievant monetary relief, but here the employer does not receive any work from the employee in exchange for the money awarded. A third approach orders that the grievant receive premium rates for regular work until he or she is made whole. The arbitrator should certainly ask the parties to address the remedy issue in their post-hearing briefs.

3.   *What questions would the arbitrator need to have answered in subcontracting cases?*[8]

Contracting out work normally performed by bargaining unit employees raises real concerns on the part of employees and their unions. Losing work means losing the opportunity to earn. At the same time, management wants to be able to make these decisions in the best interest of the business organization. The arbitrator again starts with the terms of the CBA to determine if the parties have reached any understanding about the issue. If management has the right to contract out without limitation, the grievance must be denied. If management's right is limited in specific ways by a contract clause, the arbitrator must find out whether those limitations are applicable in the case at hand.

The much more difficult case involves subcontracting when the CBA is silent on the issue. Here the arbitrator needs to know why management decided to subcontract work. There are many possible reasons, such as the absence of available employees with the skills to perform the work in question, the lack of the necessary equipment in the plant, or the need to have the work performed expeditiously. The union wants the arbitrator to understand the risk that management's action

---

[8]Roger Abrams & Dennis Nolan, *Subcontracting Disputes in Labor Arbitration: Productive Efficiency versus Job Security*, 17 Toledo L. Rev. 7 (1983).

undermines contract promises on wages and other benefits. Could management be contracting out in an effort to undermine the union and the agreement? If so, the arbitrator is going to grant the grievance.

4. What other kinds of cases does an arbitrator face?

An arbitrator will face a broad variety of contract-based issues, but the approach to decision making will remain the same whether the issue is wage adjustments following changes in operations, crew size, scheduling work, seniority as applied in layoffs and promotions, or matters of compensation, such as bonuses and pensions. In each instance, the arbitrator starts and ends with the CBA. Its terms set the parameters for the arbitrator's inquiry. The contract may be silent on the issue at hand, and here the arbitrator will have to fill in the gaps consistent with the evidence of the parties' intent, including their past practice.

IV. IMPLICATIONS OF ARBITRAL DECISION MAKING

The method that experienced arbitrators use to decide cases raises a series of questions. One primary concern parties may have is whether, by following this method, the arbitrator is prejudging the dispute without hearing evidence and reviewing documents. The fact that an arbitrator knows the questions he or she will have to ultimately address, however, does not mean that the neutral has prejudged what the answers are. Arbitrators have a fairly good sense of what the possible answers are or likely are, but each case presents unique facts that may take the entire hearing to pin down. If a particular answer is possible, but not likely, it may prove to be true after all the evidence is in.

The implication of this approach to arbitral decision making is that the parties must think in terms of what their arbitrator needs in order to decide their case. Experienced parties and advocates can be surprised by what an arbitrator later decides was an important point of evidence, but that should be rare with an experienced arbitrator. The arbitrator's goal in deciding a dispute must be to avoid such surprises.

1. If every experienced arbitrator knows the questions that must be answered, why doesn't he or she just ask the parties those questions after opening statements?

It would seem to be simple for the experienced arbitrator to just ask the parties the questions he or she has after opening statements and let them answer those questions. It would save an enormous amount of hearing time and spare the arbitrator from listening to hours of testimony, much of which is beside the point. However, there are a number of significant problems with that approach.

Even the most experienced arbitrator may be uncertain what the real issues are until much later in a hearing. The case might involve a novel puzzle to be solved, although that is not likely. Also, only joint exhibits are in evidence at this point, and the parties have not yet presented all their documents. Those documents may reveal a variety of new matters to be explored.

The arbitrator's questions are likely to evolve during the course of a hearing. The opening statements may point in one direction and witness testimony will answer some of the original questions, but that testimony may also offer new tangents. The decisional process does not change, however—the arbitrator is still listening for certain categories of evidence that he or she knows are needed to resolve a dispute of this kind.

The parties, and not the arbitrator, own the arbitration process, and they present their own cases. This understanding of how the arbitrator makes a decision still leaves work for the arbitrator in addressing the significant differences the parties may have regarding facts in dispute. Hearing the arbitrator's questions would accomplish nothing to resolve factual matters. In addition, the parties might not agree that the arbitrator is asking the correct questions, especially before they present their evidence. In any case, there is real therapeutic value in the hearing process itself, as Justice Douglas recognized in the *Steelworkers Trilogy*.

2.   *If the experienced arbitrator knows the questions, don't the advocates know the same questions?*

Some experienced advocates will know the questions an arbitrator will need to have answered in order to resolve their dispute. It is likely that the parties differ on the correct answers and on the facts that support them. Thus, there is considerable work for the arbitrator and the parties to do at the hearing.

The practice of labor law is adversarial by nature, and opposing advocates may fundamentally disagree on the correct questions that must be answered for the arbitrator. Some management-side advocates believe that management must be given almost unlimited discretion in the workplace, contract restrictions notwithstanding. Some pro-union advocates believe that the arbitrator must provide justice to the workers even if the contract and past practice do not support their claims.

Parties should know that the arbitrator will have his or her own set of questions to be answered at the hearing that may not coincide with either of their partisan points of view.

3.   How can advocates determine what questions an experienced arbitrator is likely to want answered?

Here is where research plays a vital role. The thousands of reported arbitration decisions set out the factors that arbitrators consider important in rendering a judgment in particular kinds of cases. The trained advocate can tease out from those decisions the likely questions an experienced arbitrator would have. Secondary sources will also prove helpful here.

Most importantly, advocates should find out if there are written opinions by the same arbitrator on a similar issue. There is no rule of precedent to be followed from one award to another by the same arbitrator or from past awards by other arbitrators. However, for reasons of fairness under the "law of the shop," stability, predictability, and simple human nature, arbitrators attempt to be consistent in their reasoning across all cases involving a similar issue. If an advocate finds a case by the arbitrator that is on point, the questions that should be answered will be there.

4.   What should an advocate do if he or she thinks arbitrators are generally wrong on a particular issue?

If the parties select an experienced arbitrator who is a member of the National Academy of Arbitrators (NAA), the chances are pretty good that the neutral will enter the arbitration with previous experience on an issue similar to the one that divides the parties. If the foreseeable set of questions does not favor one party, settlement is a viable option.

It may be possible, however, to convince the arbitrator at the hearing that an alternative approach is preferable to a well-established default position. For example, in recent years some advocates have convinced some arbitrators that an award of interest should accompany a back pay remedy as a regular matter. Previously, arbitrators had not awarded interest except on proof of bad faith by management, but some now do.

Although the basic principles of the common law of the labor agreement have remained fairly stable over the decades, they are not embodied in concrete. This is an area where, again, advocates are well-advised to research past decisions by various arbitrators, assuming there is not a preselected arbitrator or a panel. It might be possible to locate an arbitrator who has already reached a favorable decision on the issue or written about it in a way that suggests that he or she might be open to different approaches depending on the facts of the case.

5.   *How does the arbitrator decide a case if the parties' evidence is deficient as a result of lack of experience or ability?*

As discussed above, the arbitrator must attempt to decide the case correctly—someone's job rights may be on the line. Yet there are good reasons why an arbitrator should not inject himself or herself into the parties' presentations by asking questions that seek out the information needed to make out the case, however dissatisfied the arbitrator may be with the information provided. There are a variety of reasons that serve to buttress this approach:

- The arbitrator's position of neutrality is better preserved by being an impartial decider rather than an inquisitor. Advocates and grievants alike will likely be more accepting of the process if an arbitrator acts in conformance with the societal expectations for a neutral adjudicator.
- The arbitrator has no idea what tactical decisions advocates have made and what can of worms might be opened if one or even both parties have decided not to air a matter for some reason. The arbitral process is intended to enhance industrial peace rather than exacerbate problems because an outsider (the arbitrator) stirs the pot.
- If the presentation is one-sided because an advocate with lesser experience does not know all the arguments that should be deployed or issues that should be explored, that is not for the arbitrator to attempt to remedy. The arbitrator must appear impartial and not act as a crusader in the cause of justice. Somebody's ox will always be gored if the arbitrator intrudes. The arbitrator should decide the case based on the record that the parties present.

V. External Law

One major controversy in arbitration concerns the role that statutory law not embodied in the CBA should play in an arbitrator's decision making. Such statutory references are referred to as *external law*, because they are outside the boundaries of the contract. The issue has been discussed repeatedly at meetings of the NAA, most memorably in the 1967 presentations of Robert Howlett[9] and Bernard Meltzer.[10]

Parties select arbitrators based on their knowledge of the law of the contract, not necessarily the law of the land. Although some arbitrators are certainly as capable as any judge, the question really is one of the intent of the parties. These issues are somewhat easier to deal with in the public sector or when the CBA language tracks the statutory law. In those situations the arbitrator must address the external law because it is not really external. Similarly, if the parties request that an arbitrator address statutory law, the arbitrator must comply.

1. Is it permissible for the arbitrator to consider external law in deciding a case?

In the third case of the *Steelworkers Trilogy*, *Steelworkers v. Enterprise Wheel & Car Corp.*,[11] Justice Douglas emphasized that the labor arbitrator's focus must be on the parties' CBA. A court will not enforce an award that is based solely on law outside of the agreement, although the neutral can look to the law "for help in determining the sense of the agreement."[12] Thus, it is certainly permissible under national labor policy to look to external law. The question remains, however, whether arbitrators should do so.

In some cases, the parties specifically request that the arbitrator apply law not embodied in the CBA in the resolution of their dispute. In the public sector, for example, enacted legislation and the rulings of courts and agencies might not be mentioned in the contract, but they are part of the context within which state and federal employment exists.

In other cases, both parties might mention external law in their opening statements, in effect calling on the arbitrator to use that source

---

[9] Robert G. Howlett, *The Role of Law in Arbitration: Reprise,* in DEVELOPMENTS IN AMERICAN & FOREIGN ARBITRATION: PROCEEDINGS OF THE TWENTY-FIRST ANNUAL MEETING, NATIONAL ACADEMY OF ARBITRATORS 64 (Charles M. Rehmus, ed., 1968).

[10] Bernard D. Meltzer, *The Role of Law in Arbitration: Rejoinder,* in DEVELOPMENTS IN AMERICAN & FOREIGN ARBITRATION: PROCEEDINGS OF THE TWENTY-FIRST ANNUAL MEETING, NATIONAL ACADEMY OF ARBITRATORS 58 (Charles M. Rehmus, ed., 1968). *See also* ELKOURI & ELKOURI: HOW ARBITRATION WORKS ch. 10 (Kenneth May, ed., 7th ed. 2012).

[11] 363 U.S. 593 (1960).

[12] *Id.* at 597.

"for help" in resolving the dispute. In still other cases, one party may reference external law and the other party not raise an objection.

**2.   *Assuming the parties have not agreed that external law applies,
how does the arbitrator decide whether to look outside the
agreement to resolve the contract dispute?***

There are some cases where an arbitrator should examine external law. For example, if the parties' CBA prohibits discrimination while tracking the language of Title VII of the Civil Rights Act of 1974, the arbitrator should look to judicial interpretations of the same language in interpreting the parties' contract. That is precisely what Justice Douglas meant when he wrote that arbitrators can use that "help" in carrying out their functions.

The use of external law would also be appropriate where an ambiguous provision of the parties' CBA might have one reading that is legal under external law and another that is illegal. The arbitrator should presume that the parties sought to write a legal provision.

It is a far more difficult situation when the contract contains clear language that would be illegal under external law, for example, compensating employees at less than the minimum wage or embodying a seniority system that violates federal antidiscrimination law. What should the arbitrator do? The better approach is for the arbitrator to read and interpret what the contract says. If the CBA provides for an illegal wage, there is another forum available to aggrieved employees under the Fair Labor Standards Act. If the seniority system violates federal law, once again a court is available for redress.

The arbitrator's power comes from the contract. When there is a direct conflict between the contract and the law (or general ethics or fairness or justice), the arbitrator reads the contract. He or she is appointed not to correct the parties' mistakes, but to let them know what their contract says.

Some might argue—and with some moment—that this approach ill-serves the parties. The arbitrator is supposed to end disputes, not push them forward to another tribunal. Some have even assumed that all external law is really part of a CBA because the contract is negotiated in the context of those laws. Either applying or refusing to apply external law in a dispute is going to send the parties to a second forum if the case is worth the time and expense. This situation arises only when the contract is sufficiently clear that the arbitrator can find no room to use external law for help, and that may occur in only a very few cases.

3.   Arbitrators are sometimes asked to hear matters that are deferred to arbitration from the National Labor Relations Board. In those cases, should the arbitrator apply federal labor law?

Under prevailing National Labor Relations Board (NLRB) law, when an unfair labor practice charge is filed raising claims that are based on alleged violations of a CBA, the NLRB likely will defer the matter to arbitration. The parties will inform the arbitrator that, in addition to resolving the grievance under the parties' CBA, the neutral must determine whether a party has violated the National Labor Relations Act. The arbitrator normally files a document with the regional director or regional attorney of the NLRB, attaching a copy of his or her opinion and award. The NLRB then determines whether it will accept the arbitrator's decision as a final resolution of the labor law dispute.

In these NLRB-deferred cases, there is no question that the arbitrator must apply external law. Labor law is quite different from the usual principles applied by a labor arbitrator, and thus these cases can present quite a challenge to the neutral, especially one not trained in the law.

4.   Does an arbitrator ever have to apply constitutional principles?

On very rare occasions, an arbitrator is asked to make a ruling based on constitutional principles. It is not unusual for a union to claim that an employee was disciplined for exercising his or her First Amendment rights of free speech. It is a hard argument to make that a worker who cursed at his or her supervisor was just expressing a protected viewpoint. In any case, unless the employing entity is a public employer, constitutional protections do not apply. The arbitrator should explain this to the union at the hearing so it does not spend time arguing a point that will not prevail. However, an employee does enjoy constitution-like privileges and protections—to be treated fairly (due process) and like other similarly situated employees (equal protection), in both private and public sector situations.

When the employer is in the public sector, its actions may be limited by, for example, First Amendment principles. This is really far afield from the expertise of most arbitrators, but they are appointed to serve the parties. In the ideal situation, the parties will select as their arbitrator someone who is capable of making an analysis under the First Amendment.

VI. RIGGED AWARDS

On same rare occasions, the parties agree privately on how their dispute should be resolved, but would prefer that their understanding be issued as an arbitration decision rather than a settlement of the matter by the parties. These situations arise when the politics and the personalities of the workplace make a settlement impossible, even if the representatives of both parties agree it is the best way to proceed.

1.   Should the arbitrator agree to issue a consent award?

The Code of Professional Responsibility allows an arbitrator to issue a *consent award,* sometimes referred to pejoratively as a *rigged award,* but only under certain conditions:

> Prior to issuance of an award, the parties may jointly request the arbitrator to include in the award certain agreements between them, concerning some or all of the issues. If the arbitrator believes that a suggested award is proper, fair, sound, and lawful, it is consistent with professional responsibility to adopt it.[13]

The Code provision then notes:

> Before complying with such a request, an arbitrator must be certain of understanding the suggested settlement adequately in order to be able to appraise its terms. If it appears that pertinent facts or circumstances may not have been disclosed, the arbitrator should take the initiative to assure that all significant aspects of the case are fully understood. To this end, the arbitrator may request additional specific information and may question witnesses at a hearing.[14]

Thus, an *agreed case,* as a consent or rigged award is also sometimes called, is perfectly permissible, but should an arbitrator acquiesce? Many arbitrators believe that consent awards are a perversion of the arbitration process, designed to deceive someone other than those persons directly involved in the hearing by masquerading as an impartial arbitration award.

---

[13]NATIONAL ACADEMY OF ARBITRATORS, AMERICAN ARBITRATION ASSOCIATION, & FEDERAL MEDIATION & CONCILIATION SERVICE, CODE OF PROFESSIONAL RESPONSIBILITY FOR ARBITRATORS OF LABOR-MANAGEMENT DISPUTES 2.I.1 (as amended and in effect Sept. 2007), *available at* http://www.naarb.org/code.html.

[14]*Id.* at 2.I.1.a.

Another section of the Code seems to raise questions as to whether the arbitrator should even participate in such a deception. It says that arbitrators should "refuse to lend approval or consent to any collusive attempt by the parties to use arbitration for an improper purpose."[15] Rigged awards are a deception.

This is not to suggest that parties should not attempt to resolve disputes themselves without arbitral intervention. In many cases—perhaps half—the parties to an arbitration will reach a settlement either before or during a hearing. The union in a discharge case may realize after hearing the employer's first witness that it would be better for the grievant to accept management's terms for a resolution of his or her grievance. In preparing for the arbitration of a dispute involving the interpretation of a contract provision, management might realize that the contract is not as clear-cut as it had thought and will be willing to resolve the case. These are appropriate settlements, and arbitrators hope that parties will reach them with or without their assistance.

The consent award is quite different. Here the parties reach a settlement and want to use the arbitrator's office as a way to portray publicly that the outcome was the result of an arbitrator's ruling and not the result of a private voluntary settlement. Even if the arbitrator is convinced that the decision is "proper, fair, sound, and lawful,"[16] it is not what it purports to be—a decision by an arbitrator. It is a fraud.

Parties have good reasons for wanting to use the power of the arbitrator's office in this way. A grievant might not be pleased by an arbitrator's decision upholding his or her discharge, but the union would prefer such a neutral's award to the announcement of a voluntary settlement. An arbitrator's decision, by virtue of the *Steelworkers Trilogy*, is subject to no review on the merits. A consent award that benefits a certain cohort of employees but not another is more likely to withstand review in a duty of fair representation lawsuit if it looks like an arbitrator's judgment.

Arbitrators must carefully protect the process they are privileged to operate. That includes making sure that parties are given the opportunity to be heard and that the hearing is fair. Although the proceeding belongs to management and the union, the arbitrator serves as a fiduciary. He or she should not allow a rigged award to pervert the arbitration process.[17]

---

[15] *Id.* at 2.A.2.

[16] *Id.* at 2.I.1.

[17] These are not new concerns. Harvard Law Professor Lon Fuller expressed the same position over 50 years ago in *Collective Bargaining and the Arbitrator*, 1963 Wis. L. Rev. 3, 20–22 (the rigged award is perhaps "the crassest infringement of adjudicative integrity").

VII. MAKING THE DECISION

The model of arbitral decision making presented in this chapter emphasizes the rational and informed method that experienced arbitrators use in deciding cases. This does not mean that arbitrators do not make mistakes—they do, and every experienced arbitrator knows the cases he or she would like back.

It would be unusual—perhaps unprecedented—for an arbitrator to admit openly that he or she has decided the dispute by the end of the hearing. It is one of the "customs of the trade" for arbitrators to emphasize how much hard work and studious thinking goes into actually making a decision. And sometimes that is true.

1.   Is it difficult to make a decision?

Most arbitration cases are fairly easy to decide, at least with regard to the ultimate outcome of whether the grievance is granted or denied. However, even the "easy" cases have twists and turns that can present significant challenges to an arbitrator when writing an opinion. Other arbitration cases are almost impossible to decide. An arbitrator may leave the hearing with some clues, but few clear paths to follow. The facts may be confusing, and the outcome can remain uncertain. There is no ignoring the job, however, of resolving the dispute, regardless of whether it is easy or hard.

2.   Does an arbitrator consider the implications of his or her award?

Junior arbitrators often find it difficult to uphold the discharge of an employee. They sometimes forget that they are not firing the employee—management did that, and their job is to decide whether that action was for just cause. Nonetheless, arbitrators are people, too, and they know what it means to an employee to lose a job.

Similarly, junior employees worry about putting a discharged employee back to work. Will management avenge the arbitration loss by discharging the employee a second time? A study by Professor Stephen Goldberg presented at the NAA annual meeting in 2006[18] reached the interesting and nonintuitive conclusion that dischargees who are returned to work by an arbitrator perform well in the workplace and

---

[18] Stephen B. Goldberg, *What Happens After the Arbitrator's Award?: Presentation,* in ARBITRATION 2006: TAKING STOCK IN A NEW CENTURY, PROCEEDINGS OF THE 59TH ANNUAL MEETING, NATIONAL ACADEMY OF ARBITRATORS 231 (Stephen F. Befort & Paul F. Gerhart, eds., 2007).

are rarely subjected to a second discharge. This study should ease an arbitrator's understandable concern about returning a worker to his or her previous job.

Contract interpretation cases can be misread by the prevailing party. If management wins in a contract case, it does not mean that it is given free rein to decide whatever it wants whenever it wants. In writing an opinion the arbitrator should indicate exactly what he or she has decided and what he or she has not decided. Arbitration decides one case at a time.

Chapter 15

Drafting an Arbitration Opinion and Award

I. Overview

The arbitrator begins the process of deciding a case from the moment the hearing begins. Opening statements will set the tone for the case to be heard, and they also begin the decisional process for the arbitrator. By the end of the hearing, the arbitrator has likely decided the case, at least tentatively. It is then time to begin the process of drafting an opinion.

II. Drafting an Arbitration Decision[1]

The experienced arbitrator leaves the arbitration hearing knowing how the dispute is likely to be decided. Many arbitrators begin the drafting process shortly thereafter. Arbitrators normally review their notes immediately after the hearing. Although they are practiced at taking notes, it is not unusual for arbitrators to find some gaps in their notes that can be filled in if done immediately. Many arbitrators write up an outline or even a tentative draft of the facts and opinion shortly after the hearing. Arbitrators who do not do this will find the task of starting with a blank sheet of paper or a blank computer screen months later to present an incredibly difficult challenge. It is likely that these will be arbitrators who issue late decisions.

1. Are there any guidelines that the arbitrator must follow in drafting an arbitration opinion?

An arbitrator must draft a decision that resolves the dispute and explains to the parties how the resolution was reached. Writing an arbitration opinion and award requires time and effort on the part of the arbitrator. In arbitration parlance, that time is referred to as *study time,* although much of it is consumed in drafting rather than in study. The arbitrator must be mindful that he or she is paid based on the time spent reviewing the record, researching issues, and crafting a decision, and thus should try to hold down the ultimate cost to the parties of his or her services.

The Code of Professional Responsibility lists a variety of issues the neutral must consider in drafting an opinion:

---

[1] *See* Roger Abrams & Dennis Nolan, *Arbitral Craftsmanship and Opinion Writing,* 5 Lab. Law. 195 (1989).

When an opinion is required, factors to be considered by an arbitrator include: desirability of brevity, consistent with the nature of the case and any expressed desires of the parties; need to use a style and form that is understandable to responsible representatives of the parties, to the grievant and supervisors, and to others in the collective bargaining relationship; necessity of meeting the significant issues; forthrightness to an extent not harmful to the relationship of the parties; and avoidance of gratuitous advice or discourse not essential to disposition of the issues.[2]

2. *If the arbitrator has decided the case by the end of the hearing, what is the purpose of the parties' briefs, which are normally filed a month later? Isn't the arbitrator jumping the gun to start work on the case before reading the parties' submissions?*

After the hearing, it generally takes a month before the parties file their briefs, and it could be two months if a transcript is taken. If the arbitrator waits that long before looking through his or her notes and thinking about how the decision will be made, he or she is at a considerable disadvantage when the briefs finally arrive. For the busy arbitrator, there have been weeks of other arbitration hearings that have filled the gap (and the arbitrator's mind).

The decisional and drafting processes do not mean that briefs are unnecessary or not considered. In fact, by reading the briefs, arbitrators will generally learn something about the dispute that they did not appreciate at the hearing. Briefs also set out the parties' arguments, and it is critical that the arbitrator respond to all arguments made by the party that does not prevail in the case. Although most briefs are too long— why do we call them briefs when they are not?—they are useful, even if they do not change the arbitrator's mind about the case. On occasion, they actually do alter the outcome.

3. *How does an arbitrator write an opinion?*

Deciding how a dispute in arbitration should be resolved is only half the arbitrator's job. The neutral must also explain to the parties how he or she reached that judgment. Writing a well-crafted opinion also helps to clarify the decisional process and enhances the legitimacy of the arbitration process in the eyes of the parties.

---

[2]NATIONAL ACADEMY OF ARBITRATORS, AMERICAN ARBITRATION ASSOCIATION, & FEDERAL MEDIATION & CONCILIATION SERVICE, CODE OF PROFESSIONAL RESPONSIBILITY FOR ARBITRATORS OF LABOR-MANAGEMENT DISPUTES 6.C.1.a (as amended and in effect Sept. 2007), *available at* http://www.naarb.org/code.html (reproduced in Appendix B).

Arbitrators will tell you that there are times when a decision "just doesn't write." These difficult cases may actually leave the arbitrator in equipoise—caught evenly between two outcomes and two sets of reasoning. Sometimes, albeit rarely, an arbitrator will write two different versions of the opinion with two different outcomes before ultimately deciding which one he or she will issue.

An arbitrator writes for a variety of audiences. The decision will be read by the parties' representatives, of course. The grievant, as well as supervisors and other witnesses involved in the case, will also likely read the decision. The opinion must be understandable to those directly affected by it. Although lawyers might appreciate a decision that looks like those issued by a court, a grievant would be unlikely to find that kind of document easily accessible.

With the permission of the parties, an arbitrator may submit his or her decisions for publication by Bloomberg BNA, Commerce Clearinghouse, or other online sites that report arbitration decisions. If an arbitrator's decision is accepted for publication, it would then be read by members of the labor bar and by academics. On rare occasions, a court on review will read a decision. Finally, the arbitrator also writes for himself or herself, hoping to express the basis for his or her judgment in clear and concise prose. It is quite a challenge for the neutral to write for such a diverse audience.

4.   *Do all arbitrators succeed in writing cogent and clear opinions?*

Based on a review of published arbitration opinions, it is obvious that arbitrators have different levels of success in writing cogent and clear opinions. Some arbitrators are born writers and understand how to convey information in short declarative sentences. It is not unusual, however, for an arbitration decision to be very long on facts and very short on reasoning. Arbitrators may express their outcomes in a conclusory fashion, stating, for example, that management's action must be upheld because it was "reasonable." What exactly does that mean? More explanation is absolutely essential. A conclusory opinion ill-serves the parties and the process.

Sometimes arbitrators seem unable to avoid offering gratuitous advice to the parties. They think they know more about the parties' situation than the parties themselves. Although that may sometimes be true, more often the arbitrator is moved by hubris rather than informed knowledge. Arbitrators must avoid giving advice to the parties—it is gratuitous, and the arbitrator generally does not know enough about the parties to offer such advice. On the other hand, if management's action was held to be reasonable, an arbitrator's opinion may suggest what an unreasonable action would be, thus explaining implicitly that management's victory is not an unlimited ticket to ride anywhere in the future. A single line in an opinion that notes that the parties can change their contract provision at the next set of bargaining is also appropriate.

Other arbitrators have remanded cases to the parties for further bargaining—clearly not what the parties wanted when they submitted the case to the arbitrator. It is a capital error for an arbitrator to fail to resolve the issue. If the parties could have reached a supplementary agreement on the matter in controversy, they would have done so during the grievance procedure or before arbitration and avoided the time and expense of pursuing a hearing.

When parties read an arbitration decision, they are led to believe that the arbitrator had no doubts. In fact, no arbitrator is ever totally convinced about the outcome of a case, although you could not tell that by reading his or her opinions. Every outcome is the arbitrator's best effort, consistent with his or her training and experience, which is exactly what the parties are paying for and what they seek from the arbitrator.

Some arbitrators are simply not skilled in the writing process. Review of the published collections of arbitrator decisions demonstrates varying abilities and success. (Remember, published decisions are those that the arbitrators *chose* to submit for publication.)

5.   Isn't expecting an arbitrator to turn in a perfect opinion in a short period of time too much to ask?

It is true that arbitrating and opinion writing is not easy work. In addition, the realities of the process preclude an arbitrator from spending extra time on polishing a decision. Writing an arbitration opinion and award must be accomplished within a short period of time—a case is only worth so much to the parties, even if it is a difficult one to resolve. Generally, for a one-day hearing an arbitrator may spend two to three days reviewing the record, researching, and crafting and proofing an opinion. The appointing parties would and should be astounded to receive a bill for eight days of study for a simple one-day case. Because of lack of time, however, perfection in drafting an opinion may not be attainable, even by the best of neutrals.

6.   Does the arbitrator owe a duty to provide the parties with a full and detailed explanation for his or her award?

It is the arbitrator's primary responsibility to resolve the dispute that the parties have submitted to arbitration. Part of fulfilling that responsibility is explaining to the parties in a written opinion the reasons why the grievance was granted or denied. The arbitrator is not expected to write a law review article on the issues presented, nor do the parties seek such an extensive writing. The complexity of the case will determine the length of the opinion, but generally something more than a few pages and something less than 20 is more than sufficient.

Regrettably, some arbitrators simply rule that management's action was reasonable or arbitrary without explaining how they reached that judgment. Although the ultimate conclusion would be the same, the arbitrator should at least explain his or her process of reasoning. What are the salient facts that the arbitrator relied on? How would the outcome have been different if one fact or another were different?

Of course, in their collective bargaining agreements (CBAs) parties can specify exactly how and when they want the arbitrator to render his or her decision. The most significant complaint parties have with arbitrators is the inordinate delay between submission of briefs and the issuance of an award. However, most arbitrators abide by the guidelines set by the appointing agencies—30 days by the American Arbitration Association (AAA) and 60 days by the Federal Mediation and Conciliation Service (FMCS).

III. Burdens of Proof

Arbitrators and advocates for the parties spend an inordinate amount of time at the hearing, in briefs, and finally in arbitration decisions worrying about which party bears the burdens of production and persuasion and what is the appropriate quantum of proof.[3] Advocates—and probably some arbitrators—think these issues are important and even determinative, but they are not. They are imported from civil or even criminal litigation and should be relegated to the refuse bin.

1.   Doesn't the moving party have the burden of producing evidence?

Some party has to proceed first at the hearing—making the opening statement and presenting its case. Over the decades, parties in arbitration have agreed as to which party proceeds first in presenting its case. In discharge and discipline disputes, management proceeds first. In all other cases, the union proceeds first. Although presumably the

---

[3]Commentators also devote many pages to issues of burden of proof. *See, e.g.,* FAIRWEATHER'S PRACTICE AND PROCEDURE IN LABOR ARBITRATION ch. 10 (Ray J. Schoonhoven, ed., 4th ed. 1999).

parties in their CBA could alter this established practice, they have not chosen to do so. The practice was likely originally created by an arbitrator in the 1940s and has since then been adopted universally.[4]

The fact that one party or the other must proceed first should mean nothing regarding the merits of the case. Unlike in a civil court proceeding, the failure of a party to produce a convincing case through its evidence will not support some form of arbitral summary judgment or directed verdict in a labor arbitration case. Every party produces abundant evidence at the arbitration hearing, but whether such evidence warrants one party prevailing in the arbitration should wait until both parties have presented their proofs and arguments.

2. Is the burden of persuasion any more useful to the arbitrator?

Both parties attempt to persuade the arbitrator as to the merits of their cases. Assigning to one party or the other some form of burden of persuasion means, apparently, that if the case turns out to be equally balanced, the decision must go to the party without the burden of persuasion. This is purely and simply a makeweight used by arbitrators in making decisions.

In fact, ultimately no case is really in equipoise. One party's argument and evidence is always more persuasive than the opposing party's—perhaps not by a lot, but certainly by enough to prevail. It is similar to the baseball rule that the "tie goes to the runner." Any umpire will tell you that there is never a tie.

3. Are the various formulations of the quantum of proof also makeweights?

Arbitrators do recognize—and correctly so—that management needs to present a convincing case in order to sustain a discharge of an employee. This simply recognizes that the parties' just cause standard means something. Does an allegation of theft require more proof than if the allegation is poor work? Can any party actually convince the arbitrator that the evidence proves "guilt" beyond a reasonable doubt? Some arbitrators say they will sustain management actions—including discipline cases—when they are supported by a preponderance of the evidence. How does an arbitrator determine "preponderance?"

---

[4]Dennis Nolan, Labor and Employment Arbitration in a Nutshell 224 (2d ed. 2006) (stating that Dean Harry Shulman of Yale Law School, the first great arbitrator and the permanent umpire at Ford Motor Company, first assigned the order of proof, and every other arbitrator simply followed his lead).

Arbitrators will use these various formulations to justify their conclusions to grant or deny a grievance. In fact, what actually happens is that the arbitrator reaches a conclusion, convinced by the evidence and the arguments to go one way or the other on a case. That is what it takes for any decision maker to reach a decision—that he or she be convinced.

IV. Late Opinions

The primary complaint labor and management have about the arbitration process is how long it takes the arbitrator to issue his or her decision. Of course, courts take their time in issuing opinions, but the parties expect their neutral to fulfill their expectations, which means a timely award. Parties are also hamstrung by the fact that, if they raise concerns with an arbitrator while the case is live, the arbitrator might hold it against them. The parties can always handle the matter after the arbitrator issues the award by never selecting that neutral again, but by then it is too late.

1.   *What can the parties do if an arbitrator is very late in issuing his or her award?*

Some arbitrators take many months to issue a decision. In the absence of extenuating circumstances, such as the arbitrator's illness, such delay is inexcusable. At the very least, the arbitrator must communicate with the parties if his or her award will be delayed. What could possibly explain such lack of diligence on the part of an arbitrator?

Some arbitrators leave the job of considering the case and drafting the opinion until after receipt of the parties' briefs. Then, and only then, do they start to think about the case, research if necessary, and draft a decision. Because of delays caused by waiting for a transcript and the normal 30 days the parties are given to draft and submit their briefs, an arbitrator may not begin to think about a case until months after a hearing. If the arbitrator has a busy docket, he or she has heard many cases in the interim and is unlikely to remember much about the case in question. Starting from scratch can be an imposing task.

In every case, the parties have a right to a prompt decision. They should jointly inquire of the arbitrator as to when they can expect his or her award. *Ex parte* communications by one party are inappropriate. When the AAA is the appointing agency, the parties should contact the tribunal administrator to communicate with the arbitrator.

To deal with this problem, a few parties have provided in their CBA that the arbitrator will receive a diminishing portion of his or her final fee if the award is unnecessarily delayed. Arbitrators will likely respond to this financial incentive. In any event, one bad experience with a neutral should be sufficient to remove his or her name from future consideration for appointment.

2. How can an arbitrator make sure that his or her awards are timely?

Under the AAA rules, an arbitrator must issue the opinion and award within 30 days after the close of the hearing.[5] The hearing is closed upon receipt of any post-hearing briefs. The FMCS sets a 60-day deadline. Both appointing agencies allow an arbitrator to request an extension of time.

Arbitrators have a distinct incentive to issue timely awards. They do not get paid for their services until they issue their decisions. Some arbitrators will even aim to issue their awards within two weeks of receipt of the parties' briefs. How is an arbitrator capable of meeting such a goal?

An arbitrator should begin the process of reviewing the record, researching where warranted, and drafting the opinion as soon as the hearing has been completed. At the very least, the arbitrator should review his or her notes of the proceeding, perhaps on the plane ride home. Unless there is a transcript—and the expense of using a court reporter has made this option increasingly costly—the arbitrator's notes are the only record of what was said. Every arbitrator develops a system of taking notes, but all systems (short of shorthand) will create a record with holes that the arbitrator can fill in with a quick review. Some arbitrators will then write out an outline of the opinion, noting both facts and arguments.

In most cases, the arbitrator should draft the factual portion of his or her opinion within days after the hearing. In addition, the arbitrator should complete a preliminary draft of the discussion and opinion section of the decision. Although these are tentative efforts and will be substantially revised when the transcript and briefs arrive, few arbitrators

---

[5] *See* AMERICAN ARBITRATION ASSOCIATION, LABOR ARBITRATION RULES (amended and effective July 1, 2013), at Rule 36, *available at* http://www.adr.org/aaa/faces/rules/searchrules/rulesdetail?doc=ADRSTG_012406&_afrLoop=422248314580768&_afrWindowMode=0&_afrWindowId=7og4tr6be_1#%40%3F_afrWindowId%3D7og4tr6be_1%26_afrLoop%3D422248314580768%26doc%3DADRSTG_012406%26_afrWindowMode%3D0%26_adf.ctrl-state%3D7og4tr6be_57 (reproduced in Appendix D).

really need these later submissions to begin the process. When post-hearing briefs are received and read, the arbitrator will revise and polish the draft. This system makes the opinion-writing phase much easier to accomplish and promotes the issuance of timely awards.

3.   How do arbitrators feel about bench awards?

Some parties specify that the arbitrator is to issue a *bench award,* that is, an oral decision at the close of the hearing. Many arbitrators are reluctant to do so, preferring to take some time to consider the outcome and the reasoning. It may also be difficult for an arbitrator to tell the parties in person how their case has turned out. If the parties intend to insist on a bench decision, they must inform the arbitrator before he or she accepts the appointment. Other parties specify that they want their arbitrator to provide a short or summary decision within a specified period of time. Under some CBAs, parties require expedited arbitration for certain types of cases, typically discharge cases. Once again, the parties write their own ticket, and arbitrators who cannot meet the parties' requirements can decline the appointment.

V. Reasoning to a Result

Arbitrators know that the parties care about how a case comes out. The parties put enormous work into presenting their cases at the hearing. Although arbitration may be cheaper than litigation, the process is expensive nonetheless. But do the parties care about the arbitrator's opinion? Wouldn't they be just as pleased with a two-sentence award? If parties do not care about an arbitrator's reasoning, they can mutually direct their neutral not to write an opinion. They may assume that this will cut down substantially on an arbitrator's study time, but that also assumes that the arbitrator can reach an outcome without demonstrating how he or she reasoned to reach the result.

1.   Do the parties only care about the ultimate outcome of the case, or are they concerned about the arbitrator's reasoning?

It is true that the parties to an arbitration often turn immediately to the last page of the arbitrator's opinion to find out whether the grievance has been granted or denied. The reasoning, however, can be vitally important to the collective relationship between the parties. It can provide legitimacy to the ultimate outcome. If the arbitrator makes sense in his or her discussion, the losing party may be more accepting of the award. At the very least, it demonstrates that the neutral thought hard about the issues rather than simply jumping to a conclusion.

2. How does an arbitrator go about crafting an opinion and award?

In the typical case, as discussed above, the arbitrator already has a very good idea of how a case will come out by the end of the hearing. The post-hearing briefs can confirm that initial judgment or create a sufficient conflict in the mind of the neutral to warrant a change in outcome. Although briefs can have that effect, in most cases involving experienced arbitrators, briefs are more likely to play a confirmatory role.

Most experienced arbitrators have developed a format for drafting their decisions. The draft will briefly explain the origin of the case, describe the grievant and the employer, and set forth the essential facts. Some arbitrators will spend an inordinate and unnecessary amount of time setting forth every bit of evidence, as if the parties had missed the hearing. Even more tedious are those decisions that detail what each witness testified to at the hearing. However, it is necessary for the arbitrator to set out those facts that will be central to his or her discussion of the parties' contentions. That recitation also reassures the parties that the arbitrator listened to the testimony and read the documents.

Most arbitration opinions quote the precise issue the parties have asked their arbitrator to decide. This is important because an arbitrator who strays from that issue, by ignoring his or her charge, has, in effect, invited the losing party to seek judicial review. In the *Steelworkers Trilogy*,[6] the U.S. Supreme Court explained that the court's role in reviewing an arbitration decision is to determine whether the arbitrator's award "draws its essence" from the terms of the CBA.[7] Failing to answer the question or questions presented by the parties for resolution constitutes a failure to "draw your essence" from the agreement.

The typical arbitration decision will then set forth the parties' contentions expressed at the hearing and in their post-hearing briefs, if any are filed. Once again, a brief summary of arguments is preferable to a long recitation of every contention raised. This lets the parties know that the arbitrator has read and digested their positions.

---

[6]Steelworkers v. American Mfg. Co., 363 U.S. 564 (1960); Steelworkers v. Warrior & Gulf Navig. Co., 363 U.S. 574 (1960); Steelworkers v. Enterprise Wheel & Car Corp., 363 U.S. 593 (1960). See the discussion of Justice Douglas' *Steelworkers Trilogy* analysis in Chapter 1, §V. The *Steelworkers Trilogy* decisions are reproduced in Appendix A.
[7]*Enterprise Wheel,* 363 U.S. at 597.

The discussion section of the decision normally follows, with the arbitrator explaining the basis for his or her opinion. The arbitrator should try to respond to every argument made by the party that will not prevail in the case. At the same time, the opinion should highlight the prevailing party's arguments that have merit and those that do not. For example, management may ultimately win the case, but an arbitrator should respond to a broad-based claim of unlimited management rights with a cautionary limitation that management rights may be limited by the express terms of the agreement and by an established past practice.

Finally, the decision must end with a section setting forth the award and remedy. Here the arbitrator responds with precision to the issue presented and sets forth what should be done with the grievance, i.e., whether it is granted or denied in full or in part. If the arbitrator grants the grievance even in part, he or she must specify the remedy. If warranted, the award should indicate that the arbitrator retains jurisdiction for a limited period of time—normally 60 days—to respond to any issues that may arise concerning the implementation or calculation of the remedy.

3.   *Is it acceptable for an arbitrator to use an occasional Latin phrase?*

Latin and other foreign languages should be avoided. Even those phrases that arbitrators have traditionally used in their opinions, such as *expressio unius est exclusion alterius*, although useful in thinking through a case, should be avoided in the opinion, unless it is explained to the reader. The Latinate phrases are all based on simple logic, but they hide the arbitrator's opinion behind a cloak of lawyerisms.

Parties select lawyers as their arbitrators because they have been trained in using logic to resolve disputes, not because they are fluent in Latin—which they are not. Lawyers have not always been skilled at writing in simple English, but an arbitration opinion is much more useful to the parties if it is sculpted in those terms and not some phrases learned in law school.

More important, the use of Latin and other imports from the civil justice system are symptoms of "creeping legalism." Arbitration was created by companies and labor unions as an informal dispute resolution process. For the most part, the parties chose lawyers as their arbitrators, trusting that they would recognize the distinctive purposes of voluntary labor arbitration as compared with civil litigation. Instead, many labor arbitrators have simply applied what they have learned in civil litigation to the arbitration setting, which has not accrued to the benefit of the parties.

An arbitrator's opinion must be written in a way that makes it accessible to the stakeholders in the proceeding. Straightforward prose in the style of Ernest Hemingway is preferable to "whereas" and "henceforth." Arbitrators who need to flaunt their erudition will not long be the choice of the parties.

4.   To what extent do arbitrators research legal issues beyond the arguments and citations presented by the parties for inclusion in their award?

Arbitrators use legal research for strategic reasons in crafting their opinions. Citing and discussing reported decisions that support the arbitrator's conclusions on issues raised by the parties demonstrates that the arbitrator's outcomes were generally consistent with what other arbitrators would conclude. The party that does not prevail in the arbitration must appreciate that this outcome was not simply the result of selecting a particular arbitrator.

The question also raises the issue of whether, in deciding a case, an arbitrator should rely on an argument not made by one party or the other. Everything else being equal, it is better for the neutral to rely on arguments made by the prevailing party. There are times when an opinion will build on an argument made by a party and add elements that normally are part of the discussion.

At times, parties argue their cases in the extreme: management is always right; labor is always treated unfairly. Neither, of course, is true, and an arbitrator cannot rely on either partisan position in resolving the case. If management has a prerogative to take certain action under the CBA and it acts for a legitimate business purpose, its operational decision should be upheld. If management acts to undermine the union and shows favoritism among employees, the grievance should be granted. The arbitrator must then construct his or her own arguments to support the ultimate award rather than rely on those offered by the parties.

5.   Should the arbitrator's award address the evidence and testimony presented at the hearing?

The arbitrator's opinion should offer a summary of the relevant facts presented in the case and provide details regarding salient facts the arbitrator will rely on in rendering his or her award. A tedious recitation of everything submitted and everything that was said makes the decision both cumbersome and unwieldy. The parties—and anyone else who might read the opinion if it is published—would lose sight of the trees while blanketed by a forest of facts. It is the trees that count.

Some arbitration opinions list all the evidence presented and recite each witness' testimony. That effort certainly demonstrates the arbitrator's ability to write things down and list items, but it does little to make the opinion more convincing. The parties should see enough in the decision to know that the arbitrator paid attention at the hearing, but arbitrators are not paid by the word.

VI. The Legitimacy of the Award

An arbitrator, as a fiduciary for the arbitration process, must write an opinion that will foster the acceptability of the eventual award. Legitimacy is the product of reasoning and a willingness to confront the parties' best arguments so that they know they were heard. Of course, an arbitrator need do nothing more than decide the case, but the way he or she decides the case and explains the result will foster the acceptability of the process in the workplace.

1. Should the arbitrator, in rendering his or her award, address each and every legal argument put forward by each of the parties? If not, why not?

In order to keep the decision of manageable length, the arbitrator must choose which arguments to address at length and which to comment on in a summary fashion. The opinion should address every argument made by the party that does not prevail, and every argument made by the prevailing party that is essential to the ultimate determination.

Parties include in their presentations, both at the hearing and in their briefs, arguments of different value. Although a union might appreciate that the arbitrator could not censure management's operational decision simply because the employees did not like the decision or disagreed with it, the union may include that argument in its presentation, especially if proponents of that point of view are in attendance. The arbitrator need not take too much time and effort to respond to such a throwaway argument. Similarly, with regard to management's arguments based on its unlimited rights, the neutral should simply say that such a position ignores provisions of the CBA. Some arguments may be so off base that the arbitrator need not mention them at all in the opinion. However, it is probably better practice to simply state that the neutral has "carefully considered" all the arguments offered by the parties.

2.   What are the inclinations of arbitrators in terms of "splitting the baby" when issuing an award?

In addition to being a gruesome Solomonic metaphor, "splitting the baby" is bad arbitrating if, and only if, such an outcome is unwarranted based on the record. In some cases, however, a "compromise" decision may be fully warranted by the evidence presented. For example, consider a discharge case where the grievant failed to meet his side of the employment bargain, but management's determination of discharge was excessive. The evidence shows that the employer has not shown that the grievant will be unable to meet his work obligations in the future. Reinstatement without back pay may be the appropriate award.

The question, however, suggests the possibility that an arbitrator would issue a compromise award in order to please both parties. Management's right to discipline is upheld and the union has been able to get the employee back to work at a time when jobs are hard to come by. Every arbitrator wants to please the parties, but a compromise award in a situation where it is not warranted by the facts pleases no one in the long run. What if the grievant punched his supervisor without provocation? Returning him to the workplace obviously does not please management, and the union may be equally unpleased by the fact that the employee spent a considerable amount of time off work without pay.

An arbitrator cannot set out to do his or her job with the goal of making everyone happy. Rather, an arbitrator's goal must be to provide the parties with what they are paying for—arbitration—in a setting that does not exacerbate their ongoing relationship. An arbitrator can please both sides in the way the hearing is conducted. Parties must feel as if they have had the opportunity to present their side of the case. The case should then be decided on the merits, and the chips should fall where they may.

3.   How should an arbitrator announce a credibility determination?

It is difficult to state in an opinion that a witness lied, even if, in fact, the witness did lie in his or her testimony at the hearing. Some cases do turn on the credibility of the witnesses' testimony.

There can be repercussions in the workplace if a case is decided based solely on the fact that a named individual lied in his or her testimony. Management officials, union leaders, and rank-and-file workers will blame that individual for losing the case. This does not aid good working relationships.

When credibility is an issue, some arbitrators use the burden of proof in crafting the opinion. This is admittedly a makeweight, but its use is designed not to exacerbate morale and productivity. The arbitrator could write: "Jones' testimony was not convincing," or "management (or the union) did not meet its burden of proof on the issue." In fact, these formulations may be less than candid, but they are written in such a way that the arbitrator is not accusing anyone of prevarication.

4.   Doesn't an arbitrator need courage rather than makeweights to perform his or her role?

An arbitrator should not shy from making hard decisions. If the grievant was discharged for just cause, the arbitrator should just say so. If management acted in a way that undermined a union right protected by the CBA, then the grievance should be granted. The issue is how the arbitrator announces an outcome, not what the proper outcome is.

The parties hire the arbitrator because they value both his or her ability in conducting a hearing and judgment in reaching an award, but also because he or she will write an opinion that, although not making everyone happy, will at least not make everyone angry. On the other hand, the arbitrator was not brought in to make the workplace a happier or more productive environment—the parties could hire a consultant to do that. The arbitrator was also not hired as an independent investigator—he or she was appointed as an arbitrator to hear and resolve disputes consistent with the parties' CBA and should do that in the easiest way possible.

This narrow approach to arbitral decision making may not be the preference of either party. If both parties agree, they can submit to the arbitrator any questions they wish. Normally, however, they are concerned primarily with having the neutral resolve the dispute at hand and nothing more. If the parties want to improve their workplace, they have the negotiation process. If they want workers to have higher morale and productivity, they can act mutually to achieve that goal. Justice Douglas in the *Steelworkers Trilogy* tells us that arbitrators know all kinds of things about worker morale and productivity, but that does not mean the arbitrator should spout off on these matters if unnecessary to the resolution of the dispute.

5.   Should the arbitrator decide the case on the narrowest grounds available?

Courts in civil actions normally will look for a narrow ground for ruling for either the plaintiff or the defendant. If a statutory provision works to resolve the dispute, there is no need to reach for a constitutional basis. If there is a way to avoid a credibility resolution, that should suffice.

Much the same should be the rule in arbitration opinion writing. An arbitrator risks doing harm to the parties' relationship if he or she makes broad pronouncements in his or her opinion that are not necessary to resolve the case. Relying on some general concept of management rights is unnecessary when the agreement provides specifically that management can act exactly as it did in the case at hand.

Normally, an arbitrator will have a variety of ways to rule on a particular grievance. For example, if the dispute is not arbitrable on the procedural grounds of untimeliness, there may be no reason to reach the substantive arbitrability claim. The arbitrator should flag the issue and note that he or she is not deciding it because it does not need to be decided to resolve the case. Reaching beyond what is needed to decide the case is a form of advisory opinion—unless the parties specifically ask the arbitrator to rule on a nonessential issue, he or she should avoid doing so.

The one exception to this practice lies in the arguments made by the party that does not prevail in the case. As previously stated, it is important that the arbitrator discuss all the arguments made by the losing party. The primary argument might be sufficient to dispose of the case, but the secondary and tertiary arguments might have been sufficient grounds for a decision in its favor. The arbitrator should address them all.

VII. Federal Sector Arbitration

The system established by Congress for collective bargaining between federal agencies and federal sector unions created a distinctive procedure that affects the arbitrator's job in deciding cases and crafting decisions. The Civil Service Reform Act of 1978[8] mandates that all federal CBAs contain a grievance and arbitration system, but it forbids agencies and federal sector unions from negotiating over wages, hours, overtime, holidays, vacations, pensions, insurance, and other topics that are mandatory subjects of bargaining in the private sector. Arbitration decisions rendered through the mandated procedures are subject to review by the Federal Labor Relations Authority (FLRA).

1.   How does the federal labor relations system affect a labor arbitrator's job?

Arbitrators who hear cases in the federal sector must focus on both the provisions of the parties' CBA and the context of federal laws and

---

[8] Pub. L. No. 95-454, 92 Stat. 1111 (1978).

regulations. In the private sector, cases normally do not involve what might be considered "external law," but in federal sector arbitration external law is very much at the heart of things. As a result, disputes in the federal sector can be very difficult to resolve.

At the hearing and in their post-hearing briefs, advocates will bring to the arbitrator's attention relevant decisions of the FLRA, the federal agency charged with administering labor-management relations in the federal sector. FLRA decisions are binding precedent.

2.   *Does an arbitrator decide cases differently in the federal sector?*

An arbitrator hearing a case in the federal sector knows that his or her decision will be appealed by the losing party to the FLRA, which will review the decision on the merits. The Civil Service Reform Act basically converted federal sector labor arbitration into something more akin to a lower court or a hearing officer. Because there is no charge (other than a party's attorneys' fees) for appealing an award, virtually every case is appealed by the losing party.

Arbitrators in the federal sector system serve the two parties best when they write an opinion that cites and discusses decisions rendered by the FLRA. It is not unusual, however, for the FLRA to change its prior reading of the law in reviewing an arbitrator's decision! The arbitrator might have been correct under FLRA law when the award was rendered, but the award, along with the previous rulings of the FLRA, might be reversed on appeal. A party not pleased with the decision of the FLRA may seek review in the U.S. Court of Appeals for the Federal Circuit.

Chapter 16

Protecting the Arbitration Process

I. Overview

The arbitrator's job is to serve the parties by resolving their dispute in a manner consistent with their reasonable expectations as to both process and outcome. The best evidence of those expectations are the terms of their collective bargaining agreement (CBA), but may also be evidenced by their past practice. Both parties may honestly believe that they will prevail in a given case, but their expectations may not be reasonable. If parties were candid, they would acknowledge that there is a range of reasonable outcomes that the arbitrator could reach in any given case.

At the same time as he or she resolves the dispute, the neutral must provide the parties with a private dispute resolution system consistent with the accepted and well-understood model of labor arbitration. Parties can fine-tune that model if they wish, but the default position is ordinary, regular arbitration as it is generally practiced across the country.

Throughout this book we have discussed the obligation that an arbitrator has to the parties that select him or her to hear their dispute. However, the arbitrator bears responsibilities not only to the parties, but also to the arbitration process itself. One party (or both) may seek to contort the arbitration process by using tactics more commonly employed in state trial courts. Occasionally a party will even verbally attack the arbitrator, accusing the neutral of bias and prejudgment. In an effort to intimidate the neutral, a party might even walk out of an arbitration hearing when the proceedings do not go its way.

The arbitrator has a fiduciary responsibility to protect the process against partisan obstruction. Evenhanded treatment of all concerned is essential, but an arbitrator must have the courage to stand up to intimidation. Arbitration works because the parties want it to work and the arbitrator fulfills his or her fiduciary responsibility to the process.

II. EXTERNAL LAW AND CREEPING LEGALISM

Some arbitrators have seen the influx of legalisms into labor arbitration as a significant threat to the essence of the process as a private, informal method of adjudication. That was foreseeable as soon as lawyers became involved in the process, both as advocates and as arbitrators. The parties to a CBA can choose to have their arbitration process operate as they wish, within ethical constraints. The arbitrator should follow their lead.

The more likely scenario is that the parties will look to their arbitrator to guide the proceeding. Ever mindful of the purposes of the process and the context in which it operates, arbitrators should avoid mimicking court proceedings and keep legalisms from creeping into the private process.

1.   What should an arbitrator do regarding a claim involving "external law?"

The work relationship is governed by numerous state and federal statutes and regulations that may not be embodied in the provisions of the CBA. What should the neutral do with regard to this so-called *external law?* Commentators have varied in their approaches, but it is clear that ignoring external law (or, even worse, rendering an award that is contrary to that law) may undermine the status of arbitration and place its autonomy at risk. An arbitrator cannot ignore external law, but recognizing its proper role in a private proceeding requires great care.[1]

Arbitrators over the years have differed on the proper place of external law. Some have argued that, if arbitration is to maintain its

---

[1] *See* ELKOURI & ELKOURI: HOW ARBITRATION WORKS ch. 10 (Kenneth May, ed., 7th ed. 2012).

autonomy, arbitrators must leave to the courts the application of external law. Others have faced the reality that external law guides the workplace as much as contract provisions and to ignore that fact undermines the parties' continuing relationship.

It is best for an arbitrator to stay as close as possible to the terms of the parties' CBA in rendering his or her award. That text is the source of the arbitrator's power, not federal or state law. On the other hand, contract provisions are not self-applying and generally require interpretation. When one reading of a contract is consistent with external law and another reading runs in a contrary direction, the arbitrator is best advised to look to external law in interpreting the parties' intentions. In the absence of compelling evidence to the contrary, it is difficult to conclude that the parties intended to create a rule that would be in violation of external law. In those rare cases where the contract is clear and in violation of external law, the arbitrator should tell the parties what their contract means. The party disadvantaged by such a reading then would have recourse to the courts (or alternate tribunals such as state or federal agencies) to seek to perfect statutory rights.

2. Why does the labor arbitration process have to mirror a court proceeding?

In fact, labor arbitration need not mirror a court proceeding. Both courts and arbitration resolve disputes, but the procedures that have developed in courts over the centuries are ill-suited for the private, informal dispute resolution procedure created under a CBA.

Courts follow uniform procedures ordained by state supreme courts and constitutional principles. As part of a pyramid of adjudicatory bodies, lower courts know their decisions are subject to appeal. The jury system generally provides for the selection of 6 or 12 laypersons to assess factual issues and, under court instruction, apply the law to those facts. Obviously, court adjudication must be regulated to assure uniformity of treatment.

Arbitration is quite different, although at first glance there are similarities to court adjudication. There is a dispute that must be resolved and an adjudicator to do so. There are witnesses who offer sworn testimony and documents with relevant information. Arbitrators issue reasoned decisions and reach awards. The similarities are only superficial, however.

Arbitration is a continuation of the collective bargaining process designed to resolve disputes that are certain to arise during the term of a CBA. Whereas courts of general jurisdiction stand ready to hear a broad variety of disputes, an arbitrator can only hear those cases the parties have agreed would be cognizable in arbitration. The common practices of labor arbitration are designed to convey information from the parties to their arbitrator so that the arbitrator can make a decision consistent with the parties' intentions as evidenced in their agreement. Court-like procedures that are not needed to achieve that primary goal are more than surplusage—they can hinder the arbitrator and the process he or she is asked to administer.

Labor arbitration offers a mechanism that allows a dispute to be resolved as the parties would have resolved it if they could have reached agreement. That sounds a bit sophistical, but it is not. The parties have agreed on many things through their negotiations and their practice over time. They have not agreed on the appropriate outcome of a particular dispute, perhaps because of matters of personalities or differences as to what actually occurred. The arbitrator, as their "joint alter ego" (to use Professor St. Antoine's phrase)[2] makes the "deal" they would have made. To accomplish this task, the arbitrator does not need to sit as a court would.

3.   It seems that arbitrators and advocates enjoy using legal terms, phrases, and rules. Does that fit in arbitration?

It is hard for lawyers to leave their legal training to one side when they enter the world of labor arbitration. In the absence of a proscribed script for a labor arbitration proceeding, arbitrators fall back on what they know, especially when they are new to the process. Similarly, advocates who are lawyers import their courtroom experiences into the arbitration hearing room, making it difficult, for example, to hear a witness spout hearsay without objecting.

When it comes to writing briefs, opinions, and awards, legal training prevails. Some briefs use arcane legalisms. Some arbitrators employ a Latin phrase or two in their opinions.

Lawyer-arbitrators are not going to penalize an advocate who writes a brief suitable for a trial court. However, arbitrators do appreciate when advocates make appropriate use of reported arbitration decisions—not as controlling precedent, but as persuasively reasoned opinion. Some arbitrators cite to reported decisions throughout their

---

[2] Theodore J. St. Antoine, *Judicial Review of Labor Arbitration Awards: A Second Look at* Enterprise Wheel *and Its Progeny,* 75 MICH. L. REV. 1137, 1140 (1977). ("Put most simply, the arbitrator is the parties' officially designated 'reader' of the contract. He (or she) is their joint alter ego for the purpose of striking whatever supplementary bargain is necessary to handle the anticipated unanticipated omissions of the initial agreement.").

opinions in order to demonstrate to the parties that the decision they are receiving from the arbitrator is the same decision they would have received from any experienced arbitrator.

Arbitrators must be mindful of the diverse group of persons who will read their opinions. Writing for legally trained advocates may make an opinion less useful for a shop steward. When in doubt about a legalism, the arbitrator should leave it out.

III. Distortions in the Arbitration Process

Parties to a labor arbitration may confuse the informality of the process with an invitation to engage in a bare-knuckle confrontation with their opponents. One party may think it can bury the opponent with motions, objections and filings, common practice in a civil court case and in employment arbitration, as discussed in Chapter 17.

It is not the responsibility of the arbitrator to protect one party from the other. It is the responsibility of the arbitrator, however, to protect the arbitration process from distortion by either party. The goal should be to have every case decided on the merits, not on the basis of who has more resources or is nastier.

1. The parties to a labor arbitration may have very different economic resources. Doesn't the potentially uneven economic status of the parties distort the arbitration process?

The union decides whether to process an unresolved grievance to arbitration after it has been denied at each step of the grievance procedure. Even unions flush with cash will decide to pursue some grievances to arbitration and withdraw others. There are political reasons why a union may have to process a case to arbitration even if the union does not think it will prevail, but normally unions make merit judgments that are informed by what resources are available.

The arbitrator has to assume that both parties want the matter heard and resolved after a hearing. He or she should be cognizant of the financial limitations that one party might have, but those facts should not keep a party from presenting its theory of the case through witnesses and documents. Unions do not receive an extra benefit from the arbitrator because they do not hire a high-priced attorney to present their cases. An experienced arbitrator can figure out what a case is about fairly quickly, and the 50-page, post-hearing brief filed by management does not make its argument any better or worse.

2.   *How does an arbitrator stop an advocate from bullying witnesses?*

An arbitrator's responsibility to the arbitration process requires that he or she take charge at the hearing. Nothing should stand in the way of the parties providing their arbitrator with the information needed to make an informed decision. Although the parties are both represented at the arbitration hearing and have come to provide their appointed arbitrator with information, they may not enjoy a particularly positive relationship in real life. There is not much an arbitrator can do about that fact, but the neutral can avoid exacerbating the situation or allowing anyone in the hearing room to use the forum for ulterior purposes.

In some cases, the representative of a party will use the arbitration hearing as an opportunity to get even with opponents. The grievant may have caused management grief. The human resource manager may be a royal pain in the union's side. When each witness takes the stand, his or her opponent might see this as time for payback. But an arbitrator cannot allow an advocate to bully a witness. Strenuous cross-examination is allowed, but when it gets close to the line, it is likely to provoke an objection from the opposing advocate. Even if that advocate does not object, the arbitrator cannot allow a hearing to become a shouting match.

3.   *How does an arbitrator address the belligerence of one advocate toward an opposing advocate and the arbitrator?*

Most advocates understand that belligerence toward the arbitrator is a foolish gambit. Experienced arbitrators will not be intimidated, nor will they stand for impertinence and disrespect. Such behavior undermines the arbitration process. Arbitrators will attempt to decide each case on the merits, but they are human and are affected by the way they are treated.

An arbitrator would be best advised to talk with the advocates outside the hearing room in the event something occurs that warrants intervention. The arbitrator should not embarrass an advocate in front of his or her client. Outside the hearing room, a brief reminder to the advocate of the role and the importance of the hearing process should be sufficient. If it is not, a second discussion might be in order.

The arbitrator need not accept the vituperations of disrespectful counsel at a hearing. At some point, when enough information has been presented, the arbitrator can adjourn the hearing. That should not be the preferred strategy for the neutral, but the arbitrator cannot allow one party to degrade the process.

4. How can an arbitrator avoid undue and unwarranted delays in the process?

One primary benefit of arbitration is that it can result in an expeditious resolution of a dispute that would otherwise fester in the workplace. An arbitrator who contributes to unnecessary delays in the process fails to meet the obligation to protect arbitration. Arbitrators bear a full measure of the responsibility for the delays. Some take many months to issue their awards after the parties have spent many months waiting for a hearing date for the arbitration.

Advocates also bear responsibility for delays in arbitration. Busy lawyers seem incapable of scheduling a hearing within a month or two even if the arbitrator has a date available. The arbitrator should consider conducting a conference call with the parties' representatives to schedule the first mutually available date.

Parties can address these types of delays in the arbitration provision of their CBA. They can provide that the arbitrator must be willing to hold a hearing within 60 days. They can also provide that the arbitrator must issue his or her award within 30 or 60 days after the receipt of briefs. Arbitrators should take charge to make sure the process provides what the parties wanted when they agreed to an arbitration procedure, but the parties must take responsibility for their process as well.

5. What about consent awards? How can a conspiracy among two lawyers and an arbitrator be a good solution to any problem?

In some situations, parties decide that they want to settle on a grievance dispute, but for political or personal reasons they are unable or unwilling to announce the settlement publicly as having been reached by the parties. They ask the arbitrator if he or she would be willing to issue their settlement as an arbitration award. They will draft exactly what they want the award to say.

These *consent awards* are expressly allowed under the Code of Professional Responsibility, with certain restrictions and limitations. An arbitrator can agree to issue a consent award "[i]f the arbitrator believes that a suggested award is proper, fair, sound, and lawful."[3] How does an arbitrator make that determination? Before complying with

---

[3]NATIONAL ACADEMY OF ARBITRATORS, AMERICAN ARBITRATION ASSOCIATION, & FEDERAL MEDIATION & CONCILIATION SERVICE, CODE OF PROFESSIONAL RESPONSIBILITY FOR ARBITRATORS OF LABOR-MANAGEMENT DISPUTES 2.I.1 (as amended and in effect Sept. 2007), *available at* http://www.naarb.org/code.html (reproduced in Appendix B). For additional discussion of consent awards, see Chapter 14, §VI.1.

such a request, under the Code an arbitrator must be certain that he or she adequately understands the suggested settlement in order to be able to appraise its terms. If it appears that pertinent facts or circumstances may not have been disclosed, the arbitrator should take the initiative to assure that all significant aspects of the case are fully understood. To this end, the arbitrator may request additional specific information and may question witnesses at a hearing.

Consent awards are a travesty that causes grievous injury to the arbitration process. All an arbitrator has is his or her reputation. If it were generally known that a neutral would accept payment—the per diem fee—in return for allowing one of the arbitrator's opinions to masquerade as a decision on the merits, that reputation is rightfully subject to question.

IV. INAPPROPRIATE CONDUCT

Experienced advocates understand the nature and limits of the arbitration process. Those new to the process, however, may not fully appreciate the essence of the enterprise and the boundaries of what is appropriate conduct. The arbitrator may play a role as a teacher in some circumstances.

1. How should the arbitrator react to ex parte *contacts with the arbitrator before the hearing?*

Representatives of the parties may not fully understand the arbitrator's role as a neutral adjudicator. Although lawyers might be more attuned to the judicial model, where it would be completely inappropriate to contact a judge *ex parte* before a hearing, representatives in arbitration might not be lawyers and therefore might not be sure what the appropriate limits are in terms of contact with the neutral. An arbitrator must recognize that he or she might be hearing a case where the parties do not have experienced representation.

If a party attempts to explain to the arbitrator before the hearing its side of the case and how important it is for them to prevail, the arbitrator should interrupt the approach. The representative might not even appreciate that what he or she has done is inappropriate and unethical. The arbitrator should calmly inform the representative that there will be plenty of time at the hearing to explain their case. There is no reason to chastise the uninformed representative.

2. What about contacts with the arbitrator by a party after the award is issued?

On occasion, the party that does not prevail in the arbitration will contact the arbitrator after the award is issued. Sometimes a party calls the arbitrator to complain about the award. Other times a genuinely confused party has questions about the decision. During the hearing, an experienced arbitrator will generally offer no hint as to how he or she is responding to the parties' arguments and evidence. Losing the case may, in fact, come as a complete surprise to a party.

After the arbitrator issues an award, he or she has no further role to play unless the parties have agreed that the arbitrator will retain jurisdiction in the case for a period of time to respond to any problems involving implementation of the award. The default position, however, is that once the decision is issued, the arbitrator has completed the requirements of the appointment.

If the representative of the losing party (or even the grievant) contacts the arbitrator to complain about the decision, the arbitrator should explain that he or she is no longer involved. If the representative has questions about the decision and not merely complaints, the arbitrator should explain that he or she would be willing to respond to questions if both parties jointly request a clarification.

If the arbitrator retains jurisdiction and the contact from a party is a timely referral back to the arbitrator of issues raised in the implementation of the award, including the calculation of back pay, the arbitrator should inform the opposing party of the contact and then schedule submissions the parties should make to the arbitrator on the contested issues. It may be sufficient simply to conduct a telephone conference call. In very rare cases, the arbitrator may need to conduct a further hearing to take evidence on an issue.

3. Do losing parties ever sue the arbitrator?

On relatively rare occasions, a losing party will seek review of an arbitrator's decision despite the Supreme Court's *Steelworkers Trilogy* standard, which provides for virtually no review on the merits. In *Steelworkers v. Enterprise Wheel & Car Corp.,*[4] Justice William O. Douglas wrote for the Court that as long as an arbitrator's award "draws its essence" from the CBA, the court should enforce the award.[5] Later decisions by the Supreme Court elaborated on this standard.

---

[4]363 U.S. 593 (1960).
[5]*Id.* at 597.

There are situations where an arbitrator's award should be set aside on appeal because of the failure of the neutral to disclose matters that might raise the impression of possible bias, as discussed in depth in Chapter 3. However, even if a court concludes that the arbitrator made errors in a decision, the award should stand.

Parties may attempt to join the arbitrator in a suit to vacate an award. The precedent is clear, however, that the arbitrator has immunity from suit for his or her actions as an arbitrator. The arbitrator will move to be dropped as a party, and the court will do so.[6]

V. Misconduct by the Arbitrator

There are times when an arbitrator's conduct is rightfully subject to criticism. For example, an arbitrator may take too much time before issuing an award. An arbitrator can also act inappropriately at a hearing, favoring one party over the other or berating both advocates without cause. Finally, in handling his or her accounts, the arbitrator might bill the parties incorrectly.

1. What should a party do if an arbitrator shows partiality at the arbitration hearing?

An arbitrator's responsibility to maintain neutrality lies at the core of his or her office. Any conduct before, at, or after the hearing that undermines this basic tenet will constitute grounds to have the resulting award set aside. More important, it constitutes an insult to the arbitration process that the neutral was appointed to administer.

There are numerous ways an arbitrator can abuse his or her office by conduct at a hearing: enforcing the rules of evidence against one party but not the other, chastising only one party's representative for conduct that both advocates engage in, and seemingly ignoring the testimony from one party's witnesses but not the other. One would hope that arbitrators would not engage in such misconduct, but what should a party do if it occurs?

In the first instance, a disadvantaged party should document the arbitral transgressions. What did the arbitrator do? A transcript will not record the tone of voice used. In the most extreme case, a party may seek a discontinuance of the hearing and raise the matter with

---

[6]*See* Dennis Nolan & Roger Abrams, *Arbitral Immunity*, 11 J. Lab. & Emp. L. 228 (1989); Charles S. Loughran, How to Prepare and Present a Labor Arbitration Case ch. 18 (2d ed. 2006) (discussion of challenging an award).

the appointing agency. The American Arbitration Association (AAA) and the Federal Mediation and Conciliation Service (FMCS) hear complaints from parties but will not interrupt a proceeding. Both appointing agencies have procedures that can be used to file a formal complaint against an arbitrator, but again that comes too late for a party in the midst of a hearing.

An advocate may ask the arbitrator for a conversation outside the hearing room with the opposing advocate present. The advocate can raise his or her concerns with the neutral at that time. That is, of course, a very risky thing to do. An arbitrator who feels wrongly accused may move securely into the other party's camp as a result of such an admonition. In any case, the hearing may already have become a travesty of due process and fairness, and there may be little to lose by making an arbitrator aware of what he or she is doing. It might even make the arbitrator avoid further partiality during the hearing.

2. **What can a party do if the arbitrator refuses to grant a postponement of a hearing or an extension of time in which to file a brief because of an untimely illness?**

It is not unusual that the press of business or the onslaught of illness may compel an advocate to seek a postponement of a hearing or a delay in the filing of a post-hearing brief. In the first instance, the advocate should contact opposing counsel with the request and an explanation. Opposing advocates are normally quite understanding, recognizing that they might need the same consideration if the circumstances arise. If the opposing advocate concurs, the parties should inform the AAA tribunal administrator in a case it administers or the arbitrator directly in a case where the neutral has been appointed through the FMCS. Some advocates, however, may see an opposing party's request for postponement of the hearing or delay in the filing of briefs as a ploy, one that a representative of the party might have played before. The AAA tribunal administrator will then contact the arbitrator with the party's request for a postponement or a delay, a request that the arbitrator normally grants.

There are times when one party contacts the arbitrator directly with the request, and arbitrators normally grant the request after making sure the opposing party has the opportunity to explain its position. However, sometimes arbitrators make mistakes, and they will deny a reasonable request. Perhaps the arbitrator senses that a party's request is not founded on facts. Perhaps the arbitrator sees the request as an effort to unduly delay the resolution of the matter.

When faced with an arbitrator's error that disadvantages the party he or she represents, an advocate does not have any good options. The advocate may request an opportunity to file a brief written motion on the matter, but in such an instance, the party must proceed—there is no interlocutory appeal.

3. What should a party do if the arbitrator engages in unprofessional practices?

There are very few full-time arbitrators who engage in unprofessional practices. One example would be scheduling two hearings in one day—one in the morning and the other (nearby) in the afternoon. The arbitrator hears the morning case and informs the parties he or she has heard enough evidence and then proceeds to the second hearing. Ultimately, the arbitrator will bill both sets of parties for the same day of hearing.

It is not likely that either set of parties will discover this double billing. In fact, they may be pleased with the time the arbitrator gave to hearing their cases. This misconduct by the arbitrator is outrageous, however, and if discovered should be reported to the relevant appointing agency. The misconduct flows in two directions: not giving either set of parties the full hearing process they paid for, and double billing for the same single day of hearing.

4. What types of problems should the parties be alert to regarding an arbitrator's bill?

An arbitrator will bill the parties for the time it took to prepare the decision. The arbitrator should keep records of that time and should share with the parties how a day's work will be calculated. (Many arbitrators will count six or seven hours of work as a day even if spread over a number of days.) The arbitrator will charge a full day for the hearing and a partial day if he or she must travel to attend the hearing the day before it is scheduled.

Problems may arise with regard to an arbitrator's charges to the parties for travel expenses. The arbitrator should maintain receipts for travel, hotel, and meals and present them to a party upon request after the bill is issued. The arbitrator has a responsibility to keep these expenses reasonable, and issues arise only rarely concerning the amounts charged.

An arbitrator may attempt to schedule two or more arbitrations in a city that requires travel from his or her hometown. In such an instance, the arbitrator must not double bill the party for the airfare but split it between the two or more arbitrations.

5. *How does an arbitrator make sure that he or she is paid?*

Although administering the arbitration process may be a privilege for the neutral, it is also a business. Full-time arbitrators who receive most of the arbitration appointments each year rely on the income from those appointments.

Sometimes parties do not pay the bills in a timely fashion. When this occurs, the appointing agencies will not effectively assist the arbitrator in obtaining payment. On very rare occasions, arbitrators might actually have to sue to obtain their fees. Some might think that the losing party would be more likely to delay paying the neutral, but that is not the case.

It is much more likely that the arbitrator's bill fell between the cracks and was simply not attended to. Many arbitrators will send reminders to the parties a few months after an opinion was issued requesting payment. Even then, arbitrators may have to wait a while to receive the amounts they are owed. When a case takes many days of hearing to complete, an arbitrator may issue interim bills covering days of hearing and travel expenses. Parties tend to pay these interim bills in a timely fashion.

Chapter 17

Employment Arbitration

I. Overview

For an employer, employment arbitration offers a private dispute resolution procedure that avoids the uncertainties, delays, and costs of court litigation. The employer can design its own arbitration system, potentially leaving employees at a significant disadvantage. Employment arbitration does offer nonunion employees an alternative to litigation as a method to protect their job rights. However, arbitration may be an alternative he or she would prefer not to pursue. Most employees would choose litigation of their statutory rights before a civil jury instead of a private arbitration procedure that might not adequately protect their statutory rights or fully compensate workers whose rights have been violated.

Unlike labor arbitration, the procedures and processes of employment arbitration in the nonunion setting generally are not the product of negotiation. Employers require their employees to pursue private employment arbitration in lieu of litigation as a condition of their employment, unilaterally inserting alternative dispute resolution (ADR) processes into contracts of employment. Some employees will sign those contracts without even reading the provision that mandates the procedures to be used for all disputes arising during their employment. Similarly, employers will include arbitration procedures in personnel manuals or employee handbooks. The growth in the use of employment arbitration has followed in the wake of the enactment of myriad federal and state laws that protect employees against discrimination based on race, color, religion, sex, national origin, age, and disability.[1] Court adjudication, with its inevitable appeals, delays the resolution

---

[1] *See* ABA Section of Labor and Employment Law, Employment Discrimination Law (Barbara T. Lindemann, Paul Grossmann, & C. Geoffrey Weirich, eds., 5th ed. 2012).

of these workplace disputes and presents an employer with the risk of large judgments awarded by lay juries. Arbitration has proven a viable alternative for management.

There is no question that private employment arbitration has achieved an important place in the nonunionized work setting. Over the past two decades, the U.S. Supreme Court has repeatedly ruled in support of private ADR of employment disputes outside of the unionized sector.[2] Most texts on employment arbitration focus on these Supreme Court cases and other lower court rulings, and some of the available texts on employment arbitration are quite good.[3] Because the employment arbitrator is not a party to these court proceedings involving the initiation of employment arbitration or the ultimate review of an employment arbitrator's decision, those issues raised in these cases are mentioned here only in passing.

Courts have generally ruled that the Federal Arbitration Act (FAA) applies to cases involving individual employment arbitration outside the unionized setting,[4] but courts have held that the FAA does not apply to labor arbitration under collective bargaining agreements (CBAs).[5] The FAA does not offer a comprehensive set of rules that can be applied to employment arbitration, but it does provide guidance on a number of issues, such as discovery, an important component in employment arbitration because, in the absence of a grievance procedure, an advocate for an employee will need a process to obtain documents for a hearing on his or her claim.[6]

The disparity in resources between an employer and an employee is a fundamental flaw of nonunion employment arbitration. Whereas labor unions may not be financially flush, a single employee with a claim of discriminatory treatment has even fewer resources at hand. Private attorneys will take statutory-based cases to court on a contingency fee basis, but the outcomes in employment arbitration are less certain. The

---

[2] *See, e.g.,* Circuit City Stores, Inc. v. Adams, 532 U.S. 105 (2001); Gilmer v. Interstate/Johnson Lane Corp., 500 U.S. 20 (1991).

[3] *See* PAUL E. STARKMAN, GAIL GOLMAN HOLTZMAN, & DONALD J. SPERO, EMPLOYMENT ARBITRATION: LAW AND PRACTICE ch. 6 (2012); THOMAS E. CARBONNEAU, EMPLOYMENT ARBITRATION (2d ed. 2006); DENNIS R. NOLAN, LABOR AND EMPLOYMENT ARBITRATION pt. II (2d ed. 2002); ABA SECTION OF LABOR AND EMPLOYMENT LAW, HOW ADR WORKS (Norman Brand, ed., 2002); FAIRWEATHER'S PRACTICE AND PROCEDURE IN LABOR ARBITRATION ch. 21 (Ray J. Schoonhoven, ed., 4th ed.1999).

[4] Federal Arbitration Act, 9 U.S.C. §1 *et seq.* Congress stated that the purpose of the statute was to "reduce the longstanding judicial hostility to arbitration agreements that had existed at English common law and had been adopted by the American courts."

[5] *See, e.g.* United Food Workers Local 7R v. Safeway Stores, Inc., 889 F.2d 940, 943–44 (10th Cir. 1989).

[6] 9 U.S.C. §7.

absence of a jury in arbitration may limit monetary recoveries. Unless the employer covers the cost of the employment arbitrator, there may also be costs in employment arbitration—such as paying a share of the arbitrator's fee—that private attorneys taking the case on a contingency fee basis may be unwilling to forward on behalf of a claimant employee.

Labor and employment arbitration serve very different purposes. As emphasized in previous chapters, labor arbitration is a continuation of the collective bargaining process, with the arbitrator serving as the alter ego of the parties, guided by their intent as evidenced in their agreement. By comparison, employment arbitration is a substitute for the judicial process, as a less formal and more expeditious system of adjudication of public rights. The employment arbitrator represents the law and carries out the intent of the framers of the statutory provisions.[7]

Prior to the arbitration hearing, there are substantial differences between labor and employment arbitration. However, the processes of labor and employment arbitration are very similar once the disputants arrive at a hearing. Although it is the goal of both labor and employment arbitration processes to resolve disputes that arise in the workplace, arbitration under a CBA has a much longer history and serves additional purposes, such as easing tensions in the workplace. Employment arbitration serves as a private court and, as such, mirrors many aspects of the judicial context. If it provides a cathartic experience for the disputants, that aspect is only incidental.

II. AT-WILL EMPLOYMENT AND ALTERNATIVE DISPUTE RESOLUTION

Employees who form a union that negotiates a CBA on their behalf normally are protected against arbitrary attacks on their job status by a "just cause" provision. The basic rule of nonunionized employment, however, is that workers serve at the pleasure of their employers. This default legal relationship is termed *at-will employment*. Traditionally, management could discharge an employee for a good reason, a bad reason, or no reason at all.

The status of at-will employment has been substantially changed, however, as a result of federal and state statutes that prohibit discrimination in a variety of situations. State courts have also recognized exceptions to the at-will doctrine for employment-related actions that are

---

[7]William B. Gould IV, *Kissing Cousins?: The Federal Arbitration Act and Modern Labor Arbitration*, 55 EMORY L.J. 609 (2006).

contrary to public policy. They have also found employee rights based on the contents of management handbooks that set forth company policy.[8]

1.   Why would a nonunionized employer unilaterally establish a private arbitration system?

Employers understand that nonunionized employees may have rights under federal or state statutory law. Litigation based on statutes can be time-consuming, expensive, and ultimately may result in significant jury awards. By comparison, employment arbitration is much quicker, does not involve a jury, and can be kept private, thus protecting the reputation of the business.

In 1991, in *Gilmer v. Interstate/Johnson Lane Corp.,*[9] the U.S. Supreme Court enforced an arbitration provision in an employment contract entered into between a broker and Interstate/Johnson Lane, Inc., a brokerage firm that dealt in securities and futures for individual and institutional investors. After he was terminated, the securities executive sued his employer for age discrimination under the federal Age Discrimination in Employment Act.[10] Relying on the provisions of the FAA, the Supreme Court enforced Gilmer's promise to arbitrate claims. Thus armed with the *Gilmer* ruling, a nonunionized employer could keep statutory cases out of court and within a process it designs. After *Gilmer*, the use of employment arbitration exploded.[11]

Management-side practitioners believe that employment arbitration offers employers protection against "runaway" jury verdicts. Lawyers who normally represent employees in discrimination cases rail against employment arbitration as biased against the rights of workers and unlikely to respect their statutory claims. There is only one comprehensive study to date of this aspect of employment arbitration, and it examined cases that were heard before the widespread adoption of employment arbitration.[12] It concluded that employees were more likely to

---

[8]Similar issues are involved regarding the enforcement of executive employment agreements in arbitration. These are more likely individually negotiated employment agreements with carefully tailored alternative resolution procedures. In general, the enforcement and operation of executive employment arbitration processes lie beyond the scope of this chapter.

[9]500 U.S. 20 (1991).

[10]29 U.S.C. §621 *et seq.*

[11]Within a decade, the U.S. Court of Appeals for the Seventh Circuit could state that employment arbitration had "become a common tool in resolving employment disputes." Penn v. Ryan's Family Steak Houses, Inc., 269 F.3d 753, 758 (7th Cir. 2001).

[12]Lewis Maltby, *Private Justice: Employment Arbitration and Civil Rights*, 30 COLUM. HUM. RTS. L. REV. 29 (1998).

prevail at employment arbitration than in court, but the amount of recovery was lower in arbitration than in court.[13] Grants of summary judgment to employers in employment arbitration cases were, however, very rare.[14]

2. What should an employer include in its design of a private arbitration system?

Courts will force an employee to pursue his or her claim against an employer through employment arbitration only if it first determines that the ADR system meets the test of basic fairness.[15] At the core of any such process is an impartial adjudicator.[16] If an employer dominates the arbitrator selection process, courts are not likely to force employees to arbitrate.[17] There are organizations available to assist in administering employment arbitration in a manner that will meet the courts' standards.[18] The AAA is the preeminent organization involved in the administration of employment arbitration procedures. It maintains a roster of employment arbitrators and has promulgated a set of rules for the conduct of employment arbitration cases.[19] Judicial Arbitration and Mediation Services (JAMS) directly provides employment arbitration services from its offices nationwide.[20] These are the two main providers of ADR services in the nonunion employment context, although there are other organizations as well.[21]

---

[13] Lewis Maltby, *The Myth of Second-Class Justice: Resolving Employment Disputes in Arbitration,* in ABA Section of Labor and Employment Law, How ADR Works 915 (Norman Brand, ed., 2002).

[14] *Id.* at 919–21.

[15] For example, in *Hooters of America, Inc. v. Phillips*, 173 F.3d 933 (4th Cir. 1999), the court refused to compel employment arbitration when the procedure was "so one-sided." *Id.* at 938.

[16] Roger I. Abrams, *The Nature of the Arbitral Process: Substantive Decision-making in Labor Arbitration*, 14 U.C. Davis L. Rev. 551 (1981).

[17] *See, e.g.,* Floss v. Ryan's Family Steak Houses, Inc., 211 F.3d 306, 314 (6th Cir. 2000) ("the neutrality of the forum is far from clear").

[18] Paul E. Starkman, Gail Golman Holtzman, & Donald J. Spero, Employment Arbitration: Law and Practice ch. 3 (2012) (lists factors to be considered when drafting employment arbitration provisions).

[19] American Arbitration Association, Employment Arbitration Rules and Mediation Procedures (amended and effective Nov. 1, 2009), *available at* http://www.adr.org/aaa/faces/rules/searchrules/rulesdetail?doc=ADRSTG_004366&_afrLoop=605675250943569&_afrWindowMode=0&_afrWindowId=null#%40%3F_afrWindowId%3Dnull%26_afrLoop%3D605675250943569%26doc%3DADRSTG_004366%26_afrWindowMode%3D0%26_adf.ctrl-state%3Ddbypk5yrf_79 (reproduced in Appendix E) [hereinafter AAA Employment Arbitration Rules].

[20] Further information about JAMS can be obtained at www.jamsadr.com.

[21] Starkman, Holtzman, & Spero, *supra* note 18, at ch. 6.

3.   *Must an employment arbitration system involve an appointing agency like the American Arbitration Association?*

An employer is not required by any law to provide for the use of an appointing agency in operating its employment arbitration procedure, and it is difficult to estimate what percentage of procedures use an outside organization to administer the private process. The employer decides whether an appointing agency will be involved. The agency, such as the AAA, can provide the resources needed to operate the system, and its inclusion in the procedure facilitates its use.

4.   *Does employment arbitration always involve a single impartial arbitrator?*

The default arrangement in employment arbitration is adjudication by a single impartial arbitrator.[22] At times, an employment arbitration procedure will provide for the appointment of a tripartite panel of arbitrators. Normally, each party would select one partisan arbitrator, and the parties would then select the neutral arbitrator who will actually decide the dispute, as is the case under tripartite labor arbitration procedures. Alternately, the procedure might call for the appointment of three impartial arbitrators, although that option does increase the costs to the parties. Under the AAA Rules, a decision and award by a tripartite panel must be made by a majority of the appointed arbitrators, unless the arbitration agreement expressly requires a unanimous decision.[23]

III. Initiating Employment Arbitration

The procedures followed for initiating employment arbitration depend on the terms of the arbitration system that the employer designs. The difficulties that courts have had in enforcing unilateral employment systems can be assuaged if management makes sure that the system is fair and adequately protects the rights of employees. This includes the right to participate meaningfully in the selection of the employment arbitrator.

---

[22] AAA Employment Arbitration Rules, *supra* note 19, at Rule 12(a) ("If the arbitration agreement does not specify the number of arbitrators or the parties do not agree otherwise, the dispute shall be heard and determined by one arbitrator."); Federal Arbitration Act, 9 U.S.C. §5 ("unless otherwise provided in the agreement the arbitration shall be by a single arbitrator").

[23] AAA Employment Arbitration Rules, *supra* note 19, at Rule 26.

1.   How does an employment arbitration normally begin?

Under the AAA Rules, the parties may submit a joint request for arbitration, or the initiating party (called the *claimant*) may file a document called a *demand* with an AAA office. The claimant must provide a copy of the demand to the opposing party (the *respondent*)[24] and must pay a filing fee to the AAA.[25] The demand is not a formal pleading subject to technical judicial pleading requirements, but it is far more court-like than a simple grievance form filed under a CBA. This document must include, among other things, a "brief statement of the nature of the dispute" and "the amount in controversy," as well as "the remedy sought."[26]

The respondent is allowed to file a brief answer to the demand within 15 days, but its failure to do so will not delay the proceeding. The respondent will be deemed to have denied the claim.[27] The respondent can also file a counterclaim within the same period.[28]

Even before the selection of the employment arbitrator, the AAA or either of the parties may request that an administrative conference be scheduled "to organize and expedite the arbitration, explore its administrative aspects, establish the most efficient means of selecting an arbitrator and consider mediation as a dispute-resolution option."[29]

IV. Selecting an Employment Arbitrator

The appointment of an employment arbitrator generally follows a procedure similar to that used in labor arbitration—the employer and the employee select their neutral from a list supplied by an appointing agency. Yet there are significant differences between the labor and employment arbitration processes that will have a substantial impact on the selection process.

1.   Who are these employment arbitrators?

Almost all employment arbitrators are attorneys, and many are retired judges. Many employment arbitrators also serve as labor arbitrators under the terms of CBAs. The skill sets of labor and employment arbitrators substantially overlap, especially if they have had experience

---

[24] *Id.* at Rule 4(b)(i)(2).
[25] *Id.* at Rule 4(b)(i)(3).
[26] *Id.* at Rule 4(b)(i)(1).
[27] *Id.* at Rule 4(b)(ii).
[28] *Id.* at Rule 4(b)(iii).
[29] *Id.* at Rule 7.

hearing federal and state public sector labor arbitrations involving statutory provisions. An employment arbitrator must be able to understand and apply federal and state statutory law, which is often involved in employment arbitration cases.

The AAA maintains a roster of employment arbitrators. Although labor arbitrators are expected to be neutral and thus are generally not allowed to practice labor law for management and unions when not arbitrating, many employment arbitrators on the AAA panel are practicing employment lawyers who represent employers or employees in other proceedings. This could raise substantial concerns about their impartiality.

2. How is an employment arbitrator selected under the American Arbitration Association Rules?

The parties to an employment dispute will follow the provisions of the arbitration procedure contained in the employment contract or the management handbook in selecting an arbitrator. If the arbitration agreement is silent on the issue and the matter is brought to the AAA, the AAA will supply the parties with a list of names on the AAA's Employment Dispute Resolution Roster. It is possible that the parties will be able to select one of those arbitrators to hear their dispute.

It is more likely that the parties will have to resort to the selection procedure that the AAA follows with regard to appointing a labor arbitrator—that is, within 15 days each party strikes the names of persons who are unacceptable and ranks the remaining names. The AAA then appoints the highest-ranking, mutually acceptable arbitrator to serve.

Much of the discussion in Chapter 2 regarding the selection of a labor arbitrator is applicable to the selection of an employment arbitrator. There is the same absence of adequate information in selecting an employment arbitrator as there is in selecting a labor arbitrator. At least among labor arbitrators there are some indicators that signal a person's acceptability, such as election to membership in the National Academy of Arbitrators (NAA). Now that the NAA has decided to invite employment arbitrators to apply for election, that deficiency might be assuaged over time. Many employment arbitrators are former judges, and thus there may be information available about how they conducted their court proceedings and ruled in employment cases when serving on the bench.

3. Are there alternative ways to select an employment arbitrator?

The parties can select any person to serve as their employment arbitrator, although there are risks in selecting a person who does not have experience in running a hearing and resolving disputes based on complex statutory references. The employer may insist on the selection of an arbitrator who has served in previous disputes involving that employer and other employees. The employee and his or her advocate must make sure that the person selected is impartial. Prior service for that employer does not seem to be a useful credential in that regard.

4. *Must an employment arbitrator make disclosures of circumstances that might give rise to doubt as to his or her impartiality?*

As discussed in Chapter 2, labor arbitrators must disclose to the parties any circumstances that might give rise to an impression of possible bias. The same is true of employment arbitrators. The employment arbitrator must disclose any financial or personal interests in the matter in dispute, as well as previous or present relationships with either of the parties.

California has enacted a statute that requires a far broader range of disclosures by an employment arbitrator. California employment arbitrators (but not labor arbitrators hearing cases under CBAs) must disclose whether they have served as a neutral arbitrator in another prior (or pending) non–collective bargaining case involving either party to the current arbitration, whether they have served as a lawyer for either party, or whether their law firm has represented either party. The employment arbitrator must disclose the results of these prior cases, including dates of arbitration awards; identification of the prevailing parties; the amount of monetary damages awarded, if any; and the names of the parties' attorneys. In addition, the employment arbitrator must disclose all employment arbitrations over which he or she has presided within the previous five years, including the results, the names of the prevailing parties, the names of the attorneys, and the amounts awarded.[30] Failure to meet these rigorous standards will lead to the vacating of any resulting award at the behest of the party that does not prevail in arbitration. This standard for disclosing personal interests with a party or an advocate involved in a proceeding is even broader than that applied to presiding judges: the employment arbitrator must disclose information where "a person aware of the facts might reasonably entertain a doubt that the proposed neutral arbitrator would be able to be impartial."[31]

---

[30] CAL. CIV. PROC. CODE §1281.9 *et seq.*
[31] *Id.* §1281.9(a).

V. The Due Process Protocol

As the use of employment arbitration grew in the 1990s, many of those involved in the process raised concerns about the integrity of the process and recognized the need to regulate the procedure to ensure that it served its intended purposes. The main concern was to promote ethical behavior by employment arbitrators and to protect procedural fairness in the arbitration processes they operated. The result of their efforts was called the *Due Process Protocol.*

1. What is the Due Process Protocol?

In 1995, a task force representing all stakeholders involved in the employment arbitration process issued the Due Process Protocol for Mediation and Arbitration of Statutory Disputes Arising out of the Employment Relationship.[32] It remains the bedrock on which employment arbitration has flourished as an alternate means of resolving employment disputes. The task force's goal was to provide "due process" in the resolution of employment disputes. Recognizing that there were risks to the fairness of any procedure created and administered unilaterally by management, the Due Process Protocol enunciated the principles that should guide the creation and implementation of employment arbitration.

The Protocol requires that only qualified employment arbitrators serve as neutrals. Although knowledge about statutory law is essential, it is equally important that persons serving as employment arbitrators know how to conduct a hearing and appreciate the distinctive nature of the workplace environment.

2. What procedural elements should management include in an arbitration system in order to comply with the Due Process Protocol?

In a nonunionized setting, an employment arbitrator operates under a procedure designed by the employer. Although an employer may be inclined to stack the deck in its favor, the procedure must ensure the fundamental fairness of the process, or courts will not compel an employee to bring his or her statutory claim to arbitration. In the first

---

[32] Task Force on Alternative Dispute Resolution in Employment, A Due Process Protocol for Mediation and Arbitration of Statutory Disputes Arising Out of the Employment Relationship (effective June 1995), *available at* http://www.ilr.cornell.edu/alliance/resources/Guide/Due_process_protocol_empdispute.html [hereinafter Due Process Protocol]. The Due Process Protocol is reproduced in Appendix F.

instance, employees should have the right to be represented within the employment arbitration process.[33] The Protocol does not require the employer to reimburse an employee for the total expense of hiring an advocate, but it does recommend that "at least a portion of the employee's attorney fees, especially for lower paid employees," should be covered by the employer.[34]

The Protocol focuses on the adequacy of the means available to an employee within the employment arbitration process to prepare and present his or her case. It insists, for example, that the employee and his or her advocate have access to all "information reasonably relevant to . . . arbitration of their claims."[35] The employee should have the right to conduct prehearing depositions. The Protocol does not suggest in any detail how the employee would cover the costs of such necessary discovery procedures.

3. How is the selection of arbitrators and their training affected by the Due Process Protocol?

The Due Process Protocol recommends that employment arbitrators be skilled, knowledgeable, and impartial.[36] Labor arbitrators without the relevant experience would have to be trained in the "statutory environment . . . and the characteristics of the non-union workplace" in order to serve as employment arbitrators.[37] This training should be ongoing to keep the neutrals up to date on statutory changes and court rulings.

The Protocol addresses the problem of informational asymmetry in arbitrator selection. It is likely that the employer will have greater knowledge concerning potential employment arbitrators than will employees. Therefore, the Protocol suggests that appointing agencies provide each party with the names, addresses, and phone numbers of the advocates who represented parties before each of the arbitrators whose names are offered for the case at hand.[38] An alternate striking method as has been used in selecting labor arbitrators would be used, but the Protocol does not speak to which party should strike first.

The Protocol emphasizes the importance of disclosure as the core strategy to avoid unfairness or bias in the arbitrator selection process.

---

[33] DUE PROCESS PROTOCOL *supra* note 32, at §B(1).

[34] *Id.* §B(2).

[35] *Id.* §B(3).

[36] *Id.* §C(1).

[37] *Id.*

[38] DUE PROCESS PROTOCOL, *supra* note 32, at §B(3).

An employment arbitrator must disclose "any relationship which might reasonably constitute or be perceived as a conflict of interest."[39]

4. Does the Due Process Protocol address the requirement that the employee bear a significant portion of the costs of employment arbitration, a seemingly major impediment to an employee's pursuit of a claim in arbitration?

The Protocol posits that "impartiality is best assured by the parties sharing the fees and expenses of the . . . arbitrator."[40] How this can be accomplished is not explained in the Protocol. Litigation based on statutory rights is made possible by the contingency fee system. Attorneys will fund the litigation in exchange for a percentage of the plaintiff's recovery, if any. The Protocol does not address whether contingency fees might make attorney representation possible in employment arbitration, but that would have to be the only way an employee could proceed with an experienced advocate serving as his or her representative.

The Protocol does suggest that "the parties should make mutually acceptable arrangements" when the employee is not capable of paying an equal share of the cost of hiring the employment arbitrator.[41] If such an arrangement is not made, "the arbitrator should determine the allocation of fees,"[42] but the Protocol does not advise the employment arbitrator as to how this allocation should be made.

5. Can an employer-created arbitration process limit the damages an employee can obtain through arbitration?

The Due Process Protocol states that an employment arbitrator should be "empowered to award whatever relief would be available in court under the law."[43] Because the Protocol is only advisory, however, management is not bound by its terms in designing its arbitration system. Similarly, the AAA Rules provide that an arbitrator "may grant any remedy or relief that would have been available to the parties had the matter been heard in court."[44] Thus, if the employment arbitration procedure calls for the use of the AAA as the appointing agency, the remedial powers of the employment arbitrator cannot be limited.

---

[39] *Id.* §C(4).

[40] *Id.* §C(6).

[41] *Id.*

[42] *Id.*

[43] Due Process Protocol, *supra* note 32, at §C(5).

[44] AAA Employment Arbitration Rules, *supra* note 19, at Rule 39(d).

VI. PREHEARING PRACTICE AND DISCOVERY

Because employment arbitration tends to be more legalistic than labor arbitration, it is not surprising to find more formality in the prehearing stage. Parties will file motions with the arbitrator (and sometimes with a court) to seek documents or quash subpoenas.[45] Under the AAA Rules, an employment arbitrator may even allow a party to file a "dispositive motion" if he or she determines that the movant "has shown substantial cause that the motion is likely to succeed and dispose of or narrow the issues in the case."[46] Thus, an employment arbitration may be resolved by what is, in effect, summary judgment, something that would never happen in a labor arbitration under a CBA.

1.   Can a party communicate directly with the employment arbitrator?

Much as it does in administering a labor arbitration, the AAA insulates an employment arbitrator from any contact with the parties other than at the Arbitration Management Conference and at the arbitration hearing. In a case not administered by the AAA, *ex parte* communication with the selected arbitrator, except regarding ministerial matters such as the location and time of the hearing, should be prohibited.

2.   Can a party obtain prehearing discovery in an employment arbitration?

The tools of discovery are widely available in employment arbitration. In labor arbitration there is almost no prehearing discovery through depositions and interrogatories because the parties are likely to have exchanged information and enunciated their positions in the grievance procedure. There is no grievance procedure in nonunion employment arbitration, and thus various methods of discovery are employed. Under the AAA Rules, upon the request of a party, an employment arbitrator may order discovery through taking depositions, responding to interrogatories and requests for admissions, and producing requested documents.[47] An employment arbitrator's willingness to order

---

[45] *See* PAUL E. STARKMAN, GAIL GOLMAN HOLTZMAN, & DONALD J. SPERO, EMPLOYMENT ARBITRATION: LAW AND PRACTICE §6:3 (2012) (motion practice in employment arbitration).

[46] AAA EMPLOYMENT ARBITRATION RULES, *supra* note 19, at Rule 27.

[47] *Id.* at Rule 9.

such discovery depends on the circumstances of the particular case and whether the discovery is necessary or simply cumulative.

It is quite common for the arbitrator to allow the employer's advocate to depose the claimant, much as would happen in a court adjudication.[48] This would be unheard of in labor arbitration—it would be seen as a way for management to intimidate a grievant before the arbitration hearing.

3. Does an employment arbitrator entertain motions prior to the hearing limiting the introduction of evidence and the like?

As a substitute for court adjudication based on statutory provisions, employment arbitration has taken on many of the trappings of court practice. Parties might file motions prior to the hearing, seeking to exclude the consideration of certain evidence it knows the opposing party will present at the hearing. Parties could even file "dispositive" motions for summary judgment. Employment arbitrators might even require the parties to submit their documentary evidence prior to the hearing and provide those documents to the opposing party.[49]

VII. The Prehearing Arbitration Management Conference

Over the decades, parties to CBAs containing a labor arbitration process have developed a well-understood set of procedures for resolving their disputes. Once an arbitrator has been selected either through the assistance of an appointing agency or by the parties themselves, the case proceeds to hearing. By comparison, in employment arbitration, where it is quite likely that neither the employer nor the employee has had previous experience with the process, it is essential that ground rules be established before the case proceeds. This is accomplished under the AAA Rules through use of a mandatory arbitration management conference before arbitration commences.

1. How does the arbitration management conference facilitate employment arbitration?

Under the AAA Rules, the parties to an employment arbitration and the arbitrator must hold an *arbitration management conference*

---

[48] *See* Robert Weil, *Employment Arbitration: A Retired Judge's View,* in ABA Section of Labor and Employment Law, How ADR Works 463 (Norman Brand, ed., 2002).
[49] *Id.*

within 60 days of the arbitrator's selection. At this conference, which can be conducted via telephone, the parties discuss with the employment arbitrator how the arbitration will proceed. During the conference, the following matters might be considered:

1. the issues to be arbitrated;
2. the date, time, place, and estimated duration of the hearing;
3. the resolution of outstanding discovery issues and establishment of discovery parameters;
4. the law, standards, rules of evidence, and burdens of proof applicable to the proceeding;
5. the exchange of stipulations and declarations regarding facts, exhibits, witnesses, and other issues;
6. the names of witnesses (including expert witnesses), the scope of each witness' testimony, and witness exclusion;
7. the value of bifurcating the arbitration into a liability phase and a damages phase;
8. the need for a stenographic record;
9. whether the parties will summarize their arguments orally or in writing;
10. the form of the award;
11. any other issues relating to the subject or conduct of the arbitration;
12. the allocation of attorneys' fees and costs;
13. the specification of undisclosed claims;
14. the extent to which documentary evidence may be submitted at the hearing;
15. the extent to which testimony may be admitted at the hearing via telephone, over the Internet, by written or videotaped deposition, by affidavit, or by any other means; and
16. any disputes over the AAA's determination regarding whether the dispute arose from an individually negotiated employment agreement or contract, or from an employer-promulgated plan.[50]

The AAA will send the parties a *case management order*, which indicates the agreements they have reached during the arbitration management conference. Advocates who are accustomed to court litigation will find the arbitration management conference quite familiar. Judges normally use pretrial conferences to clarify issues to be tried. By comparison, those advocates and arbitrators schooled in labor arbitration

---

[50] AAA EMPLOYMENT ARBITRATION RULES, *supra* note 19, at Rule 8.

may find the arbitration management conference superfluous.[51] As a practical matter, the management conference allows the advocates for the parties to size up their arbitrator and adequately prepare for the hearing. Thus, it might be preferable for the session to be held in person rather than by telephone. The arbitrator will set the ground rules for prehearing discovery and determine the dates by which prehearing matters must be concluded. The purpose of the management conference is to avoid surprises at the arbitration hearing.

2.   Do employment arbitrators require the parties to file prehearing briefs?

Some employment arbitrators require the advocates for the parties to file a brief that sets forth the party's position and specify what remedy it seeks in the arbitration.[52] The submission requires the employee to explain the basis for his or her claim. The employment arbitrator may also ask the parties to submit a stipulation of uncontested facts by a certain date prior to the hearing.[53]

VIII. The Employment Arbitration Hearing

Prior to the employment arbitration hearing, each party normally will submit to the arbitrator and the opposing party a list of the witnesses it intends to call, along with a brief recitation of the subject matter of their expected testimony. Unlike at a typical labor arbitration hearing, it is not unusual in an employment arbitration case for parties to present some evidence in the form of affidavits.

1.   How are employment arbitration hearings, labor arbitration hearings, and court proceedings different from each other?

Employment arbitration normally involves parties who no longer have an employer-employee relationship and are quite unlikely to enjoy such a relationship in the future. In this regard, an employment arbitration hearing mirrors a court proceeding. By comparison, a labor arbitration under the terms of a CBA involves parties who have an ongoing relationship. The way the labor arbitration hearing is conducted can

---

[51] JAMS has its own set of rules for employment arbitration that basically parallel those of the AAA. *See* http://www.jamsadr.com/rules-employment-arbitration/.

[52] *See* Weil, *supra* note 48.

[53] *Id.*

have spillover effects on morale and productivity in the workplace and the parties' continuing relationship.[54]

An employment arbitration hearing is more like a court proceeding than a labor arbitration hearing. The parties are more likely to be represented by litigators rather than labor lawyers. There is a formality to the employment arbitration proceeding that would be out of place in a labor arbitration. For example, a stenographic record is much more common in employment arbitration. Also, many employment arbitrators see themselves as "judges" in the arbitral forum.[55] On the other hand, in some ways, an employment arbitration hearing is more informal than a judicial proceeding. It is held at a hotel or office conference room, not in a courthouse; the employment arbitrator wears business attire, not a robe; and the proceeding is private, not open to the public. In fact, the employment arbitrator is required under the AAA Rules to "maintain the confidentiality of the arbitration."[56]

It is possible that an employment arbitration hearing will be conducted in accordance with the rules of evidence, a practice that is unheard of in labor arbitration and not required by the AAA Rules.[57] The arbitrator, or the chairperson of a three-person panel, will likely commence the hearing with a review of the procedures that will be followed. The AAA Rules require the employment arbitrator to record the date, time, and place of the hearing; the names of the parties and their advocates; and the demand for arbitration and the answer.[58] Parties will present opening and closing statements and offer documents and testimonial evidence. As in a labor arbitration, the arbitrator may ask questions.

The employment arbitrator must be prepared to rein in the excesses of the advocates, something judges have learned to do through experience. Scorched-earth tactics that would be out of bounds in a labor arbitration may be the prevailing scenario in some employment cases.

At the close of the hearing, the employment arbitrator is required under the AAA Rules to "specifically inquire of all parties whether they have any further proofs to offer or witnesses to be heard."[59] The

---

[54] *See* Janet Maleson Spencer, *How Arbitrators Run a Hearing: An Arbitrator's View*, in ABA SECTION OF LABOR AND EMPLOYMENT LAW, HOW ADR WORKS 611 (Norman Brand, ed., 2002). .

[55] *See* Alfred G. Feliu, *How Arbitrators Decide Cases: An Arbitrator's View*, in ABA SECTION OF LABOR AND EMPLOYMENT LAW, HOW ADR WORKS 527 (Norman Brand, ed., 2002) (an employment arbitrator is a "surrogate judge").

[56] AAA EMPLOYMENT ARBITRATION RULES, *supra* note 19, at Rule 23.

[57] *Id.* at Rule 24.

[58] *Id.* at Rule 28.

[59] *Id.* at Rule 33.

arbitrator will then formally declare the hearing closed, unless the parties seek to file briefs. If briefs are filed, the hearing is closed when the briefs are received.

2.   What challenges does the arbitrator face in an employment arbitration that might not be present in a labor arbitration?

At an employment arbitration hearing, the arbitrator must obtain the information he or she needs to resolve the dispute. However, the employee may be at a significant disadvantage in an employment arbitration because of the lack of financial resources. He or she might not even be able to afford an attorney or find an advocate willing to take the case on a contingency fee basis. Thus, the employment arbitrator must determine whether he or she will ask a witness questions that might make out the employee's case and, in turn, supply the arbitrator with the information he or she needs to accurately resolve the dispute.

3.   Is an employment arbitration more formal than a labor arbitration?

There is a distinct possibility that the advocates who represent the employer and the employee (if he or she has hired an advocate) may not be familiar with the customs and practices of employment arbitration, but have more experience in court adjudication. Therefore, the advocates would expect the hearing to be court-like in nature, which may include applying the rules of evidence to limit the admissibility of evidence. In any case, an employment arbitrator should be prepared to field objections to the admissibility of evidence based on hearsay or lack of relevance.

However, there is a possibility that, as a result of the costs involved, the employee would not be represented at the hearing, which would lend itself to a more informal hearing. The employee would not likely be schooled in cross-examination, for example. The employee would simply tell his or her story, with the employment arbitrator asking questions to obtain the information needed to resolve the employment dispute.

4.   Which party bears the burden of proof in an employment arbitration case?

Because employment arbitration is an alternative to court adjudication, the burdens of proof in employment arbitration mirror those that would apply in court adjudication. For example, the discharged employee would bear the burden of proving discrimination, as he or she would in court. This turns the normal practice in labor arbitration on its head. In a labor arbitration involving the discipline or discharge of an employee, management bears the burden of proof.

IX. THE AWARD

Under the AAA Rules, the employment arbitrator must issue the award "promptly" and "no later than 30 days from the close of the hearing."[60] The arbitrator is expressly allowed to award any relief that would be available in a court proceeding, including attorneys' fees and costs.[61] The arbitrator's award is final and binding. The AAA Rules provide for the agency to collect the arbitrator's fee in advance of the hearing and pay that amount to the employment arbitrator, a practice the AAA does not follow with regard to labor arbitrators' fees.[62]

1.   *How does an employment arbitrator decide a case?*

Theoretically, employment arbitrators will decide statutory cases the same way a court would resolve the same type of dispute. That must be the goal of any such proceeding. Although quicker and more efficient than litigation, arbitration of claims of employment discrimination, for example, should not be decided any differently simply because the adjudicator is an employment arbitrator and not a judge.[63]

This means, of course, that the broad range of skills and abilities that Supreme Court Justice William O. Douglas said a labor arbitrator brings to the resolution of a labor dispute are not applicable in employment arbitration.[64] The law of the shop[65] and the therapeutic effects of arbitration[66] are irrelevant in employment arbitration. The employment

---

[60] *Id.* at Rule 39(a).

[61] AAA EMPLOYMENT ARBITRATION RULES, *supra* note 19, at Rule 39(d).

[62] *Id.* at Rules 44 and 46.

[63] Alfred G. Feliu, *How Arbitrators Decide Cases: An Arbitrator's View,* in ABA SECTION OF LABOR AND EMPLOYMENT LAW, HOW ADR WORKS 527 (Norman Brand, ed., 2002).

[64] *See* Steelworkers v. American Mfg. Co., 363 U.S. 564 (1960); Steelworkers v. Warrior & Gulf Navig. Co., 363 U.S. 574 (1960); Steelworkers v. Enterprise Wheel & Car Corp., 363 U.S. 593 (1960). See the discussion of Justice Douglas' *Steelworkers Trilogy* analysis in Chapter 1, §V. The *Steelworkers Trilogy* decisions are reproduced in Appendix A.

[65] Steelworkers v. American Mfg. Co., 363 U.S. 564 (1960); Steelworkers v. Warrior & Gulf Navig. Co., 363 U.S. 574, 582 (1960); Steelworkers v. Warrior & Gulf Navig. Co., 363 U.S. 574, 579 (1960).

[66] *American Manufacturing,* 363 U.S. at 568.

arbitrator might disagree with how the courts have interpreted a statute, but that is irrelevant. The parties want a judicial reading by a nonjudge, and they should get it.

This does not mean that an employment arbitrator does not consider fairness and due process in conducting the proceeding. It is essential that both parties feel they have had a full opportunity to present their cases. The adjudicator, however, cannot vary from or modify the law as set externally. The employment arbitrator does not make public policy; he or she simply administers it in a private forum.

2. Does the employment arbitrator always issue an opinion?

At the arbitration management conference held before the hearing, the parties to the proceeding can discuss the form of the award they seek from their employment arbitrator. Many employment arbitrators in the past simply announced the outcome of the case without an opinion. With the growth of employment arbitration, however, parties are more likely to seek what is referred to as a *reasoned opinion* that explains how the arbitrator reached his or her judgment. A reasoned opinion supports the legitimacy of the employment arbitration process, increasing the likelihood that the result will not be contested in court.

X. Judicial Review

As is the case with labor arbitration awards, the decisions of the employment neutral (or a majority of a tripartite panel) are subject to very limited judicial review. Employment arbitrators are not involved in any post-arbitration court proceedings.[67] Thus, courts will defer to the results reached in both labor and employment arbitration. With regard to employment arbitration, the grounds for review are set forth in the FAA.

1. What are the grounds for vacating an employment arbitration award?

Under the provisions of the FAA, a court may vacate an arbitrator's award only in very limited circumstances:

---

[67] Once having issued his or her award, an employment arbitrator's authority is terminated. He or she is considered *functus officio:* he or she has served as the neutral, and the appointment has expired.

1. where the award was procured by corruption, fraud, or undue means;
2. where there was evident partiality or corruption in the arbitrators, or either of them;
3. where the arbitrators were guilty of misconduct in refusing to postpone the hearing, upon sufficient cause shown, or in refusing to hear evidence pertinent and material to the controversy; or of any other misbehavior by which the rights of any party have been prejudiced; or
4. where the arbitrators exceeded their powers, or so imperfectly executed them that a mutual, final, and definite award upon the subject matter submitted was not made.[68]

2. *What should a court do when an employment arbitrator's decision is wrong?*

Courts have recognized that the purposes of arbitration—both labor and employment—are ill-served by judicial review of the details of arbitration decisions. Justice William O. Douglas explained the policy bases for this limited review of labor arbitration awards in the *Steelworkers Trilogy*.[69] Limited review of employment arbitration decisions is solidly based on the terms of the FAA.

However, an employment arbitrator has likely interpreted state or federal law. His or her decision cannot evidence a "manifest disregard" of that law and withstand judicial review.[70]

3. *Do courts ever set aside employment arbitration awards?*

As a general matter, courts will give great deference to an employment arbitrator's procedural decisions and rulings on admissibility and relevancy of evidence.[71] Judicial review of arbitration awards is "among the narrowest known to the law."[72] Courts must be careful not to allow a

---

[68] 9 U.S.C. §10(a).

[69] *See* Steelworkers v. American Mfg. Co., 363 U.S. 564 (1960); Steelworkers v. Warrior & Gulf Navig. Co., 363 U.S. 574 (1960); Steelworkers v. Enterprise Wheel & Car Corp., 363 U.S. 593 (1960). See the discussion of Justice Douglas' *Steelworkers Trilogy* analysis in Chapter 1, §V. The *Steelworkers Trilogy* decisions are reproduced in Appendix A.

[70] *See, e.g.,* Merrill Lynch, Pierce, Fenner & Smith v. Bobker, 808 F.2d 930 (2d Cir. 1986).

[71] Hoteles Condado Beach v. Union De Tronquistas Local 901, 763 F.2d 34 (1st Cir. 1985).

[72] U.S. Postal Serv. v. American Postal Workers Union, 204 F.3d 523, 527 (4th Cir. 2000).

mere objection to the outcome of a proceeding to masquerade as an alleged perversion of the process. Even a decision that an objecting party considers "irrational" should withstand appeal.[73]

The easiest way to obtain judicial reversal of an employment arbitration award is by proving that the employment arbitrator failed to disclose material personal information, thus supporting a conclusion of evident partiality or even corruption. In *Commonwealth Coatings Corp. v. Continental Casualty Co.*,[74] the U.S. Supreme Court ruled that an arbitration award should be vacated when the neutral chair of a tripartite arbitration panel failed to disclose that he had served as an engineering consultant to the party that ultimately prevailed in the arbitration.

On occasion, courts have reached beyond the provisions of the FAA to set aside employment arbitration awards, finding a decision to be in manifest disregard of the law,[75] arbitrary and capricious,[76] or contrary to public policy.[77] These cases reject the finality of arbitration awards and recognize that statutory rights are more important than the autonomy of the employment arbitration process.

---

[73] Ario v. Lloyds, 618 F.3d 277 (3d Cir. 2010).
[74] 393 U.S. 145 (1968).
[75] Wilko v. Swan, 346 U.S. 427 (1953).
[76] United States Postal Serv. v. Letter Carriers, 847 F.2d 775 (11th Cir. 1988).
[77] Perma-Line Corp. v. Painters Union, 639 F.2d 890 (2d Cir. 1981).

Chapter 18

Mediation

I. Overview

Mediation is one of the most commonly used means of alternative dispute resolution (ADR). Parties who have a dispute—whether in matters affecting an employment relationship, a divorce, or a construction contract—will turn to a neutral to help them settle any differences they have. Some see the mediator as a magician who can make settlements appears out of an empty top hat, but no mediator would claim to have mystical powers. Mediators do not settle cases—parties settle disputes with a mediator's assistance. Parties settle disputes because they want to, reaching agreement when the real costs of settlement are less than the projected costs of continued disagreement. If mediators play a role in that process of accommodation, it is based primarily on their ability to get disputing parties to recognize the benefits of agreement and the detriments of continued disagreement.

Almost all cases set for litigation will eventually settle. Very few cases actually go to trial. The difference between mediation and litigation, therefore, is when a dispute will be settled and whether one party or the other believes it will obtain a better outcome by waiting to settle on the courthouse steps. An earlier settlement certainly saves the parties money.

A case set for labor arbitration may or may not settle, although a significant percentage of grievance disputes are resolved privately by the parties before the arbitration hearing. There may be political reasons with regard to grievance disputes why one party or the other cannot voluntarily settle a matter, and therefore they must leave it to an arbitrator to resolve their differences. In those cases, mediation may not prove successful. On the other hand, mediation does preserve the continuing relationship between the parties by allowing the mediator to take the heat, thus avoiding personal confrontations between the parties.

This chapter addresses mediation of labor arbitration cases, although many of the observations also apply to mediation of employment cases. One exception is that mediating an employment case requires the neutral to be fluent in the statutory law that is the basis of the employee's claim: while labor mediators seek a settlement that satisfies the parties, employment mediators seek a settlement that satisfies the law as well as the parties. While labor mediators are generalists, able to use mediation to resolve any type of labor arbitration or collective bargaining dispute, in employment mediation the intricacies of federal and state statutes might require an employment mediator who is well-versed in a specific area of employment law, such as age or gender discrimination. Employment mediators cannot rely on the parties to teach them about current law; it is unlikely that the "lessons" would be other than partisan. Further, an ability to independently analyze the legal strengths and weaknesses of each party's case can be a distinct advantage when an employment mediator attempts in separate caucuses to persuade parties at opposite ends of the spectrum to move toward a middle ground where settlement can be achieved. For a detailed discussion of both labor and employment mediation issues and practices, see Part II of *How ADR Works,* published by Bloomberg BNA/American Bar Association and edited by Norman Brand (2002).

1. What is the difference between mediation and arbitration?

It is surprising how many informed people, including lawyers, confuse mediation and arbitration. Both provide alternative methods of resolving labor and employment disputes, but the processes are quite distinct. Arbitration—either labor arbitration or employment arbitration—provides a final, binding method of adjudication. Pending disputes are resolved by an outside impartial neutral. Mediation provides the parties to a dispute with an outside impartial party whose task is to facilitate an agreement between the parties to resolve their dispute. The mediator does not have the power to resolve the dispute himself or herself. A mediator is not a decision maker—he or she is a facilitator, influencing the parties' relationship with each other.[1]

On occasion, parties to an arbitration will ask their appointed neutral to mediate their dispute in lieu of immediately hearing the matter

---

[1] *See* EVA ROBINS, A GUIDE FOR LABOR MEDIATORS 1 (1976).

in arbitration. Other times the arbitrator will offer to mediate. In either case, the parties must clarify what happens if the parties are unable to settle their dispute. Does the arbitrator resume his or her role as the decision maker? This topic is discussed in more detail later in this chapter.

Those who are successful at mediation describe their methodology more as an art than as a skill. They vary greatly in the way they approach their tasks. However, there are some aspects of mediation that are universal and worthy of discussion.

2. Why would parties select one process of dispute resolution over another?

Mediation offers disputing parties the opportunity to resolve their own dispute with the help, but not at the direction, of an outside neutral. There are distinct benefits to keeping "ownership" of the resolution process. An arbitrator's award may resolve a dispute in a manner that one or both parties find unacceptable. The arbitrator's decision, however, is normally final and binding, and as such the parties are stuck with it, unless they can mutually agree to another resolution. If they had been able to agree on a mutually acceptable arrangement in the first place, they would not have had to proceed to arbitration.

There are times when one party or the other is unwilling or unable to voluntarily agree to a particular resolution of a dispute. If the company fires a union steward, it is difficult for the union to accept the termination without a fight through the grievance and arbitration procedure. If an important supervisor makes a decision on the shop floor, management may feel it necessary to stand behind its representative. Both the union in the steward discharge case and the company in the supervisory decision case may appreciate the weakness of their positions, but they will leave it to an arbitrator to uphold the discharge and reverse the supervisor's decision. Mediation would not work; arbitration is the only viable alternative.

On the other hand, there are disputes that are too important to be left in the hands of an impartial arbitrator. Fundamental workplace issues, like the extent of management's right to subcontract work and the limitations imposed on the exercise of that right, are best resolved through negotiation. Here mediation may prove useful. An experienced mediator will know about alternatives other parties have used that can best protect the core interests of both parties.

Mediation is a better alternative when the preferable resolution of a dispute is an agreement that the parties can reach but a labor arbitrator is unlikely to be able to order. Consider a typical discharge case where the company absolutely refuses to allow the grievant to return to work. Assume an arbitrator finds that management did not have just cause for the termination, but the grievant's involvement in the incident warrants reinstatement without back pay. The parties can accomplish what the arbitrator cannot—reach an agreement that the grievant does not return to work but receives a significant payment from the company and a promise to inform any future inquiring employers that the grievant was employed between certain dates without explaining the grounds the company had proffered when it discharged the worker. This is a situation when mediation might help the parties to reach a mutually acceptable result, but arbitration might not.

3. Are labor disputes more difficult to resolve than other types of disputes where mediation is involved?

Resolving a simple grievance over a single issue involving single variable, such as money, is not difficult to resolve if the parties desire a voluntary agreement. By comparison, mediating collective bargaining negotiations with multiple issues in dispute can be extremely complicated. The labor context increases the complexity because both parties have multiple constituencies. A union is a political institution with a diverse membership with varying interests. Senior employees will seek greater protection for seniority; skilled employees may favor increments based on skills and abilities. The same is true on management's side. Human resources and operational leadership may seek conflicting goals. A labor mediator may find that he or she must first find out who from each party can make a deal, while recognizing the conflicting interests within each party.

II. Selecting a Mediator

1. How do the disputing parties select a mediator?

If the parties have agreed to use a mediator appointed under the auspices of the American Arbitration Association (AAA), either party (or both) will submit a *request for mediation* to any AAA regional office, along with the following:

1. a copy of the mediation provision of the parties' contract or the parties' stipulation to mediate;
2. the names, regular mail addresses, e-mail addresses (if available), and telephone numbers of all parties to the dispute and representatives, if any, in the mediation;
3. a brief statement of the nature of the dispute and the relief requested; and

4.   any specific qualifications the mediator should possess.[2]

The parties can review the profiles of mediators available through the AAA to seek agreement on who will serve as their neutral.[3] In the absence of agreement, the AAA will provide a list of mediators. If the parties are unable to agree on a mediator, each party will strike the names of mediators who are unacceptable and rank the remaining names. The AAA will then "invite" the highest-ranking mediator to serve.[4]

Judicial Arbitration and Mediation Services (JAMS) does not use the AAA striking process in the selection of a mediator. In fact, it denigrates that process as "outdated."[5] Instead, JAMS has the parties individually submit to JAMS a list of three to five preferred mediators in the region. Some of the mediators may be eliminated due to conflicts of interest. Then JAMS will determine which names appear on both parties' lists. This list of overlapping candidates is then distributed to the parties, who prioritize the remaining candidates. The highest-ranking choice is appointed.[6]

There are times when one party to a dispute will contact a neutral expressing interest in mediation. That party may be concerned that to directly suggest mediation to the opposing party would indicate a weakness. If the mediator is interested in serving, he or she will make contact with the opposing party, perhaps through a third-party intermediary, to inquire whether it would be interested in pursuing the possibility of settlement if the opposing party were interested. (Of course, the opposing party has already indicated to the mediator that it is interested in mediation.) With this conditional approach, the mediator can assess whether there is mutual interest in using his or her services.[7] If there is, the parties can proceed to mediation.

[2] AMERICAN ARBITRATION ASSOCIATION, EMPLOYMENT ARBITRATION RULES AND MEDIATION PROCEDURES, at Rule M-2, *available at* www.adr.org/aaa/faces/rules/searchrules/rulesdetail?doc=ADRSTG_004366&_afrLoop=1815657372636161&_afrWindowMode=0&_afrWindowId=null#%40%3F_afrWindowId%3Dnull%26_afrLoop%3D1815657372636161%26doc%3DADRSTG_004366%26_afrWindowMode%3D0%26_adf.ctrl-state%3D16ms7sywi_4 (reproduced in Appendix E).
[3] *See* AMERICAN ARBITRATION ASSOCIATION, ARBITRATOR AND MEDIATOR SELECTION, http://www.adr.org/aaa/faces/arbitratorsmediators/arbitratormediatorselection?_afrLoop=2501776630500620&_afrWindowMode=0&_afrWindowId=fwn4z6q3p_23#%40%3F_afrWindowId%3Dfwn4z6q3p_23%26_afrLoop%3D2501776630500620%26_afrWindowMode%3D0%26_adf.ctrl-state%3Dx1dtdpkbc_4.
[4] AMERICAN ARBITRATION ASSOCIATION, *supra* note 2, at Rule M-5.
[5] *See* JAMS, Selecting an Experienced Neutral for the Complex, Highly Sensitive or Multi-Jurisdictional Case, http://www.jamsadr.com/selecting-an-experienced-neutral-for-the-complex-highly-sensitive-or-multi-jurisdictional-case-09-01-2002/.
[6] *Id.*
[7] George Nicolau, *How Mediators Operate: A Mediator's View*, in ABA SECTION OF LABOR AND EMPLOYMENT LAW, HOW ADR WORKS 141 (Norman Brand, ed., 2002).

2. How do the parties determine who would be a good mediator?

A good mediator is experienced in the process of facilitating voluntary settlements and is a quick learner when it comes to understanding the nature of the parties' dispute and their conflicting interests. A good mediator has strong interpersonal skills in developing rapport and building relationships with the parties. Trust in the neutral will be essential to the success of the process, and the mediator must earn that trust. A good mediator will be skilled in listening and learning as well as devising creative alternatives that move the parties closer to common ground and, ultimately, to agreement.

A good mediator demonstrates to the parties that he or she is interested in them and not just in their dispute. He or she must have an enormous reservoir of patience, but must be willing to probe to distinguish between a party's stated position and its genuine interests. A good mediator is honest, respectful, nonjudgmental, upbeat, active, and hardworking in bringing the parties toward agreement. Every mediator has his or her own variety of styles and will choose an approach that fits the needs of a particular case. A good mediator must be persuasive, persistent, tenacious, and willing to deal rationally in what often starts out as an irrational situation. Ultimately, with the help of a good mediator, people will generally solve their own problems.

III. How Does the Mediation Process Work?

Mediation works by facilitating the negotiation process between two parties to a dispute who genuinely seek to settle their differences. If there is an obstinate refusal to reach a resolution, there is little even the most skilled mediator can accomplish. On the other hand, some parties who enter mediation not intending to reach a voluntary settlement may discover information that makes a private resolution preferable to its alternatives. Facts may be revealed or even changed during a mediation in a way that may allow both parties to reevaluate their initial assessment of the utility of a particular outcome. *Utility* is a measure of value, satisfaction, and preferences, both personal and economic. One role of the mediator is to make the parties see the benefits of a resolution—the *utility*—and the disadvantages of a failure to settle.

1. Why don't parties just settle all of their differences?

In some other world, it is possible that people would not have disagreements. Parties would share the same set of values and interests and be able to communicate their needs in a nonadversarial manner.

But that is not the real world, the place where parties do have different perspectives and interests. That does not mean that an accommodation is impossible, however—only that the parties may need to work on their differences through negotiation.

Each party to a labor dispute—whether the dispute is over the terms of a new or revised collective bargaining agreement (CBA) or the resolution of a pending grievance—will obtain varying levels of benefit from different outcomes of their negotiations. Management, for example, will find great utility in controlling costs; a union will identify more value in an adequate (or even generous) rate of pay. A similar evaluation is possible on all issues that divide the parties, from seniority to management rights. In fact, on any given issue there may be no point or position where both parties would find positive utility in an agreement. If management wants to pay employees at the minimum wage, the union may find that outcome completely unacceptable and without utility. If the union seeks a pay rate at triple the wage paid by competitors to their employees, management may find that outcome completely unacceptable. If the parties are unable to reassess their positions, perhaps by combining disputed issues in a way that allows each to claim value, no agreement will be reached. Here is where a mediator may do some good work.

2.   *Does the mediator enter the dispute with certain assumptions?*

In her short, but insightful, monograph, *A Guide for Labor Mediators*, the late Eva Robins posed a series of assumptions that most mediators bring to an appointment:

1.   There is no issue that people of good will and infinite patience cannot resolve, given the desire to settle.
2.   The parties want to reach agreement. . . .
3.   The parties do not want a strike. . . .
4.   The parties will at one time or another try to "con" the mediator but by and large will be as cooperative as their legitimate interests allow them to be.
5.   There is "fat" in the union's and employer's proposals which needs to be identified by the mediator and which will be removed as the mediation efforts proceed.[8]

3.   *After appointment, how does a mediator initiate the process?*

There are administrative matters that the mediator should take care of even before mediation begins. They should be addressed early so they do not encumber the mediation process. In an initial pre-mediation

---

[8] EVA ROBINS, A GUIDE FOR LABOR MEDIATORS 50–51 (1976).

conference, usually a teleconference, involving the mediator and the parties, the mediator should disclose any prior business or personal relationships with either party or their advocates or firms. After such disclosures are made, the mediator must make sure that the parties wish that he or she continue to serve.[9]

At this initial conference, the mediator must ascertain the sophistication of the parties regarding the use of mediation and whether they have selected mediation voluntarily or by order of a court or an agency. This information will give the mediator a better idea of whether settlement is a real possibility. In addition, the mediator must make sure that the parties know the mediator's fee arrangements. If appointed through the AAA or JAMS procedures, the parties will already have this information, but there is no reason why parties cannot contact a mediator directly to secure his or her services. Some experienced mediators will even require the parties to provide a retainer for mediation services.[10]

The mediator may request that the parties submit pre-mediation position papers with relevant documents to inform the mediator of the nature of the dispute and the position of the parties. It is important that these papers be sufficiently informal so they do not freeze a party's position in place. Finally, the pre-mediation conference will address the issue of scheduling based on the complexity of the dispute and the number of persons involved. The mediation should be held at a location where the parties can have their own "breakout" rooms as well as a large room where the parties can come together at one time. Scheduling a mediation session may prove difficult with a large group of participants.

All persons may not be able to participate in all sessions, and therefore it is critical for the mediator to make sure that each party has in attendance someone who can actually make a decision regarding an interim settlement. The right people have to be there—those who are able to make decisions to move toward an agreement.[11] Mediating with persons of limited authority may prove useless.[12] It is also preferable to have the parties themselves speak up rather than only express a

---

[9]Rosemary A. Townley, *How Mediators Operate: A Mediator's View* in ABA SECTION OF LABOR AND EMPLOYMENT LAW, HOW ADR WORKS 113 (Norman Brand, ed., 2002). This insightful article is a useful resource on many of the concepts addressed in this chapter.

[10]*Id.*

[11]*See* John R. Van Winkle, *How Mediators Operate: A Mediator's View*, in ABA SECTION OF LABOR AND EMPLOYMENT LAW, HOW ADR WORKS 155 (Norman Brand, ed., 2002). ROBINS, *supra* note 8, at 25 ("It is enormously valuable for the mediator to know who is present and in what capacity, who is influential and whether the influential person is the principle negotiator.").

[12]*See* Anthony C. Piazza, *How Mediators Operate: A Mediator's View*, in ABA SECTION OF LABOR AND EMPLOYMENT LAW, HOW ADR WORKS 127 (Norman Brand, ed., 2002).

viewpoint through their advocates. After all, they will have to live with any settlement that is achieved, and they should claim ownership of the process through which settlement is reached.[13]

4. How does the mediator go about his or her job?

Mediation generally proceeds in stages, gradually building momentum that will lead toward settlement. It is generally useful for the mediator first to convene a joint meeting of the parties to hear their positions on contested matters. This session will not only introduce the mediator to the dispute, it will also help to set the agenda for discussion. The representatives will relate their positions in narrative form. There are no witnesses, although there may be documents that contain the parties' written proposals.

At the initial joint meeting, both sides will not only hear the opposing side's positions (which they probably know already), but they will also hear from each other the intensity of their commitment to their positions. Every issue in dispute is not of equal importance to a party, although at the initial stage a party would not be prepared to remove a matter from contention. This is important information for the mediator to learn.

At some point the mediator will separate the parties to be able to speak with them in confidence and to gain their trust. As a facilitator, the mediator will have to use the same interpersonal skills involved in conducting an arbitration hearing, actively listening to each of the parties in an effort to determine their real interests and genuine preferences. A mediator will also learn at these separate meetings who the active and influential players are for each party on certain issues. He or she will assess whether and when a productive dialogue is possible. As negotiations proceed, the mediator may talk with the people who have both power and a willingness to seek alternatives in sidebar sessions, out in the hallway away from other members of the negotiating group, in an effort to solicit their support for moving the process forward.

5. What skills must a mediator bring to a dispute?

A mediator must be able to listen to the parties and watch them carefully. Although like an arbitrator a mediator must keep control over the process, there are additional skills required for mediation. A mediator must have enormous patience and sensitivity to the conflicting

---

[13] *See* George Nicolau, *How Mediators Operate: A Mediator's View*, in ABA SECTION OF LABOR AND EMPLOYMENT LAW, HOW ADR WORKS 141 (Norman Brand, ed., 2002).

interests of the parties and must engage in empathic listening. The parties must believe that the mediator is listening.

The parties enter into mediation with different interest and values. The mediator's job is first to understand those interests and values. The opposing parties attach different levels of utility to different outcomes. At the commencement of mediation, there may be no outcome on any issue where both parties would achieve value. The mediator's job after ascertaining this information is to help the parties rethink their utility assessments. A particular outcome on an issue may not produce utility, but if the issue can be joined with another where a party could obtain abundant utility, the mediator may have facilitated a zone within which an agreement can be reached. That will be one measure of the success of the mediation process.

The mediator must be persistent, tenacious, and able to communicate well. Mediation is hard work, much more difficult than arbitrating a dispute. The mediator must be willing to walk away from the process if the parties are unwilling or unable to explore alternatives to their stated positions. One way a mediator gets the parties to consider options is by raising doubts in their own minds as to whether their current positions will ultimately prevail in court or before an arbitrator, assuming further proceedings are scheduled. The higher the perceived risk of not prevailing in another forum, the better the prospects for settlement through mediated negotiations. That process may take some time, however, and the mediator will pace the negotiations.

6.   *What happens on the first day of the mediation?*

At the start of the first day of mediation, the mediator is likely to convene a brief joint session with both parties in attendance. He or she will set the tone for the process, reviewing how the mediation will proceed and what role the mediator will play. The mediator will also reiterate the ground rules to be followed, including a promise of confidentiality for any discussions the mediator has with each party away from the opposing party, called a *caucus*.[14] The mediator will likely ask the parties to make a brief opening statement so the neutral can clarify any questions he or she may have about what matters are in dispute and on what issues the parties agree. The mediator should make sure that the parties and their advocates understand the mediator's role, emphasizing that the mediator is neutral and will attempt to assist the parties

---

[14] Eva Robins, A Guide for Labor Mediators 35 (1976).

in reaching an acceptable agreement.[15] The mediator should emphasize that it is not his or her job to dictate the terms of that settlement.[16]

It is not unusual for the parties to try to convince the mediator both at this opening session and as the mediation proceeds that its position on contested matters is the correct one. There is normally a full measure of positioning, posturing, and even anger at these early stages. The mediator must clarify that it is not his or her prerogative to decide who is correct, but rather to find ways for the parties to reach an agreement that will resolve the dispute.

Some mediators insist that the process should take only one day.[17] This does not mean, however, that the mediator finishes at 5:00 p.m. Successful mediation often takes place when fatigue hits the parties, and a resolution in the wee hours of the morning is not unusual. Rushing the process may not be the most successful approach. It may take time for the parties to accept the fact that they will not achieve all they desire in a settlement and that compromise is essential. It will also take time for the mediator to assess the personalities and their disparate positions in order to help the parties forge the compromises needed for settlement.

7. *How does a mediator gain the confidence of the parties?*

After the initial joint session, the mediator is likely to move the parties into separate rooms and meet with each caucus privately. Here the process of gaining the confidence of the parties begins. The mediator should reiterate that the conversations they will have are strictly confidential.[18] This is part of the process of gaining the trust of both parties. The mediator must develop his or her credibility. He or she should listen more than speak, gathering the information that will be essential in forging the compromises from which a settlement can be made. The mediator should expect that some participants might become quite emotional in expressing their views, but it is important that they be allowed to say what they wish to the mediator. After that, however, there should be no need to repeat those outbursts in the future.

---

[15] *Id.*

[16] *Id.*

[17] *See* Piazza, *supra* note 12.

[18] *See* Kay McMurray, *The Role of Mediation and Conciliation in Collective Bargaining,* in Max Zimny, William F. Dolson, & Christopher A. Barreca, Labor Arbitration: A Practical Guide for Advocates 43 (1990) (emphasizing the critical importance of maintaining confidentiality). If the parties are going to proceed toward a settlement in a positive fashion, they must be able to provide the neutral with information in separate meetings that will not be disclosed to the opposing party.

The process of negotiating a settlement to a dispute is based not only on the objective positions expressed by the parties but also on the personalities of the participants. The mediator must figure out who he or she is dealing with. Both parties will likely have to move from their initial positions in order to reach a settlement. It is the mediator's job to make sure that a party can save face when it alters its position on contested issues. Thus, a mediator must develop both parties' trust.

8.   How can a mediator alter a party's initial position?

In separate meetings with each of the parties, the mediator attempts to ascertain each party's real positions, as opposed to the ones they expressed in the joint meeting or initially expressed in caucus to the mediator. Here the mediator begins to explore whether something less than a party's optimum outcome would still provide utility and whether there are any genuine bottom lines that may have to be adjusted in order to reach a settlement. The mediator might then begin to explore alternatives that might prove to be acceptable.

Sometimes the mediator will group issues together to develop natural tradeoffs. After learning the utility one party places on a particular issue, the mediator may attempt to find a counterpart that is of particular value to the opposing party. These can be grouped together in an effort to move negotiations forward through interim agreements. The established protocol in collective bargaining is that interim agreements on pieces of the deal are all tentative until the entire contract is completed. The mediator can reach back into the pile of interim agreements to find sweeteners for later trades.[19]

Mediating a grievance dispute or an employment dispute without a union may also involve grouping and trading, but that only works effectively once the mediator learns the value that the opposing parties place on certain issues and outcomes. For example, an employer may be willing to pay an employee a substantial settlement as long as he or she does not return to the workplace. The mediator's job is to ascertain how much a "substantial" amount is and whether it is sufficient to settle the dispute.

There will be times when the mediator will want to talk privately with just the principal negotiator of a party, and at other times bring the principal negotiators of both parties together for a meeting. Working with a large negotiating group may prove dysfunctional to the process and prevent progress. The mediator should let the parties know what is

---

[19] ROBINS, *supra* note 14, at 43.

going on, without blaming any individual or group for stopping progress. Everyone should be assured that no deal is reached until the deal is complete and agreed to.

It is important for the mediator to keep each party from committing to a position that will make settlement impossible. A party should be encouraged never to say "never," because it might have to move in that direction to make a deal.[20] The mediator can suggest that the facts may change and make the impossible now possible. By encouraging each party to be realistic about its position and where a settlement might be reached, the mediator leaves open the door to compromise without suggesting in any way that a party's position is wrong. Mediation is not intended to find fault or assign blame—it is designed simply to generate a "climate of settlement."[21]

The parties' transition from aspirational and emotional to realistic and practical is the critical transformation in the mediation process. The reality is that it is most unlikely that the "winner" will take all. It is most unlikely, in fact, that there will even be a "winner." Winning comes from settling.

Part of the mediator's box of tools is explaining separately to each party what the impact of not reaching an agreement could be. The mediator can portray the uncertainties of life in litigation or in arbitration without hyperbole. If the mediator is not able to accomplish a transition in a party's position, a settlement zone will not be created, and the parties will be left not far from where the mediator first found them. The process at times does not work.

Timing is of utmost importance as the mediator goes about his or her job. What issues should be raised for discussion, and in what order? Has a party had a sufficient catharsis in explaining its positions in confidence to the mediator to now get down to the business of settlement? The mediator must be sensitive to the slightest changes in tone, and strike when the iron has sufficiently cooled.[22] The mediator will have to really get to know the parties in order to reach this judgment.

At times, one party will insist that a particular issue—what Eva Robins called a "boulder" issue—be resolved before the parties move on to settle other matters in dispute.[23] These issues are sufficiently significant that they might generate a work stoppage. One way to handle boulder issues is for the mediator to suggest the creation of a joint

---

[20] *Id.* at 32.
[21] *Id.* at 3.
[22] *Id.* at 21.
[23] *Id.* at 48.

subcommittee to study the matter in terms of current practices in the industry and report back to the full negotiating committees. While this diversion is occurring, the parties can move on to other matters in contention. If this does not work, the mediator may have to get the parties to address the issue head-on.[24]

A mediator may find that the parties need some time away from negotiations to reconsider their positions. The mediator might send the parties off to obtain economic data that might prove useful. When a dispute does not have a deadline, as it would if a CBA were going to expire, a mediator might use an adjournment strategically to change the atmospherics. While away from the mediation, the parties might gain a new appreciation of the positive role the mediator is playing in their settlement process and return with a changed attitude and increased investment in the mediation process.[25]

9.   *How can a mediator serve as a resource for the parties?*

During the confidential meetings with each party, the mediator may play the role of devil's advocate, asking questions and presenting points of view that make that party's initial position untenable. This can be uncomfortable, but the mediator should explain that he or she is doing the same thing with the opposing party, seeking to bring objective realism to the table.[26]

In the confidential caucus, a party might express a willingness to explore a certain avenue of settlement but may be unwilling to make that offer to the opposing party lest it demonstrate weakness. The mediator may offer to carry the proposal to the opposing side as his or her own suggestion to see if it might have any traction. If it does have traction, the mediator has served the parties well. The neutral may have induced "a settlement psychology."[27] Even if it does not have traction, the mediator has learned either that it will take more to make a deal or that a deal is not in the offing at all.

At other times, the mediator will realize that an offer one party is developing will not move the negotiations forward. In fact, it may make settlement more difficult, even if proposed in good faith. The mediator likely knows how the opposing side will take the proposal but

---

[24] *Id.* at 49–50.

[25] *Id.* at 39–40.

[26] *See* Anthony C. Piazza, *How Mediators Operate: A Mediator's View,* in ABA Section of Labor and Employment Law, How ADR Works 127 (Norman Brand, ed., 2002).

[27] *See* Eva Robins, A Guide for Labor Mediators 3 (1976).

cannot reveal any information obtained in confidence. At this point, the mediator will have to draw on the legitimacy he or she has developed with a party and suggest holding off on the offer until a later point. This suggestion does not reveal confidences, and it may be sufficient to keep the negotiations on track. The "poison" proposal might never be made.

It is rare that a dispute is the result of only one party being unreasonable. Both parties are likely at fault for the dispute. They are fortunate to have made it to mediation. The mediator will convey information from one party to the other, seeking to find areas of commonality. These transmittals should be accompanied by a reminder to each party of the costs of not reaching a voluntary agreement in terms of litigation expenses or the risks involved in arbitration or court proceedings. The selective and well-timed use of tension, while the mediator remains calm, can be a persuasive tool as well.[28]

10. Does the mediator present his or her own proposals?

At some point, the mediator may begin to express his or her own opinions about the parties' positions in a manner than does not risk losing his or her legitimacy as a neutral. To spur movement, a mediator may be able to present the parties with options for resolving their dispute that they had not previously considered. The mediator must recognize that an effective mediated settlement provides each party with utility, but not necessarily a victory.

Ultimately, the mediator, based on the various positions expressed in the separate meetings, may put together a package that the neutral thinks the parties could accept. Unlike earlier exchanges of proposals, neither party owns this package; it is a package offered by the mediator, who is neutral and seeks only a settlement of the dispute.

11. What happens when the parties are ready to reach an agreement?

An experienced mediator will be able to sense when the parties are close enough in their opposing positions to reach a settlement. He or she will not adjourn the negotiating session because the momentum to wrap up the deal may evaporate.

If the mediation results in an agreement, it should immediately be written down, likely by the mediator who can phrase the settlement in a manner that encourages the parties to abide by their commitments.

---

[28] *Id.* at 30.

Representatives of the parties should then sign it in a joint session. This document prevents later disagreement as to what was agreed to. It is not unusual for a party (or even both parties) at some later point to have "buyer's remorse," but the signed document signifies the binding arrangement.

12. Does a mediator become invested in a dispute? Does a mediator care if the settlement the parties reach is fair?

Obviously, a mediator seeks an agreement, yet he or she should not really care about the contents of that agreement. There are too many unknowns to determine whether a deal is a good one or a bad one. It is not the mediator's responsibility to determine whether the bargain the parties reach is wise and beneficial. His or her goal should be to get them to reach an agreement they think they can live with.[29]

A mediator must convince each party that he or she wants to achieve an agreement, but settlement will depend on the parties, not the neutral. Although a party might want to have the mediator acknowledge the correctness of its stance, that can lead to trouble when, in order to achieve a settlement, some other outcome is necessary. The mediator is invested in the process, not in a particular outcome of the process other than a settlement. When the parties do not reach an agreement, that does not mean that the process failed—it may simply mean that agreement was not in the offing at that point. The parties may need some further time to think about where they stand, and an agreement may come later. The mediation process only fails if the parties are not given every possibility to reach a settlement of their dispute by exploring all options.[30]

During the course of mediation, a mediator must appear to become invested in the parties, but not in the positions they take. The parties must believe that the mediator is listening to what they say and is understanding the nature of their arguments. The mediator has no power to compel agreement—only the ability to persuade, influence, and propose alternatives. Ultimately, of course, a successful outcome is totally within the control of the parties.[31]

---

[29] *Id.* at 4.

[30] John R. Van Winkle, *How Mediators Operate: A Mediator's View*, in ABA Section of Labor and Employment Law, How ADR Works 155 (Norman Brand, ed., 2002).

[31] George Nicolau, *How Mediators Operate: A Mediator's View*, in ABA Section of Labor and Employment Law, How ADR Works 141 (Norman Brand, ed., 2002).

13. Are there any behavioral guidelines that are useful in understanding mediation?

George Nicolau, one of the nation's finest labor arbitrators and mediators, has explained his "Iron Laws" of mediation in these terms:

1. Parties will rarely make a decision if there is any way to avoid it.
2. All disputes have got to end sometime.
3. No settlement is entered into without doubt.
4. People don't like to be told what to do.
5. People usually act out of self-interest.
6. A dispute can't be resolved until the parties make a decision that they really want to resolve it.
7. People tend to carry out only those decisions they have helped to formulate.[32]

Using these tools, the mediator can help forge a settlement.

IV. MEDIATION AS PART OF ARBITRATION[33]

At the start of an arbitration hearing—both labor and employment arbitration—some neutrals always ask the parties if they have thoroughly explored the possibilities of settlement. Some arbitrators, however, recognize that if the parties have come to the arbitration hearing, they likely are seeking arbitration and they have failed to reach a voluntary resolution of their dispute. If the parties suggest that they might want to spend more time trying to settle the matter, the arbitrator might offer to help by serving as a mediator.

1. When does an arbitrator offer to mediate? Should an arbitrator mediate a dispute that he or she has been appointed to arbitrate?

The offer to mediate, if it is to be made, should be tendered before evidence is presented at the arbitration. The arbitrator may hear something in opening statements that suggests that pursuing a voluntary settlement may be both possible and preferable to a hearing on the merits.

---

[32] *Id.*

[33] *See* Susan L. Stewart, Janice K. Frankman, Bill Houlihan, & John E. Sands, *Mediation During Arbitration,* in ARBITRATION 2012: OUTSIDE IN: HOW THE EXTERNAL ENVIRONMENT IS SHAPING ARBITRATION, PROCEEDINGS OF THE 65TH ANNUAL MEETING, NATIONAL ACADEMY OF ARBITRATORS 285 (Nancy Kauffman & Matthew M. Franckiewicz, eds., 2013) (discussing whether arbitrators should switch roles at an arbitration hearing and "don the hat of a mediator").

Before mediation commences, the parties and the arbitrator (now mediator) have to clarify what happens if the mediation fails to achieve a settlement of the grievance dispute. Mediation works on the premise of trust and confidentiality, and, to be successful, the mediator will likely learn things he or she would not learn through arbitration. This is why some arbitrators feel that, if they engage in mediation at the direction of the parties, they cannot later reassume the position of neutral arbitrator if settlement is not reached.

Other arbitrators recognize the value of retaining the ultimate power to resolve a dispute in arbitration if mediation fails. Referred to as "med-arb," this hybrid form of ADR is particularly successful because the mediator has the ability in caucusing with a party to state that the position the party is taking will not prevail in arbitration. Nothing is a more powerful and coercive tool in altering a party's position than knowing that a position will be a loser before the mediator when he or she once again becomes the arbitrator.

Everything a neutral says to a party in med-arb is a "fist in a velvet glove." The parties know that and seek to obtain through mediation a better outcome than the mediator suggests is awaiting them in arbitration. However, the fact that the mediator may ultimately hear the case as an arbitrator may keep the parties from being fully candid in what they tell the neutral in mediation.

2. When the arbitrator serves as a mediator, is it appropriate to tell one side or the other that its position is untenable and that it should settle?

As discussed in Chapter 1, Justice William O. Douglas emphasized in the *Steelworkers Trilogy*[34] that arbitration offers a therapeutic effect even if the grievance in question was frivolous. A mediator who tells a party that its position is frivolous and it should settle seems to undercut this important potential cathartic value of arbitration.

3. What are the ultimate benefits and disadvantages of combining mediation and arbitration?

Parties pursue ADR processes in an effort to resolve their dispute. Although it might be preferable for the parties to do so voluntarily

---

[34] *See* Steelworkers v. American Mfg. Co., 363 U.S. 564 (1960); Steelworkers v. Warrior & Gulf Navig. Co., 363 U.S. 574 (1960); Steelworkers v. Enterprise Wheel & Car Corp., 363 U.S. 593 (1960). See the discussion of Justice Douglas' *Steelworkers Trilogy* analysis in Chapter 1, §V. The *Steelworkers Trilogy* decisions are reproduced in Appendix A.

through mediation, the major benefit of med-arb is that the dispute will be resolved one way or the other. A hybrid process is also cheaper than two independent processes—mediation followed by arbitration by a different neutral. When the processes are combined, the parties will not have to spend much time educating their mediator regarding the nature of the dispute when he or she assumes the role of arbitrator.

The disadvantage of combining the two processes under the purview of one person is clear, however. It is easier for a mediator-arbitrator to push the parties to settlement because he or she retains the power to ultimately issue an award in the dispute, but the parties may be giving up too much in the process. They are certainly giving up some measure of control over the settlement process. The mediator is able to coerce a settlement with the threat of a negative outcome in the arbitration to follow.

All things considered, it would be preferable if the parties select one person to serve as a mediator, with a second neutral ready to take over the case and commence arbitration if a settlement is not reached. The best mediator in such a situation would be someone who the party could also have selected as an arbitrator. Thus, as a mediator, he or she could say with some confidence that a position a party was taking in mediation would not likely prevail in arbitration. Because the mediator in this hybrid procedure would not be the actual arbitrator, the parties would maintain a measure of control over the settlement process. Med-arb with a single neutral should not be used unless the parties need a resolution more than they need to maintain their autonomy and protect their own interests.

Chapter 19

A Look to the Future[1]

---

[1] *See* Dennis Nolan & Roger Abrams, *The Future of Labor Arbitration*, 37 LAB. L.J. 437 (1986).

I. Overview

Few can doubt that labor arbitration has been a great invention of the American labor movement. It has provided workers with an efficient means for seeking redress for their workplace complaints. It has allowed unions to demonstrate to their membership the value of organization. At the same time, it provides management with a relatively inexpensive means of protecting its discretionary rights to administer the workplace. Experienced labor arbitrators have served as informed but impartial neutrals, operating a process so successful that no parties that have ever adopted arbitration have chosen to return to the previous system of resolving disputes in court or through the use of economic power. Labor arbitration may not always be cheap, quick, and informal, but it is cheaper, quicker, and more comfortable to participants than the alternative, litigation.

Employment arbitration is still in its adolescence, although it has experienced a "growth spurt" assisted by supportive U.S. Supreme Court decisions. Many labor arbitrators also serve as employment arbitrators, so there is a skilled group of neutrals available to make the nonunion process operate fairly and efficiently. Other employment arbitrators, such as retired judges, do not come with workplace credentials, but they have adjudication experience that may prove valuable depending on the nature of the dispute. Practicing lawyers sitting as employment arbitrators may also bring to employment arbitration the trappings of the court system to resolve employment disputes based on state and federal statutes.

Mediators, whether employed directly by private parties, appointed through an agency such as the American Arbitration Association

(AAA), or employed full time by the Federal Mediation and Concilia-tion Service (FMCS), bring a variety of interpersonal skills and finely tuned experiences to the resolution of workplace disputes. They enter a dispute when the parties are unable to resolve their differences without some outside and impartial assistance. Although mediators cannot as-sure success, when parties genuinely seek to reach a settlement, media-tors can help make that happen.

What then is the future of labor and employment arbitration and mediation? What can the parties to collective bargaining agreements (CBAs) do to make sure these systems of alternative dispute resolution (ADR) continue to prosper? How can nonunion employers use employ-ment arbitration in a manner that enhances its legitimacy and accept-ability and is not seen as an elaborate and pernicious scheme to divest employees of their statutory rights?

The future of ADR in the employment field depends on the ability to train skilled neutrals to operate both arbitration and mediation. We cur-rently have no systematic way of educating the next generation of neu-trals that will replace those who adjudicate and facilitate the resolution of workplace disputes today. Now is the time to focus on this absence of institutionalized training and credentialing of neutral specialists.

II. A Cloudy Future for Labor Arbitration

The future of traditional labor arbitration remains cloudy. In some heavily unionized parts of the country, the private system of dispute resolution continues to flourish, but there are ominous signs of trouble ahead as unions continue to lose membership and management contin-ues to voice objections to unionization.

1.   Will labor arbitration wither away?

The future of labor arbitration depends, of course, on whether there is a future for American labor unions. Labor union density con-tinues to decrease.[2] Organized labor grew dramatically during the pre- and post-war years as workers sought to protect their collective rights

---

[2]The Bureau of Labor Statistic reports that, in 2012, labor union density stood at 11.3%, a drop of 2% in the previous decade, with public sector unionization leading the way with more than a third of government employees unionized. By comparison, the private sector union density has fallen below 7%. *See* Press Release, U.S. Depart-ment of Labor, Bureau of Labor Statistics, Union Members Summary (Jan 23, 2013), *available at* http://www.bls.gov/news.release/union2.nr0.htm.

and benefits. Without a union, employers could and did act to disadvantage workers, who did not have much recourse. Arbitration became the preferred method to protect worker rights, and the procedure spread to eventually cover all unionized settings.

All of the conditions that prompted unionization during that earlier period exist today. Despite conditions that might favor collective action by employees, the percentage of private sector American workers who are unionized has dropped to single digits. Workers face invigorated management often committed to and successful in resisting unionization. Labor unions regularly vow to spread organization to the unorganized. If they fulfill that promise, labor arbitration will regain lost ground.

It is not unthinkable that the American labor movement will rebound. It has done so in the past. Union membership dropped by almost half from 1920 to 1933, but then almost tripled in the next four years as New Deal legislation aided organization.[3] Although it is seems unlikely that Congress will enact statutes that would aid unions, management could so overreach its position of primacy as to drive workers back into unions. Unionization and collective bargaining will lead to greater use of arbitration.

2. *Will there be any changes in the* Steelworkers Trilogy*'s edict that labor arbitration should be autonomous?*

The norm of nonintervention into the merits and procedures of labor arbitration established by the U.S. Supreme Court more than half a century ago has proven to be durable and efficient.[4] Most important, it meets the needs of the parties to collective relationships. There is no apparent reason why the judiciary would want to reassume a role of appellate review over private systems of labor adjudication, especially as the Supreme Court continues to be supportive of arbitration in employment and other fields. The system works—there is no need to fix it.

3. *Will legalisms and judicial procedure continue their creep into labor arbitration?*

Periodically, arbitrators express concern about "creeping legalisms" in labor arbitration.[5] They protest that the procedure is a continuation

---

[3] U.S. DEPARTMENT OF LABOR, BUREAU OF LABOR STATISTICS, HANDBOOK OF LABOR STATISTICS 1975—REFERENCE EDITION 389, BULLETIN 1865 (1975).

[4] See the discussion of Justice William O. Douglas' *Steelworkers Trilogy* analysis in Chapter 1, §V. The *Steelworkers Trilogy* decisions are reproduced in Appendix A.

[5] *See, e.g.,* Perry A. Zirkel & Andriy Krahmal, *Creeping Legalism in Grievance Arbitration: Fact or Fiction?* 16 OHIO ST. J. DISP. RESOL. 243 (2001).

of the collective bargaining process rather than a quasi-court proceeding. The informal adjudication of rights embodied in a CBA should not be encumbered by judicial procedures. Some labor arbitrators, however, have succumbed to the infestation of legalisms—their opinions sound like judicial pronouncements—whereas others have successfully resisted them. However, there has been little discourse recently on the prospect that labor arbitrators are being transmuted into "judges without robes."

Labor arbitrators should remain sufficiently flexible to address the changing needs and specific requests of the parties on a case-by-case basis. Some cases, especially in the public sector and cases involving statutory rights, may require more legalisms. Others that arise on the shop floor can be handled more informally as the parties would likely prefer. The same cannot be said of employment arbitration, as is discussed below.

4. Will federal sector arbitration awards continue to be reviewed by the Federal Labor Relations Authority?

The federal labor relations system provides for the review of labor arbitration awards by the Federal Labor Relations Authority (FLRA). As a result, an arbitrator who hears federal public sector cases will write his or her opinion in recognition of the fact that review by the FLRA is almost a certainty. This tends to increase the arbitrator's study time and alters the focus of the decision from the agreement to the prevailing legal doctrine announced by the FLRA. As a result, in the federal public sector, the arbitrator serves more as a hearing officer than as a private impartial contract reader.

It is unlikely that this federal public sector status quo will change any time soon. Federal public sector unions have learned to operate under the law that severely limits the scope of bargaining but mandates arbitration of disputes. Both management and labor make repeated use of the FLRA to review awards they see as unfavorable. Although the current federal public sector arbitration system includes a court-like rigidity, there is no political consensus that it needs to be changed.

III. A BRIGHT FUTURE FOR EMPLOYMENT ARBITRATION

The future of employment arbitration looks rosy, as employers find private adjudication of statutory rights using a procedure they design and control much more inviting than public adjudication in court. Although the advent of nonunion employment arbitration might offer hope to many workers that their rights can be protected outside of a traditional union setting, individual employees may not have sufficient financial resources to adequately protect their rights in employment arbitration. In the absence of legislation that mandates workplace rights and requires universal arbitration, employment dispute resolution will grow as long as the alternative—traditional court litigation—continues to prove unsuitable for employers.

1. Will courts intervene to ensure evenhanded fairness in employment arbitration procedures?

Courts have shown a willingness to scrutinize employment arbitration procedures to ensure that employees are treated fairly by the process that employers design to replace litigation over statutory rights. This trend of case-by-case adjudication will continue unless legislatures intervene to enact uniform guidelines for employment arbitration. A standard procedure for fair and adequate employment arbitration might even evolve, much as has happened in labor arbitration without legislative intervention. As long as employers do not abuse their power, it is unlikely that legislatures will mandate such procedures.

Some states, such as California, have already addressed what are seen as the failures of employment arbitration systems. Starting with enhanced disclosure requirements imposed on employment arbitrators, other states may experiment with optional or required elements for ADR in nonunion settings. However, it is unlikely that Congress will join the reform movement.

2. Will employers and employees continue to appoint former judges to hear employment arbitration cases?

Retired judges offer their judicial expertise to employers and employees in addressing employment arbitration cases based on federal and state statutory provisions. They come to employment arbitration with courtroom experience and familiarity in handling statutory issues. Although not necessarily skilled in addressing workplace disputes, these judges certainly bring a legitimacy that makes their decisions more acceptable to a losing party.

The use of former judges to hear employment arbitration cases may be simply a transitional phase for nonunion cases as more experienced labor arbitrators demonstrate their skills in handling statutory matters in the nonunion sector. The advantages of informality may be something these experienced labor neutrals can bring to employment arbitration cases. The ultimate decision on who will serve, of course, is that of the parties, and they will decide whether they would prefer more court-like proceedings and appoint former judges to administer their processes.

3.   *How will employees be assured of a fair shake in employment arbitration cases?*

Employees have little influence in controlling the design and operation of employment arbitration procedures. They are required to pursue arbitration under provisions they were not likely to have appreciated when they were hired. As long as employment arbitration produces fair results, however, employees will have little choice under existing law. By creating their own arbitration procedures, employers can shut the courthouse door to keep statutory cases away from juries.

The employment arbitration process is yet to reach its final stages of development. Although the legal framework for enforcing arbitration procedures has been set by Supreme Court decisions, as the use of ADR continues to expand in the nonunion sector there will be opportunity for parties—in particular, for employers—to seek changes that will ensure that employment arbitration awards are the final word. However, finality will be conditioned on proof of the fairness of the process used to reach the ultimate award.

IV. Growth of Mediation as the ADR Procedure of First Choice

Mediation is a low-cost alternative to both arbitration and litigation. As the corps of experienced, talented, and available mediators continues to grow, more parties will pursue mediation as an ordinary and customary step in their process of resolving disputes. In nonunion settings, the mediator can replace the grievance procedure as a step where matters can be settled short of litigation or arbitration. In unionized settings, mediation will reduce delays and backlogs.

1.   *What are some new ways that mediation will be used to resolve disputes?*

Changing an established system of ADR is difficult to accomplish through negotiations in the unionized workplace. Unless the parties experience a mutual dissatisfaction with the system in place, contract modifications can be difficult to implement. Yet adding a mediation step to a pre-arbitration grievance system seems like an idea that parties might explore, if only as a pilot project for identifiable cases.

Professor Emeritus Stephen Goldberg created such a system as an experimental project for the coal industry and the United Mine Workers union; it proved a remarkable success.[6] Other industries with a backlog of grievances should experiment with using mediation as a way to make sure that only cases that have to be arbitrated are brought to formal arbitration.

There has been less success with judges mandating mediation as a preliminary step before court adjudication. Imposed mediation may not offer the conditions conducive to the voluntary resolution of workplace disputes. Yet mediation may prove valuable when the parties pursue conciliation on their own initiative.

Mediation may be a preliminary step to employment arbitration that would enhance the fairness of the process. Courts and legislatures should consider whether mediation might balance the scales of justice in a process that is otherwise unilaterally established and enforced by employers.

V. Becoming a Labor Arbitrator

The single defining personal characteristic of labor arbitrators is that they are quite advanced in age. It is not likely that there are many other professions in the country where the average age is in the mid 60s. This suggests that many experienced neutrals will be leaving the profession in the coming decades.

Assuming that arbitration continues to serve the interests of the parties, there will be a need for new arbitrators to take the place of those who have gone before.

1. How does someone become a labor arbitrator?

The process of becoming an acceptable labor arbitrator can take many years and requires some good fortune. The AAA maintains a roster of labor arbitrators and administers a rigorous set of qualifications for those who seek inclusion.[7] The same is true for the FMCS.[8]

---

[6] Jeanne M. Brett & Stephen B. Goldberg, *Grievance Mediation in the Coal Industry: A Field Experiment,* 37 INDUS. & LAB. REL. REV. 49 (1983).

[7] *See* AMERICAN ARBITRATION ASSOCIATION, QUALIFICATION CRITERIA FOR ADMITTANCE TO THE AAA LABOR PANEL, *available at* http://www.adr.org/aaa/ShowPDF? doc=ADRSTG_003879.

[8] *See* FEDERAL MEDIATION AND CONCILIATION SERVICE, BECOMING AN FMCS ARBITRATOR: JOINING THE FMCS ROSTER, http://www.fmcs.gov/internet/itemDetail.asp?cate goryID=184&itemID=16436.

Securing a place on these rosters, however, does not mean that an arbitrator receives appointments to hear cases.

For most arbitrators, it can take years to develop a reputation for good service as a neutral. For many on the rosters, arbitration appointments are rare, if they come at all. Parties tend, for good reason, to appoint neutrals they have used in the past. Experienced arbitrators bring skills to the resolution of workplace disputes that junior arbitrators might not yet have developed.

2.   *Where will the next generation of arbitrators come from?*

The average age of an active labor arbitrator today is 66. Many members of the corps of neutrals are in their 80s. They continue to hear cases and resolve disputes, although there is a question of how well they can continue to perform the required tasks and accomplish the travel that is sometimes necessary. Regretfully, each issue of the newsletter of the National Academy of Arbitrators (NAA) contains pages of obituaries. At some point, the parties, as part of their selection process, will decide whether senior arbitrators can continue to serve them as well as they have in the past.

Arbitrators have an obligation to train the next generation of arbitrators. That is easy to say, but as the number of grievance disputes brought to arbitration decreases with the decline in the labor movement, it is difficult to ask full-time arbitrators to prepare others to take their places. The Code of Professional Responsibility, however, makes this obligation clear: "An experienced arbitrator should cooperate in the training of new arbitrators."[9]

3.   *Is there a better way to train new arbitrators?*

Little attention has been paid to the systematic training of the next generation of neutrals, perhaps because there is great uncertainty as to the size of the caseload and the future demand for new arbitrators in the labor-management community. Of course, labor and management will require some new arbitrators, although it is unclear how many will be needed. As stated earlier, there is no established mechanism for educating new arbitrators.

---

[9]NATIONAL ACADEMY OF ARBITRATORS, AMERICAN ARBITRATION ASSOCIATION, & FEDERAL MEDIATION & CONCILIATION SERVICE, CODE OF PROFESSIONAL RESPONSIBILITY FOR ARBITRATORS OF LABOR-MANAGEMENT DISPUTES §1.C.4 (as amended and in effect Sept. 2007), *available at* http://www.naarb.org/code.html (reproduced in Appendix B).

Many members of the next generation of arbitrators currently work as labor relations professionals, in human resources, for international unions, and as labor relations academics. Others serve as practitioners who represent unions or management, and that may be where they receive their initial exposure to the arbitration process. When they become arbitrators, these neutrals struggle to become "acceptable" to the parties who might select them to serve as their arbitrators. Today there is no deficit in the number of arbitrators. Thousands who have been admitted to the labor panels of the AAA and the FMCS receive only a few (if any) appointments per year.

The problem with the corps of labor arbitrators is not that there are too few willing to pursue the occupation. The problem is that too few arbitrators are appointed to hear cases. Labor and management have focused on a few hundred neutrals to hear the bulk of their cases, and those men and women continue to move toward retirement. The problem is determining how those other arbitrators can take their places.

4.   How does a new arbitrator become recognized?

Labor arbitration is a learned profession, like the practice of law. A successful neutral understands not only the practices of the workplace and the intricacies of the CBA, but also how to run an efficient hearing, research a complex record, and write a cogent, understandable, and timely opinion for the parties.

Although appointing agencies serve as gatekeepers, their review of potential neutrals is cursory. Their central concern is to make sure that members of their panels are truly impartial. However, a person who is completely unbiased with regard to the interests of labor and management may also be completely incompetent in terms of performing the obligations of an arbitrator.

The marketplace controls who is chosen to serve as arbitrators—the parties decide. Although the alternative of having an arbitrator appointed by some authority outside of the collective relationship undermines one of the core distinctions of arbitration—the legitimacy that flows from the parties selecting their own neutral—and the selecting parties generally do not have enough information to make an informed choice.

Parties do review the credentials of the list of potential arbitrators who are presented to them by an appointing agency. They look at potential arbitrators' education, experience, per diem, and likely their age. They may seek input from many sources. In the final analysis, however, the most compelling data will be prior experience with a particular neutral. A bad experience will blackball a candidate. A good experience may put him or her at the top of a party's list.

The parties need more information, especially when it comes to new arbitrators. Currently, it is unclear how parties decide whether to take a chance on someone who is quite junior in the field.

VI. Credentialing Arbitrators

The current system of arbitral selection suffers from information failure. The future of the labor arbitration process depends on the selection of new arbitrators based on valid criteria. One way to accomplish this goal is by credentialing new neutrals.

1.   Might there be some way to credential new arbitrators with the greatest potential?

There are two ways to credential new professionals in any field. The first is by providing specialized training; the second is by mandating accreditation. In the legal profession, credentialing is accomplished by requiring lawyers to pursue advanced training in a law school accredited by the American Bar Association and then mandating that they pass a state bar examination.[10]

How would this work in the field of labor arbitration? Persons seeking credentialing would pursue a year-long training program that includes lectures, field work, and interning. Upon completion of the course, participants could include this credential on their résumés and biographies. Parties would be able to recognize the value of the credential in making their selections from among new arbitrators. This educational effort could be hosted by, for example, the Cornell University School of Industrial and Labor Relations, which would serve as a center for the study of arbitration and the training of future arbitrators.

2.   Are there other possible credentials that could assist parties when they select neutrals?

Parties have long relied on membership in the NAA as a useful credential in the selection of arbitrators. In fact, some CBAs require that the arbitrator be a member of the NAA. To become a member, an

---

[10]These two steps could be collapsed into a single stage. In Wisconsin, for example, students who graduate from a law school in the state need not take the state bar examination. Under the so-called *diploma privilege,* such graduates are automatically admitted to the Wisconsin bar. *See* Wisconsin Court System, For Attorneys: Admission to the Practice of Law in Wisconsin, http://www.wicourts.gov/services/attorney/bardiploma.htm.

arbitrator must demonstrate substantial acceptability as a neutral in the field.[11] The problem with the NAA credential is that it is both over- and under-inclusive.

There are longtime, very senior NAA members who are no longer able to perform well as arbitrators. Similarly, there are terrific junior arbitrators who have not yet accumulated the caseload to qualify for membership consideration. The NAA could identify a group of "potential future candidates" who have enjoyed substantial acceptability and will likely be nominated and qualify for membership in a few years, with the appropriate disclaimer as to this being either exhaustive or an endorsement of the individuals listed. Much as the construction trades use an apprenticeship program, the NAA could help these arbitrators through this recognition.

The NAA could also operate a live training program for junior arbitrators that would expose these new neutrals to ideas and experiences of the best of the country's corps of neutrals.[12] The program would include the observation of arbitration hearings conducted by experienced NAA members and the writing of mock awards that would be reviewed and critiqued. The program would offer a certificate of completion that parties could look to in choosing among junior arbitrators. In this regard, it should be noted that the FMCS currently offers a not-for-profit, noncommercial course titled "Becoming a Labor Arbitrator" that seeks to assist with the education and training of aspiring labor arbitrators for inclusion on the FMCS roster. The course materials include excerpts from NAA writings.

It is important for the current corps of labor arbitrators to pass on what they have learned to the next generation of impartial neutrals. Whether this is accomplished through formal courses in a certificate program or informal sessions where experienced arbitrators work with junior arbitrators, the process must go on. Much like the Inns of Court in England, the transmittal of information and experiences to those who will serve the parties in the decades to come is critical. One purpose of this book has been to record some of that data, and, it is hoped, that goal has been accomplished.

---

[11] *See* NATIONAL ACADEMY OF ARBITRATORS, NAA MEMBERSHIP GUIDELINES, http://naarb.org/member_guidelines.asp. The threshold requirement is "at least five years of arbitration experience and a minimum of 60 written decisions in a time period not to exceed six years, at least 40 of which must be 'countable labor-management arbitration awards.'" *Id.*

[12] Such a training program is described in CHRISTOPHER BARRECA, ANNE HARMON MILLER, & MAX ZIMNY, LABOR ARBITRATION DEVELOPMENT: A HANDBOOK (1983).

Appendices

Appendix A

The *Steelworkers Trilogy*

STEELWORKERS V. AMERICAN MANUFACTURING CO., 363 U.S. 564, 34 LA 559 (1960)

STEELWORKERS v. AMERICAN MFG. CO.   **34 LA 559**

STEELWORKERS v. AMERICAN MFG. CO.

Supreme Court of the United States

UNITED STEELWORKERS OF AMERICA v. AMERICAN MANUFACTURING COMPANY, No. 360, June 20, 1960

LABOR - MANAGEMENT RELATIONS ACT

—Arbitration agreement—Enforcement—Role of courts ▶ 94.09 ▶ 94.750
US SupCt

In actions under Section 301 of LMRA for specific performance of agreements to arbitrate all questions of contract interpretation, the function of courts is limited to ascertaining whether the party seeking arbitration is making a claim which on its face is governed by contract; the courts may not undertake to determine the merits of grievance under guise of interpreting arbitration clause of contract. Arbitration therefore should be ordered if dispute involves a claim that substantive provision of contract has been violated. (US SupCt)—United Steelworkers of America v. American Mfg. Co., 34 LA 559.

—Arbitration agreement — Enforcement—Contract interpretation ▶ 94.117
US SupCt

In suit under Section 301 of LMRA for specific performance of agreement to arbitrate all questions of contract interpretation, arbitration should have been ordered of union's claim that company violated contract's seniority provisions by refusing to reinstate employee who had settled workmen's compensation claim against company on basis that he was permanently partially disabled, since dispute necessarily involves interpretation of contract. (US SupCt)—United Steelworkers of America v. American Mfg. Co., 34 LA 559.

On writ of certiorari to the U. S. Court of Appeals for the Sixth Circuit (43 LRRM 2757, 32 LA 238, 264 F.2d 624). Reversed.

David E. Feller (Arthur J. Goldberg, Elliot Bredhoff, and Jerry D. Anker with him on the brief), Washington, D.C., for petitioner.

John S. Carriger (John S. Fletcher with him on the brief), Chattanooga, Tenn., for respondent.

Full Text of Opinion

Mr. Justice DOUGLAS delivered the opinion of the Court.

This suit was brought by petitioner union in the District Court to compel arbitration of a "grievance" that petitioner, acting for one Sparks, a union member, had filed with the respondent, Sparks' employer. The employer defended on the ground (1) that Sparks is estopped from making his claim because he had a few days previously settled a workmen's compensation claim against the company on the basis that he was permanently partially disabled, (2) that Sparks is not physically able to do the work, and (3) that this type of dispute is not arbitrable under the collective bargaining agreement in question.

[PROVISIONS OF CONTRACT]

The agreement provided that during its term there would be "no strike," unless the employer refused to abide by a decision of the arbitrator. The agreement sets out a detailed grievance procedure with a provision for arbitration (regarded as the standard form) of all disputes between the parties "as to the meaning, interpretation and application of the provisions of this agreement."[1]

The agreement also reserves to the management power to suspend or discharge any employee "for cause."[2] It also contains a provision that the employer will employ and promote em-

---

[1] The relevant arbitration provisions read as follows:

"Any disputes, misunderstandings, differences or grievances arising between the parties as to the meaning, interpretation and application of the provisions of this agreement, which are not adjusted as herein provided, may be submitted to the Board of Arbitration for decision. * * *

"The arbitrator may interpret this agreement and apply it to the particular case under consideration but shall, however, have no authority to add to, subtract from, or modify the terms of the agreement. Disputes relating to discharges or such matters as might involve a loss of pay for employees may carry an award of back pay in whole or in part as may be determined by the Board of Arbitration.

"The decision of the Board of Arbitration shall be final and conclusively binding upon both parties, and the parties agree to observe and abide by same. * * *"

[2] "The Management of the works, the direction of the working force, plant layout and routine of work, including the right to hire, suspend, transfer, discharge or otherwise discipline any employee for cause, such cause being: infraction of company rules, inefficiency, insubordination, contagious disease harmful to others, and any other ground or reason that would tend to reduce or impair the efficiency of plant operation; and to lay off employees because of lack of work, is reserved to the Company, provided it does not conflict with this agreement. * * *"

Symbol ▶ *indicates number under Index-Digest*

Decisions and Recommendations

ployees on the principle of seniority "where ability and efficiency are equal."[3] Sparks left his work due to an injury and while off work brought an action for compensation benefits. The case was settled, Sparks' physician expressing the opinion that the injury had made him 25% permanently partially disabled. That was on September 9. Two weeks later the union filed a grievance which charged that Sparks was entitled to return to his job by virtue of the seniority provision of the collective bargaining agreement. Respondent refused to arbitrate and this action was brought. The District Court held that Sparks, having accepted the settlement on the basis of permanent partial disability was estopped to claim any seniority or employment rights and granted the motion for summary judgment. The Court of Appeals affirmed, 264 F.2d 624, 43 LRRM 2757, for different reasons. After reviewing the evidence it held that the grievance is "a frivolous, patently baseless one, not subject to arbitration under the collective bargaining agreement." Id., at 628. The case is here on a writ of certiorari, 361 U.S. 881.

[POLICY OF LMRA]

Section 203(d) of the Labor Management Relations Act, 1947, 61 Stat. 154, 29 U.S.C. § 173(d) states, "Final adjustment by a method agreed upon by the parties is hereby declared to be the desirable method for settlement of grievance disputes arising over the application or interpretation of an existing collective-bargaining agreement. * * *" That policy can be effectuated only if the means chosen by the parties for settlement of their differences under a collective bargaining agreement is given full play. A state decision that held to the contrary announced a principle that could only have a crippling effect on grievance arbitration. The case was International Assn. of Machinists v. Cutler-Hammer, Inc., 271 App.Div. 917, 19 LRRM 2232, aff'd 297 N.Y. 519, 20 LRRM 2445. It held that "If the meaning of the provision of the contract sought to be arbitrated is beyond dispute, there cannot be anything to arbitrate and the contract cannot be

said to provide for arbitration." 271 App.Div., at 918. The lower courts in the instant case had a like preoccupation with ordinary contract law. The collective agreement requires arbitration of claims that courts might be unwilling to entertain. Yet in the context of the plant or industry the grievance may assume proportions of which judges are ignorant. Moreover, the agreement is to submit all grievances to arbitration, not merely those that a court may deem to be meritorious. There is no exception in the "no strike" clause and none therefore should be read into the grievance clause, since one is the *quid pro quo* for the other.[4] The question is not whether in the mind of a court there is equity in the claim. Arbitration is a stabilizing influence only as it serves as a vehicle for handling every and all disputes that arise under the agreement.

[FUNCTION OF COURT]

The collective agreement calls for the submission of grievances in the categories which it describes irrespective of whether a court may deem them to be meritorious. In our role of developing a meaningful body of law to govern the interpretation and enforcement of collective bargaining agreements, we think special heed should be given to the context in which collective bargaining agreements are negotiated and the purpose which they are intended to serve. See Lewis v. Benedict Coal Corp., 361 U. S. 459, 468, 45 LRRM 2719. The function of the court is very limited when the parties have agreed to submit all questions of contract interpretation to the arbitrator. It is then confined to ascertaining whether the party seeking arbitration is making a claim which on its face is governed by the contract. Whether the moving party is right or wrong is a question of contract interpretation for the arbitrator. In these circumstances the moving party should not be deprived of the arbitrator's judgment, when it was his judgment and all that it connotes that was bargained for.

The courts therefore have no business weighing the merits of the grievance,[5] considering whether there

---

[3] This provision provides in relevant part: "The Company and the Union fully recognize the principle of seniority as a factor in the selection of employees for promotion, transfer, lay-off, re-employment, and filling of vacancies, where ability and efficiency are equal. It is the policy of the Company to promote employees on that basis."

[4] Cf. Structural Steel & Ornament Assn. v. Shopmen's Local Union, 172 F.Supp. 354, 43 LRRM 2868, where the employer sued for breach of the "no strike" agreement.

[5] See New Bedford Defense Products Division v. Local No. 1113, 258 F.2d 522, 526, 42 LRRM 2518 (C.A. 1st Cir.).

STEELWORKERS V. WARRIOR & GULF NAVIGATION CO., 363 U.S. 593, 34 LA 561 (1960)

STEELWORKERS v. WARRIOR NAVIGATION CO.   34 LA 561

is equity in a particular claim, or determining whether there is particular language in the written instrument which will support the claim. The agreement is to submit all grievances to arbitration, not merely those the court will deem meritorious. The processing of even frivolous claims may have therapeutic values which those who are not a part of the plant environment may be quite unaware.[6]

The union claimed in this case that the company had violated a specific provision of the contract. The company took the position that it had not violated that clause. There was, therefore, a dispute between the parties as to "the meaning, interpretation and application" of the collective bargaining agreement. Arbitration should have been ordered. When the judiciary undertakes to determine the merits of a grievance under the guise of interpreting the grievance procedure of collective bargaining agreements, it usurps a function which under that regime is entrusted to the arbitration tribunal.

Reversed.

Mr. Justice FRANKFURTER concurs in the result.

Mr. Justice WHITTAKER, believing that the District Court lacked jurisdiction to determine the merits of the claim which the parties had validly agreed to submit to the exclusive jurisdiction of a Board of Arbitrators (Textile Workers v. Lincoln Mills, 353 U. S. 448, 40 LRRM 2113, 2120), concurs in the result of this opinion.

Mr. Justice BLACK took no part in the consideration or decision of this case.

---

[6] Cox, Current Problems in the Law of Grievance Arbitration, 30 Rocky Mt. L. Rev. 247, 261 (1958), writes:
"The typical arbitration clause is written in words which cover, without limitation, all disputes concerning the interpretation or application of a collective bargaining agreement. Its words do not restrict its scope to meritorious disputes or two-sided disputes, still less are they limited to disputes which a judge will consider two-sided. Frivolous cases are often taken, and are expected to be taken, to arbitration. What one man considers frivolous another may find meritorious, and it is common knowledge in industrial relations circles that grievance arbitration often serves as a safety valve for troublesome complaints. Under these circumstances it seems proper to read the typical arbitration clause as a promise to arbitrate every claim, meritorious or frivolous, which the complainant bases upon the contract. The objection that equity will not order a party to do a useless act is outweighed by the cathartic value of arbitrating even a frivolous grievance and by the dangers of excessive judicial intervention."

STEELWORKERS v. WARRIOR NAVIGATION CO.

Supreme Court of the United States

UNITED STEELWORKERS OF AMERICA v. WARRIOR AND GULF NAVIGATION COMPANY, No. 443, June 20, 1960

LABOR - MANAGEMENT RELATIONS ACT

—Arbitration agreement — Enforcement—Role of courts ▶ 94.09 ▶ 94.750
US SupCt

In suits under Section 301 of LMRA for specific performance of collectively-bargained arbitration agreements, arbitration should be ordered unless it may be said with positive assurance that the arbitration clause is not susceptible to an interpretation that covers the asserted dispute. Doubts should be resolved in favor of coverage. (US SupCt)—United Steelworkers of America v. Warrior & Gulf Navigation Co., 34 LA 561.

—Arbitration agreement—Arbitrable issue—Subcontracting of work ▶ 94. 166 ▶ 2.01 ▶ 117.38
US SupCt

Union is entitled, in action brought under Section 301 of LMRA, to an order requiring employer to arbitrate grievance alleging that its contracting-out of work violated collective bargaining agreement, notwithstanding provision excluding from arbitration matters which are "strictly a function of management." Such phrase must be interpreted as excluding only matters over which contract gives management complete control and unfettered discretion, and contracting-out of work does not fall within this category. Grievance therefore involves a dispute as to contract's meaning and application which the parties had agreed would be determined by arbitration. (US SupCt)—United Steelworkers of America v. Warrior & Gulf Navigation Co., 34 LA 561.

On writ of certiorari to the U. S. Court of Appeals for the Fifth Circuit (44 LRRM 2567, 32 LA 944, 269 F.2d 633). Reversed.

David E. Feller (Arthur J. Goldberg, Elliot Bredhoff, and Jerry D. Anker with him on the brief), Washington, D.C., for petitioner.

Samuel Lang, New Orleans, La., (Richard C. Keenan, New Orleans, La., and T. K. Jackson, Jr., Mobile, Ala., with him on the brief), for respondent.

34 LA 562   STEELWORKERS v. WARRIOR NAVIGATION CO.

Full Text of Opinion

Mr. Justice DOUGLAS delivered the opinion of the Court.

Respondent transports steel and steel products by barge and maintains a terminal at Chickasaw, Alabama, where it performs maintenance and repair work on its barges. The employees at that terminal constitute a bargaining unit covered by a collective bargaining agreement negotiated by petitioner union. Respondent between 1956 and 1958 laid off some employees, reducing the bargaining unit from 42 to 23 men. This reduction was due in part to respondent contracting maintenance work, previously done by its employees, to other companies. The latter used respondent's supervisors to lay out the work and hired some of the laid-off employees of respondent (at reduced wages). Some were in fact assigned to work on respondent's barges. A number of employees signed a grievance which petitioner presented to respondent, the grievance reading:

"We are hereby protesting the Company's actions, of arbitrarily and unreasonably contracting out work to other concerns, that could and previously has been performed by Company employees.

"This practice becomes unreasonable, unjust and discriminatory in view of the fact that at present there are a number of employees that have been laid off for about 1 and ½ years or more for allegedly lack of work.

"Confronted with these facts we charge that the Company is in violation of the contract by inducing a partial lockout, of a number of the employees who would otherwise be working were if not for this unfair practice."

[GRIEVANCE PROCEDURE]

The collective agreement had both a "no strike" and a "no lockout" provision. It also had a grievance procedure which provided in relevant part as follows:

"Issues which conflict with any Federal statute in its application as established by Court procedure or matters which are strictly a function of management shall not be subject to arbitration under this section.

"Should differences arise between the Company and the Union or its members employed by the Company as to the meaning and application of the provisions of this Agreement, or should any local trouble of any kind arise, there shall be no suspension of work on account of such differences but an earnest effort shall be made to settle such differences immediately in the following manner:

"A. For Maintenance Employees:

"First, between the aggrieved employees, and the Foreman involved; Second, between a member or members of the Grievance Committee designated by the Union and the Foreman and Master Mechanic."

* * *

"Fifth, if agreement has not been reached the matter shall be referred to an impartial umpire for decision. The parties shall meet to decide on an umpire acceptable to both. If no agreement on selection of an umpire is reached, the parties shall jointly petition the United States Conciliation Service for suggestion of a list of umpires from which selection will be made. The decision of the umpire shall be final."

Settlement of this grievance was not had and respondent refused arbitration. This suit was then commenced by the union to compel it.[1]

[THEORY OF COURTS BELOW]

The District Court granted respondent's motion to dismiss the complaint. 168 F. Supp. 702, 43 LRRM 2328. It held after hearing evidence, much of which went to the merits of the grievance, that the agreement did not "confide in an arbitrator the right to review the defendant's business judgment in contracting out work." Id., at 705. It further held that "the contracting out of repair and maintenance work, as well as construction work, is strictly a function of management not limited in any respect by the labor agreement involved here." Ibid. The Court of Appeals affirmed by a divided vote, 269 F.2d 633, 44 LRRM 2567, the majority holding that the collective agreement had withdrawn from the grievance procedure "matters which are strictly a function of management" and that contracting-out fell in that exception. The case is here on a writ of certiorari. 361 U.S. 912.

We held in Textile Workers v. Lincoln Mills, 353 U.S. 448, 40 LRRM 2113, 2120, that a grievance arbitration provision in a collective agreement could be enforced by reason of § 301(a) of the Labor Management Relations Act[2] and that the policy to be applied in enforcing this type of arbitration was that reflected in our national

---

1 Section 301(a) of the Labor Management Relations Act, 1947, 61 Stat. 156, 29 U.S.C. § 185 (a), provides:

"Suits for violation of contracts between an employer and a labor organization representing employees in an industry affecting commerce as defined in this Act, or between any such labor organizations, may be brought in any district court of the United States having jurisdiction of the parties, without respect to the amount in controversy or without regard to the citizenship of the parties." See Textile Workers v. Lincoln Mills, 353 U.S. 448, 40 LRRM 2113, 2120.

2 Note 1, supra.

STEELWORKERS v. WARRIOR NAVIGATION CO.   **34 LA 563**

labor laws. Id., at 456-457. The present federal policy is to promote industrial stabilization through the collective bargaining agreement.[3] Id., at 453-454. A major factor in achieving industrial peace is the inclusion of a provision for arbitration of grievances in the collective bargaining agreement.[4]

Thus the run of arbitration cases, illustrated by Wilko v. Swan, 346 U.S. 427, become irrelevant to our problem. There the choice is between the adjudication of cases or controversies in courts with established procedures or even special statutory safeguards on the one hand and the settlement of them in the more informal arbitration tribunal on the other. In the commercial case, arbitration is the substitute for litigation. Here arbitration is the substitute for industrial strife. Since arbitration of labor disputes has quite different functions from arbitration under an ordinary commercial agreement, the hostility evinced by courts toward arbitration of commercial agreements has no place here. For arbitration of labor disputes u n d e r collective bargaining agreements is part and parcel of the collective bargaining process itself.

[COLLECTIVE AGREEMENT]

The collective bargaining agreement states the rights and duties of the parties. It is more than a contract; it is a generalized code to govern a myriad of cases which the draftsmen cannot wholly anticipate. See Shulman, Reason, Contract, and Law in Labor Relations, 68 Harv. L. Rev. 999, 1004-1005. The collective agreement covers the whole employment relationship.[5] It calls into being a new

common law—the common law of a particular industry or of a particular plant. As one observer has put it:[6]

"* * * [I] t is not unqualifiedly true that a collective-bargaining agreement is simply a document by which the union and employees have imposed upon management limited, express restrictions of its otherwise absolute right to manage the enterprise, so that an employee's claim must fail unless he can point to a specific contract provision upon which the claim is founded. There are too many people, too many problems, too many unforeseeable contingencies to make the words of the contract the exclusive source of rights and duties. One cannot reduce all the rules governing a community like an industrial plant to fifteen or even fifty pages. Within the sphere of collective bargaining, the institutional characteristics and the governmental nature of the collective-bargaining process demand a common law of the shop which implements and furnishes the context of the agreement. We must assume that intelligent negotiators acknowledged so plain a need unless they stated a contrary rule in plain words."

A collective bargaining agreement is an effort to erect a system of in dustrial self-government. When most parties enter into contractual relationship they do so voluntarily, in the sense that there is no real compulsion to deal with one another, as opposed to dealing with other parties. This is not true of the labor agreement. The choice is generally not between entering or refusing to enter into a relationship, for that in all probability pre-exists the negotiations. Rather it is between having that relationship governed by an agreed upon rule of law or leaving each and every matter subject to a temporary resolution dependent solely upon the relative strength, at any given moment, of the contending forces. The mature labor agreement may attempt to regulate all aspects of the complicated relationship, from the most crucial to the most

---

3 In § 8(d) of the 1947 Act, 29 U.S.C. § 158 (d), Congress indeed provided that where there was a collective agreement for a fixed term the duty to bargain did not require either party "to discuss or agree to any modification of the terms and conditions contained in" the contract. And see Labor Board v. Sands Mfg. Co., 306 U.S. 332, 4 LRRM 530.

4 Complete effectuation of the federal policy is achieved when the agreement contains both an arbitration provision for all unresolved grievances and an absolute prohibition of strikes, the arbitration agreement being the *"quid pro quo"* for the agreement not to strike. Textile Workers v. Lincoln Mills, 353 U.S. 448, 455, 40 LRRM 2113, 2120.

5 "Contracts which ban strikes often provide for lifting the ban under certain conditions. Unconditional pledges against strikes are, however, somewhat more frequent than conditional ones. Where conditions are attached to no-strike pledges, one or both of two approaches may be used: certain *subjects* may be exempted from the scope of the pledge, or the pledge may be lifted after certain *procedures* are followed by the union.

(Similar qualifications may be made in pledges against lockouts.)

"Most frequent conditions for lifting no-strike pledges are: (1) The occurrence of a deadlock in wage reopening negotiations; and (2) violation of the contract, especially noncompliance with the grievance procedure and failure to abide by an arbitration award.

"No-strike pledges may also be lifted after compliance with specified procedures. Some contracts permit the union to strike after the grievance procedure has been exhausted without a settlement, and where arbitration is not prescribed as the final recourse. Other contracts permit a strike if mediation efforts fail, or after a specified cooling-off period." Collective Bargaining Negotiations and Contracts, Bureau of National Affairs, Inc., 77:101.

6 Cox, Reflections Upon Labor Arbitration, 72 Harv. L. Rev. 1482, 1498-1499 (1959).

minute over an extended period of time. Because of the compulsion to reach agreement and the breadth of the matters covered, as well as the need for a fairly concise and readable instrument, the product of negotiations (the written document) is, in the words of the late Dean Shulman, "a compilation of diverse provisions; some provide objective criteria almost automatically applicable; some provide more or less specific standards which require reason and judgment in their application; and some do little more than leave problems to future consideration with an expression of hope and good faith." Shulman, supra, at 1005. Gaps may be left to be filled in by reference to the practices of the particular industry and of the various shops covered by the agreement. Many of the specific practices which underlie the agreement may be unknown, except in hazy form, even to the negotiators. Courts and arbitration in the context of most commercial contracts are resorted to because there has been a breakdown in the working relationship of the parties; such resort is the unwanted exception. But the grievance machinery under a collective bargaining agreement is at the very heart of the system of industrial self-government. Arbitration is the means of solving the unforeseeable by molding a system of private law for all the problems which may arise and to provide for their solution in a way which will generally accord with the variant needs and desires of the parties. The processing of disputes through the grievance machinery is actually a vehicle by which meaning and content is given to the collective bargaining agreement.

[SCOPE OF ARBITRATION CLAUSE]

Apart from matters that the parties specifically exclude, all of the questions on which the parties disagree must therefore come within the scope of the grievance and arbitration provisions of the collective agreement. The grievance procedure is, in other words, a part of the continuous collective bargaining process. It, rather than a strike, is the terminal point of a disagreement.

"A proper conception of the arbitrator's function is basic. He is not a public tribunal imposed upon the parties by superior authority which the parties are obliged to accept. He has no general charter to administer justice for a community which transcends the parties. He is rather part of a system of self-government created by and confined to the parties. * * *" Shulman, supra, at 1016.

The labor arbitrator performs functions which are not normal to the courts; the considerations which help him fashion judgments may indeed be foreign to the competence of courts. The labor arbitrator's source of law is not confined to the express provisions of the contract, as the industrial common law—the practices of the industry and the shop—is equally a part of the collective bargaining agreement although not expressed in it. The labor arbitrator is usually chosen because of the parties' confidence in his knowledge of the common law of the shop and their trust in his personal judgment to bring to bear considerations which are not expressed in the contract as criteria for judgment. The parties expect that his judgment of a particular grievance will reflect not only what the contract says but, insofar as the collective bargaining agreement permits, such factors as the effect upon productivity of a particular result, its consequence to the morale of the shop, his judgment whether tensions will be heightened or diminished. For the parties' objective in using the arbitration process is primarily to further their common goal of uninterrupted production under the agreement, to make the agreement serve their specialized needs. The ablest judge cannot be expected to bring the same experience and competence to bear upon the determination of a grievance, because he cannot be similarly informed.

[JUDICIAL INQUIRY]

The Congress, however, has by § 301 of the Labor Management Relations Act, assigned the courts the duty of determining whether the reluctant party has breached his promise to arbitrate. For arbitration is a matter of contract and a party cannot be required to submit to arbitration any dispute which he has not agreed so to submit. Yet, to be consistent with congressional policy in favor of settlement of disputes by the parties through the machinery of arbitration, the judicial inquiry under § 301 must be strictly confined to the question whether the reluctant party did agree to arbitrate the grievance or agreed to give the arbitrator power to make the award he made. An order to arbitrate the particular grievance should not be denied unless it may be said with posi-

STEELWORKERS v. WARRIOR NAVIGATION CO. **34 LA 565**

tive assurance that the arbitration clause is not susceptible to an interpretation that covers the asserted dispute. Doubts should be resolved in favor of coverage.[7]

We do not agree with the lower courts that contracting-out grievances were necessarily excepted from the grievance procedure of this agreement. To be sure the agreement provides that "matters which are strictly a function of management shall not be subject to arbitration." But it goes on to say that if "differences" arise or if "any local trouble of any kind" arises, the grievance procedure shall be applicable.

Collective bargaining agreements regulate or restrict the exercise of management functions; they do not oust management from the performance of them. Management hires and fires, pays and promotes, supervises and plans. All these are part of its function, and absent a collective bargaining agreement, it may be exercised freely except as limited by public law and by the willingness of employees to work under the particular, unilaterally imposed conditions. A collective bargaining agreement may treat only with certain specific practices, leaving the rest to management but subject to the possibility of work stoppages. When, however, an absolute no-strike clause is included in the agreement, then in a very real sense everything that management does is subject to the agreement, for either management is prohibited or limited in the action it takes, or if not, it is protected from interference by strikes. This comprehensive reach of the collective bargaining agreement does not mean, however, that the language, "strictly a function of management" has no meaning.

"Strictly a function of management" might be thought to refer to any practice of management in which, under particular circumstances prescribed by the agreement, it is permitted to indulge. But if courts, in order to determine arbitrability, were

allowed to determine what is permitted and what is not, the arbitration clause would be swallowed up by the exception. Every grievance in a sense involves a claim that management has violated some provision of the agreement.

[FUNCTION OF MANAGEMENT]

Accordingly, "strictly a function of management" must be interpreted as referring only to that over which the contract gives management complete control and unfettered discretion. Respondent claims that the contracting-out of work falls within this category. Contracting-out work is the basis of many grievances; and that type of claim is grist in the mills of the arbitrators.[8] A specific collective bargaining agreement may exclude contracting-out from the grievance procedure. Or a written collateral agreement may make clear that contracting-out was not a matter for arbitration. In such a case a grievance based solely on contracting-out would not be arbitrable. Here, however, there is no such provision. Nor is there any showing that the parties designed the phrase "strictly a function of management" to encompass any and all forms of contracting-out. In the absence of any express provision excluding a particular grievance from arbitration, we think only the most forceful evidence of a purpose to exclude the claim from arbitration can prevail, particularly where, as here, the exclusion clause is vague and the arbitration clause quite broad. Since any attempt by a court to infer such a purpose necessarily comprehends the merits, the court should view with suspicion an attempt to persuade it to become entangled in the construction of the substantive provisions of a labor agreement, even through the back door of interpreting the arbitration clause, when the alternative is to utilize the services of an arbitrator.

The grievance alleged that the contracting-out was a violation of the collective bargaining agreement. There was, therefore, a dispute "as to the meaning and application of the provisions of this Agreement" which the

[7] It is clear that under both the agreement in this case and that involved in American Manufacturing Co., ante. p.—, 46 LRRM 2414, the question of arbitrability is for the courts to decide. Cf. Cox, Reflections Upon Labor Arbitration, 72 Harv. L. Rev. 1482, 1508-1509. Where the assertion by the claimant is that the parties excluded from court determination not merely the decision of the merits of the grievance but also the question of its arbitrability, vesting power to make both decisions in the arbitrator, the claimant must bear the burden of a clear demonstration of that purpose.

[8] See Celanese Corp. of America, 33 LA 925, 941 (1959), where the arbiter in a grievance growing out of contracting-out work said:
"In my research I have located 64 published decisions which have been concerned with this issue covering a wide range of factual situations but all of them with the common characteristic—i. e., the contracting-out of work involved occurred under an Agreement that contained no provision that specifically mentioned contracting-out of work."

parties had agreed would be determined by arbitration.

The judiciary sits in these cases to bring into operation an arbitral process which substitutes a regime of peaceful settlement for the older regime of industrial conflict. Whether contracting-out in the present case violated the agreement is the question. It is a question for the arbiter, not for the courts.

Reversed.

Mr. Justice FRANKFURTER concurs in the result.

Mr. Justice BLACK took no part in the consideration or decision of this case.

Dissenting Opinion

Mr. Justice WHITTAKER, dissenting.

Until today, I have understood it to be the unquestioned law, as this Court has consistently held, that arbitrators are private judges chosen by the parties to decide particular matters specifically submitted;[1] that the contract under which matters are submitted to arbitrators is at once the source and limit of their authority and power;[2] and that their power to decide issues with finality, thus ousting the normal functions of the courts, must rest upon a clear, definitive agreement of the parties, as such powers can never be implied. United States v. Moorman, 338 U.S. 457, 462;[3] Mercantile Trust Co. v. Hensey, 205 U.S. 298, 309.[4] See also Fernandez & Hnos v. Rickert Mills, 119 F.2d 809, 815 (C.A. 1st Cir.);[5] Marchant v. Mead-Morrison Mfg. Co., 252 N.Y.

[1] "Arbitrators are judges chosen by the parties to decide the matter submitted to them." Burchell v. Marsh, 17 How. 334, 349.

[2] "The agreement under which [the arbitrators] were selected *was at once the source and limit of their authority,* and the award, to be binding, must, in substance and form, conform to the submission." Continental Ins. Co. v. Garrett, 125 F. 589, 590 (C.A. 6th Cir.)—Opinion by Judge, later Mr. Justice, Lurton. (Emphasis added.)

[3] "It is true that *the intention of the parties to submit their contractual disputes to final determination outside the courts should be made manifest by plain language."* United States v. Moorman, 338 U.S. 457, 462. (Emphasis added.)

[4] "To make such [an arbitrator's] certificate conclusive *requires plain language in the contract.* It is not to be implied." Mercantile Trust Co. v. Hensey, 205 U. S. 298, 309. (Emphasis added.)

[5] "A party is never required to submit to arbitration any question which he has not agreed so to submit, and contracts providing for arbitration *will be carefully construed in order not to force a party to submit to arbitration a question which he did not intend to be submitted."* Fernandez & Hnos v. Rickert Rice Mills, 119 F. 2d 809, 815 (C.A. 1st Cir.). (Emphasis added.)

284, 299, 169 N.E. 386, 391;[6] Continental Milling & Feed Co. v. Doughnut Corp., 186 Md. 669, 48 A.2d 447, 450;[7] Jacob v. Weisser, 207 Pa. 484, 56 A. 1065, 1067.[8] I believe that the Court today departs the established principles announced in these decisions.

Here, the employer operates a shop for the normal maintenance of its barges, but it is not equipped to make major repairs, and accordingly the employer has, from the beginning of its operations more than 19 years ago, contracted out its major work. During most, if not all, of this time the union has represented the employees in that unit. The District Court found that "[t]hroughout the successive labor agreements between these parties, including the present one, * * * [the union] has unsuccessfully sought to negotiate changes in the labor contract, and particularly during the negotiation of the present labor agreement, * * * which would have limited the right of the [employer] to continue the practice of contracting out such work." 168 F.Supp. 702, 704-705, 43 LRRM 2328.

[ARBITRATION CLAUSE]

The labor agreement involved here provides for arbitration of disputes respecting the interpretation and application of the agreement and, arguably,

[6] In this leading case, Judge, later Mr. Justice, Cardozo said:

"The question is one of intention, to be ascertained by the same tests that are applied to contracts generally. * * * No one is under a duty to resort to these conventional tribunals, however helpful their processes, *except to the extent that he has signified his willingness.* Our own favor or disfavor of the cause of arbitration is not to count as a factor in the appraisal of the thought of others." Marchant v. Mead-Morrison Mfg. Co., 252 N.Y. 284, 299, 169 N.E. 386, 391. (Emphasis added.)

[7] In this case, the Court, after quoting Judge Cardozo's language in Marchant, supra, saying that "the question is one of intention," said:

"Sound policy demands that the terms of an arbitration *must not be strained to discover power to pass upon matters in dispute,* but the terms must be clear and unmistakable to oust the jurisdiction of the Court, for trial by jury cannot be taken away in any case merely by implication." Continental Milling & Feed Co. v. Doughnut Corp., 186 Md. 669, 676, 48 A.2d 447, 450. (Emphasis added.)

[8] "But, under any circumstances, before the decision of an arbitrator can be held final and conclusive, it must appear, as was said in Chandley Bros. v. Cambridge Springs, 200 Pa. 230, 49 Atl. 772, *that power to pass upon the subject-matter, is clearly given to him. 'The terms of the agreement are not to be strained to discover it. They must be clear and unmistakable to oust the jurisdiction of the courts; for trial by jury cannot be taken away by implication merely in any case.'"* Jacob v. Weisser, 207 Pa. 484, 489, 56 A. 1065, 1067. (Emphasis added.)

STEELWORKERS v. WARRIOR NAVIGATION CO.   **34 LA 567**

also some other things. But the first paragraph of the arbitration section says: [M]atters which are strictly a function of management shall not be subject to arbitration under this section." Although acquiescing for 19 years in the employer's interpretation that contracting out work was "strictly a function of management," and having repeatedly tried—particularly in the negotiation of the agreement involved here—but unsuccessfully, to induce the employer to agree to a covenant that would prohibit it from contracting out work, the union, after having agreed to and signed the contract involved, presented a "grievance" on the ground that the employer's contracting out work, at a time when some employees in the unit were laid off for lack of work, constituted a partial "lockout" of employees in violation of the antilockout provision of the agreement.

Being unable to persuade the employer to agree to cease contracting out work or to agree to arbitrate the "grievance," the union brought this action in the District Court, under § 301 of the Labor Management Relations Act, 29 U.S.C. § 185, for a decree compelling the employer to submit the "grievance" to arbitration. The District Court, holding that the contracting out of work was, and over a long course of dealings had been interpreted and understood by the parties to be, "strictly a function of management," and was therefore specifically excluded from arbitration by the terms of the contract, denied the relief prayed, 168 F.Supp. 702, 43 LRRM 2328. The Court of Appeals affirmed, 269 F.2d 633, 44 LRRM 2567, and we granted certiorari. 361 U.S. 912.

The Court now reverses the judgment of the Court of Appeals. It holds that the arbitrator's source of law is "not confined to the express provisions of the contract," that arbitration should be ordered "unless it may be said with positive assurance that the arbitration clause is not susceptible to an interpretation that covers the asserted dispute," that "[d]oubts [of arbitrability] should be resolved in favor of coverage," and that when, as here, "a no-strike clause is included in the agreement, then * * * everything that management does is subject to [arbitration]." I understand the Court thus to hold that the arbitrators are not confined to the express provisions of the contract, that arbitration is to

be ordered unless it may be said with positive assurance that arbitration of a particular dispute is excluded by the contract, that doubts of arbitrability are to be resolved in favor of arbitration, and that when, as here, the contract contains a no-strike clause, everything that management does is subject to arbitration.

[STRANGE DOCTRINE]

This is an entirely new and strange doctrine to me. I suggest, with deference, that it departs both the contract of the parties and the controlling decisions of this Court. I find nothing in the contract that purports to confer upon arbitrators any such general breadth of private judicial power. The Court cites no legislative or judicial authority that creates for or gives to arbitrators such broad general powers. And I respectfully submit that today's decision cannot be squared with the statement of Judge, later Mr. Justice, Cardozo in Marchant that "no one is under a duty to resort to these conventional tribunals, however helpful their process, *except to the extent that he has signified his willingness.* Our own favor or disfavor of the cause of arbitration is not to count as a factor in the appraisal of the thoughts of others," 252 N.Y., at 299, 169 N.E., at 391 (emphasis added); nor with his statement in that case that "[t]he question is one of intention, to be ascertained by the same tests that are applied to contracts generally," id., nor with this Court's statement in Moorman, "that the intention of the parties to submit their contractual disputes to final determination outside the courts *should be made manifest by plain language,*" 338 U.S., at 462 (emphasis added); nor with this Court's statement in Hensey that: "To make such [an arbitrator's] certificate conclusive *requires plain language in the contract.* It is not to be implied." 205 U.S., at 309. (Emphasis added.) "A party is never required to submit to arbitration any question which he has not agreed so to submit, and *contracts providing for arbitration will be carefully construed in order not to force a party to submit to arbitration a question which he did not intend to be submitted.*" Fernandez & Hnos v. Rickert Rice Mills, supra, 119 F.2d, at 815 (C. A. 1st Cir). (Emphasis added.)

With respect, I submit that there is nothing in the contract here to indicate that the employer "signified [its] willingness" (Marchant, supra, at

391) to submit to arbitrators whether it must cease contracting out work. Certainly no such intention is "made manifest by plain language" (Moorman, supra, at 462), as the law "requires," because such consent "is not to be implied." (Hensley, supra, at 309). To the contrary, the parties by their conduct over many years interpreted the contracting out of major repair work to be "strictly a function of management," and if, as the concurring opinion suggests, the words of the contract can "be understood only by reference to the background which gave rise to their inclusion," then the interpretation given by the parties over 19 years to the phrase "matters which are strictly a function of management" should logically have some significance here. By their contract, the parties agreed that "matters which are strictly a function of management shall not be subject to arbitration." The union over the course of many years repeatedly tried to induce the employer to agree to a covenant prohibiting the contracting out of work, but was never successful. The union again made such an effort in negotiating the very contract involved here, and, failing of success, signed the contract, knowing, of course, that it did not contain any such covenant, but that, to the contrary, it contained, just as had the former contracts, a covenant that "matters which are strictly a function of management shall not be subject to arbitration." Does not this show that, instead of signifying a willingness to submit to arbitration the matter of whether the employer might continue to contract out work, the parties fairly agreed to exclude at least that matter from arbitration? Surely it cannot be said that the parties agreed to such a submission by any "plain language." Moorman, supra, at 462, and Hensey, supra, at 309. Does not then the Court's opinion compel the employer "to submit to arbitration [a] question which [it] has not agreed so to submit"? (Fernandez & Hnos, supra, at 815.)

[JUDICIAL QUESTION]

Surely the question whether a particular subject or class of subjects are or are not made arbitrable by a contract is a judicial question, and if, as the concurring opinion suggests, "the Court may conclude that [the contract] commits to arbitration any [subject or class of subjects]," it may likewise conclude that the contract does not commit such subject or class

of subjects to arbitration, and "[w]ith that finding the Court will have exhausted its function" no more nor less by denying arbitration than by ordering it. Here the District Court found, and the Court of Appeals approved its finding, that by the terms of the contract, as interpreted by the parties over 19 years, the contracting out of work was "strictly a function of management" and "not subject to arbitration." That finding, I think, should be accepted here. Acceptance of it requires affirmance of the judgment.

I agree with the Court that courts have no proper concern with the "merits" of claims which by contract the parties have agreed to submit to the exclusive jurisdiction of arbitrators. But the question is one of jurisdiction. Neither may entrench upon the jurisdiction of the other. The test is: Did the parties in their contract "manifest by plain language" (Moorman, supra, at 462) their willingness to submit the issue in controversy to arbitrators? If they did, then the arbitrators have exclusive jurisdiction of it, and the courts, absent fraud or the like, must respect that exclusive jurisdiction and cannot interfere. But if they did not, then the courts must exercise their jurisdiction, when properly invoked, to protect the citizen against the attempted use by arbitrators of pretended powers actually never conferred. That question always is, and from its very nature must be, a judicial one. Such was the question presented to the District Court and the Court of Appeals here. They found the jurisdictional facts, properly applied the settled law to those facts, and correctly decided the case. I would therefore affirm the judgment.

STEELWORKERS V. ENTERPRISE WHEEL & CAR CORP., 363 U.S. 574, 34 LA 569 (1960)

STEELWORKERS v. ENTERPRISE WHEEL & CAR CORP. 34 LA 569

STEELWORKERS v. ENTERPRISE WHEEL & CAR CORP.

Supreme Court of the United States

UNITED STEELWORKERS OF AMERICA v. ENTERPRISE WHEEL AND CAR CORPORATION, No. 538, June 20, 1960

LABOR-MANAGEMENT RELATIONS ACT

—Arbitration—Enforcement of award—Role of courts ▶ 94.7052
US SupCt

Courts should refuse enforcement of arbitration awards in suits brought under Section 301 of LMRA when it appears that arbitrator's decision was not based on collective bargaining contract, but so far as decision concerns construction of contract, the courts should not overrule arbitrator merely because their interpretation differs from his. Mere ambiguity in opinion accompanying award which permits inference that arbitrator may have exceeded his authority is not a reason for refusing to enforce the award. (US SupCt)—United Steelworkers of America v. Enterprise Wheel & Car Corp., 34 LA 569.

—Arbitration—Enforcement of award—Period of back pay ▶94.559 ▶94.707 ▶ 118.806
US SupCt

Arbitration award directing employer to reinstate and pay back pay to discharged employees for period before and after expiration of collective bargaining agreement is enforceable in suit brought under Section 301 of LMRA, since it is not apparent that arbitrator went beyond submission which restricted him to construction and application of the contract. Award may be resubmitted to arbitrator, however, so that amounts due employees may be definitely determined. (US SupCt)—United Steelworkers of America v. Enterprise Wheel & Car Corp., 34 LA 569.

On writ of certiorari to the U. S. Court of Appeals for the Fourth Circuit (44 LRRM 2349, 32 LA 814, 269 F.2d 327). Reversed except for a modification, and case remanded to District Court.

Elliot Bredhoff and David E. Feller (Arthur J. Goldberg and Jerry D. Anker with them on the brief), Washington, D.C., for petitioner.

William C. Beatty (Jackson N. Huddleston and E. Jackson Boggs with him on the brief), Huntington, W.Va., for respondent.

Full Text of Opinion

Mr. Justice DOUGLAS delivered the opinion of the Court.

Petitioner union and respondent during the period relevant here had a collective bargaining agreement which provided that any differences "as to the meaning and application" of the agreement should be submitted to arbitration and that the arbitrator's decision "shall be final and binding on the parties." Special provisions were included concerning the suspension and discharge of employees. The agreement stated:

"Should it be determined by the Company or by an arbitrator in accordance with the grievance procedure that the employee has been suspended unjustly or discharged in violation of the provisions of this Agreement, the Company shall reinstate the employee and pay full compensation at the employee's regular rate of pay for the time lost."

The agreement also provided:

"* * * It is understood and agreed that neither party will institute *civil suits or legal proceedings* against the other for alleged violation of any of the provisions of this labor contract; instead all disputes will be settled in the manner outlined in this Article III—Adjustment of Grievances."

[FACTS OF CASE]

A group of employees left their jobs in protest against the discharge of one employee. A union official advised them at once to return to work. An official of respondent at their request gave them permission and then rescinded it. The next day they were told they did not have a job any more "until this thing was settled one way or the other."

A grievance was filed; and when respondent finally refused to arbitrate, this suit was brought for specific enforcement of the arbitration provisions of the agreement. The District Court ordered arbitration. The arbitrator found that the discharge of the men was not justified, though their conduct, he said, was improper. In his view the facts warranted at most a suspension of the men for 10 days each. After their discharge and before the arbitration award the collective bargaining agreement had expired. The union, however, continued to represent the workers at the plant. The arbitrator rejected the conten-

34 LA 570   STEELWORKERS v. ENTERPRISE WHEEL & CAR CORP.

tion that expiration of the agreement barred reinstatement of the employees. He held that the provision of the agreement above quoted imposed an unconditional obligation on the employer. He awarded reinstatement with back pay, minus pay for a 10-day suspension and such sums as these employees received from other employment.

Respondent refused to comply with the award. Petitioner moved the District Court for enforcement. The District Court directed respondent to comply. 168 F.Supp. 308, 43 LRRM 2291. The Court of Appeals, while agreeing that the District Court had jurisdiction to enforce an arbitration award under a collective bargaining agreement, [1] held that the failure of the award to specify the amounts to be deducted from the back pay rendered the award unenforceable. That defect, it agreed, could be remedied by requiring the parties to complete the arbitration. It went on to hold, however, that an award for back pay subsequent to the date of termination of the collective bargaining agreement could not be enforced. It also held that the requirement for reinstatement of the discharged employees was likewise unenforceable because the collective agreement had expired. 269 F.2d 327, 44 LRRM 2349.

[MERITS OF AWARDS]

The refusal of courts to review the merits of an arbitration award is the proper approach to arbitration under collective bargaining agreements. The federal policy of settling labor disputes by arbitration would be undermined if courts had the final say on the merits of the awards. As we stated in United Steelworkers of America v. Warrior & Gulf Navigation Co., ante, p. ——, 46 LRRM 2416, decided this day, the arbitrators under these collective agreements are indispensable agencies in a continuous collective bargaining process. They sit to settle disputes at the plant level—disputes that require for their solution knowledge of the custom and practices of a particular factory or of a particular industry as reflected in particular agreements. [2]

When an arbitrator is commissioned to interpret and apply the collective bargaining agreement, he is to bring his informed judgment to bear in order to reach a fair solution of a problem. This is especially true when it comes to formulating remedies. There the need is for flexibility in meeting a wide variety of situations. The draftsmen may never have thought of what specific remedy should be awarded to meet a particular contingency. Nevertheless, an arbitrator is confined to interpretation and application of the collective bargaining agreement; he does not sit to dispense his own brand of industrial justice. He may of course look for guidance from many sources, yet his award is legitimate only so long as it draws its essence from the collective bargaining agreement. When the arbitrator's words manifest an infidelity to this obligation, courts have no choice but to refuse enforcement of the award.

[OPINION OF ARBITRATOR]

The opinion of the arbitrator in this case, as it bears upon the award of back pay beyond the date of the agreement's expiration and reinstatement, is ambiguous. It may be read as based solely upon the arbitrator's view of the requirements of enacted legislation, which would mean that he exceeded the scope of the submission. Or it may be read as embodying a construction of the agreement itself, perhaps with the arbitrator looking to "the law" for help in determining the sense of the agreement. A mere ambiguity in the opinion accompanying an award, which permits the infer-

---

the 'green hand,' is gradually initiated into what amounts to a miniature society. There he finds himself in a strange environment that assaults his senses with unusual sounds and smells and often with different 'weather conditions' such as sudden drafts of heat, cold, or humidity. He discovers that the society of which he only gradually becomes a part has of course a formal government of its own—the rules which management and the union have laid down—but that it also differs from or parallels the world outside in social classes, folklore, ritual, and traditions.

"Under the process in the old mills a very real 'miniature society' had grown up, and in important ways the technological revolution described in this case history shattered it. But a new society or work community was born immediately, though for a long time it developed slowly. As the old society was strongly molded by the *discontinuous* process of making pipe, so was the new one molded by the *continuous* process and strongly influenced by the characteristics of new high-speed automatic equipment." Walker, Life in the Automatic Factory, 36 Harv. Bus. Rev. 111, 117.

---

1 See Textile Workers v. Cone Mills Corp., 268 F.2d 920, 44 LRRM 2345 (C. A. 4th Cir.).

2 "Persons unfamiliar with mills and factories—farmers or professors, for example— often remark upon visiting them that they seem like another world. This is particularly true if, as in the steel industry, both tradition and technology have strongly and uniquely molded the ways men think and act when at work. The newly hired employee,

ence that the arbitrator may have exceeded his authority, is not a reason for refusing to enforce the award. Arbitrators have no obligation to the court to give their reasons for an award. To require opinions[3] free of ambiguity may lead arbitrators to play it safe by writing no supporting opinions. This would be undesirable for a well reasoned opinion tends to engender confidence in the integrity of the process and aids in clarifying the underlying agreement. Moreover, we see no reason to assume that this arbitrator has abused the trust the parties confided in him and has not stayed within the areas marked out for his consideration. It is not apparent that he went beyond the submission. The Court of Appeal's opinion refusing to enforce the reinstatement and partial back pay portions of the award was not based upon any finding that the arbitrator did not premise his award on his construction of the contract. It merely disagreed with the arbitrator's construction of it.

The collective bargaining agreement could have provided that if any of the employees were wrongfully discharged, the remedy would be reinstatement and back pay up to the date they were returned to work. Respondent's major argument seems to be that by applying correct principles of law to the interpretation of the collective bargaining agreement it can be determined that the agreement did not so provide, and that therefore the arbitrator's decision was not based upon the contract. The acceptance of this view would require courts, even under the standard arbitration clause, to review the merits of every construction of the contract. This plenary review by a court of the merits would make meaningless the provisions that the arbitrator's decision is final, for in reality it would almost never be final. This underlines the fundamental error which we have alluded to in United States Steelworkers of America v. American Manufacturing Co., ante, p. —, 46 LRRM 2414, decided this day. As we there emphasized the question of interpretation of the collective bargaining agreement is a question for the arbitrator. It is the arbitrator's construction which was bargained for; and so far as the arbitrator's decision concerns construction of the contract, the courts have no business overruling

ing him because their interpretation of the contract is different from his.

We agree with the Court of Appeals that the judgment of the District Court should be modified so that the amounts due the employees may be definitely determined by arbitration. In all other respects we think the judgment of the District Court should be affirmed. Accordingly, we reverse the judgment of the Court of Appeals, except for that modification, and remand the case to the District Court for proceedings in conformity with this opinion.

It is so ordered.

Mr. Justice FRANKFURTER concurs in the result.

Mr. Justice BLACK took no part in the consideration or decision of this case.

Dissenting Opinion

Mr. Justice WHITTAKER, dissenting.

Claiming that the employer's discharge on January 18, 1957, of 11 employees violated the provisions of its collective bargaining contract with the employer—covering the period beginning April 5, 1956, and ending April 5, 1957—the union sought and obtained arbitration, under the provisions of the contract, of the issues whether these employees had been discharged in violation of the agreement and, if so, should be ordered reinstated and awarded wages from the time of their wrongful discharge. In August 1957 more than four months after the collective agreement had expired, these issues were tried before and submitted to a Board of Arbitrators. On April 10, 1958, the arbitrators made their award, finding that the 11 employees had been discharged in violation of the agreement and ordering their reinstatement with back pay at their regular rates from a time 10 days after their discharge to the time of reinstatement. Over the employer's objection that the collective agreement and the submission under it did not authorize nor empower the arbitrators to award reinstatement or wages for any period after the date of expiration of the contract (April 5, 1957), the District Court ordered enforcement of the award. The Court of Appeals modified the judgment by eliminating the requirement that the employer reinstate the employees and

---

[3] See Jalet, Judicial Review of Arbitration: The Judicial Attitude, 45 Cornell L. Q. 519, 522.

pay them wages for the period *after* expiration of the collective agreement, and affirmed it in all other respects, 269 F.2d 327, 44 LRRM 2349, and we granted certiorari, 361 U.S. 929.

That the propriety of the discharges, under the collective agreement, was arbitrable under the provisions of that agreement, even after its expiration, is not in issue. Nor is there any issue here as to the power of the arbitrators to award reinstatement status and back pay to the discharged employees to the date of expiration of the collective agreement. It is conceded, too, that the collective agreement expired by its terms on April 5, 1957, and was never extended or renewed.

The sole question here is whether the arbitrators exceeded the submission and their powers in awarding reinstatement and back pay for any period after expiration of the collective agreements. Like the Court of Appeals, I think they did. I find nothing in the collective agreement that purports to so authorize. Nor does the Court point to anything in the agreement that purports to do so. Indeed, the union does not contend that there is any such covenant in the contract. Doubtless all rights that accrued to the employees under the collective agreement during its term, and that were made arbitrable by its provisions, could be awarded to them by the arbitrators, even though the period of the agreement had ended. But surely no rights *accrued* to the employees under the agreement after it had expired. Save for the provisions of the collective agreement, and in the absence, as here, of any applicable rule of law or contrary covenant between the employer and the employees, the employer had the legal right to discharge the employees at will. The collective agreement, however, protected them against discharge, for specified reasons, during its continuation. But when that agreement expired, it did not continue to afford rights *in futuro* to the employees—as though still effective and governing. After the agreement expired the employment status of these 11 employees was terminable at the will of the employer, as the Court of Appeals quite properly held, 269 F.2d, at 331, 44 LRRM 2349, and see Meadows v. Radio Industries, 222 F.2d 347, 349, 36 LRRM 2147 (C. A. 7th Cir); Atchison, T. & S. F. R. Co. v. Andrews,

211 F.2d 264, 265 (C.A. 10th Cir); Warden v. Hinds, 163 F. 201 (C.A. 4th Cir.), and the announced discharge of these 11 employees then became lawfully effective.

Once the contract expired, no rights continued to accrue under it to the employees. Thereafter they had no contractual right to demand that the employer continue to employ them, and *a fortiori* the arbitrators did not have power to order the employer to do so; nor did the arbitrators have power to order the employer to pay wages to them after the date of termination of the contract, which was also the effective date of their discharges.

The judgment of the Court of Appeals, affirming so much of the award as required reinstatement of the 11 employees to employment status and payment of their wages until expiration of the contract, but not thereafter, seems to me to be indubitably correct, and I would affirm it.

Concurring Opinion

[To decisions in United Steelworkers v. American Mfg. Co.; United Steelworkers v. Warrior and Gulf Navigation Co.; and United Steelworkers v. Enterprise Wheel and Car Corp.]

Mr. Justice BRENNAN, with whom Mr. Justice HARLAN joins, concurring.

While I join the Court's opinions in Nos. 443, 360 and 538, I add a word in Nos. 443 and 360.

In each of these two cases the issue concerns the enforcement of but one promise—the promise to arbitrate in the context of an agreement dealing with a particular subject matter, the industrial relations between employers and employees. Other promises contained in the collective bargaining agreements are beside the point unless, by the very terms of the arbitration promise, they are made relevant to its interpretation. And I emphasize this, for the arbitration promise is itself a contract. The parties are free to make that promise as broad or as narrow as they wish for there is no compulsion in law requiring them to include any such promise in their agreement. The meaning of the arbitration promise is not to be found simply by reference to the dictionary definitions of the words the parties use, or by reference to the interpretation of commercial arbi-

CONCURRING OPINION   34 LA 573

tration clauses. Words in a collective bargaining agreement, rightly viewed by the Court to be the charter instrument of a system of industrial self-government, like words in a statute, are to be understood only by reference to the background which gave rise to their inclusion. The Court therefore avoids the prescription of inflexible rules for the enforcement of arbitration promises. Guidance is given by identifying the various considerations which a court should take into account when construing a particular clause—considerations of the milieu in which the clause is negotiated and of the national labor policy. It is particularly underscored that the arbitral process in collective bargaining presupposes that the parties wanted the informed judgment of an arbitrator, precisely for the reason that judges cannot provide it. Therefore, a court asked to enforce a promise to arbitrate should ordinarily refrain from involving itself in the interpretation of the substantive provisions of the contract.

[QUESTION FOR COURT]

To be sure, since arbitration is a creature of contract, a court must always inquire, when a party seeks to invoke its aid to force a reluctant party to the arbitration table, whether the parties have agreed to arbitrate the particular dispute. In this sense, the question of whether a dispute is "arbitrable" is inescapably for the court.

On examining the arbitration clause, the court may conclude that it commits to arbitration any "dispute, difference, disagreement, or controversy of any nature or character." With that finding the court will have exhausted its function, except to order the reluctant party to arbitration. Similarly, although the arbitrator may be empowered only to interpret and apply the contract, the parties may have provided that any dispute as to whether a particular claim is within the arbitration clause is itself for the arbitrator. Again the court, without more, must send any dispute to the arbitrator, for the parties have agreed that the construction of the arbitration promise itself is for the arbitrator, and the reluctant party has breached his promise by refusing to submit the dispute to arbitration.

[AMERICAN CASE]

In American, the Court deals with a request to enforce the "standard"

form of arbitration clause, one that provides for the arbitration of "any disputes, misunderstandings, differences or grievances arising between the parties as to the meaning, interpretation and application of this agreement.* * *" Since the arbitration clause itself is part of the agreement, it might be argued that a dispute as to the meaning of that clause is for the arbitrator. But the Court rejects this position, saying that the threshold question, the meaning of the arbitration clause itself, is for the judge unless the parties clearly state to the contrary. However, the Court finds that the meaning of that "standard" clause is simply that the parties have agreed to arbitrate any dispute which the moving party asserts to involve construction of the substantive provisions of the contract, because such a dispute necessarily does involve such a construction.

[WARRIOR CASE]

The issue in the Warrior case is essentially no different from that in American, that is, it is whether the company agreed to arbitrate a particular grievance. In contrast to American, however, the arbitration promise here excludes a particular area from arbitration—"matters which are strictly a function of management." Because the arbitration promise is different, the scope of the court's inquiry may be broader. Here, a court may be required to examine the substantive provisions of the contract to ascertain whether the parties have provided that contracting out shall be a "function of management." If a court may delve into the merits to the extent of inquiring whether the parties have expressly agreed whether or not contracting out was a "function of management," why was it error for the lower court here to evaluate the evidence of bargaining history for the same purpose? Neat logical distinctions do not provide the answer. The Court rightly concludes that appropriate regard for the national labor policy and the special factors relevant to the labor arbitral process, admonish that judicial inquiry into the merits of this grievance should be limited to the search for an explicit provision which brings the grievance under the cover of the exclusion clause since "the exclusion clause is vague and arbitration clause quite broad." The hazard of going further into the merits is amply demonstrated by what the courts below did. On the basis of inconclusive evidence, those courts found that Warrior was in no way limited by any implied covenants of good faith and fair dealing from contracting out as it pleased — which would necessarily mean that Warrior was free completely to destroy the collective bargaining agreement by contracting out all the work.

The very ambiguity of the Warrior exclusion clause suggests that the parties were generally more concerned with having an arbitrator render decisions as to the meaning of the contract than they were in restricting the arbitrator's jurisdiction. The case might of course be otherwise were the arbitration clause very narrow, or the exclusion clause quite specific, for the inference might then be permissible that the parties had manifested a greater interest in confining the arbitrator; the presumption of arbitrability would then not have the same force and the Court would be somewhat freer to examine into the merits.

The Court makes reference to an arbitration clause being the *quid pro quo* for a no-strike clause. I do not understand the Court to mean that the application of the principles announced today depends upon the presence of a no-strike clause in the agreement.

Mr. Justice FRANKFURTER joins these observations.

Appendix B

Code of Professional Responsibility for Arbitrators of Labor-Management Disputes

National Academy of Arbitrators
American Arbitration Association
Federal Mediation and Conciliation Service
(As Amended and in Effect September 2007)

Source: National Academy of Arbitrators, http://naarb.org/code.asp

First instituted in 1951 as the Code of Ethics and Procedural Standards for Labor-Management Arbitration, the Code of Professional Responsibility for Arbitrators of Labor-Management Disputes has been revised periodically by a Joint Steering Committee with representatives from the National Academy of Arbitrators, American Arbitration Association, and the Federal Mediation and Conciliation Service.

Since its adoption there has been considerable analysis and discussion of the Code, most notably in the Proceedings of the National Academy of Arbitrators (see Appendix G) and in NAA Advisory Opinions that specifically address interpretation of the Code. These Advisory Opinions are available at http://naarb.org/advisoryopinions.asp.

CODE

OF PROFESSIONAL RESPONSIBILITY FOR ARBITRATORS OF LABOR-MANAGEMENT DISPUTES

OF THE
NATIONAL ACADEMY OF ARBITRATORS
AMERICAN ARBITRATION ASSOCIATION
FEDERAL MEDIATION AND CONCILIATION SERVICE

As amended and in effect September 2007

FOREWORD

This "Code of Professional Responsibility for Arbitrators of Labor-Management Disputes" supersedes the "Code of Ethics and Procedural Standards for Labor-Management Arbitration," approved in 1951 by a Committee of the American Arbitration Association, by the National Academy of Arbitrators, and by representatives of the Federal Mediation and Conciliation Service.

Revision of the 1951 Code was initiated officially by the same three groups in October, 1972. The following members of a Joint Steering Committee were designated to draft a proposal:

Chair
William E. Simkin

Representing American Arbitration Association
Frederick H. Bullen
Donald B. Straus

Representing Federal Mediation and Conciliation Service
Lawrence B. Babcock, Jr.
L. Lawrence Schultz

Representing National Academy of Arbitrators
Sylvester Garrett
Ralph T. Seward

The proposal of the Joint Steering Committee was issued on November 30, 1974, and thereafter adopted by all three sponsoring organizations. Reasons for Code revision should be noted briefly. Ethical considerations and procedural standards were deemed to be sufficiently intertwined to warrant combining the subject matter of Parts I and II of the 1951 Code under the caption of "Professional Responsibility." It also seemed advisable to eliminate admonitions to the parties (Part III of the 1951 Code) except as they appear incidentally in connection with matters primarily involving responsibilities of arbitrators. The substantial growth of third-party participation in dispute resolution in the public sector required consideration, as did the fact that the arbitration of new contract terms had become more significant. Finally, during the interval of more than two decades, new problems had emerged as private-sector grievance arbitration matured and became more diversified.

In 1985, the provisions of 2 C. 1. c. were amended to specify certain procedures, deemed proper, which could be followed by an arbitrator seeking to determine if the parties are willing to consent to publication of an award.

In 1996, the wording of the Preamble was amended to reflect the intent that the provisions of the Code apply to covered arbitrators who agree to serve as impartial third parties in certain arbitration and related procedures, dealing with the rights and interests of employees in connection with their employment and/or representation by a union. Simultaneously, the provisions of 2 A. 3. were amended to make clear that an arbitrator has no obligation to accept an appointment to arbitrate under dispute procedures adopted unilaterally by an employer or union and to identify additional disclosure responsibilities for arbitrators who agree to serve under such procedures.

In 2001, the provisions of 1 C. were amended to eliminate the general prohibition of advertising, along with certain qualifying statements added in 1996, and replace them with a provision that permits advertising except that which is false or deceptive.

In 2003, 1 C. was amended further to reflect that the same standard applies to written solicitations of arbitration work, but that care must be taken to avoid compromising or giving the appearance of compromising the arbitrator's neutrality.

In 2007, a new 6 E. was added and the previous 6 E. was re-designated 6 F. The purpose of the revision was to make clear that an arbitrator does not violate the Code by retaining jurisdiction in an award over application or interpretation of a remedy.

NOTE: From time to time, the Committee on Professional Responsibility and Grievances of the National Academy of Arbitrators prepares Advisory Opinions relating to issues arising under the Code which are adopted upon approval by the Academy's Board of Governors. These Advisory Opinions can be found on the Academy's website: naarb.org.

TABLE OF CONTENTS

PREAMBLE

Background

The provisions of this Code deal with the voluntary arbitration of labor-management disputes and certain other arbitration and related procedures which have developed or become more common since it was first adopted.

Voluntary arbitration rests upon the mutual desire of management and labor in each collective bargaining relationship to develop procedures for dispute settlement which meet their own particular needs and obligations. No two voluntary systems, therefore, are likely to be identical in practice. Words used to describe arbitrators (Arbitrator, Umpire, Impartial Chair, Chair of Arbitration Board, etc.) may suggest typical approaches, but actual differences within any general type of arrangement may be as great as distinctions often made among the several types.

Arbitrators of labor-management disputes are sometimes asked to serve as impartial third parties under a variety of arbitration and related procedures dealing with the rights and interests of employees in connection with their employment and/or representation by a union. In some cases these procedures may not be the product of voluntary agreement between management and labor. They may be established by statute or ordinance, *ad hoc* agreement, individual employment contract, or through procedures unilaterally adopted by employers and unions. Some of the procedures may be designed to resolve disputes over new or revised contract terms, where the arbitrator may be referred to as a Fact Finder or a member of an Impasse Panel or Board of Inquiry, or the like. Others may be designed to resolve disputes over wrongful termination or other employment issues arising under the law, an implied or explicit individual employment contract, or an agreement to resolve a lawsuit. In some such cases the arbitrator may be referred to as an Appeal Examiner, Hearing Officer, Referee, or other like titles. Finally, some procedures may be established by employers to resolve employment disputes under personnel policies and handbooks or established by unions to resolve disputes with represented employees in agency shop or fair share cases.

The standards of professional responsibility set forth in this Code are intended to guide the impartial third party serving in all of these diverse procedures.

Scope of Code

This Code is a privately developed set of standards of professional behavior for arbitrators who are subject to its provisions. It applies to voluntary arbitration of labor-management disputes and the other arbitration and related procedures described in the Preamble, hereinafter referred to as "covered arbitration dispute procedures."

The word "arbitrator," as used hereinafter in the Code, is intended to apply to any impartial person, irrespective of specific title, who serves in a covered arbitration dispute procedure in which there is conferred authority to decide issues or to make formal recommendations.

The Code is not designed to apply to mediation or conciliation, as distinguished from arbitration, nor to other procedures in which the third party is not authorized in advance to make decisions or recommendations. It does not apply to partisan representatives on tripartite boards. It does not apply to commercial arbitration or to uses of arbitration other than a covered arbitration dispute procedure as defined above.

Format of Code

Bold Face type, sometimes including explanatory material, is used to set forth general principles. *Italics* are used for amplification of general principles. Ordinary type is used primarily for illustrative or explanatory comment.

Application of Code

Faithful adherence by an arbitrator to this Code is basic to professional responsibility.

The National Academy of Arbitrators will expect its members to be governed in their professional conduct by this Code and stands ready, through its Committee on Professional Responsibility and Grievances, to advise its members as to the Code's interpretation. The American Arbitration Association and the Federal Mediation and Conciliation Service will apply the Code to the arbitrators on their rosters in cases handled under their respective appointment or referral procedures. Other arbitrators and administrative agencies may, of course, voluntarily adopt the Code and be governed by it.

In interpreting the Code and applying it to charges of professional misconduct, under existing or revised procedures of the National Academy of Arbitrators and of the administrative agencies, it should be recognized that while some of its standards express ethical principles basic to the arbitration profession, others rest less on ethics than on considerations of good practice. Experience has shown the difficulty of drawing rigid lines of distinction between ethics and good practice, and this Code does not attempt to do so. Rather, it leaves the gravity of alleged misconduct and the extent to which ethical standards have been violated to be assessed in the light of the facts and circumstances of each particular case.

1

ARBITRATOR'S QUALIFICATIONS AND RESPONSIBILITIES TO THE PROFESSION

A. General Qualifications

1. **Essential personal qualifications of an arbitrator include honesty, integrity, impartiality and general competence in labor relations matters.**

   An arbitrator must demonstrate ability to exercise these personal qualities faithfully and with good judgment, both in procedural matters and in substantive decisions.

   a. Selection by mutual agreement of the parties or direct designation by an administrative agency are the effective methods of appraisal of this combination of an individual's potential and performance, rather than the fact of placement on a roster of an administrative agency or membership in a professional association of arbitrators.

2. **An arbitrator must be as ready to rule for one party as for the other on each issue, either in a single case or in a group of cases. Compromise by an arbitrator for the sake of attempting to achieve personal acceptability is unprofessional.**

B. Qualifications for Special Cases

1. **When an arbitrator decides that a case requires specialized knowledge beyond the arbitrator's competence, the arbitrator must decline appointment, withdraw, or request technical assistance.**

   a. An arbitrator may be qualified generally but not for specialized assignments. Some types of incentive, work standard, job evaluation, welfare program, pension, or insurance cases may require specialized knowledge, experience or competence. Arbitration of contract terms also may require distinctive background and experience.

   b. Effective appraisal by an administrative agency or by an arbitrator of the need for special qualifications requires that both parties make known the special nature of the case prior to appointment of the arbitrator.

C. Responsibilities to the Profession

1. **An arbitrator must uphold the dignity and integrity of the office and endeavor to provide effective service to the parties.**

    a. To this end, an arbitrator should keep current with principles, practices and developments that are relevant to the arbitrator's field of practice.

2. **An arbitrator shall not make false or deceptive representations in the advertising and/or solicitation of arbitration work.**

3. **An arbitrator shall not engage in conduct that would compromise or appear to compromise the arbitrator's impartiality.**

    a. Arbitrators may disseminate or transmit truthful information about themselves through brochures or letters, among other means, provided that such material and information is disclosed, disseminated or transmitted in good faith to representatives of both management and labor.

4. **An experienced arbitrator should cooperate in the training of new arbitrators.**

2

RESPONSIBILITIES TO
THE PARTIES

A. Recognition of Diversity in Arbitration Arrangements

1. An arbitrator should conscientiously endeavor to understand and observe, to the extent consistent with professional responsibility, the significant principles governing each arbitration system in which the arbitrator serves.

   a. Recognition of special features of a particular arbitration arrangement can be essential with respect to procedural matters and may influence other aspects of the arbitration process.

2. Such understanding does not relieve an arbitrator from a corollary responsibility to seek to discern and refuse to lend approval or consent to any collusive attempt by the parties to use arbitration for an improper purpose.

3. An arbitrator who is asked to arbitrate a dispute under a procedure established unilaterally by an employer or union, to resolve an employment dispute or agency shop or fair share dispute, has no obligation to accept such appointment. Before accepting such an appointment, an arbitrator should consider the possible need to disclose the existence of any ongoing relationships with the employer or union.

   a. If the arbitrator is already serving as an umpire, permanent arbitrator or panel member under a procedure where the employer or union has the right unilaterally to remove the arbitrator from such a position, those facts should be disclosed.

B. Required Disclosures

1. Before accepting an appointment, an arbitrator must disclose directly or through the administrative agency involved, any current or past managerial, representational, or consultative relationship with any company or union involved in a proceeding in which the arbitrator is being considered for appointment or has been tentatively designated to serve. Disclosure must also be made of any pertinent pecuniary interest.

   a. The duty to disclose includes membership on a Board of Directors, full-time or part-time service as a representative or advocate, consultation work for a fee, current stock or bond ownership (other than mutual fund shares or appropriate trust arrangements) or any other pertinent form of managerial, financial or immediate family interest in the company or union involved.

8

2. **When an arbitrator is serving concurrently as an advocate for or representative of other companies or unions in labor relations matters, or has done so in recent years, such activities must be disclosed before accepting appointment as an arbitrator.**

   An arbitrator must disclose such activities to an administrative agency if on that agency's active roster or seeking placement on a roster. Such disclosure then satisfies this requirement for cases handled under that agency's referral.

   a. It is not necessary to disclose names of clients or other specific details. It is necessary to indicate the general nature of the labor relations advocacy or representational work involved, whether for companies or unions or both, and a reasonable approximation of the extent of such activity.

   b. *An arbitrator on an administrative agency's roster has a continuing obligation to notify the agency of any significant changes pertinent to this requirement.*

   c. When an administrative agency is not involved, an arbitrator must make such disclosure directly unless the arbitrator is certain that both parties to the case are fully aware of such activities.

3. **An arbitrator must not permit personal relationships to affect decision-making.**

   Prior to acceptance of an appointment, an arbitrator must disclose to the parties or to the administrative agency involved any close personal relationship or other circumstance, in addition to those specifically mentioned earlier in this section, which might reasonably raise a question as to the arbitrator's impartiality.

   a. Arbitrators establish personal relationships with many company and union representatives, with fellow arbitrators, and with fellow members of various professional associations. There should be no attempt to be secretive about such friendships or acquaintances but disclosure is not necessary unless some feature of a particular relationship might reasonably appear to impair impartiality.

4. **If the circumstances requiring disclosure are not known to the arbitrator prior to acceptance of appointment, disclosure must be made when such circumstances become known to the arbitrator.**

5. **The burden of disclosure rests on the arbitrator. After appropriate disclosure, the arbitrator may serve if both parties so desire. If the arbitrator believes or perceives that there is a clear conflict of interest, the arbitrator should withdraw, irrespective of the expressed desires of the parties.**

9

C. Privacy of Arbitration

1. **All significant aspects of an arbitration proceeding must be treated by the arbitrator as confidential unless this requirement is waived by both parties or disclosure is required or permitted by law.**

   a. Attendance at hearings by persons not representing the parties or invited by either or both of them should be permitted only when the parties agree or when an applicable law requires or permits. Occasionally, special circumstances may require that an arbitrator rule on such matters as attendance and degree of participation of counsel selected by a grievant.

   b. *Discussion of a case at any time by an arbitrator with persons not involved directly should be limited to situations where advance approval or consent of both parties is obtained or where the identity of the parties and details of the case are sufficiently obscured to eliminate any realistic probability of identification.*

   A commonly recognized exception is discussion of a problem in a case with a fellow arbitrator. *Any such discussion does not relieve the arbitrator who is acting in the case from sole responsibility for the decision and the discussion must be considered as confidential.*

   Discussion of aspects of a case in a classroom without prior specific approval of the parties is not a violation provided the arbitrator is satisfied that there is no breach of essential confidentiality.

   c. *It is a violation of professional responsibility for an arbitrator to make public an award without the consent of the parties.*

   An arbitrator may ask the parties whether they consent to the publication of the award either at the hearing or at the time the award is issued.

   (1) If such question is asked at the hearing it should be asked in writing as follows:

   "Do you consent to the submission of the award in this matter for publication?
        (   )   (   )
         YES   *NO*

   If you consent you have the right to notify the arbitrator within 30 days after the date of the award that you revoke your consent."

   It is desirable but not required that the arbitrator remind the parties at the time of the issuance of the award of their right to withdraw their consent to publication.

(2) If the question of consent to the publication of the award is raised at the time the award is issued, the arbitrator may state in writing to each party that failure to answer the inquiry within 30 days will be considered an implied consent to publish.

d. It is not improper for an arbitrator to donate arbitration files to a library of a college, university or similar institution without prior consent of all parties involved. When the circumstances permit, there should be deleted from such donations any cases concerning which one or both of the parties have expressed a desire for privacy. As an additional safeguard, an arbitrator may also decide to withhold recent cases or indicate to the donee a time interval before such cases can be made generally available.

e. *Applicable laws, regulations, or practices of the parties may permit or even require exceptions to the above noted principles of privacy.*

D. Personal Relationships with the Parties

1. **An arbitrator must make every reasonable effort to conform to arrangements required by an administrative agency or mutually desired by the parties regarding communications and personal relationships with the parties.**

    a. *Only an "arm's-length" relationship may be acceptable to the parties in some arbitration arrangements or may be required by the rules of an administrative agency. The arbitrator should then have no contact of consequence with representatives of either party while handling a case without the other party's presence or consent.*

    b. *In other situations, both parties may want communications and personal relationships to be less formal. It is then appropriate for the arbitrator to respond accordingly.*

E. Jurisdiction

1. **An arbitrator must observe faithfully both the limitations and inclusions of the jurisdiction conferred by an agreement or other submission under which the arbitrator serves.**

2. **A direct settlement by the parties of some or all issues in a case, at any stage of the proceedings, must be accepted by the arbitrator as removing further jurisdiction over such issues.**

F. Mediation by an Arbitrator

1. **When the parties wish at the outset to give an arbitrator authority both to mediate and to decide or submit recommendations regarding residual issues, if any, they should so advise the arbitrator prior to appointment. If the appointment is accepted, the arbitrator must perform a mediation role consistent with the circumstances of the case.**

    a. Direct appointments, also, may require a dual role as mediator and arbitrator of residual issues. This is most likely to occur in some public sector cases.

2. **When a request to mediate is first made after appointment, the arbitrator may either accept or decline a mediation role.**

    a. *Once arbitration has been invoked, either party normally has a right to insist that the process be continued to decision.*

    b. *If one party requests that the arbitrator mediate and the other party objects, the arbitrator should decline the request.*

    c. *An arbitrator is not precluded from suggesting mediation. To avoid the possibility of improper pressure, the arbitrator should not so suggest unless it can be discerned that both parties are likely to be receptive. In any event, the arbitrator's suggestion should not be pursued unless both parties readily agree.*

G. Reliance by an Arbitrator on Other Arbitration Awards or on Independent Research

1. **An arbitrator must assume full personal responsibility for the decision in each case decided.**

    a. *The extent, if any, to which an arbitrator properly may rely on precedent, on guidance of other awards, or on independent research is dependent primarily on the policies of the parties on these matters, as expressed in the contract, or other agreement, or at the hearing.*

    b. When the mutual desires of the parties are not known or when the parties express differing opinions or policies, the arbitrator may exercise discretion as to these matters, consistent with the acceptance of full personal responsibility for the award.

H. Use of Assistants

1. **An arbitrator must not delegate any decision-making function to another person without consent of the parties.**

   a. *Without prior consent of the parties, an arbitrator may use the services of an assistant for research, clerical duties, or preliminary drafting under the direction of the arbitrator, which does not involve the delegation of any decision-making function.*

   b. *If an arbitrator is unable, because of time limitations or other reasons, to handle all decision-making aspects of a case, it is not a violation of professional responsibility to suggest to the parties an allocation of responsibility between the arbitrator and an assistant or associate. The arbitrator must not exert pressure on the parties to accept such a suggestion.*

I. Consent Awards

1. **Prior to issuance of an award, the parties may jointly request the arbitrator to include in the award certain agreements between them, concerning some or all of the issues. If the arbitrator believes that a suggested award is proper, fair, sound, and lawful, it is consistent with professional responsibility to adopt it.**

   a. *Before complying with such a request, an arbitrator must be certain of understanding the suggested settlement adequately in order to be able to appraise its terms. If it appears that pertinent facts or circumstances may not have been disclosed, the arbitrator should take the initiative to assure that all significant aspects of the case are fully understood. To this end, the arbitrator may request additional specific information and may question witnesses at a hearing.*

J. Avoidance of Delay

1. **It is a basic professional responsibility of an arbitrator to plan a work schedule so that present and future commitments will be fulfilled in a timely manner.**

   a. *When planning is upset for reasons beyond the control of the arbitrator, every reasonable effort should nevertheless be exerted to fulfill all commitments. If this is not possible, prompt notice at the arbitrator's initiative should be given to all parties affected. Such notices should include reasonably accurate estimates of any additional time required. To the extent possible, priority should be given to cases in process so that other parties may make alternative arbitration arrangements.*

2. **An arbitrator must cooperate with the parties and with any administrative agency involved in avoiding delays.**

   a. *An arbitrator on the active roster of an administrative agency must take the initiative in advising the agency of any scheduling difficulties that can be foreseen.*

13

b. *Requests for services, whether received directly or through an administrative agency, should be declined if the arbitrator is unable to schedule a hearing as soon as the parties wish. If the parties, nevertheless, jointly desire to obtain the services of the arbitrator and the arbitrator agrees, arrangements should be made by agreement that the arbitrator confidently expects to fulfill.*

c. *An arbitrator may properly seek to persuade the parties to alter or eliminate arbitration procedures or tactics that cause unnecessary delay.*

3. Once the case record has been closed, an arbitrator must adhere to the time limits for an award, as stipulated in the labor agreement or as provided by regulation of an administrative agency or as otherwise agreed.

a. *If an appropriate award cannot be rendered within the required time, it is incumbent on the arbitrator to seek an extension of time from the parties.*

b. If the parties have agreed upon abnormally short time limits for an award after a case is closed, the arbitrator should be so advised by the parties or by the administrative agency involved, prior to acceptance of appointment.

K. Fees and Expenses

1. An arbitrator occupies a position of trust in respect to the parties and the administrative agencies. In charging for services and expenses, the arbitrator must be governed by the same high standards of honor and integrity that apply to all other phases of arbitration work.

An arbitrator must endeavor to keep total charges for services and expenses reasonable and consistent with the nature of the case or cases decided.

Prior to appointment, the parties should be aware of or be able readily to determine all significant aspects of an arbitrator's bases for charges for fees and expenses.

a. *Services Not Primarily Chargeable on a Per Diem Basis*

By agreement with the parties, the financial aspects of many "permanent" arbitration assignments, of some interest disputes, and of some "ad hoc" grievance assignments do not include a per diem fee for services as a primary part of the total understanding. *In such situations, the arbitrator must adhere faithfully to all agreed-upon arrangements governing fees and expenses.*

14

b. *Per Diem Basis for Charges for Services*

(1) *When an arbitrator's charges for services are determined primarily by a stipulated per diem fee, the arbitrator should establish in advance the bases for application of such per diem fee and for determination of reimbursable expenses.*

Practices established by an arbitrator should include the basis for charges, if any, for:

(a) hearing time, including the application of the stipulated basic per diem hearing fee to hearing days of varying lengths;
(b) study time;
(c) necessary travel time when not included in charges for hearing time;
(d) postponement or cancellation of hearings by the parties and the circumstances in which such charges will normally be assessed or waived;
(e) office overhead expenses (secretarial, telephone, postage, etc.);
(f) the work of paid assistants or associates.

(2) *Each arbitrator should be guided by the following general principles:*

(a) *Per diem charges for a hearing should not be in excess of actual time spent or allocated for the hearing.*
(b) *Per diem charges for study time should not be in excess of actual time spent.*
(c) *Any fixed ratio of study days to hearing days, not agreed to specifically by the parties, is inconsistent with the per diem method of charges for services.*
(d) *Charges for expenses must not be in excess of actual expenses normally reimbursable and incurred in connection with the case or cases involved.*
(e) *When time or expense are involved for two or more sets of parties on the same day or trip, such time or expense charges should be appropriately prorated.*
(f) *An arbitrator may stipulate in advance a minimum charge for a hearing without violation of (a) or (e) above.*

(3) *An arbitrator on the active roster of an administrative agency must file with the agency the individual bases for determination of fees and expenses if the agency so requires. Thereafter, it is the responsibility of each such arbitrator to advise the agency promptly of any change in any basis for charges.*

Such filing may be in the form of answers to a questionnaire devised by an agency or by any other method adopted by or approved by an agency.

Having supplied an administrative agency with the information noted above, an arbitrator's professional responsibility of disclosure under this Code with respect to fees and expenses has been satisfied for cases referred by that agency.

(4) *If an administrative agency promulgates specific standards with respect to any of these matters which are in addition to or more restrictive than an individual arbitrator's standards, an arbitrator on its active roster must observe the agency standards for cases handled under the auspices of that agency, or decline to serve.*

(5) *When an arbitrator is contacted directly by the parties for a case or cases, the arbitrator has a professional responsibility to respond to questions by submitting the bases for charges for fees and expenses.*

(6) *When it is known to the arbitrator that one or both of the parties cannot afford normal charges, it is consistent with professional responsibility to charge lesser amounts to both parties or to one of the parties if the other party is made aware of the difference and agrees.*

(7) *If an arbitrator concludes that the total of charges derived from the normal basis of calculation is not compatible with the case decided, it is consistent with professional responsibility to charge lesser amounts to both parties.*

2. **An arbitrator must maintain adequate records to support charges for services and expenses and must make an accounting to the parties or to an involved administrative agency on request.**

Code of Professional Responsibility

3

RESPONSIBILITIES TO ADMINISTRATIVE AGENCIES

A. General Responsibilities

1. **An arbitrator must be candid, accurate, and fully responsive to an administrative agency concerning qualifications, availability, and all other pertinent matters.**

2. **An arbitrator must observe policies and rules of an administrative agency in cases referred by that agency.**

3. **An arbitrator must not seek to influence an administrative agency by any improper means, including gifts or other inducements to agency personnel.**

   a. It is not improper for a person seeking placement on a roster to request references from individuals having knowledge of the applicant's experience and qualifications.

   b. Arbitrators should recognize that the primary responsibility of an administrative agency is to serve the parties.

17

4

PREHEARING CONDUCT

1. **All prehearing matters must be handled in a manner that fosters complete impartiality by the arbitrator.**

   a. The primary purpose of prehearing discussions involving the arbitrator is to obtain agreement on procedural matters so that the hearing can proceed without unnecessary obstacles. If differences of opinion should arise during such discussions and, particularly, if such differences appear to impinge on substantive matters, the circumstances will suggest whether the matter can be resolved informally or may require a prehearing conference or, more rarely, a formal preliminary hearing. When an administrative agency handles some or all aspects of the arrangements prior to a hearing, the arbitrator will become involved only if differences of some substance arise.

   b. *Copies of any prehearing correspondence between the arbitrator and either party must be made available to both parties.*

18

5

HEARING CONDUCT

A. General Principles

1. **An arbitrator must provide a fair and adequate hearing which assures that both parties have sufficient opportunity to present their respective evidence and argument.**

   a. *Within the limits of this responsibility, an arbitrator should conform to the various types of hearing procedures desired by the parties.*

   b. An arbitrator may: encourage stipulations of fact; restate the substance of issues or arguments to promote or verify understanding; question the parties' representatives or witnesses, when necessary or advisable, to obtain additional pertinent information; and request that the parties submit additional evidence, either at the hearing or by subsequent filing.

   c. *An arbitrator should not intrude into a party's presentation so as to prevent that party from putting forward its case fairly and adequately.*

B. Transcripts or Recordings

1. **Mutual agreement of the parties as to use or non-use of a transcript must be respected by the arbitrator.**

   a. *A transcript is the official record of a hearing only when both parties agree to a transcript or an applicable law or regulation so provides.*

   b. An arbitrator may seek to persuade the parties to avoid use of a transcript, or to use a transcript if the nature of the case appears to require one. *However, if an arbitrator intends to make appointment to a case contingent on mutual agreement to a transcript, that requirement must be made known to both parties prior to appointment.*

   c. If the parties do not agree to a transcript, an arbitrator may permit one party to take a transcript at its own cost. The arbitrator may also make appropriate arrangements under which the other party may have access to a copy, if a copy is provided to the arbitrator.

   d. Without prior approval, an arbitrator may seek to use a personal tape recorder to supplement note taking. The arbitrator should not insist on such a tape recording if either or both parties object.

C. Ex Parte Hearings

1. In determining whether to conduct an ex parte hearing, an arbitrator must consider relevant legal, contractual, and other pertinent circumstances.

2. An arbitrator must be certain, before proceeding ex parte, that the party refusing or failing to attend the hearing has been given adequate notice of the time, place, and purposes of the hearing.

D. Plant Visits

1. An arbitrator should comply with a request of any party that the arbitrator visit a work area pertinent to the dispute prior to, during, or after a hearing. An arbitrator may also initiate such a request.

   a. *Procedures for such visits should be agreed to by the parties in consultation with the arbitrator.*

E. Bench Decisions or Expedited Awards

1. When an arbitrator understands, prior to acceptance of appointment, that a bench decision is expected at the conclusion of the hearing, the arbitrator must comply with the understanding unless both parties agree otherwise.

   a. *If notice of the parties' desire for a bench decision is not given prior to the arbitrator's acceptance of the case, issuance of such a bench decision is discretionary.*

   b. *When only one party makes the request and the other objects, the arbitrator should not render a bench decision except under most unusual circumstances.*

2. When an arbitrator understands, prior to acceptance of appointment, that a concise written award is expected within a stated time period after the hearing, the arbitrator must comply with the understanding unless both parties agree otherwise.

6

POST HEARING CONDUCT

A. Post Hearing Briefs and Submissions

1. **An arbitrator must comply with mutual agreements in respect to the filing or nonfiling of post hearing briefs or submissions.**

   a. An arbitrator may either suggest the filing of post hearing briefs or other submissions or suggest that none be filed.

   b. When the parties disagree as to the need for briefs, an arbitrator may permit filing but may determine a reasonable time limitation.

2. **An arbitrator must not consider a post hearing brief or submission that has not been provided to the other party.**

B. Disclosure of Terms of Award

1. **An arbitrator must not disclose a prospective award to either party prior to its simultaneous issuance to both parties or explore possible alternative awards unilaterally with one party, unless both parties so agree.**

   a. Partisan members of tripartite boards may know prospective terms of an award in advance of its issuance. Similar situations may exist in other less formal arrangements mutually agreed to by the parties. In any such situation, the arbitrator should determine and observe the mutually desired degree of confidentiality.

C. Awards and Opinions

1. **The award should be definite, certain, and as concise as possible.**

   a. When an opinion is required, factors to be considered by an arbitrator include: desirability of brevity, consistent with the nature of the case and any expressed desires of the parties; need to use a style and form that is understandable to responsible representatives of the parties, to the grievant and supervisors, and to others in the collective bargaining relationship; necessity of meeting the significant issues; forthrightness to an extent not harmful to the relationship of the parties; and avoidance of gratuitous advice or discourse not essential to disposition of the issues.

D. Clarification or Interpretation of Awards

1. No clarification or interpretation of an award is permissible without the consent of both parties.

2. Under agreements which permit or require clarification or interpretation of an award, an arbitrator must afford both parties an opportunity to be heard.

E. Retaining Remedial Jurisdiction

1. An arbitrator may retain remedial jurisdiction in the award to resolve any questions that may arise over application or interpretation of a remedy.

   a. Unless otherwise prohibited by agreement of the parties or applicable law, an arbitrator may retain remedial jurisdiction without seeking the parties' agreement. If the parties disagree over whether remedial jurisdiction should be retained, an arbitrator may retain such jurisdiction in the award over the objection of a party and subsequently address any remedial issues that may arise.

2. The retention of remedial jurisdiction is limited to the question of remedy and does not extend to any other parts of the award. An arbitrator who retains remedial jurisdiction is still bound by Paragraph D above, entitled "Clarification or Interpretation of Awards," which prohibits the clarification or interpretation of any other parts of an award unless both parties consent.

F. Enforcement of Award

1. The arbitrator's responsibility does not extend to the enforcement of an award.

2. In view of the professional and confidential nature of the arbitration relationship, an arbitrator should not voluntarily participate in legal enforcement proceedings.

Appendix C

Federal Mediation and Conciliation Service Arbitration Policies and Procedures

Source: http://www.fmcs.gov/assets/files/Arbitration/arbppoliciesand procedures.pdf

PART 1404 -- ARBITRATION SERVICES

AUTHORITY: 29 U.S.C. 172 and 29 U.S.C. 173 et seq.

Subpart A -- Arbitration Policy; Administration of Roster

1404.1 Scope and Authority

This chapter is issued by the Federal Mediation and Conciliation Service (FMCS) under Title II of the Labor Management Relations Act of 1947 (Pub L. 80-101) as amended. It applies to all arbitrators listed on the FMCS Roster of Arbitrators, to all applicants for listing on the Roster, and to all persons or parties seeking to obtain from FMCS either names or panels of names of arbitrators listed on the Roster in connection with disputes which are to be submitted to arbitration or factfinding.

1404.2 Policy

The labor policy of the United States promotes and encourages the use of voluntary arbitration to resolve disputes over the interpretation or application of collective bargaining agreements. Voluntary arbitration and fact-finding are important features of constructive employment relations as alternatives to economic strife.

1404.3 Administrative Responsibilities

a. *Director.* The Director of FMCS has responsibility for all aspects of FMCS arbitration activities and is the final agency authority on all questions concerning the Roster and FMCS arbitration procedures.

b. *Office of Arbitration Services.* The Office of Arbitration Services (OAS) maintains a Roster of Arbitrators (the Roster); administers Subpart C of this part (Procedures for Arbitration Services); assists, promotes, and cooperates in the establishment of programs for training and developing new arbitrators; and provides names or panels of names of listed arbitrators to parties requesting them.

c. *Arbitrator Review Board.* The Arbitrator Review Board shall consist of a chairman and members appointed by the Director who shall serve at the Director's pleasure. The Board shall be composed entirely of full-time officers or employees of the Federal Government and shall establish procedures for carrying out its duties.

    1. *Duties of the Board.* The Board shall:

        i.   Review the qualifications of all applicants for listing on the Roster, interpreting and applying the criteria set forth in Section 1404.5;

        ii. Review the status of all persons whose continued eligibility for listing on the Roster has been questioned under subsection 1404.5;

        iii. Recommend to the Director the acceptance or rejection of applicants for listing on the Roster, or the withdrawal of listing on the Roster for any of the reasons set forth in this part;

        iv. At the request of the Director of FMCS, review arbitration policies and procedures, including all regulations and written guidance regarding the use of the FMCS arbitrators, and make recommendations regarding such policies and procedures to the Director.

    2. [Reserved]

Subpart B -- Roster of Arbitrators; Admission and Retention

1404.4 Roster and Status of Members

a. *The Roster.* FMCS shall maintain a Roster of labor arbitrators consisting of persons who meet the criteria for listing contained in 1404.5 and who remain in good standing.

b. *Adherence of Standards and Requirements.* Persons listed on the Roster shall comply with FMCS rules and regulations pertaining to arbitration and with such guidelines and procedures as may be issued by the OAS pursuant to Subpart C of this part. Arbitrators shall conform to the ethical standards and procedures set forth in the Code of Professional Responsibility for Arbitrators of Labor Management Disputes, as approved by the National Academy of Arbitrators, Federal Mediation and Conciliation Service, and the American Arbitration Association.

c. *Status of Arbitrators.* Persons who are listed on the Roster and are selected or appointed to hear arbitration matters or to serve as fact-finders do not become employees of the Federal Government by virtue of their selection or appointment. Following selection or appointment, the arbitrator's relationship is solely with the parties to the dispute, except that arbitrators are subject to certain reporting requirements and to standards of conduct as set forth in this Part.

d. *Role of FMCS.* FMCS has no power to:
    1. Compel parties to appear before an arbitrator;
    2. Enforce an agreement to arbitrate;
    3. Compel parties to arbitrate any issue;
    4. Influence, alter, or set aside decisions of arbitrators on the Roster;
    5. Compel, deny, or modify payment of compensation to an arbitrator.

e. *Nominations and Panels.* On request of the parties to an agreement to arbitrate or engage in fact-finding, or where arbitration or fact-finding may be provided for by statute, OAS will provide names or panels of names for a nominal fee. Procedures for obtaining these services are outlined in Subpart C of this part. Neither the submission of a nomination or panel nor the appointment of an arbitrator constitutes a determination by FMCS that an agreement to arbitrate or enter fact-finding proceedings exists; nor does such action constitute a ruling that the matter in controversy is arbitrable under any agreement.

f. *Rights of Persons Listed on the Roster.* No person shall have any right to be listed or to remain listed on the Roster. FMCS retains its authority and responsibility to assure that the needs of the parties using its services are served. To accomplish this purpose, FMCS may establish procedures for the preparation of panels or the appointment of arbitrators or fact-finders which include consideration of such factors as background and experience, availability, acceptability, geographical location, and the expressed preferences of the parties. FMCS may also establish procedures for the removal from the Roster of those arbitrators who fail to adhere to provisions contained in this part.

1404.5 Listing on the Roster; Criteria for Listing and Retention

Persons seeking to be listed on the Roster must complete and submit an application form which may be obtained from OAS. Upon receipt of an executed application, OAS will review the application, assure that it is complete, make such inquiries as are necessary, and submit the application to the Arbitrator Review Board. The Board will review the completed application under the criteria in paragraphs (a), (b), and 8 of this section, and will forward to the FMCS Director its recommendation as to whether or not the applicant meets the criteria for listing on the Roster. The Director shall make all final decisions as to whether an applicant may be listed on the Roster. Each applicant shall be notified in writing of the Director's decision and the reasons therefore.

    a. *General Criteria.* Applicants for the Roster will be listed on the Roster upon a determination that they are experienced, competent, and acceptable in decision-making roles in the resolution of labor relations disputes.

    b. *Proof of Qualification.* Qualifications for listing on the Roster may be demonstrated by submission of five (5) arbitration awards prepared by the applicant while serving as an impartial arbitrator of record chosen by the parties to labor disputes arising under collective bargaining agreements. The Board will consider experience in relevant positions in collective bargaining or as a judge or hearing examiner in labor relations controversies as a substitute for such awards.

    c. Advocacy. Any person who at the time of application is an advocate as defined in paragraph (c)(1) of this section, must agree to cease such activity before being recommended for listing on the Roster by the Board. Except in the case of persons listed on the Roster as advocates before November 17, 1976, any person who did not divulge his or her advocacy at the time of listing or who becomes an advocate while listed on the Roster, shall be recommended for removal by the Board after the fact of advocacy is revealed.

        1. *Definition of Advocacy.* An advocate is a person who represents employers, labor organizations, or individuals as an employee, attorney, or consultant, in matters of labor relations, including but not limited to the subjects of union representation and recognition matters, collective bargaining, arbitration, unfair labor practices, equal employment opportunity, and other areas generally recognized as constituting labor relations. The definition includes representatives of employers or employees in individual cases or controversies involving worker's compensation, occupational health or safety, minimum wage, or other labor standards matters. This definition of advocate also includes a person who is directly associated with an advocate in a business or professional relationship as, for example, partners or employees of a law firm. Consultants engaged only in joint education or training or other non-adversarial activities will not be deemed as advocates.

    d. *Duration of Listing, Retention.* Listing on the Roster shall be by decision of the Director of FMCS based upon the recommendations of the Arbitrator Review Board. The Board may recommend, and the Director may remove, any person listed on the Roster, for violation of this part and/or the Code of Professional

Responsibility. Notice of cancellation or suspension shall be given to a person listed on the Roster whenever a Roster member:

1. No longer meets the criteria for admission;
2. Has become an advocate as defined in paragraph 8 of this section;
3. Has been repeatedly or flagrantly delinquent in submitting awards;
4. Has refused to make reasonable and periodic reports in a timely manner to FMCS, as required in Subpart C of this part, concerning activities pertaining to arbitration;
5. Has been the subject of complaints by parties who use FMCS services, and the Board after appropriate inquiry, concludes that just cause for cancellation has been shown;
6. Is determined by the Director to be unacceptable to the parties who use FMCS arbitration services; the Director may base a determination of unacceptability on FMCS records which show the number of times the arbitrator's name has been proposed to the parties and the number of times it has been selected. Such cases will be reviewed for extenuating circumstances, such as length of time on the Roster or prior history.

e. The Board may, at its discretion, conduct an inquiry into the facts of any proposed removal from the Roster. An arbitrator listed on the Roster may only be removed after 60-day notice and an opportunity to submit a response or information showing why the listing should not be canceled. The Board may recommend to the Director whether to remove an arbitrator from the Roster. All determinations to remove an arbitrator from the Roster shall be made by the Director. Removals may be for a period of up to two (2) years, after which the arbitrator may seek reinstatement.

f. The director of OAS may suspend for a period not to exceed 180 days any person listed on the Roster who has violated any of the criteria in paragraph (d) of this section. Arbitrators shall be promptly notified of a suspension. They may appeal a suspension to the Arbitrator Review Board, which shall make a recommendation to the Director of FMCS. The decision of the Director of FMCS shall constitute the final action of the agency.

1404. 6 Inactive Status

A member of the Roster who continues to meet the criteria for listing on the Roster may request that he or she be put in an inactive status on a temporary basis because of ill health, vacation, schedule, or other reasons.

1404.7 Listing Fee

All arbitrators will be required to pay an annual fee for listing on the Roster as set forth in the Appendix to this part.

Subpart C -- Procedures for Arbitration Services

1404.8 Freedom of Choice

Nothing contained in this part should be construed to limit the rights of parties who use FMCS arbitration services to jointly select any arbitrator or arbitration procedure acceptable to them. Once a request is made to OAS, all parties are subject to the procedures contained in this part.

1404.9 Procedures for Requesting Arbitration Lists and Panels

a. The Office of Arbitration Services (OAS) has been delegated the responsibility for administering all requests for arbitration services. Requests should be addressed to the Federal Mediation and Conciliation Service, Office of Arbitration Services, Washington, DC 20427.

b. The OAS will refer a panel of arbitrators to the parties upon request. The parties are encouraged to make joint requests. In the event, however, that the request is made by only one party, the OAS will submit a panel of arbitrators. However, the issuance of a panel -- pursuant to either joint or unilateral request -- is nothing more than a response to a request. It does not signify the adoption of any position by the FMCS regarding the arbitrability of any dispute or the terms of the parties' contract.

c. As an alternative to a request for a panel of names, OAS will, upon written request, submit a list of all arbitrators and their biographical sketches from a designated geographical area. The parties may then select and deal directly with an arbitrator of their choice, with no further involvement of FMCS with the parties or the arbitrator. The parties may also request FMCS to make a direct appointment of their selection. In such a situation, a case number will be assigned.

d. The OAS reserves the right to decline to submit a panel or make appointments of arbitrators, if the request submitted is overly burdensome or otherwise impracticable. The OAS, in such circumstances, may refer the parties to an FMCS mediator to help in the design of an alternative solution. The OAS may also decline to service any requests from parties with a demonstrated history of non-payment of arbitrator fees or other behavior which constrains the spirit or operation of the arbitration process.

e. The parties are required to use the Request for Arbitration Panel (Form R-43), which has been prepared by the OAS and is available in quantity upon request to the Federal Mediation and Conciliation Service, Office of Arbitration Services, Washington, DC 20427, or by calling (202) 606-5111 or at www.fmcs.gov. Requests that do not contain all required information requested on the R-43 in typewritten form may be rejected.

f. Requests made by only one party, for a service other than the furnishing of a standard list or panel of seven (7) arbitrators, will not be honored unless authorized by the applicable collective bargaining agreement. This includes unilateral requests for a second or third panel or for a direct appointment of an arbitrator.

g. The OAS will charge a nominal fee for all requests for lists, panels, and other major services. Payments for these services must be received with the request for services before the service is delivered and may be paid by either labor or management or both. A schedule of fees is listed in the Appendix to this part.

1404.10 Arbitrability

The OAS will not decide the merits of a claim by either party that a dispute is not subject to arbitration.

1404.11 Nominations of Arbitrators

a. The parties may also request a randomly selected panel containing the names of seven (7) arbitrators accompanied by a biographical sketch for each member of the panel. This sketch states the background, qualifications, experience, and all fees as furnished to the OAS by the arbitrator. Requests for a panel of seven (7) arbitrators, whether joint or unilateral, will be honored. Requests for a panel of other than seven (7) names, for a direct appointment of an arbitrator, for special qualifications or other service will not be honored unless jointly submitted or authorized by the applicable collective bargaining agreement. Alternatively, the parties may request a list and biographical sketches of some or all arbitrators in one or more designated geographical areas. If the parties can agree on the selection of an arbitrator, they may appoint their own arbitrator directly without any further case tracking by FMCS. No case number will be assigned.
b. All panels submitted to the parties by the OAS, and all letters issued by the OAS making a direct appointment, will have an assigned FMCS case number. All future communications between the parties and the OAS should refer to this case number.
c. The OAS will provide a randomly selected panel of arbitrators located in state (s) in proximity of the hearing site. The parties may request special qualifications of arbitrators experienced in certain issues or industries or that possess certain backgrounds. The OAS has no obligation to put an individual on any given panel, or on a minimum number of panels in any fixed period. In general:
   1. The geographic location of arbitrators placed on panels is governed by the site of the dispute as stated on the request received by the OAS.
   2. If at any time both parties request that a name or names be included, or omitted, from a panel, such name or names will be included, or omitted, unless the number of names is excessive. These inclusions/exclusions may not discriminate against anyone because of age, race, gender, ethnicity or religious beliefs.
d. If the parties do not agree on an arbitrator from the first panel, the OAS will furnish a second and third panel to the parties upon joint request and payment of an additional fee. Requests for a second or third panel should be accompanied by a brief explanation as to why the previous panel(s) was

inadequate. If parties are unable to agree on a selection after having received three panels, the OAS will make a direct appointment upon joint request.

1404.12 Selection by Parties and Appointments of Arbitrators

a. After receiving a panel of names, the parties must notify the OAS of their selection of an arbitrator or of the decision not to proceed with arbitration. Upon notification of the selection of an arbitrator, the OAS will make a formal appointment of the arbitrator. The arbitrator, upon notification of appointment, is expected to communicate with the parties within 14 days to arrange for preliminary matters, such as the date and place of hearing. Should an arbitrator be notified directly by the parties that he or she has been selected, the Arbitrator must promptly notify the OAS of the selection and his or her willingness to serve. If the parties settle a case prior to the hearing, the parties must inform the arbitrator as well as the OAS. Consistent failure to follow these procedures may lead to a denial of future OAS service.

b. If the parties request a list of names and biographical sketches rather than a panel, they may choose to appoint and contact an arbitrator directly. In this situation, neither the parties nor the arbitrator is required to furnish any additional information to FMCS and no case number will be assigned.

c. Where the parties' collective bargaining agreement is silent on the manner of selecting arbitrators, the parties may wish to consider any jointly determined method or one of the following methods for selection of an arbitrator from a panel:

    1. Each party alternately strikes a name from the submitted panel until one remains, **or**
    2. Each party advises the OAS of its order of preference by numbering each name on the panel and submitting the numbered lists in writing to the OAS. The name that has the lowest combined number will be appointed.
    3. In those situations where the parties separately notify the OAS of their preferred selections, once the OAS receives the preferred selection from one party, it will notify the other party that it has fourteen (14) days in which to submit its selections. If that party fails to respond within the deadline, the first party's choice will be honored. If, within 14 days, a second panel is requested and is allowed by the collective bargaining agreement, the requesting party must pay a fee for the second panel.

d. The OAS will make a direct appointment of an arbitrator only upon joint request unless authorized by the applicable collective bargaining agreement.

e. The issuance of a panel of names or a direct appointment in no way signifies a determination on arbitrability or an interpretation of the terms and conditions of the collective bargaining agreement. The resolution of such disputes rests solely with the parties.

1404.13 Conduct of Hearings

All proceedings conducted by the arbitrators shall be in conformity with the contractual obligations of the parties. The arbitrator shall comply with 1404.4(b). The conduct of the arbitration proceeding is under the arbitrator's jurisdiction and control, and the arbitrator's decision shall be based upon the evidence and testimony presented at the hearing or otherwise incorporated in the record of the proceeding. The arbitrator may, unless prohibited by law, proceed in the absence of any party who, after due notice, fails to be present or to obtain a postponement. An award rendered in an <u>ex parte</u> proceeding of this nature must be based upon evidence presented to the arbitrator.

1404.14 Decision and Award

a. Arbitrators shall make awards no later than 60 days from the date of the closing of the record as determined by the arbitrator, unless otherwise agreed upon by the parties or specified by the collective bargaining agreement or law. However, failure to meet the 60 day deadline will not invalidate the process or award. A failure to render timely awards reflects upon the performance of an arbitrator and may lead to removal from the FMCS Roster.
b. The parties should inform the OAS whenever a decision is unduly delayed. The arbitrator shall notify the OAS if and when the arbitrator (1) cannot schedule, hear, and render decisions promptly, or (2) learns a dispute has been settled by the parties prior to the decision.
c. Within 15 days after an award has been submitted to the parties, the arbitrator shall submit an Arbitrator's Report and Fee Statement (Form R-19) to OAS showing a breakdown of the fee and expense charges so that the OAS may review conformance with stated charges under Section 1404.11(a). The Form R-19 is not to be used to invoice the parties.
d. While FMCS encourages the publication of arbitration awards, arbitrators should not publicize awards if objected to by one of the parties.

1404.15 Fees and Charges of Arbitrators

a. FMCS will charge all arbitrators an annual fee to be listed on the Roster. All arbitrators listed on the Roster may charge a per diem and other predetermined fees for services, if the amount of such fees have been provided in advance to FMCS. Each arbitrator's maximum per diem and other fees are set forth on a biographical sketch which is sent to the parties when panels are submitted. The arbitrator shall not change any fee or add charges without giving at least 30 days advance written notice to FMCS. Arbitrators with dual business addresses must bill the parties for expenses from the least expensive business address to the hearing site.
b. In cases involving unusual amounts of time and expenses relative to the pre-hearing and post-hearing administration of a particular case, an administrative charge may be made by the arbitrator.
c. Arbitrators shall divulge all charges to the parties and obtain agreement thereto immediately after appointment.

d. The OAS requests that it be notified of any arbitrator's deviation from the policies expressed in this part. While the OAS does not resolve individual fee disputes, repeated complaints concerning the fees charged by an arbitrator will be brought to the attention of the Arbitrator Review Board for consideration. Similarly, repeated complaints by arbitrators concerning non-payment of fees by the parties may lead to the denial of services or other actions by the OAS.

1404.16 Reports and Biographical Sketches

a. Arbitrators listed on the Roster shall execute and return all documents, forms and reports required by the OAS. They shall also keep the OAS informed of changes of address, telephone number, availability, and of any business or other connection or relationship which involves labor-management relations or which creates or gives the appearance of advocacy as defined in Section 1404.5 (c) (1).
b. The OAS will provide biographical sketches on each person admitted to the Roster from information supplied by applicants. Arbitrators may request revision of biographical information at later dates to reflect changes in fees, the existence of additional charges, or other relevant data. The OAS reserves the right to decide and approve the format and content of biographical sketches.

Subpart D - Expedited Arbitration

1404.17 Policy.

In an effort to reduce the time and expense of some grievance arbitrations, FMCS is offering expedited procedures that may be appropriate in certain non-precedential cases or those that do not involve complex or unique issues. Expedited Arbitration is intended to be a mutually agreed upon process whereby arbitrator appointments, hearings and awards are acted upon quickly by the parties, FMCS, and the arbitrators. The process is streamlined by mandating short deadlines and eliminating requirements for transcripts, briefs and lengthy opinions.

1404.18 Procedures for Requesting Expedited Panels.

a. With the exception of the specific changes noted in this Subpart, all FMCS rules and regulations governing its arbitration services shall apply to Expedited Arbitration.
b. Upon receipt of a joint Request for Arbitration Panel (Form R-43) indicating that expedited services are desired by both parties, the OAS will refer a panel of arbitrators.
c. A panel of arbitrators submitted by the OAS in expedited cases shall be valid for up to 30 days. Only one panel will be submitted per case. If the parties are

unable to mutually agree upon an arbitrator or if prioritized selections are not received from both parties within 30 days, the OAS will make a direct appointment of an arbitrator not on the original panel.

d. If the parties mutually select an arbitrator, but the arbitrator is not available, the parties may select a second name from the same panel or the OAS will make a direct appointment of another arbitrator not listed on the original panel.

1404.19 Arbitration Process.

a. Once notified of the expedited case appointment by the OAS, the arbitrator must contact the parties within seven (7) calendar days.
b. The parties and the arbitrator must attempt to schedule a hearing within 30 days of the appointment date.
c. Absent mutual agreement, all hearings will be concluded within one day. No transcripts of the proceedings will be made and the filing of post-hearing briefs will not be allowed.
d. All awards must be completed within seven (7) working days after the hearing. These awards are expected to be brief, concise, and not require extensive written opinion or research time.

1404.20 Arbitrator Eligibility.

In an effort to increase exposure for new arbitrators, those arbitrators who have been listed on the Roster of Arbitrators for a period of five (5) years or less will be automatically placed on expedited panels submitted to the parties. However, all panels will also contain the names of at least two more senior arbitrators. In addition, the parties may jointly request a larger pool of arbitrators or a direct appointment of any arbitrator of their choice who is listed on the Roster.

1404.21 Proper Use of Expedited Arbitration.

a. FMCS reserves the right to cease honoring requests for Expedited Arbitration if a pattern of misuse of this process becomes apparent. Misuse may be indicated by the parties' frequent delaying of the process or referral of inappropriate cases.
b. Arbitrators who exhibit a pattern of unavailability for appointments or who are repeatedly unable to schedule hearings or render awards within established deadlines will, after written warning, be considered ineligible for appointment for this service.

Appendix Schedule of Fees

Annual listing fee for all arbitrators: $100 for the first address; $50 for second address

Request for panel of arbitrators: $30 for each panel request (includes subsequent appointment)

Direct appointment of arbitrator $20 per appointment when a panel is not used

List and biographical sketches of $10 per request plus $.10 per page arbitrators in a specific area

Appendix D

American Arbitration Association Labor Arbitration Rules*

(Including Expedited Labor Arbitration Rules)
(Amended and Effective July 1, 2013)

Labor Arbitration Rules

(Including Expedited Labor Arbitration Rules)

 AMERICAN ARBITRATION ASSOCIATION®

Available online at **adr.org/labor**

Rules Amended and Effective July 1, 2013.

Table of Contents

Labor Arbitration Rules
(Including Expedited Labor Arbitration Rules)

Introduction

Every year, labor and management enter into thousands of collective bargaining agreements. Virtually all of these agreements provide for arbitration of unresolved grievances. For decades, the American Arbitration Association® (AAA) has been a leading administrator of labor-management disputes.

The American Arbitration Association is a public-service, not-for-profit organization offering a broad range of dispute resolution services to business executives, attorneys, individuals, trade associations, unions, management, consumers, families, communities, and all levels of government. Services are available through AAA headquarters in New York City and through offices located in major cities throughout the United States. Hearings may be held at locations convenient for the parties and are not limited to cities with AAA offices. In addition, the AAA serves as a center for education and training, issues specialized publications, and conducts research on all forms of out-of-court dispute settlement.

Arbitration is a tool of industrial relations. Like other tools, it has limitations as well as advantages. In the hands of an expert, it produces useful results. When abused or made to do things for which it was never intended, the outcome can be disappointing. For these reasons, all participants in the process — union officials, employers, personnel executives, attorneys, and the arbitrators themselves — have an equal stake in orderly, efficient, and constructive arbitration procedures. The AAA's Labor Arbitration Rules provide a time-tested method for efficient, fair, and economical resolution of labor-management disputes. By referring to them in a collective bargaining agreement, the parties can take advantage of these benefits.

The parties can provide for arbitration of future disputes by inserting the following clause into their contracts:

Any dispute, claim, or grievance arising from or relating to the interpretation or application of this agreement shall be submitted to arbitration administered by the American Arbitration Association under its Labor Arbitration Rules. The parties further agree to accept the arbitrator's award as final and binding on them.

For relatively uncomplicated grievances, parties who use the labor arbitration services of the American Arbitration Association may agree to use expedited procedures that provide a prompt and inexpensive method for resolving disputes. This option responds to a concern about rising costs and delays in processing grievance arbitration cases. The AAA's Expedited Labor Arbitration Procedures, by eliminating or streamlining certain steps, are intended to resolve cases within a month of the appointment of the arbitrator. The procedures are in the following pages.

Labor Arbitration Rules

1. Agreement of Parties

The parties shall be deemed to have made these rules a part of their arbitration agreement whenever, in a collective bargaining agreement or submission, they have provided for arbitration by the American Arbitration Association (hereinafter the AAA) or under its rules. These rules and any amendment of them shall apply in the form in effect at the time the administrative requirements are met for a demand for arbitration or submission agreement received by the AAA. The parties, by written agreement, may vary the procedures set forth in these rules.

2. AAA and Delegation of Duties

When parties agree to arbitrate under these rules or when they provide for arbitration by the AAA and an arbitration is initiated under these rules, they thereby authorize the AAA to administer the arbitration. The authority and duties of the AAA are prescribed in the agreement of the parties and in these rules, and may be carried out through such of the AAA's representatives as it may direct. The AAA may, in its discretion, assign the administration of an arbitration to any of its offices.

3. Jurisdiction

a. The arbitrator shall have the power to rule on his or her own jurisdiction, including any objections with respect to the existence, scope, or validity of the arbitration agreement.

b. The arbitrator shall have the power to determine the existence or validity of a contract of which an arbitration clause forms a part. Such an arbitration clause shall be treated as an agreement independent of the other terms of the contract. A decision by the arbitrator that the contract is null and void shall not for that reason alone render invalid the arbitration clause.

c. A party must object to the jurisdiction of the arbitrator or to the arbitrability of a claim or counterclaim no later than the filing of the answering statement to the claim or counterclaim that gives rise to the objection. The arbitrator may rule on such objections as a preliminary matter or as part of the final award.

4. Panel of Neutral Labor Arbitrators

The AAA shall establish and maintain a National Roster of Labor Arbitrators and shall appoint arbitrators as provided in these rules.

5. Initiation under an Arbitration Clause in a Collective Bargaining Agreement

Arbitration under an arbitration clause in a collective bargaining agreement under these rules may be initiated by either party in the following manner:

a. by giving written notice to the other party of its intention to arbitrate (demand), which notice shall contain a statement setting forth the nature of the dispute, the names and addresses of all other parties, including phone number and email address, the remedy sought, and the hearing locale requested.

b. by filing at any regional office of the AAA a copy of the notice, together with a copy of the collective bargaining agreement or other relevant documents that relate to the dispute, including the arbitration provisions, together with the appropriate filing fee as provided in the schedule included with the rules. After the arbitrator is appointed, no new or different claim may be submitted except with the consent of the arbitrator and all other parties.

6. Answer

The party upon whom the demand for arbitration is made may file an answering statement with the AAA within 10 days after notice from the AAA, simultaneously sending a copy to the other party. If no answer is filed within the stated time, it will be treated as a denial of the claim. Failure to file an answer shall not operate to delay the arbitration.

7. Initiation under a Submission

Parties to any collective bargaining agreement may initiate an arbitration under these rules by filing at any regional office of the AAA a copy of a written agreement to arbitrate under these rules (submission), signed by the parties and setting forth the nature of the dispute, the names and addresses of all other parties, including phone number and email address, the remedy sought and the hearing locale requested.

8. Fixing of Locale

The parties may mutually agree on the geographic region (locale) where the arbitration is to be held. If the locale is not designated in the collective bargaining agreement or submission, and if the parties disagree as to the locale, the AAA may initially determine the place of arbitration, subject to the power of the arbitrator(s), after their appointment, to make a final determination on the locale. All such determinations shall be made having regard for the contentions of the parties and the circumstances of the arbitration.

9. Qualifications of Arbitrator

Any neutral arbitrator appointed pursuant to Section 10, 11, or 12, or selected by mutual agreement of the parties or their appointees, shall be subject to disqualification for the reasons specified in Section 15. If the parties specifically agree in writing, the arbitrator shall not be subject to disqualification for those reasons. Unless the parties agree otherwise, an arbitrator selected unilaterally by one party is a party-appointed arbitrator and is not subject to disqualification pursuant to Section 15.

The term "arbitrator" in these rules refers to the arbitration panel, whether composed of one or more arbitrators and whether the arbitrators are neutral or party appointed.

10. Appointment from National Roster

If the parties have not appointed an arbitrator and have not provided any other method of appointment, the arbitrator shall be appointed in the following manner: immediately after the filing of the demand or submission, the AAA shall submit simultaneously to each party an identical list of names of persons chosen from the National Roster of Labor Arbitrators. The Parties are encouraged to agree to an arbitrator from the submitted list and to advise the AAA of their agreement. If the parties are unable to agree upon an arbitrator, each party shall have 10 days from the transmittal date in which to strike names objected to, number the remaining names to indicate the order of preference, and return the list to the AAA.

If a party does not return the list within the time specified, all persons named therein shall be deemed acceptable.

From among the persons who have been approved on both lists, and in accordance with the designated order of mutual preference, the AAA shall invite the acceptance of an arbitrator to serve. If the parties fail to agree upon any of the persons named, or if acceptable arbitrators are unable to act, or if for any other reason the appointment cannot be made from the submitted lists, the AAA shall have the power to make the appointment from among other members of the National Roster without the submission of any additional list.

11. Direct Appointment by Parties

If the agreement of the parties names an arbitrator or specifies a method of appointing an arbitrator, that designation or method shall be followed. The notice of appointment, with the name and address of the arbitrator, shall be filed with the AAA by the appointing party. Upon the request of any appointing party, the AAA shall submit a list of members of the National Roster from which the party may, if it so desires, make the appointment.

If the agreement specifies a period of time within which an arbitrator shall be appointed and any party fails to make an appointment within that period, the AAA may make the appointment.

If no period of time is specified in the agreement, the AAA shall notify the parties to make the appointment and if within 10 days thereafter such arbitrator has not been so appointed, the AAA shall make the appointment.

12. Appointment of Neutral Arbitrator by Party-Appointed Arbitrators

If the parties have appointed their arbitrators or if either or both of them have been appointed as provided in Section 11, and have authorized those arbitrators to appoint a neutral arbitrator within a specified time and no appointment is made within that time or any agreed extension thereof, the AAA may appoint a neutral arbitrator who shall act as chairperson.

If no period of time is specified for appointment of the neutral arbitrator and the parties do not make the appointment within 10 days from the date of the appointment of the last party-appointed arbitrator, the AAA shall appoint a neutral arbitrator who shall act as chairperson.

If the parties have agreed that the arbitrators shall appoint the neutral arbitrator from the National Roster, the AAA shall furnish to the party-appointed arbitrators, in the manner prescribed in Section 10, a list selected from the National Roster, and the appointment of the neutral arbitrator shall be made as prescribed in that section.

13. Number of Arbitrators

If the arbitration agreement does not specify the number of arbitrators, the dispute shall be heard and determined by one arbitrator, unless the parties otherwise agree.

14. Notice to Arbitrator of Appointment

Notice of the appointment of the neutral arbitrator shall be sent to the arbitrator by the AAA and the signed acceptance of the arbitrator shall be filed with the AAA prior to the opening of the first hearing.

15. Disclosure and Challenge Procedure

Any person appointed or to be appointed as an arbitrator shall disclose to the AAA any circumstance likely to give rise to justifiable doubt as to the arbitrator's impartiality or independence, including any bias or any financial or personal interest in the result of the arbitration. Such obligation shall remain in effect throughout the arbitration. Upon receipt of this information from the arbitrator or another source, the AAA shall communicate the information to the parties and, if it deems it appropriate to do so, to the arbitrator. Upon objection of a party to the continued service of a neutral arbitrator, the AAA, after consultation with the parties and the arbitrator, shall determine whether the arbitrator should be disqualified and shall inform the parties of its decision, which shall be conclusive.

16. Vacancies

If for any reason an arbitrator is unable to perform the duties of the office, the AAA may, on proof satisfactory to it, declare the office vacant. Vacancies shall be filled in accordance with the applicable provisions of these rules, and the matter shall be reheard by the new arbitrator unless the parties agree upon an alternative arrangement.

17. Date, Time, and Place of Hearing

The parties shall respond to requests for hearing dates in a timely manner, be cooperative in scheduling the earliest practicable date, and adhere to established deadlines and hearing schedules. Upon the request of either party or the AAA, the arbitrator shall have the authority to convene a scheduling conference call and/or issue a Notice of Hearing setting the date, time and place for each hearing.

The parties will receive a formal written Notice of Hearing detailing the arrangements agreed to by the parties or ordered by the arbitrator at least five days in advance of the hearing date, unless otherwise agreed by the parties.

18. Representation

Any party may be represented by counsel or other authorized representative.

19. Stenographic Record

Any party desiring a stenographic record shall make arrangements directly with a stenographer and shall notify the other parties of such arrangements in advance of the hearing. The requesting party or parties shall pay the cost of the record. If the transcript is agreed by the parties to be or, in appropriate cases, determined by the arbitrator to be the official record of the proceeding, it must be made available to the arbitrator and to the other party for inspection, at a time and place determined by the arbitrator even if one party does not agree to pay for the transcript.

20. Interpreters

Any party wishing an interpreter shall make all arrangements directly with the interpreter and shall assume the costs of the service.

21. Attendance at Hearing

The arbitrator and the AAA shall maintain the privacy of the hearing unless the law provides to the contrary. Any person having a direct interest in the arbitration is entitled to attend hearings. The arbitrator shall otherwise have the power to require the exclusion of any witness, other than a party, during the testimony of other witnesses. It shall be discretionary with the arbitrator to determine the propriety of the attendance of any other person other than a party and its representatives.

22. Postponements

The arbitrator may postpone any hearing upon agreement of the parties, upon request of a party for good cause shown, or upon the arbitrator's own initiative.

23. Oaths

Before proceeding with the first hearing, each arbitrator may take an oath of office and, if required by law, shall do so. The arbitrator may require witnesses to testify under oath administered by any duly qualified person and, if required by law or requested by either party, shall do so.

24. Majority Decision

When the panel consists of more than one arbitrator, unless required by law or by the arbitration agreement, a majority of the arbitrators must make all decisions.

25. Order of Proceedings

A hearing shall be opened by the filing of the oath of the arbitrator, where required; by the recording of the date, time, and place of the hearing and the presence of the arbitrator, the parties, and counsel, if any; and by the receipt by the arbitrator of the demand and answer, if any, or the submission.

Exhibits may, when offered by either party, be received in evidence by the arbitrator. The names and addresses of all witnesses and exhibits in the order received shall be made a part of the record.

The arbitrator may vary the normal procedure under which the initiating party first presents its claim, but in any case shall afford full and equal opportunity to all parties for the presentation of relevant proofs.

The arbitrator, exercising his or her discretion, shall conduct the proceedings with a view to expediting the resolution of the dispute and may direct the order of proof, bifurcate proceedings and direct the parties to focus their presentations on issues the decision on which could dispose of all or part of the case.

26. Arbitration in the Absence of a Party or Representative

Unless the law provides to the contrary, the arbitration may proceed in the absence of any party or representative who, after due notice, fails to be present or fails to obtain a postponement. An award shall not be made solely on the default of a party. The arbitrator shall require the other party to submit such evidence as may be required for the making of an award.

27. Evidence and Filing of Documents

The parties may offer such evidence as is relevant and material to the dispute, and shall produce such evidence as the arbitrator may deem necessary to an understanding and determination of the dispute. An arbitrator or other person authorized by law to subpoena witnesses and documents may do so independently or upon the request of any party. The arbitrator shall determine the admissibility, the relevance, and materiality of the evidence offered and may exclude evidence deemed by the arbitrator to be cumulative or irrelevant and conformity to legal rules of evidence shall not be necessary. All evidence shall be taken in the presence of all of the arbitrators and all of the parties, except where any of the parties is absent, in default, or has waived the right to be present.

All documents that are not filed with the arbitrator at the hearing, but arranged at the hearing or subsequently by agreement of the parties to be submitted, shall be filed with the AAA for transmission to the arbitrator or transmitted to the arbitrator directly if the parties agree. All parties shall be afforded the opportunity to examine such documents.

Documents may be filed by regular or electronic mail or telephone facsimile, and will be deemed timely if postmarked or otherwise transmitted to the arbitrator or the AAA on or before the due date.

28. Evidence by Affidavit

The arbitrator may receive and consider the evidence of witnesses by affidavit, giving it only such weight as the arbitrator deems proper after consideration of any objection made to its admission.

29. Inspection

Whenever the arbitrator deems it necessary, he or she may make an inspection in connection with the subject matter of the dispute after notice to the parties, who may, if they so desire, be present at the inspection.

30. Closing of Hearing

The arbitrator shall inquire of all parties whether they have any further proof to offer or witnesses to be heard. Upon receiving negative replies or if satisfied that the record is complete, the arbitrator shall declare the hearing closed.

If briefs or other documents are to be filed, the hearing shall be declared closed as of the final date set by the arbitrator for the receipt of briefs. If documents are to be filed as provided in Section 27 and the date for their receipt is later than the date set for the receipt of briefs, the later date shall be the date of closing the hearing. The time limit within which the arbitrator is required to make an award shall commence to run, in the absence of another agreement by the parties, upon the closing of the hearings.

31. Reopening of Hearing

The hearing may be reopened on the arbitrator's initiative, or upon application of a party, at any time before the award is made. If reopening of the hearing would prevent the making of the award within the specific time agreed upon by the parties in the contract out of which the controversy has arisen, the matter may not be reopened unless the parties agree on an extension of time. When no specific date is fixed in the contract, the arbitrator may reopen the hearings and shall have 30 days from the closing of the reopened hearing within which to make an award.

32. Waiver of Oral Hearing

The parties may provide, by written agreement, for the waiver of oral hearing. If the parties are unable to agree as to the procedure, the AAA shall specify a fair and equitable procedure.

33. Waiver of Rules

Any party who proceeds with the arbitration after knowledge that any provision or requirement of these rules has not been complied with and who fails to state an objection thereto in writing shall be deemed to have waived the right to object.

34. Extensions of Time

The parties may modify any period of time by mutual agreement. The AAA or the arbitrator may for good cause extend any period of time established by these rules, except the time for making the award. The AAA shall notify the parties of any such extension.

35. Serving of Notice

Any papers, notices, or process necessary or proper for the initiation or continuation of an arbitration under these rules, for any court action in connection therewith, or for the entry of judgment on any award made under these rules, may be served on a party by mail addressed to the party or its representative at the last known address or by personal service, in or outside the state where the arbitration is to be held, provided that reasonable opportunity to be heard with regard to the dispute is or has been granted to the party. The AAA, the arbitrator and the parties may also use overnight delivery or electronic facsimile transmission, or other written forms of electronic communication to give the notices required by these rules.

Unless otherwise instructed by the AAA or by the arbitrator, any documents submitted by any party to the AAA or to the arbitrator shall simultaneously be provided to the other party or parties to the arbitration.

36. Time of Award

The award shall be rendered promptly by the arbitrator and, unless otherwise agreed by the parties or specified by law, no later than 30 days from the date of closing the hearing or, if oral hearings have been waived, the award shall be rendered no later than 30 days from the date of transmitting the final statements and proofs to the arbitrator.

37. Form of Award

The award shall be in writing and shall be signed (electronic signature acceptable) either by the neutral arbitrator or by a concurring majority if there is more than one arbitrator. The parties shall advise the AAA whenever they do not require the arbitrator to accompany the award with an opinion.

38. Award Upon Settlement

If the parties settle their dispute during the course of the arbitration and if the parties so request, the arbitrator may set forth the terms of the settlement in a "consent award".

39. Delivery of Award to Parties

Parties shall accept as legal delivery of the award the placing of the award or a true copy thereof in the mail, addressed to the party at its last known address or to its representative; personal or electronic service of the award; or the filing of the award in any other manner that is permitted by law.

40. Modification of Award

Within 20 days after the transmittal of an award, any party, upon notice to the other parties, may request the arbitrator, through the AAA, to correct any clerical, typographical, technical, or computational errors in the award. The arbitrator is not empowered to redetermine the merits of any claim already decided. The other parties shall be given 10 days to respond to the request. The arbitrator shall dispose of the request within 20 days after transmittal by the AAA to the arbitrator of the request and any response thereto. If applicable law requires a different procedural time frame, that procedure shall be followed.

41. Release of Documents for Judicial Proceedings

The AAA shall, upon the written request of a party, furnish to such party, at its expense, certified copies of documents contained in the arbitration case file in the AAA's possession that may be required in judicial proceedings relating to the arbitration.

42. Judicial Proceedings and Exclusion of Liability

a. Neither the AAA nor any arbitrator in a proceeding under these rules is a necessary or proper party in judicial proceedings relating to the arbitration.

b. Parties to an arbitration under these rules shall be deemed to have consented that neither the AAA nor any arbitrator shall be liable to any party in any action for damages or injunctive relief for any act or omission in connection with any arbitration conducted under these rules.

43. Administrative Fees

As a not-for-profit organization, the AAA shall prescribe an administrative fee schedule to compensate it for the cost of providing administrative services. The schedule in effect at the time of filing shall be applicable.

44. Expenses

The expenses of witnesses for either side shall be paid by the party producing such witnesses. Expenses of the arbitration, other than the cost of the stenographic record, including required traveling and other expenses of the arbitrator and of AAA representatives and the expenses of any witness or the cost of any proof produced at the direct request of the arbitrator, shall be borne equally by the parties, unless they agree otherwise, or unless the arbitrator, in the award, assesses such expenses or any part thereof against any specified party or parties.

45. Suspension for Non-Payment

If administrative charges have not been paid in full, the AAA may so inform the parties in order that one of them may advance the required payment. If such payments are not made, the AAA may suspend or terminate the proceedings.

46. Communication with Arbitrator

There shall be no direct communication between the parties and a neutral arbitrator on substantive matters relating to the case other than at oral hearings, unless the parties and the arbitrator agree otherwise. Any other oral or written communication from the parties to the arbitrator shall be directed to the AAA for transmittal to the arbitrator.

This rule does not prohibit communications on non-substantive matters such as travel arrangements and driving directions, nor does it prohibit direct communications in special circumstances (such as emergency delays) when the AAA is unavailable.

47. Interpretation and Application of Rules

The arbitrator shall interpret and apply these rules insofar as they relate to the arbitrator's powers and duties. When there is more than one arbitrator and a difference arises among them concerning the meaning or application of any such rule, it shall be decided by a majority vote. If that is not possible, the arbitrator or either party may refer the question to the AAA for final decision. All other rules shall be interpreted and applied by the AAA.

Administrative Fees

Full Service Administrative Fee

The initial administrative fee is $250 for each party, due and payable at the time of filing. No refund of the initial fee is made when a matter is withdrawn or settled after the filing of the demand for arbitration or submission.

Arbitrator Compensation

Unless mutually agreed otherwise, the arbitrator's compensation shall be borne equally by the parties, in accordance with the fee structure disclosed in the arbitrator's biographical profile submitted to the parties.

Hearing Room Rental

Hearing rooms are available on a rental basis at AAA offices. Please check with your Case Management Center or local AAA office for specific availability and rates.

Postponement Fees

A fee of $150 is payable by a party causing a postponement of any scheduled hearing that is subsequently rescheduled by the AAA.

Expedited Labor Arbitration Procedures

In response to the concern of parties over rising costs and delays in grievance arbitration, the American Arbitration Association has established expedited procedures under which cases are scheduled promptly and awards rendered no later than seven days after the hearings. In return for giving up certain features of traditional labor arbitration, such as transcripts, briefs, and extensive opinions, the parties using these simplified procedures can obtain quick decisions and realize certain cost savings.

Leading labor arbitrators have indicated a willingness to offer their services under these procedures, and the Association makes every effort to assign the best possible arbitrators with early available hearing dates. Since the establishment of these procedures, an ever increasing number of parties have taken advantage of them.

E1. Agreement of Parties

The Streamlined Labor Arbitration Rules, or the Expedited Labor Arbitration Rules of the American Arbitration Association, in the form obtaining when the arbitration is initiated, shall apply whenever the parties have agreed to arbitrate under them.

These procedures shall be applied as set forth below, in addition to any other portion of the Labor Arbitration Rules not in conflict with these expedited procedures.

E2. Appointment of Neutral Arbitrator

The AAA shall appoint a single neutral arbitrator from its National Roster of Labor Arbitrators, who shall hear and determine the case promptly.

E3. Qualifications of Neutral Arbitrator

Any person appointed or to be appointed as an arbitrator shall disclose to the AAA any circumstance likely to give rise to justifiable doubt as to the arbitrator's impartiality or independence, including any bias or any financial or personal interest in the result of the arbitration. The prospective arbitrator shall also disclose any circumstance likely to prevent a prompt hearing. The disclosure obligations in this section shall remain in effect throughout the arbitration. Upon receipt of such information, the AAA shall determine whether the arbitrator should be disqualified and shall inform the parties of its decision, which shall be conclusive.

E4. Vacancies

The AAA is authorized to substitute another arbitrator if a vacancy occurs or if an appointed arbitrator is unable to serve promptly.

E5. Date, Time, and Place of Hearing

The arbitrator shall fix the date, time, and place of the hearing, notice of which must be given at least 24 hours in advance. Such notice may be given orally, electronically or by facsimile.

E6. No Stenographic Record

There shall be no stenographic record of the proceedings.

E7. Proceedings

The hearing shall be conducted by the arbitrator in whatever manner will most expeditiously permit full presentation of the evidence and arguments of the parties. The arbitrator shall make an appropriate minute of the proceedings. Normally, the hearing shall be completed within one day. In unusual circumstances and for good cause shown, the arbitrator may schedule an additional hearing to be held within seven days.

E8. Post-hearing Briefs

There shall be no post-hearing briefs.

E9. Time of Award

The award shall be rendered promptly by the arbitrator and, unless otherwise agreed by the parties, no later than seven days from the date of the closing of the hearing.

E10. Form of Award

The award shall be in writing and shall be signed by the arbitrator. If the arbitrator determines that an opinion is necessary, it shall be in summary form.

Administrative Fees

Expedited Administrative Fee

The initial administrative fee is $150 for each party, due and payable at the time of filing. No refund of the initial fee is made when a matter is withdrawn or settled after the filing of the demand for arbitration or submission.

An additional fee of $25.00 for each party shall apply if a list of arbitrators is requested.

Arbitrator Compensation

Unless mutually agreed otherwise, the arbitrator's compensation shall be borne equally by the parties, in accordance with the fee structure disclosed in the arbitrator's biographical profile submitted to the parties.

Hearing Room Rental

Hearing rooms are available on a rental basis at AAA offices. Please check with your Case Management Center or local AAA office for specific availability and rates.

Postponement Fees

A fee of $150 is payable by a party causing a postponement of any scheduled hearing that is subsequently rescheduled by the AAA.

Optional Labor Services

Parties who use the labor arbitration services of the American Arbitration Association may mutually agree to use any of the Optional Labor Services, as opposed to the process being managed under the standard Labor Rules.

These options respond to a concern about rising costs and delays in processing grievance-arbitration cases and were designed to give the parties more economical considerations to resolve their dispute. Any issue not specifically identified under these Optional Labor Services will default to the Labor Rules.

O1. List Only Service

Parties can contact the AAA and request one list of no more than 15 names. Within 48 hours of receipt of the joint request, the AAA will submit the list of names and then the AAA closes its file. The administrative fee for a list only is $75 per party.

O2. List with Appointment

Parties can contact the AAA and request one list of no more than 15 names. Within 48 hours of receipt of the joint request, the AAA will submit a list with a return date of 10 days, for review and appointment of the arbitrator based on the parties' mutual selection. The AAA will notify the parties of the selection of the arbitrator. The administrative fee for list with appointment is $100 per party.

O3. Rapid Resolve Procedure

For relatively uncomplicated grievances, this procedure provides a prompt and inexpensive method for resolving labor disputes. Under this procedure, the parties have the option of filing up to three grievances in one demand. The same Arbitrator will hear all grievances within a single day of hearing being set aside. The written award will be rendered within 48 hours and is limited to a one-paragraph decision on each grievance, unless the Arbitrator determines otherwise. The total cost is $750.00 per party, which includes the AAA's Administrative Fee and the Fee of the Arbitrator.

O4. Documents Only Procedure

Under this procedure, the parties may agree to waive in-person hearings and resolve the dispute through the submission of documents. This is a simple process for the resolution of grievances where a face-to-face hearing is not necessary. The Arbitrator determines the time frame for the submission of written evidence, the record is closed and the award is issued within 14 days. A telephonic conference is optional. The total cost is $650.00 per party, which includes the AAA's Administrative Fee and the Fee of the Arbitrator.

O5. Emergency Scheduling Procedure

This procedure allows the parties the opportunity to schedule hearing dates very quickly. Under this procedure, the parties will have the ability to file a demand and receive a limited list of experienced neutrals who have confirmed they are available for a hearing on a specific date within a 14-day time period. By agreement of the parties, a grievance can be scheduled within 24 hours of filing a demand. The procedures can be utilized on existing cases filed with the AAA. There are no additional costs for using these procedures *(regular fees apply)*.

O6. Administration of Permanent Panels

For parties who are engaged in an ad-hoc or non-administered arbitration system, the AAA can assist the parties with the management of their Permanent Panels. The AAA can identify new panel members, assist in rotating the panel members off their roster, or assist in appointing the arbitrator from their roster. The cost varies depending on the services provided.

O7. Grievance Mediation Services

When negotiations are at an impasse, the AAA's Grievance Mediation Services can provide an informal, effective and confidential means of reaching settlement. These procedures can assist unions and management to define and clarify issues, understand differences, identify interests and explore solutions to reach mutually satisfactory agreements that preserve important relationships. Mediation is very cost-effective when compared to other dispute resolution options. At the AAA, there is no cost to search the AAA's roster of labor neutrals to identify an appropriate mediator for the case at hand. The total cost is $150.00 per party plus the fee of the Mediator.

O8. Customized Services

The AAA's role in the dispute resolution process is to administer cases from filing to closing. Additional AAA services include assistance in the design and development of alternative dispute resolution (ADR) systems for corporations, unions, government agencies, law firms and courts. By agreement of the parties, they can customize the administration of their case, which can include limitations, identification of an alternative method for the appointment of the arbitrator, a specific process for the scheduling of the hearing, or to simply define the specific services needed on their case. Ultimately, the AAA aims to move cases through the arbitration process in a fair and impartial manner that is agreed upon by the parties.

For more information about any of these services, please contact **1.888.774.6904,** or send an email to **labormediation@adr.org.**

Rules, forms, procedures, and guides, as well as information about applying for a fee reduction or deferral, are subject to periodic change and updating. To ensure that you have the most current information, see our website at **www.adr.org.**

Appendix E

American Arbitration Association Employment Arbitration Rules and Mediation Procedures*

(Rules Amended and Effective November 1, 2009; Fee Schedule Amended and Effective May 15, 2013)

Employment Arbitration Rules and Mediation Procedures

Rules Amended and Effective November 1, 2009

Fee Schedule Amended and Effective May 15, 2013

To access the AAA Employment Arbitration Rules and Mediation Procedures with the previous versions of Fee Schedules, visit the Archived Rules area of the site -- click here.

TABLE OF CONTENTS

1

3

Introduction

Federal and state laws reflecting societal intolerance for certain workplace conduct, as well as court decisions interpreting and applying those statutes, have redefined responsible corporate practice and employee relations. Increasingly, employers and employees face workplace disputes involving alleged wrongful termination, sexual harassment, or discrimination based on race, color, religion, sex, national origin, age and disability.

As courts and administrative agencies become less accessible to civil litigants, employers and their employees now see alternative dispute resolution ("ADR") as a way to promptly and effectively resolve workplace disputes. ADR procedures are becoming more common in contracts of employment, personnel manuals, and employee handbooks.

Increasingly, corporations and their employees look to the American Arbitration Association as a resource in developing prompt and effective employment procedures for employment-related disputes.

These Rules have been developed for employers and employees who wish to use a private alternative to resolve their disputes, enabling them to have complaints heard by an impartial person with expertise in the employment field. These procedures benefit both the employer and the individual employee by making it possible to resolve disputes without extensive litigation.

Role of the American Arbitration Association

The American Arbitration Association, founded in 1926, is a not-for-profit, public service organization dedicated to the resolution of disputes through mediation, arbitration, elections and other voluntary dispute resolution procedures. Millions of workers are now covered by employment ADR plans administered by the AAA.

In addition, the AAA provides education and training, specialized publications, and research on all forms of dispute settlement. With 30 offices worldwide and cooperative agreements with arbitral institutions in 63 other nations, the American Arbitration Association is the nation's largest private provider of ADR services.

For over 80 years, the American Arbitration Association has set the standards for the development of fair and equitable dispute resolution procedures. The development of the Employment Arbitration Rules and Mediation Procedures and the reconstitution of a select and diverse roster of expert neutrals to hear and resolve disputes, are the most recent initiatives of the Association to provide private, efficient and cost-effective procedures for out-of-court settlement of workplace disputes.

Legal Basis of Employment ADR

Since 1990, Congress has twice re-affirmed the important role of ADR in the area of employment discrimination -- in the Americans with Disabilities Act in 1990, and a year later in Section 118 of the Civil Rights Act of 1991.

The United States Supreme Court has also spoken on the importance of ADR in the employment context. In Gilmer v. Interstate/Johnson Lane , 500 U.S. 20, 111 S.Ct. 1647 (1991), the Supreme Court refused to invalidate Gilmer's agreement with the New York Stock Exchange that he would arbitrate disputes with his employer (Interstate/Johnson Lane) simply because he was obliged to sign it in order to work as a securities dealer whose trades were executed on the Exchange. Although the Gilmer Court found that the Age Discrimination in Employment Act did not preclude arbitration of age discrimination claims, it specifically declined to decide whether employment arbitration agreements were "contracts of employment" excluded under the Federal Arbitration Act.

The specific issue left open by Gilmer was decided 10 years later by the United States Supreme Court in Circuit City Stores, Inc. v. Adams , 532 U.S. 105, 121 S. Ct. 1302, 149 L. Ed. 2d 234 (2001). In Circuit City, the Supreme Court concluded that except for transportation workers such as seamen or railroad workers, the FAA covers all contracts of employment and that the Act may be used to compel arbitration of employment-related claims. While Circuit City involved only state law claims, the Supreme Court had determined previously in Gilmer that federal age discrimination claims (and presumably other federal civil rights claims) were arbitrable under the FAA.

The Fairness Issue: The Due Process Protocol

The Due Process Protocol for Mediation and Arbitration of Statutory Disputes Arising Out of the Employment Relationship was developed in 1995 by a special task force composed of individuals representing management, labor, employment, civil rights organizations, private administrative agencies, government, and the American Arbitration Association. The Due Process Protocol, which was endorsed by the Association in 1995, seeks to ensure fairness and equity in resolving workplace disputes. The Due Process Protocol encourages mediation and arbitration of statutory disputes, provided there are due process safeguards. It conveys the hope that ADR will reduce delays caused by the huge backlog of cases pending before administrative agencies and the courts. The Due Process Protocol "recognizes the dilemma inherent in the timing of an agreement to mediate and/or arbitrate statutory disputes" but does not take a position on whether an employer can require a pre-dispute, binding arbitration program as a condition of employment.

The Due Process Protocol has been endorsed by organizations representing a broad range of constituencies. They include the American Arbitration Association, the American Bar

Association Labor and Employment Section, the American Civil Liberties Union, the Federal Mediation and Conciliation Service, the National Academy of Arbitrators, and the National Society of Professionals in Dispute Resolution. The National Employment Lawyers Association has endorsed the substantive provisions of the Due Process Protocol.

It has been incorporated into the Report of the United States Secretary of Labor's Task Force in Excellence in State and Local Government and cited with approval in numerous court opinions.

AAA's Employment ADR Rules

On June 1, 1996, the Association issued National Rules for the Resolution of Employment Disputes (now known as the Employment Arbitration Rules and Mediation Procedures). The rules reflected the guidelines outlined in the Due Process Protocol and were based upon the AAA's California Employment Dispute Resolution Rules, which were developed by a committee of employment management and plaintiff attorneys, retired judges and arbitrators, in addition to Association executives. The revised rules were developed for employers and employees who wish to use a private alternative to resolve their disputes. The rules enabled parties to have complaints heard by an impartial person of their joint selection, with expertise in the employment field. Both employers and individual employees benefit by having experts resolve their disputes without the costs and delay of litigation. The rules included procedures which ensure due process in both the mediation and arbitration of employment disputes. After a year of use, the rules were amended to address technical issues.

AAA's Policy on Employment ADR

The AAA's policy on employment ADR is guided by the state of existing law, as well as its obligation to act in an impartial manner. In following the law, and in the interest of providing an appropriate forum for the resolution of employment disputes, the Association administers dispute resolution programs which meet the due process standards as outlined in its Employment Arbitration Rules and Mediation Procedures and the Due Process Protocol. If the Association determines that a dispute resolution program on its face substantially and materially deviates from the minimum due process standards of the Employment Arbitration Rules and Mediation Procedures and the Due Process Protocol, the Association may decline to administer cases under that program. Other issues will be presented to the arbitrator for determination.

Notification

If an employer intends to utilize the dispute resolution services of the Association in an employment ADR plan, it shall, at least 30 days prior to the planned effective date of the program: (1) notify the Association of its intention to do so; and (2) provide the Association with a copy of the employment dispute resolution plan. If an employer does not comply with this requirement, the Association reserves the right to decline its administrative services. Copies of all plans should be sent to the American Arbitration Association, 725 South Figueroa Street, Suite 2400, Los Angeles, CA 90017; FAX: 213.622.6199.

Costs of Employment Arbitration

These Rules contain two separate and distinct arbitration costs sections; one for disputes arising out of employer-promulgated plans and the other for disputes arising out of individually-negotiated employment agreements and contracts. When the arbitration is filed, the AAA makes an initial administrative determination as to whether the dispute arises from an employer-promulgated plan or an individually-negotiated employment agreement or contract. This determination is made by reviewing the documentation provided to the AAA by the parties, including, but not limited to, the demand for arbitration, the parties' arbitration program or agreement, and any employment agreements or contracts between the parties.

When making its determination on the applicable costs of arbitration section in a given arbitration, the AAA's review is focused on two primary issues. The first component of the review focuses on whether the arbitration program and/or agreement between the individual employee and the employer is one in which it appears that the employer has drafted a standardized arbitration clause with its employees. The second aspect of the review focuses on the ability of the parties to negotiate the terms and conditions of the parties' agreement.

If a party disagrees with the AAA's initial determination, the parties may bring the issue to the attention of the arbitrator for a final determination.

Designing an ADR Program

The guiding principle in designing a successful employment ADR system is that it must be fair in fact and perception. The American Arbitration Association has considerable experience in administering and assisting in the design of employment ADR plans, which gives it an informed perspective on how to effectively design ADR systems, as well as the problems to avoid. Its guidance to those designing employment ADR systems is summarized as follows:

»The American Arbitration Association encourages employers to consider the wide range of legally-available options to resolve workplace disputes outside the courtroom.

»A special emphasis is placed by the Association on encouraging the development of in-house dispute resolution procedures, such as open door policies, ombuds, peer review and internal mediation.

»The Association recommends an external mediation component to resolve disputes not settled by the internal dispute resolution process.

»Programs which use arbitration as a final step may employ:

- pre-dispute, voluntary final and binding arbitration;
- pre-dispute, mandatory nonbinding arbitration;
- pre-dispute, mandatory final and binding arbitration; or
- post-dispute, voluntary final and binding arbitration.

»Although the AAA administers binding arbitration systems that have been required as a condition of initial or continued employment, such programs must be consistent with the Association's Employment Arbitration Rules and Mediation Procedures.

8

Specific guidance on the responsible development and design of employment ADR systems is contained in the Association's publication, Resolving Employment Disputes: A Practical Guide, which is available from the AAA's website, www.adr.org.

Alternative Dispute Resolution Options

Open Door Policy

Employees are encouraged to meet with their immediate manager or supervisor to discuss problems arising out of the workplace environment. In some systems, the employee is free to approach anyone in the chain of command.

Ombuds

A neutral third party (either from within or outside the company) is designated to confidentially investigate and propose settlement of employment complaints brought by employees.

Peer Review

A panel of employees (or employees and managers) works together to resolve employment complaints. Peer review panel members are trained in the handling of sensitive issues.

Internal Mediation

A process for resolving disputes in which a neutral third person from within the company, trained in mediation techniques, helps the disputing parties negotiate a mutually acceptable settlement. Mediation is a nonbinding process in which the parties discuss their disputes with an impartial person who assists them in reaching a settlement. The mediator may suggest ways of resolving the dispute but may not impose a settlement on the parties.

Fact-Finding

The investigation of a complaint by an impartial third person (or team) who examines the complaint and the facts and issues a nonbinding report. Fact-finding is particularly helpful for allegations of sexual harassment, where a fact-finding team, composed of one male and one female neutral, investigates the allegations and presents its findings to the employer and the employee.

Arbitration

Arbitration is generally defined as the submission of disputes to one or more impartial persons for final and binding determination. It can be the final step in a workplace program that includes other dispute resolution methods. There are many possibilities for designing this final step.

They include:

» Pre-Dispute, Voluntary Final and Binding Arbitration

The parties agree in advance, on a voluntary basis, to use arbitration to resolve disputes and they are bound by the outcome.

9

» **Pre-Dispute, Mandatory Nonbinding Arbitration**

The parties must use the arbitration process to resolve disputes, but they are not bound by the outcome.

» **Pre-Dispute, Mandatory Final and Binding Arbitration**

The parties must arbitrate unresolved disputes and they are bound by the outcome.

» **Post-Dispute, Voluntary Final and Binding Arbitration**

The parties have the option of deciding whether to use final and binding arbitration after a dispute arises.

Types of Disputes Covered

The dispute resolution procedures contained in this booklet were developed for arbitration agreements contained in employee personnel manuals, an employment application of an individual employment agreement, other types of employment agreements, or can be used for a specific dispute. They do not apply to disputes arising out of collective bargaining agreements or independent contractor agreements.

Employment Arbitration

Rules and Mediation Procedures

1. Applicable Rules of Arbitration

The parties shall be deemed to have made these rules a part of their arbitration agreement whenever they have provided for arbitration by the American Arbitration Association (hereinafter "AAA") or under its Employment Arbitration Rules and Mediation Procedures or for arbitration by the AAA of an employment dispute without specifying particular rules*. If a party establishes that an adverse material inconsistency exists between the arbitration agreement and these rules, the arbitrator shall apply these rules.

If, within 30 days after the AAA's commencement of administration, a party seeks judicial intervention with respect to a pending arbitration and provides the AAA with documentation that judicial intervention has been sought, the AAA will suspend administration for 60 days to permit the party to obtain a stay of arbitration from the court. These rules, and any amendment of them, shall apply in the form in effect at the time the demand for arbitration or submission is received by the AAA.

*The National Rules for the Resolution of Employment Disputes have been re-named the Employment Arbitration Rules and Mediation Procedures. Any arbitration agreements providing for arbitration under its National Rules for the Resolution of Employment Disputes shall be administered pursuant to these Employment Arbitration Rules and Mediation Procedures.

10

2. Notification

An employer intending to incorporate these rules or to refer to the dispute resolution services of the AAA in an employment ADR plan, shall, at least 30 days prior to the planned effective date of the program:

  i.   notify the Association of its intention to do so and,

  ii. provide the Association with a copy of the employment dispute resolution plan.

Compliance with this requirement shall not preclude an arbitrator from entertaining challenges as provided in Section 1. If an employer does not comply with this requirement, the Association reserves the right to decline its administrative services.

3. AAA as Administrator of the Arbitration

When parties agree to arbitrate under these rules, or when they provide for arbitration by the AAA and an arbitration is initiated under these rules, they thereby authorize the AAA to administer the arbitration. The authority and duties of the AAA are prescribed in these rules, and may be carried out through such of the AAA's representatives as it may direct. The AAA may, in its discretion, assign the administration of an arbitration to any of its offices.

4. Initiation of Arbitration

Arbitration shall be initiated in the following manner.

  a.   The parties may submit a joint request for arbitration.

  b.   In the absence of a joint request for arbitration:

(i) The initiating party (hereinafter "Claimant[s]") shall:

(1) File a written notice (hereinafter "Demand") of its intention to arbitrate at any office of the AAA, within the time limit established by the applicable statute of limitations. Any dispute over the timeliness of the demand shall be referred to the arbitrator. The filing shall be made in duplicate, and each copy shall include the applicable arbitration agreement. The Demand shall set forth the names, addresses, and telephone numbers of the parties; a brief statement of the nature of the dispute; the amount in controversy, if any; the remedy sought; and requested hearing location.

(2) Simultaneously provide a copy of the Demand to the other party (hereinafter "Respondent[s]").

(3) Include with its Demand the applicable filing fee, unless the parties agree to some other method of fee advancement.

(ii) The Respondent(s) may file an Answer with the AAA within 15 days after the date of the letter from the AAA acknowledging receipt of the Demand. The Answer shall provide the Respondent's brief response to the claim and the issues presented. The Respondent(s) shall make its filing in duplicate with the AAA, and simultaneously shall send a copy of the Answer to the Claimant. If no answering statement is filed within the stated time, Respondent will be deemed to deny the claim. Failure to file an answering statement shall not operate to delay the arbitration.

11

(iii) The Respondent(s):

(1) May file a counterclaim with the AAA within 15 days after the date of the letter from the AAA acknowledging receipt of the Demand. The filing shall be made in duplicate. The counterclaim shall set forth the nature of the claim, the amount in controversy, if any, and the remedy sought.

(2) Simultaneously shall send a copy of any counterclaim to the Claimant.

(3) Shall include with its filing the applicable filing fee provided for by these rules.

(iv) The Claimant may file an Answer to the counterclaim with the AAA within 15 days after the date of the letter from the AAA acknowledging receipt of the counterclaim. The Answer shall provide Claimant's brief response to the counterclaim and the issues presented. The Claimant shall make its filing in duplicate with the AAA, and simultaneously shall send a copy of the Answer to the Respondent(s). If no answering statement is filed within the stated time, Claimant will be deemed to deny the counterclaim. Failure to file an answering statement shall not operate to delay the arbitration.

c. The form of any filing in these rules shall not be subject to technical pleading requirements.

5. Changes of Claim

Before the appointment of the arbitrator, if either party desires to offer a new or different claim or counterclaim, such party must do so in writing by filing a written statement with the AAA and simultaneously provide a copy to the other party(s), who shall have 15 days from the date of such transmittal within which to file an answer with the AAA. After the appointment of the arbitrator, a party may offer a new or different claim or counterclaim only at the discretion of the arbitrator.

6. Jurisdiction

    a. The arbitrator shall have the power to rule on his or her own jurisdiction, including any objections with respect to the existence, scope or validity of the arbitration agreement.

    b. The arbitrator shall have the power to determine the existence or validity of a contract of which an arbitration clause forms a part. Such an arbitration clause shall be treated as an agreement independent of the other terms of the contract. A decision by the arbitrator that the contract is null and void shall not for that reason alone render invalid the arbitration clause.

    c. A party must object to the jurisdiction of the arbitrator or to the arbitrability of a claim or counterclaim no later than the filing of the answering statement to the claim or counterclaim that gives rise to the objection. The arbitrator may rule on such objections as a preliminary matter or as part of the final award.

7. Administrative and Mediation Conferences

Before the appointment of the arbitrator, any party may request, or the AAA, in its discretion, may schedule an administrative conference with a representative of the AAA and the parties and/or their representatives. The purpose of the administrative conference is to organize and expedite the arbitration, explore its administrative aspects, establish the most efficient means of

12

selecting an arbitrator, and to consider mediation as a dispute resolution option. There is no administrative fee for this service.

At any time after the filing of the Demand, with the consent of the parties, the AAA will arrange a mediation conference under its Mediation Procedures to facilitate settlement. The mediator shall not be any arbitrator appointed to the case, except by mutual written agreement of the parties. There is no additional filing fee for initiating a mediation under the AAA Mediation Procedures for parties to a pending arbitration.

8. Arbitration Management Conference

As promptly as practicable after the selection of the arbitrator(s), but not later than 60 days thereafter, an arbitration management conference shall be held among the parties and/or their attorneys or other representatives and the arbitrator(s). Unless the parties agree otherwise, the Arbitration Management Conference will be conducted by telephone conference call rather than in person. At the Arbitration Management Conference the matters to be considered shall include, without limitation

i. the issues to be arbitrated;

ii. the date, time, place, and estimated duration of the hearing;

iii. the resolution of outstanding discovery issues and establishment of discovery parameters;

iv. the law, standards, rules of evidence and burdens of proof that are to apply to the proceeding;

v. the exchange of stipulations and declarations regarding facts, exhibits, witnesses, and other issues;

vi. the names of witnesses (including expert witnesses), the scope of witness testimony, and witness exclusion;

vii. the value of bifurcating the arbitration into a liability phase and damages phase;

viii. the need for a stenographic record;

ix. whether the parties will summarize their arguments orally or in writing;

x. the form of the award;

xi. any other issues relating to the subject or conduct of the arbitration;

xii. the allocation of attorney's fees and costs;

xiii. the specification of undisclosed claims;

xiv. the extent to which documentary evidence may be submitted at the hearing;

xv. the extent to which testimony may be admitted at the hearing telephonically, over the internet, by written or video-taped deposition, by affidavit, or by any other means;

13

xvi.   any disputes over the AAA's determination regarding whether the dispute arose from an individually-negotiated employment agreement or contract, or from an employer-promulgated plan (see Costs of Arbitration section).

The arbitrator shall issue oral or written orders reflecting his or her decisions on the above matters and may conduct additional conferences when the need arises.

There is no AAA administrative fee for an Arbitration Management Conference.

9. Discovery

The arbitrator shall have the authority to order such discovery, by way of deposition, interrogatory, document production, or otherwise, as the arbitrator considers necessary to a full and fair exploration of the issues in dispute, consistent with the expedited nature of arbitration.

The AAA does not require notice of discovery related matters and communications unless a dispute arises. At that time, the parties should notify the AAA of the dispute so that it may be presented to the arbitrator for determination.

10. Fixing of Locale (the city, county, state, territory, and/or country of the Arbitration)

If the parties disagree as to the locale, the AAA may initially determine the place of arbitration, subject to the power of the arbitrator(s), after their appointment to make a final determination on the locale. All such determinations shall be made having regard for the contentions of the parties and the circumstances of the arbitration.

11. Date, Time and Place (the physical site of the hearing within the designated locale) of Hearing

The arbitrator shall set the date, time, and place for each hearing. The parties shall respond to requests for hearing dates in a timely manner, be cooperative in scheduling the earliest practicable date, and adhere to the established hearing schedule. The AAA shall send a notice of hearing to the parties at least 10 days in advance of the hearing date, unless otherwise agreed by the parties.

12. Number, Qualifications and Appointment of Neutral Arbitrators

a.   If the arbitration agreement does not specify the number of arbitrators or the parties do not agree otherwise, the dispute shall be heard and determined by one arbitrator.

b.   Qualifications

     i.   Neutral arbitrators serving under these rules shall be experienced in the field of employment law.

     ii.   Neutral arbitrators serving under these rules shall have no personal or financial interest in the results of the proceeding in which they are appointed and shall have no relation to the underlying dispute or to the parties or their counsel that may create an appearance of bias.

     iii.   The roster of available arbitrators will be established on a non-discriminatory basis, diverse by gender, ethnicity, background, and qualifications.

iv.   The AAA may, upon request of a party within the time set to return their list or upon its own initiative, supplement the list of proposed arbitrators in disputes arising out of individually-negotiated employment contracts with persons from the Commercial Roster, to allow the AAA to respond to the particular need of the dispute. In multi-arbitrator disputes, at least one of the arbitrators shall be experienced in the field of employment law.

c.   If the parties have not appointed an arbitrator and have not provided any method of appointment, the arbitrator shall be appointed in the following manner:

i.   Shortly after it receives the Demand, the AAA shall send simultaneously to each party a letter containing an identical list of names of persons chosen from the Employment Dispute Resolution Roster. The parties are encouraged to agree to an arbitrator from the submitted list and to advise the AAA of their agreement.

ii.   If the parties are unable to agree upon an arbitrator, each party to the dispute shall have 15 days from the transmittal date in which to strike names objected to, number the remaining names in order of preference, and return the list to the AAA. If a party does not return the list within the time specified, all persons named therein shall be deemed acceptable.

iii. From among the persons who have been approved on both lists, and in accordance with the designated order of mutual preference, the AAA shall invite the acceptance of an arbitrator to serve. If the parties fail to agree on any of the persons named, or if acceptable arbitrators are unable to act, or if for any other reason the appointment cannot be made from the submitted list, the AAA shall have the power to make the appointment from among other members of the panel without the submission of additional lists.

13. Party Appointed Arbitrators

a.   If the agreement of the parties names an arbitrator or specifies a method of appointing an arbitrator, that designation or method shall be followed.
b.   Where the parties have agreed that each party is to name one arbitrator, the arbitrators so named must meet the standards of Section R-16 with respect to impartiality and independence unless the parties have specifically agreed pursuant to Section R-16(a) that the party-appointed arbitrators are to be non-neutral and need not meet those standards. The notice of appointment, with the name, address, and contact information of the arbitrator, shall be filed with the AAA by the appointing party. Upon the request of any appointing party, the AAA shall submit a list of members of the National Roster from which the party may, if it so desires, make the appointment.
c.   If the agreement specifies a period of time within which an arbitrator shall be appointed and any party fails to make the appointment within that period, the AAA shall make the appointment.
d.   If no period of time is specified in the agreement, the AAA shall notify the party to make the appointment. If within 15 days after such notice has been sent, an arbitrator has not been appointed by a party, the AAA shall make the appointment.

14. Appointment of Chairperson by Party-Appointed Arbitrators or Parties

a.   If, pursuant to Section R-13, either the parties have directly appointed arbitrators, or the arbitrators have been appointed by the AAA, and the parties have authorized them to

15

appoint a chairperson within a specified time and no appointment is made within that time or any agreed extension, the AAA may appoint the chairperson.

b. If no period of time is specified for appointment of the chairperson and the party-appointed arbitrators or the parties do not make the appointment within 15 days from the date of the appointment of the last party-appointed arbitrator, the AAA may appoint the chairperson.

c. If the parties have agreed that their party-appointed arbitrators shall appoint the chairperson from the National Roster, the AAA shall furnish to the party-appointed arbitrators, in the manner provided in Section R-12, a list selected from the National Roster, and the appointment of the chairperson shall be made as provided in that Section.

15. Disclosure

a. Any person appointed or to be appointed as an arbitrator shall disclose to the AAA any circumstance likely to give rise to justifiable doubt as to the arbitrator's impartiality or independence, including any bias or any financial or personal interest in the result of the arbitration or any past or present relationship with the parties or their representatives. Such obligation shall remain in effect throughout the arbitration.

b. Upon receipt of such information from the arbitrator or another source, the AAA shall communicate the information to the parties and, if it deems it appropriate to do so, to the arbitrator and others.

c. In order to encourage disclosure by arbitrators, disclosure of information pursuant to this Section R-15 is not to be construed as an indication that the arbitrator considers that the disclosed circumstance is likely to affect impartiality or independence.

16. Disqualification of Arbitrator

a. Any arbitrator shall be impartial and independent and shall perform his or her duties with diligence and in good faith, and shall be subject to disqualification for:

 i.   partiality or lack of independence,

 ii. inability or refusal to perform his or her duties with diligence and in good faith, and

 iii. any grounds for disqualification provided by applicable law. The parties may agree in writing, however, that arbitrators directly appointed by a party pursuant to Section R-13 shall be nonneutral, in which case such arbitrators need not be impartial or independent and shall not be subject to disqualification for partiality or lack of independence.

b. Upon objection of a party to the continued service of an arbitrator, or on its own initiative, the AAA shall determine whether the arbitrator should be disqualified under the grounds set out above, and shall inform the parties of its decision, which decision shall be conclusive.

17. Communication with Arbitrator

a. No party and no one acting on behalf of any party shall communicate ex parte with an arbitrator or a candidate for arbitrator concerning the arbitration, except that a party, or someone acting on behalf of a party, may communicate ex parte with a candidate for direct appointment pursuant to Section R-13 in order to advise the candidate of the general nature of the controversy and of the anticipated proceedings and to discuss the candidate's qualifications, availability, or independence in relation to the parties or to discuss the suitability of candidates for selection as a third arbitrator where the parties or party-designated arbitrators are to participate in that selection.

b. Section R-17(a) does not apply to arbitrators directly appointed by the parties who, pursuant to Section R-16(a), the parties have agreed in writing are non-neutral. Where the parties have so agreed under Section R-16(a), the AAA shall as an administrative practice suggest to the parties that they agree further that Section R-17(a) should nonetheless apply prospectively.

18. Vacancies

a. If for any reason an arbitrator is unable to perform the duties of the office, the AAA may, on proof satisfactory to it, declare the office vacant. Vacancies shall be filled in accordance with applicable provisions of these Rules.

b. In the event of a vacancy in a panel of neutral arbitrators after the hearings have commenced, the remaining arbitrator or arbitrators may continue with the hearing and determination of the controversy, unless the parties agree otherwise.

c. In the event of the appointment of a substitute arbitrator, the panel of arbitrators shall determine in its sole discretion whether it is necessary to repeat all or part of any prior hearings.

19. Representation

Any party may be represented by counsel or other authorized representatives. For parties without representation, the AAA will, upon request, provide reference to institutions which might offer assistance. A party who intends to be represented shall notify the other party and the AAA of the name and address of the representative at least 10 days prior to the date set for the hearing or conference at which that person is first to appear. If a representative files a Demand or an Answer, the obligation to give notice of representative status is deemed satisfied.

20. Stenographic Record

Any party desiring a stenographic record shall make arrangements directly with a stenographer and shall notify the other parties of these arrangements at least three days in advance of the hearing. The requesting party or parties shall pay the cost of the record. If the transcriptis agreed by the parties, or determined by the arbitrator to be the official record of the proceeding, it must be provided to the arbitrator and made available to the other parties for inspection, at a date, time, and place determined by the arbitrator.

21. Interpreters

Any party wishing an interpreter shall make all arrangements directly with the interpreter and shall assume the costs of the service.

22. Attendance at Hearings

The arbitrator shall have the authority to exclude witnesses, other than a party, from the hearing during the testimony of any other witness. The arbitrator also shall have the authority to decide whether any person who is not a witness may attend the hearing.

23. Confidentiality

The arbitrator shall maintain the confidentiality of the arbitration and shall have the authority to make appropriate rulings to safeguard that confidentiality, unless the parties agree otherwise or the law provides to the contrary.

24. Postponements

The arbitrator: (1) may postpone any hearing upon the request of a party for good cause shown; (2) must postpone any hearing upon the mutual agreement of the parties; and (3) may postpone any hearing on his or her own initiative.

25. Oaths

Before proceeding with the first hearing, each arbitrator shall take an oath of office. The oath shall be provided to the parties prior to the first hearing. The arbitrator may require witnesses to testify under oath administered by any duly qualified person and, if it is required by law or requested by any party, shall do so.

26. Majority Decision

All decisions and awards of the arbitrators must be by a majority, unless the unanimous decision of all arbitrators is expressly required by the arbitration agreement or by law.

27. Dispositive Motions

The arbitrator may allow the filing of a dispositive motion if the arbitrator determines that the moving party has shown substantial cause that the motion is likely to succeed and dispose of or narrow the issues in the case.

28. Order of Proceedings

A hearing may be opened by: (1) recording the date, time, and place of the hearing; (2) recording the presence of the arbitrator, the parties, and their representatives, if any; and (3) receiving into the record the Demand and the Answer, if any. The arbitrator may, at the beginning of the hearing, ask for statements clarifying the issues involved.

The parties shall bear the same burdens of proof and burdens of producing evidence as would apply if their claims and counterclaims had been brought in court.

Witnesses for each party shall submit to direct and cross examination.

With the exception of the rules regarding the allocation of the burdens of proof and going forward with the evidence, the arbitrator has the authority to set the rules for the conduct of the proceedings and shall exercise that authority to afford a full and equal opportunity to all parties to present any evidence that the arbitrator deems material and relevant to the resolution of the dispute. When deemed appropriate, the arbitrator may also allow for the presentation of evidence by alternative means including web conferencing, internet communication, telephonic conferences and means other than an in-person presentation of evidence. Such alternative means must still afford a full and equal opportunity to all parties to present any evidence that the arbitrator deems material and relevant to the resolution of the dispute and when involving witnesses, provide that such witness submit to direct and cross-examination.

The arbitrator, in exercising his or her discretion, shall conduct the proceedings with a view toward expediting the resolution of the dispute, may direct the order of proof, bifurcate proceedings, and direct the parties to focus their presentations on issues the decision of which could dispose of all or part of the case.

Documentary and other forms of physical evidence, when offered by either party, may be received in evidence by the arbitrator.

The names and addresses of all witnesses and a description of the exhibits in the order received shall be made a part of the record.

29. Arbitration in the Absence of a Party or Representative

Unless the law provides to the contrary, the arbitration may proceed in the absence of any party or representative who, after due notice, fails to be present or fails to obtain a postponement. An award shall not be based solely on the default of a party. The arbitrator shall require the party who is in attendance to present such evidence as the arbitrator may require for the making of the award.

30. Evidence

The parties may offer such evidence as is relevant and material to the dispute and shall produce such evidence as the arbitrator deems necessary to an understanding and determination of the dispute. All evidence shall be taken in the presence of all of the arbitrators and all of the parties, except where any party or arbitrator is absent, in default, or has waived the right to be present, however "presence" should not be construed to mandate that the parties and arbitrators must be physically present in the same location.

An arbitrator or other person authorized by law to subpoena witnesses or documents may do so upon the request of any party or independently.

The arbitrator shall be the judge of the relevance and materiality of the evidence offered, and conformity to legal rules of evidence shall not be necessary. The arbitrator may in his or her discretion direct the order of proof, bifurcate proceedings, exclude cumulative or irrelevant testimony or other evidence, and direct the parties to focus their presentations on issues the decision of which could dispose of all or part of the case. All evidence shall be taken in the presence of all of the arbitrators and all of the parties, except where any party is absent, in default, or has waived the right to be present.

If the parties agree or the arbitrator directs that documents or other evidence may be submitted to the arbitrator after the hearing, the documents or other evidence shall be filed with the AAA for transmission to the arbitrator, unless the parties agree to a different method of distribution. All parties shall be afforded an opportunity toexamine such documents or other evidence and to lodge appropriate objections, if any.

31. Inspection

Upon the request of a party, the arbitrator may make an inspection in connection with the arbitration. The arbitrator shall set the date and time, and the AAA shall notify the parties. In the event that one or all parties are not present during the inspection, the arbitrator shall make an oral or written report to the parties and afford them an opportunity to comment.

32. Interim Measures

At the request of any party, the arbitrator may grant any remedy or relief that would have been available to the parties had the matter been heard in court, as stated in Rule 39(d), Award.

A request for interim measures addressed by a party to a judicial authority shall not be deemed incompatible with the agreement to arbitrate or a waiver of the right to arbitrate.

33. Closing of Hearing

The arbitrator shall specifically inquire of all parties whether they have any further proofs to offer or witnesses to be heard. Upon receiving negative replies or if satisfied that the record is complete, the arbitrator shall declare the hearing closed.

If briefs are to be filed, the hearing shall be declared closed as of the final date set by the arbitrator for the receipt of briefs. If documents are to be filed as provided in Rule 30 and the date set for their receipt is later than that set for the receipt of briefs, the later date shall be the date of closing the hearing. The time limit within which the arbitrator is required to make the award shall commence to run, in the absence of other agreements by the parties, upon closing of the hearing.

34. Reopening of Hearing

The hearing may be reopened by the arbitrator upon the arbitrator's initiative, or upon application of a party for good cause shown, at any time before the award is made. If reopening the hearing would prevent the making of the award within

the specific time agreed on by the parties in the contract(s) out of which the controversy has arisen, the matter may not be reopened unless the parties agree on an extension of time. When no specific date is fixed in the contract, the arbitrator may reopen the hearing and shall have 30 days from the closing of the reopened hearing within which to make an award.

35. Waiver of Oral Hearing

The parties may provide, by written agreement, for the waiver of oral hearings. If the parties are unable to agree as to the procedure, upon the appointment of the arbitrator, the arbitrator shall specify a fair and equitable procedure.

36. Waiver of Objection/Lack of Compliance with These Rules

Any party who proceeds with the arbitration after knowledge that any provision or requirement of these rules has not been complied with, and who fails to state objections thereto in writing or in a transcribed record, shall be deemed to have waived the right to object.

37. Extensions of Time

The parties may modify any period of time by mutual agreement. The AAA or the arbitrator may for good cause extend any period of time established by these Rules, except the time for making the award. The AAA shall notify the parties of any extension.

38. Serving of Notice

a. Any papers, notices, or process necessary or proper for the initiation or continuation of an arbitration under these rules, for any court action in connection therewith, or for the entry of judgment on any award made under these rules may be served on a party by mail addressed to the party, or its representative at the last known address or by personal service, in or outside the state where the arbitration is to be held, provided that reasonable opportunity to be heard with regard to the dispute is or has been granted to the party.

b. The AAA, the arbitrator, and the parties may also use overnight delivery or electronic facsimile transmission (fax), to give the notices required by these rules. Where all parties and the arbitrator agree, notices may be transmitted by electronic mail (e-mail), or other methods of communication.

c. Unless otherwise instructed by the AAA or by the arbitrator, any documents submitted by any party to the AAA or to the arbitrator shall simultaneously be provided to the other party or parties to the arbitration.

39. The Award

a. The award shall be made promptly by the arbitrator and, unless otherwise agreed by the parties or specified by law, no later than 30 days from the date of closing of the hearing or, if oral hearings have been waived, from the date of the AAA's transmittal of the final statements and proofs to the arbitrator. Three additional days are provided if briefs are to be filed or other documents are to be transmitted pursuant to Rule 30.

b. An award issued under these rules shall be publicly available, on a cost basis. The names of the parties and witnesses will not be publicly available, unless a party expressly agrees to have its name made public in the award.

c. The award shall be in writing and shall be signed by a majority of the arbitrators and shall provide the written reasons for the award unless the parties agree otherwise. It shall be executed in the manner required by law.

d. The arbitrator may grant any remedy or relief that would have been available to the parties had the matter been heard in court including awards of attorney's fees and costs, in accordance with applicable law. The arbitrator shall, in the award, assess arbitration fees, expenses, and compensation as provided in Rules 43, 44, and 45 in favor of any party and, in the event any administrative fees or expenses are due the AAA, in favor of the AAA, subject to the provisions contained in the Costs of Arbitration section.

21

e. If the parties settle their dispute during the course of the arbitration and mutually request, the arbitrator may set forth the terms of the settlement in a consent award.

f. The parties shall accept as legal delivery of the award the placing of the award or a true copy thereof in the mail, addressed to a party or its representative at the last known address, personal service of the award, or the filing of the award in any manner that may be required by law.

g. The arbitrator's award shall be final and binding.

40. Modification of Award

Within 20 days after the transmittal of an award, any party, upon notice to the other parties, may request the arbitrator to correct any clerical, typographical, technical, or computational errors in the award. The arbitrator is not empowered to redetermine the merits of any claim already decided. The other parties shall be given 10 days to respond to the request. The arbitrator shall dispose of the request within 20 days after transmittal by the AAA to the arbitrator of the request and any response thereto. If applicable law requires a different procedural time frame, that procedure shall be followed.

41. Release of Documents for Judicial Proceedings

The AAA shall, upon the written request of a party, furnish to the party, at that party's expense, certified copies of any papers in the AAA's case file that may be required in judicial proceedings relating to the arbitration.

42. Applications to Court

a. No judicial proceeding by a party relating to the subject matter of the arbitration shall be deemed a waiver of the party's right to arbitrate.

b. Neither the AAA nor any arbitrator in a proceeding under these rules is or shall be considered a necessary or proper party in judicial proceedings relating to the arbitration.

c. Parties to these procedures shall be deemed to have consented that judgment upon the arbitration award may be entered in any federal or state court having jurisdiction.

d. Parties to an arbitration under these rules shall be deemed to have consented that neither the AAA nor any arbitrator shall be liable to any party in any action for damages or injunctive relief for any act or omission in connection with any arbitration under these rules.

43. Administrative Fees

As a not-for-profit organization, the AAA shall prescribe filing and other administrative fees to compensate it for the cost of providing administrative services. The AAA administrative fee schedule in effect at the time the demand for arbitration or submission agreement is received shall be applicable.

AAA fees shall be paid in accordance with the Costs of Arbitration Section (see pages 45-53).

The AAA may, in the event of extreme hardship on any party, defer or reduce the administrative fees. (To ensure that you have the most current information, see our website at www.adr.org).

22

44. Neutral Arbitrator's Compensation

Arbitrators shall charge a rate consistent with the arbitrator's stated rate of compensation. If there is disagreement concerning the terms of compensation, an appropriate rate shall be established with the arbitrator by the AAA and confirmed to the parties.

Any arrangement for the compensation of a neutral arbitrator shall be made through the AAA and not directly between the parties and the arbitrator. Payment of the arbitrator's fees and expenses shall be made by the AAA from the fees and moneys collected by the AAA for this purpose.

Arbitrator compensation shall be borne in accordance with the Costs of Arbitration section.

45. Expenses

Unless otherwise agreed by the parties or as provided under applicable law, the expenses of witnesses for either side shall be borne by the party producing such witnesses.

All expenses of the arbitrator, including required travel and other expenses, and any AAA expenses, as well as the costs relating to proof and witnesses produced at the direction of the arbitrator shall be borne in accordance with the Costs of Arbitration section.

46. Deposits

The AAA may require deposits in advance of any hearings such sums of money as it deems necessary to cover the expenses of the arbitration, including the arbitrator's fee, if any, and shall render an accounting and return any unexpended balance at the conclusion of the case.

47. Suspension for Non-Payment

If arbitrator compensation or administrative charges have not been paid in full, the AAA may so inform the parties in order that one of them may advance the required payment. If such payments are not made, the arbitrator may order the suspension or termination of the proceedings. If no arbitrator has yet been appointed, the AAA may suspend or terminate the proceedings.

48. Interpretation and Application of Rules

The arbitrator shall interpret and apply these rules as they relate to the arbitrator's powers and duties. When there is more than one arbitrator and a difference arises among them concerning the meaning or application of these Rules, it shall be resolved by a majority vote. If that is not possible, either an arbitrator or a party may refer the question to the AAA for final decision. All other procedures shall be interpreted and applied by the AAA.

Costs of Arbitration (including AAA Administrative Fees)

This Costs of Arbitration section contains two separate and distinct sub-sections. Initially, the AAA shall make an administrative determination as to whether the dispute arises from an employer-promulgated plan or an individually-negotiated employment agreement or contract.

If a party disagrees with the AAA's determination, the parties may bring the issue to the attention of the arbitrator for a final determination. The arbitrator's determination will be made on documents only, unless the arbitrator deems a hearing is necessary.

23

For Disputes Arising Out of Employer-Promulgated Plans*:

Arbitrator compensation is not included as part of the administrative fees charged by the AAA. Arbitrator compensation is based on the most recent biography sent to the parties prior to appointment. The employer shall pay the arbitrator's compensation unless the employee, post dispute, voluntarily elects to pay a portion of the arbitrator's compensation. Arbitrator compensation, expenses as defined in section (iv) below, and administrative fees are not subject to reallocation by the arbitrator(s) except upon the arbitrator's determination that a claim or counterclaim was filed for purposes of harassment or is patently frivolous.

*Pursuant to Section 1284.3 of the California Code of Civil Procedure, consumers with a gross monthly income of less than 300% of the federal poverty guidelines are entitled to a waiver of arbitration fees and costs, exclusive of arbitrator fees. This law applies to all consumer agreements subject to the California Arbitration Act, and to all consumer arbitrations conducted in California. If you believe that you meet these requirements, you must submit to the AAA a declaration under oath regarding your monthly income and the number of persons in your household. Please contact Case Filing Services at 877-495-4185 if you have any questions regarding the waiver of administrative fees. (Effective January 1, 2003.)

A party making a demand for treatment of a claim, counterclaim, or additional claim as a collective action arbitration will be subject to the administrative fees as outlined in the standard and flexible fee schedules below. Arbitrator compensation is not included as a part of the administrative fees charged by the AAA. Arbitrator compensation in cases involving a collective action claim will be charged in accordance with the determination as to whether the dispute arises from an employer-promulgated plan or an individually negotiated employment agreement or contract.

(i) Filing Fees

Cases Filed by Employee Against Employer

In cases before a single arbitrator, a non-refundable filing fee capped in the amount of $200 is payable in full by the employee when a claim is filed, unless the plan provides that the employee pay less. A non-refundable fee in the amount of $1350 is payable in full by the employer, unless the plan provides that the employer pay more.

In cases before three or more arbitrators, a non-refundable filing fee capped in the amount of $200 is payable in full by the employee when a claim is filed, unless the plan provides that the employee pay less. A non-refundable fee in the amount of $1,800 is payable in full by the employer, unless the plan provides that the employer pay more.

The employer's share is due as soon as the employee meets his or her filing requirements, even if the matter settles.

There shall be no filing fee charged for a counterclaim. If a determination is made that the dispute arises out of an individually-negotiated employment agreement, the filing fee for a counterclaim will be charged in accordance with the fee schedules below for disputes arising out of individually negotiated employment agreements.

The above fee schedule will also apply where the employer files on behalf of the employee pursuant to the terms of the employer promulgated plan.

Cases Filed by Employer Against Employee

24

In cases before a single arbitrator, a non-refundable fee in the amount of $1550 is payable in full by the employer.

In cases before three or more arbitrators, a non-refundable fee in the amount of $2000 is payable in full by the employer.

There shall be no filing fee charged for a counterclaim. If a determination is made that the dispute arises out of an individually-negotiated employment agreement, the filing fee for a counterclaim will be charged in accordance with the fee schedules below for disputes arising out of individually-negotiated employment agreements.

(ii) Hearing Fees

For each day of hearing held before a single arbitrator, an administrative fee of $350 is payable by the employer.

For each day of hearing held before a multi-arbitrator panel, an administrative fee of $500 is payable by the employer.

There is no AAA hearing fee for the initial Arbitration Management Conference.

(iii) Postponement/Cancellation Fees

A fee of $150 is payable by a party causing a postponement of any hearing scheduled before a single arbitrator.

A fee of $250 is payable by a party causing a postponement of any hearing scheduled before a multi-arbitrator panel.

(iv) Hearing Room Rental

The hearing fees described above do not cover the rental of hearing rooms. The AAA maintains hearing rooms in most offices for the convenience of the parties. Check with the administrator for availability and rates. Hearing room rental fees will be borne by the employer.

(v) Abeyance Fee

Parties on cases held in abeyance for one year will be assessed an annual abeyance fee of $300. A case may only be held in abeyance after the initial filing fees have been paid. If a party refuses to pay the assessed fee, the other party or parties may pay the entire fee on behalf of all parties, otherwise the matter will be administratively closed.

(vi) Expenses

All expenses of the arbitrator, including required travel and other expenses, and any AAA expenses, as well as the costs relating to proof and witnesses produced at the direction of the arbitrator, shall be borne by the employer.

For Disputes Arising Out of Individually-Negotiated Employment Agreements and Contracts:

The AAA's Fee Schedule, as modified below, will apply to disputes arising out of individually-negotiated employment agreements and contracts, even if such agreements and contracts

25

reference or incorporate an employer-promulgated plan.   Arbitrator compensation is not included as part of the administrative fees charged by the AAA. Arbitrator compensation is based on the most recent biography sent to the parties prior to appointment.

Administrative Fee Schedules (Standard and Flexible Fee)

The AAA has two administrative fee options for parties filing claims or counterclaims, the Standard Fee Schedule and Flexible Fee Schedule. The Standard Fee Schedule has a two-payment schedule, and the Flexible Fee Schedule has a three-payment schedule which offers lower initial filing fees, but potentially higher total administrative fees of approximately 12% to 19% for cases that proceed to a hearing. The administrative fees of the AAA are based on the amount of the claim or counterclaim. Arbitrator compensation is not included in this schedule. Unless the parties agree otherwise, arbitrator compensation and administrative fees are subject to allocation by the arbitrator in the award.

In an effort to make arbitration costs reasonable for consumers, the AAA has a separate fee schedule for consumer-related disputes. Please refer to Section C-8 of the Supplementary Procedures for Consumer-Related Disputes when filing a consumer-related claim. Note that the Flexible Fee Schedule is not available on cases administered under these supplementary procedures.

The AAA applies the Supplementary Procedures for Consumer-Related Disputes to arbitration clauses in agreements between individual consumers and businesses where the business has a standardized, systematic application of arbitration clauses with customers and where the terms and conditions of the purchase of standardized, consumable goods or services are non-negotiable or primarily non-negotiable in most or all of its terms, conditions, features, or choices. The product or service must be for personal or household use. The AAA will have the discretion to apply or not to apply the Supplementary Procedures and the parties will be able to bring any disputes concerning the application or non-application to the attention of the arbitrator. Consumers are not prohibited from seeking relief in a small claims court for disputes or claims within the scope of its jurisdiction, even in consumer arbitration cases filed by the business.

Fees for incomplete or deficient filings: Where the applicable arbitration agreement does not reference the AAA, the AAA will attempt to obtain the agreement of the other parties to the dispute to have the arbitration administered by the AAA. However, where the AAA is unable to obtain the agreement of the parties to have the AAA administer the arbitration, the AAA will administratively close the case and will not proceed with the administration of the arbitration. In these cases, the AAA will return the filing fees to the filing party, less the amount specified in the fee schedule below for deficient filings.

Parties that file demands for arbitration that are incomplete or otherwise do not meet the filing requirements contained in these Rules shall also be charged the amount specified below for deficient filings if they fail or are unable to respond to the AAA's request to correct the deficiency.

Fees for additional services: The AAA reserves the right to assess additional administrative fees for services performed by the AAA beyond those provided for in these Rules which may be required by the parties' agreement or stipulation.

(i) Standard Fee Schedule

An Initial Filing Fee is payable in full by a filing party when a claim, counterclaim, or additional claim is filed. A Final Fee will be incurred for all cases that proceed to their first hearing. This fee will be payable in advance at the time that the first hearing is scheduled. This fee will be refunded at the conclusion of the case if no hearings have occurred. However, if the Association is not notified at least 24 hours before the time of the scheduled hearing, the Final Fee will remain due and will not be refunded.

These fees will be billed in accordance with the following schedule:

Amount of Claim	Initial Filing Fee	Final Fee
Above $0 to $10,000	$775	$200
Above $10,000 to $75,000	$975	$300
Above $75,000 to $150,000	$1,850	$750
Above $150,000 to $300,000	$2,800	$1,250
Above $300,000 to $500,000	$4,350	$1,750
Above $500,000 to $1,000,000	$6,200	$2,500
Above $1,000,000 to $5,000,000	$8,200	$3,250
Above $5,000,000 to $10,000,000	$10,200	$4,000
Above $10,000,000	Base fee of $12,800 plus .01% of the amount above $10,000,000 Fee Capped at $65,000	$6,000
Nonmonetary Claims[1]	$3,350	$1,250
Collective Action Claims[2]	$3,350	$1,250
Deficient Claim Filing Fee[3]	$350	
Additional Services[4]		

[1]This fee is applicable when a claim or counterclaim is not for a monetary amount. Where a monetary claim amount is not known, parties will be required to state a range of claims or be subject to a filing fee of $10,200.

[2]This fee is applicable where a party makes a demand for treatment of a claim, counterclaim, or additional claim as a collective action arbitration.

[3]The Deficient Claim Filing Fee shall not be charged in cases filed by a consumer in an arbitration governed by the Supplementary Procedures for the Resolution of Consumer-Related Disputes, or in cases filed by an Employee who is submitting their dispute to arbitration pursuant to an employer promulgated plan.

27

[4]*The AAA may assess additional fees where procedures or services outside the Rules sections are required under the parties' agreement or by stipulation.*

Fees are subject to increase if the amount of a claim or counterclaim is modified after the initial filing date. Fees are subject to decrease if the amount of a claim or counterclaim is modified before the first hearing.

The minimum fees for any case having three or more arbitrators are $2,800 for the Initial Filing Fee, plus a $1,250 Final Fee. Expedited Procedures are applied in any case where no disclosed claim or counterclaim exceeds $75,000, exclusive of interest and arbitration costs.

Parties on cases filed under either the Flexible Fee Schedule or the Standard Fee Schedule that are held in abeyance for one year will be assessed an annual abeyance fee of $300. A case may only be held in abeyance after the filing fees have been paid. If a party refuses to pay the assessed fee, the other party or parties may pay the entire fee on behalf of all parties, otherwise the matter will be administratively closed.

For more information, please contact your local AAA office, case management center, or our Customer Service desk at 1-800-778-7879.

(ii) Refund Schedule for Standard Fee Schedule

The AAA offers a refund schedule on filing fees connected with the Standard Fee Schedule. For cases with claims up to $75,000, a minimum filing fee of $350 will not be refunded. For all other cases, a minimum fee of $600 will not be refunded. Subject to the minimum fee requirements, refunds will be calculated as follows:

> 100% of the filing fee, above the minimum fee, will be refunded if the case is settled or withdrawn within five calendar days of filing.

> 50% of the filing fee, will be refunded if the case is settled or withdrawn between six and 30 calendar days of filing.

> 25% of the filing fee will be refunded if the case is settled or withdrawn between 31 and 60 calendar days of filing.

No refund will be made once an arbitrator has been appointed (this includes one arbitrator or a three-arbitrator panel). No refunds will be granted on awarded cases.

Note: The date of receipt of the demand for arbitration with the AAA will be used to calculate refunds of filing fees for both claims and counterclaims.

(iii) Flexible Fee Schedule

A non-refundable Initial Filing Fee is payable in full by a filing party when a claim, counterclaim, or additional claim is filed. Upon receipt of the Demand for Arbitration, the AAA will promptly initiate the case and notify all parties as well as establish the due date for filing of an Answer, which may include a Counterclaim. In order to proceed with the further administration of the arbitration and appointment of the arbitrator(s), the appropriate, non-refundable Proceed Fee outlined below must be paid.

If a Proceed Fee is not submitted within ninety (90) days of the filing of the Claimant's Demand for Arbitration, the Association will administratively close the file and notify all parties.

28

No refunds or refund schedule will apply to the Filing or Proceed Fees once received.

The Flexible Fee Schedule below also may be utilized for the filing of counterclaims. However, as with the Claimant's claim, the counterclaim will not be presented to the arbitrator until the Proceed Fee is paid.

A Final Fee will be incurred for all claims and/or counterclaims that proceed to their first hearing. This fee will be payable in advance when the first hearing is scheduled, but will be refunded at the conclusion of the case if no hearings have occurred. However, if the Association is not notified of a cancellation at least 24 hours before the time of the scheduled hearing, the Final Fee will remain due and will not be refunded.

All fees will be billed in accordance with the following schedule:

Amount of Claim	Initial Filing Fee	Proceed Fee	Final Fee
Above $0 to $10,000	$400	$475	$200
Above $10,000 to $75,000	$625	$500	$300
Above $75,000 to $150,000	$850	$1250	$750
Above $150,000 to $300,000	$1,000	$2125	$1,250
Above $300,000 to $500,000	$1,500	$3,400	$1,750
Above $500,000 to $1,000,000	$2,500	$4,500	$2,500
Above $1,000,000 to $5,000,000	$2,500	$6,700	$3,250
Above $5,000,000 to $10,000,000	$3,500	$8,200	$4,000
Above $10,000,000	$4,500	$10,300 plus .01% of claim amount over $10,000,000 up to $65,000	$6,000
Nonmonetary[1]	$2,000	$2,000	$1,250
Collective Action Claims[2]	$2,000	$2,000	$1,250
Deficient Claim Filing Fee	$350		
Additional Services[3]			

[1]*This fee is applicable when a claim or counterclaim is not for a monetary amount. Where a monetary claim amount is not known, parties will be required to state a range of claims or be subject to a filing fee of $3,500 and a proceed fee of $8,200.*

[2]*This fee is applicable where a party makes a demand for treatment of a claim, counterclaim, or additional claim as a collective action arbitration.*

[3]*The AAA reserves the right to assess additional administrative fees for services performed by the AAA beyond those provided for in these Rules and which may be required by the parties' agreement or stipulation.*

For more information, please contact your local AAA office, case management center, or our Customer Service desk at 1-800-778-7879. All fees are subject to increase if the amount of a claim or counterclaim is modified after the initial filing date. Fees are subject to decrease if the amount of a claim or counterclaim is modified before the first hearing.

The minimum fees for any case having three or more arbitrators are $1,000 for the Initial Filing Fee; $2,125 for the Proceed Fee; and $1,250 for the Final Fee.

Under the Flexible Fee Schedule, a party's obligation to pay the Proceed Fee shall remain in effect regardless of any agreement of the parties to stay, postpone or otherwise modify the arbitration proceedings. Parties that, through mutual agreement, have held their case in abeyance for one year will be assessed an annual abeyance fee of $300. If a party refuses to pay the assessed fee, the other party or parties may pay the entire fee on behalf of all parties, otherwise the matter will be closed.

Note: The date of receipt by the AAA of the demand for arbitration will be used to calculate the ninety (90) day time limit for payment of the Proceed Fee.

There is no Refund Schedule in the Flexible Fee Schedule.

(iv) Hearing Room Rental

The fees described above do not cover the cost of hearing rooms, which are available on a rental basis. Check with the AAA for availability and rates.

(v) Abeyance Fee

Parties on cases filed under the Standard Fee Schedule that are held in abeyance for one year will be assessed an annual abeyance fee of $300. A case may only be held in abeyance after the filing fees have been paid. If a party refuses to pay the assessed fee, the other party or parties may pay the entire fee on behalf of all parties, otherwise the matter will be administratively closed.

(vi) Expenses

All expenses of the arbitrator, including required travel and other expenses, and any AAA expenses, as well as the costs relating to proof and witnesses produced at the direction of the arbitrator, shall be borne equally by the parties.

For Disputes Proceeding Under the Supplementary Rules for Class Action Arbitration ("Supplementary Rules"):

The AAA's Administered Fee Schedule, as listed in Section 11 of the Supplementary Rules for Class Action Arbitration, shall apply to disputes proceeding under the Supplementary Rules.

Optional Rules for Emergency Measures of Protection

O-1. Applicability

Where parties by special agreement or in their arbitration clause have adopted these rules for emergency measures of protection, a party in need of emergency relief prior to the constitution of the panel shall notify the AAA and all other parties in writing of the nature of the relief sought and the reasons why such relief is required on an emergency basis. The application shall also set forth the reasons why the party is entitled to such relief. Such notice may be given by facsimile transmission, or other reliable means, but must include a statement certifying that all other parties have been notified or an explanation of the steps taken in good faith to notify other parties.

O-2. Appointment of Emergency Arbitrator

Within one business day of receipt of notice as provided in Section O-1, the AAA shall appoint a single emergency arbitrator from a special AAA panel of emergency arbitrators designated to rule on emergency applications. The emergency arbitrator shall immediately disclose any circumstance likely, on the basis of the facts disclosed in the application, to affect such arbitrator's impartiality or independence. Any challenge to the appointment of the emergency arbitrator must be made within one business day of the communication by the AAA to the parties of the appointment of the emergency arbitrator and the circumstances disclosed.

O-3. Schedule

The emergency arbitrator shall as soon as possible, but in any event within two business days of appointment, establish a schedule for consideration of the application for emergency relief. Such schedule shall provide a reasonable opportunity to all parties to be heard, but may provide for proceeding by telephone conference or on written submissions as alternatives to a formal hearing.

O-4. Interim Award

If after consideration the emergency arbitrator is satisfied that the party seeking the emergency relief has shown that immediate and irreparable loss or damage will result in the absence of emergency relief, and that such party is entitled to such relief, the emergency arbitrator may enter an interim award granting the relief and stating the reasons therefore.

O-5. Constitution of the Panel

Any application to modify an interim award of emergency relief must be based on changed circumstances and may be made to the emergency arbitrator until the panel is constituted; thereafter such a request shall be addressed to the panel. The emergency arbitrator shall have no further power to act after the panel is constituted unless the parties agree that the emergency arbitrator is named as a member of the panel.

O-6. Security

Any interim award of emergency relief may be conditioned on provision by the party seeking such relief of appropriate security.

O-7. Special Master

A request for interim measures addressed by a party to a judicial authority shall not be deemed incompatible with the agreement to arbitrate or a waiver of the right to arbitrate. If the AAA is directed by a judicial authority to nominate a special master to consider and report on an application for emergency relief, the AAA shall proceed as provided in Section O-1 of this article and the references to the emergency arbitrator shall be read to mean the special master, except that the special master shall issue a report rather than an interim award.

O-8. Costs

The costs associated with applications for emergency relief shall be apportioned in the same manner as set forth in the Costs of Arbitration section.

Employment Mediation Procedures

M-1. Agreement of Parties

Whenever, by stipulation or in their contract, the parties have provided for mediation or conciliation of existing or future disputes under the auspices of the American Arbitration Association (AAA) or under these procedures, the parties and their representatives, unless agreed otherwise in writing, shall be deemed to have made these procedures , as amended and in effect as of the date of filing of a request for mediation, a part of their agreement and designate the AAA as the administrator of their mediation.

The parties by mutual agreement may vary any part of these procedures including, but not limited to, agreeing to conduct the mediation via telephone or other electronic or technical means.

M-2. Initiation of Mediation

Any party or parties to a dispute may initiate mediation under the AAA's auspices by making a Request for Mediation to any of the AAA's regional offices or case management centers via telephone, email, regular mail or fax. Requests for Mediation may also be filed online via AAA WebFile at www.adr.org.

The party initiating the mediation shall simultaneously notify the other party or parties of the request. The initiating party shall provide the following information to the AAA and the other party or parties as applicable:

   i.   A copy of the mediation provision of the parties' contract or the parties' stipulation to mediate.

   ii.   ii. The names, regular mail addresses, email addresses (if available), and telephone numbers of all parties to the dispute and representatives, if any, in the mediation.

   iii. A brief statement of the nature of the dispute and the relief requested.

   iv.   Any specific qualifications the mediator should possess.

Where there is no preexisting stipulation or contract by which the parties have provided for mediation of existing or future disputes under the auspices of the AAA, a party may request the

AAA to invite another party to participate in "mediation by voluntary submission". Upon receipt of such a request, the AAA will contact the other party or parties involved in the dispute and attempt to obtain a submission to mediation.

M-3. Fixing of Locale (the city, county, state, territory and, if applicable, country of the mediation)

i. When the parties' agreement to mediate is silent with respect to locale and the parties are unable to agree upon a locale, the AAA shall have the authority to consider the parties' arguments and determine the locale.

ii. When the parties' agreement to mediate requires a specific locale, absent the parties' agreement to change it, the locale shall be that specified in the agreement to mediate.

iii. If the reference to a locale in the agreement to mediate is ambiguous, the AAA shall have the authority to consider the parties' arguments and determine the locale.

M-4. Representation

Any party may participate without representation (pro-se), or by any representative of that party's choosing, or by counsel, unless such choice is prohibited by applicable law. A party intending to have representation shall notify the other party and the AAA of the name, telephone number and address, and email address if available of the representative.

M-5. Appointment of the Mediator

Parties may search the online profiles of the AAA's Panel of Mediators at www.aaamediation.com in an effort to agree on a mediator. If the parties have not agreed to the appointment of a mediator and have not provided any other method of appointment, the mediator shall be appointed in the following manner:

i. Upon receipt of a request for mediation, the AAA will send to each party a list of mediators from the AAA's Panel of Mediators. The parties are encouraged to agree to a mediator from the submitted list and to advise the AAA of their agreement.

ii. ii. If the parties are unable to agree upon a mediator, each party shall strike unacceptable names from the list, number the remaining names in order of preference, and return the list to the AAA. If a party does not return the list within the time specified, all mediators on the list shall be deemed acceptable to that party. From among the mediators who have been mutually approved by the parties, and in accordance with the designated order of mutual preference, the AAA shall invite a mediator to serve.

iii. If the parties fail to agree on any of the mediators listed, or if acceptable mediators are unable to serve, or if for any other reason the appointment cannot be made from the submitted list, the AAA shall have the authority to make the appointment from among other members of the Panel of Mediators without the submission of additional lists.

M-6. Mediator's Impartiality and Duty to Disclose

AAA mediators are required to abide by the Model Standards of Conduct for Mediators in effect at the time a mediator is appointed to a case. Where there is a conflict between the Model Standards and any provision of these Mediation Procedures, these Mediation Procedures shall govern. The Standards require mediators to (i) decline a mediation if the mediator cannot conduct it in an impartial manner, and (ii) disclose, as soon as practicable, all actual and potential conflicts of interest that are reasonably known to the mediator and could reasonably be seen as raising a question about the mediator's impartiality.

Prior to accepting an appointment, AAA mediators are required to make a reasonable inquiry to determine whether there are any facts that a reasonable individual would consider likely to create a potential or actual conflict of interest for the mediator. AAA mediators are required to disclose any circumstance likely to create a presumption of bias or prevent a resolution of the parties' dispute within the time-frame desired by the parties. Upon receipt of such disclosures, the AAA shall immediately communicate the disclosures to the parties for their comments.

The parties may, upon receiving disclosure of actual or potential conflicts of interest of the mediator, waive such conflicts and proceed with the mediation. In the event that a party disagrees as to whether the mediator shall serve, or in the event that the mediator's conflict of interest might reasonably be viewed as undermining the integrity of the mediation, the mediator shall be replaced.

M-7. Vacancies

If any mediator shall become unwilling or unable to serve, the AAA will appoint another mediator, unless the parties agree otherwise, in accordance with section M-5.

M-8. Duties and Responsibilities of the Mediator

i.   The mediator shall conduct the mediation based on the principle of party self-determination. Self-determination is the act of coming to a voluntary, uncoerced decision in which each party makes free and informed choices as to process and outcome.

ii. ii. The mediator is authorized to conduct separate or ex parte meetings and other communications with the parties and/or their representatives, before, during, and after any scheduled mediation conference. Such communications may be conducted via telephone, in writing, via email, online, in person or otherwise.

iii. The parties are encouraged to exchange all documents pertinent to the relief requested. The mediator may request the exchange of memoranda on issues, including the underlying interests and the history of the parties' negotiations. Information that a party wishes to keep confidential may be sent to the mediator, as necessary, in a separate communication with the mediator.

iv. The mediator does not have the authority to impose a settlement on the parties but will attempt to help them reach a satisfactory resolution of their dispute. Subject to the discretion of the mediator, the mediator may make oral or written recommendations for settlement to a party privately or, if the parties agree, to all parties jointly.

v.   In the event a complete settlement of all or some issues in dispute is not achieved within the scheduled mediation session(s), the mediator may continue to communicate with the parties, for a period of time, in an ongoing effort to facilitate a complete settlement.

vi. The mediator is not a legal representative of any party and has no fiduciary duty to any party.

vii. The mediator shall set the date, time, and place for each session of the mediation conference. The parties shall respond to requests for conference dates in a timely manner, be cooperative in scheduling the earliest practicable date, and adhere to the established conference schedule. The AAA shall provide notice of the conference to the parties in advance of the conference date, when timing permits.

M-9. Responsibilities of the Parties

The parties shall ensure that appropriate representatives of each party, having authority to consummate a settlement, attend the mediation conference.

Prior to and during the scheduled mediation conference session(s) the parties and their representatives shall, as appropriate to each party's circumstances, exercise their best efforts to prepare for and engage in a meaningful and productive mediation.

M-10. Privacy

Mediation sessions and related mediation communications are private proceedings. The parties and their representatives may attend mediation sessions. Other persons may attend only with the permission of the parties and with the consent of the mediator.

M-11. Confidentiality

Subject to applicable law or the parties' agreement, confidential information disclosed to a mediator by the parties or by other participants (witnesses) in the course of the mediation shall not be divulged by the mediator. The mediator shall maintain the confidentiality of all information obtained in the mediation, and all records, reports, or other documents received by a mediator while serving in that capacity shall be confidential.

The mediator shall not be compelled to divulge such records or to testify in regard to the mediation in any adversary proceeding or judicial forum.

The parties shall maintain the confidentiality of the mediation and shall not rely on, or introduce as evidence in any arbitral, judicial, or other proceeding the following, unless agreed to by the parties or required by applicable law:

   i.   Views expressed or suggestions made by a party or other participant with respect to a possible settlement of the dispute;

   ii.   Admissions made by a party or other participant in the course of the mediation proceedings;

   iii. Proposals made or views expressed by the mediator; or

   iv. The fact that a party had or had not indicated willingness to accept a proposal for settlement made by the mediator.

M-12. No Stenographic Record

There shall be no stenographic record of the mediation process.

M-13. Termination of Mediation

The mediation shall be terminated:

   i.   By the execution of a settlement agreement by the parties; or

35

ii.   By a written or verbal declaration of the mediator to the effect that further efforts at mediation would not contribute to a resolution of the parties' dispute; or

iii.   By a written or verbal declaration of all parties to the effect that the mediation proceedings are terminated; or

iv.   When there has been no communication between the mediator and any party or party's representative for 21 days following the conclusion of the mediation conference.

M-14. Exclusion of Liability

Neither the AAA nor any mediator is a necessary party in judicial proceedings relating to the mediation. Neither the AAA nor any mediator shall be liable to any party for any error, act or omission in connection with any mediation conducted under these procedures. Parties to a mediation under these procedures may not call the mediator, the AAA or AAA employees as a witness in litigation or any other proceeding relating to the mediation. The mediator, the AAA and AAA employees are not competent to testify as witnesses in any such proceeding.

M-15. Interpretation and Application of Procedures

The mediator shall interpret and apply these procedures insofar as they relate to the mediator's duties and responsibilities. All other procedures shall be interpreted and applied by the AAA.

M-16. Deposits

Unless otherwise directed by the mediator, the AAA will require the parties to deposit in advance of the mediation conference such sums of money as it, in consultation with the mediator, deems necessary to cover the costs and expenses of the mediation and shall render an accounting to the parties and return any unexpended balance at the conclusion of the mediation.

M-17. Expenses

All expenses of the mediation, including required traveling and other expenses or charges of the mediator, shall be borne equally by the parties unless they agree otherwise. The expenses of participants for either side shall be paid by the party requesting the attendance of such participants.

M-18. Cost of the Mediation

There is no filing fee to initiate a mediation or a fee to request the AAA to invite parties to mediate.

The cost of mediation is based on the hourly or daily mediation rate published on the mediator's AAA profile. This rate covers both mediator compensation and an allocated portion for the AAA's services. There is a four-hour or one half-day minimum charge for a mediation conference. Expenses referenced in Section M-17 may also apply.

If a matter submitted for mediation is withdrawn or cancelled or results in a settlement after the request to initiate mediation is filed but prior to the mediation conference the cost is $200 plus any mediator time and charges incurred. These costs shall be borne by the initiating party unless the parties agree otherwise.

If you have questions about mediation costs or services visit www.aaamediation.com or contact your local AAA office.

Appendix F

Due Process Protocol for Mediation and Arbitration of Statutory Disputes Arising Out of the Employment Relationship

Source: ARBITRATION 1995: NEW CHALLENGES AND EXPANDING RESPONSIBILITIES, PROCEEDINGS OF THE 48TH ANNUAL MEETING, NATIONAL ACADEMY OF ARBITRATORS 298–304 (Joyce M. Najita, ed., 1996).

A DUE PROCESS PROTOCOL FOR MEDIATION AND ARBITRATION OF STATUTORY DISPUTES ARISING OUT OF THE EMPLOYMENT RELATIONSHIP

The following protocol is offered by the undersigned individuals, members of the Task Force on Alternative Dispute Resolution in Employment, as a means of providing due process in the resolution by mediation and binding arbitration of employment disputes involving statutory rights. The signatories were designated by their respective organizations, but the protocol reflects their personal views and should not be construed as representing the policy of the designating organizations.

Genesis

This Task Force was created by individuals from diverse organizations involved in labor and employment law to examine questions of due process arising out of the use of mediation and arbitration for resolving employment disputes. In this protocol we confine ourselves to statutory disputes.

The members of the Task Force felt that mediation and arbitration of statutory disputes conducted under proper due process safeguards should be encouraged in order to provide expeditious, accessible, inexpensive and fair private enforcement of statutory employment disputes for the 100,000,000 members of the workforce who might not otherwise have ready, effective access to administrative or judicial relief. They also hope that such a system will serve to reduce the delays which now arise out of the huge backlog of cases pending before administrative agencies and courts and that it will help forestall an even greater number of such cases.

A. Pre or Post Dispute Arbitration

The Task Force recognizes the dilemma inherent in the timing of an agreement to mediate and/or arbitrate statutory disputes. It did not achieve consensus on this difficult issue. The views in this spectrum are set forth randomly, as follows:

Employers should be able to create mediation and/or arbitration systems to resolve statutory claims, but any agreement to mediate and/or arbitrate disputes should be informed, voluntary, and not a condition of initial or continued employment.

Employers should have the right to insist on an agreement to mediate and/or arbitrate statutory disputes as a condition of initial or continued employment. Postponing such an agreement until a dispute actually arises, when there will likely exist a stronger predisposition to litigate, will result in very few agreements to mediate and/or arbitrate, thus negating the likelihood of effectively utilizing alternative dispute resolution and overcoming the problems of administrative and judicial delays which now plague the system.

Employees should not be permitted to waive their right to judicial relief of statutory claims arising out of the employment relationship for any reason.

Employers should be able to create mediation and/or arbitration systems to resolve statutory claims, but the decision to mediate and/or arbitrate individual cases should not be made until after the dispute arises.

The Task Force takes no position on the timing of agreements to mediate and/or arbitrate statutory employment disputes, though it agrees that such agreements be knowingly made. The focus of this protocol is on standards of exemplary due process.

B.   *Right of Representation*

1.   Choice of Representative

Employees considering the use of or, in fact, utilizing mediation and/or arbitration procedures should have the right to be represented by a spokesperson of their own choosing. The mediation and arbitration procedure should so specify and should include reference to institutions which might offer assistance, such as bar associations, legal service associations, civil rights organizations, trade unions, etc.

2.   Fees for Representation

The amount and method of payment for representation should be determined between the claimant and the representative. We recommend, however, a number of existing systems which provide employer reimbursement of at least a portion of the employee's attorney fees, especially for lower paid employees. The arbitrator should have the authority to provide for fee reimbursement, in whole or in part, as part of the remedy in accordance with applicable law or in the interests of justice.

3. Access to Information

One of the advantages of arbitration is that there is usually less time and money spent in pre-trial discovery. Adequate but limited pre-trial discovery is to be encouraged and employees should have access to all information reasonably relevant to mediation and/or arbitration of their claims. The employees' representative should also have reasonable pre-hearing and hearing access to all such information and documentation. Necessary pre-hearing depositions consistent with the expedited nature of arbitration should be available.

We also recommend that prior to selection of an arbitrator, each side should be provided with the names, addresses and phone numbers of the representatives of the parties in that arbitrator's six most recent cases to aid them in selection.

C. *Mediator and Arbitrator Qualification*

1. Roster Membership

Mediators and arbitrators selected for such cases should have skill in the conduct of hearings, knowledge of the statutory issues at stake in the dispute, and familiarity with the workplace and employment environment. The roster of available mediators and arbitrators should be established on a non-discriminatory basis, diverse by gender, ethnicity, background, experience, etc., to satisfy the parties that their interest and objectives will be respected and fully considered. Our recommendation is for selection of impartial arbitrators and mediators. We recognize the right of employers and employees to jointly select as mediator and/or arbitrator one in whom both parties have requisite trust, even though not possessing the qualifications here recommended, as most promising to bring finality and to withstand judicial scrutiny.

The existing cadre of labor and employment mediators and arbitrators, some lawyers, some not, although skilled in conducting hearings and familiar with the employment milieu is unlikely, without special training, to consistently possess knowledge of the statutory environment in which these disputes arise and of the characteristics of the non-union workplace.

There is a manifest need for mediators and arbitrators with expertise in statutory requirements in the employment field who may, without special training, lack experience in the employment area and in the conduct of arbitration hearings and mediation sessions. Reexamination of rostering eligibility by designating agencies, such as the American Arbitration Association, may permit the expedited inclusion in the pool of this most valuable source of expertise. The roster of arbitrators and mediators should contain representatives with all such skills in order to meet the diverse needs of this caseload.

Regardless of their prior experience, mediators and arbitrators on the roster must be independent of bias toward either party. They should reject cases if they believe the procedure lacks requisite due process.

2. Training

The creation of a roster containing the foregoing qualifications dictates the development of a training program to educate existing and potential labor and employment mediators and arbitrators as to the statutes, including substantive, procedural and remedial issues to be confronted and to train experts in the statutes as to employer procedures governing the employment relationship as well as due process and fairness in the conduct and control of arbitration hearings and mediation sessions.

Training in the statutory issues should be provided by the government agencies, bar associations, academic institutions, etc., administered perhaps by the designating agency, such as the AAA, at various locations throughout the country. Such training should be updated periodically and be required of all mediators and arbitrators. Training in the conduct of mediation and arbitration could be provided by a mentoring program with experienced panelists.

Successful completion of such training would be reflected in the resume or panel cards of the arbitrators supplied to the parties for their selection process.

3. Panel Selection

Upon request of the parties, the designating agency should utilize a list procedure such as that of the AAA or select a panel composed of an odd number of mediators and arbitrators from its roster or pool. The panel cards for such individuals should be submitted to the parties for their perusal prior to alternate striking of the names on the list, resulting in the designation of the remaining mediator and/or arbitrator. The selection process could empower the designating agency to appoint a mediator and/or arbitrator if the striking procedure is unacceptable or unsuccessful. As noted above, subject to the consent of the parties, the designating agency should provide the names of the parties and their representatives in recent cases decided by the listed arbitrators.

4.   Conflicts of Interest

The mediator and arbitrator for a case has a duty to disclose any relationship which might reasonably constitute or be perceived as a conflict of interest. The designated mediator and/or arbitrator should be required to sign an oath provided by the designating agency, if any, affirming the absence of such present or preexisting ties.

5.   Authority of the Arbitrator

The arbitrator should be bound by applicable agreements, statutes, regulations and rules of procedure of the designating agency, including the authority to determine the time and place of the hearing, permit reasonable discovery, issue subpoenas, decide arbitrability issues, preserve order and privacy in the hearings, rule on evidentiary matters, determine the close of the hearing and procedures for post-hearing submissions, and issue an award resolving the submitted dispute. The arbitrator should be empowered to award whatever relief would be available in court under the law. The arbitrator should issue an opinion and award setting forth a summary of the issues, including the type(s) of dispute(s), the damages and/or other relief requested and awarded, a statement of any other issues resolved, and a statement regarding the disposition of any statutory claim(s).

6.   Compensation of the Mediator and Arbitrator

Impartiality is best assured by the parties sharing the fees and expenses of the mediator and arbitrator. In cases where the economic condition of a party does not permit equal sharing, the parties should make mutually acceptable arrangements to achieve that goal if at all possible. In the absence of such agreement, the arbitrator should determine allocation of fees. The designating agency, by negotiating the parties' share of costs and collecting such fees, might be able to reduce the bias potential of disparate contributions by forwarding payment to the mediator and/or arbitrator without disclosing the parties' share therein.

D.   Scope of Review

The arbitrator's award should be final and binding and the scope of review should be limited.

Dated: May 9, 1995

/s/Christopher A. Barreca

Christopher A. Barreca,
Co-Chair
Partner
Paul, Hastings, Janofsky &
Walker
Rep., Council of Labor &
Employment Section,
American Bar Association

/s/Arnold Zack

Arnold Zack, Co-Chair
President, National Academy of
Arbitrators

/s/W. Bruce Newman

W. Bruce Newman
Rep., Society of Professionals in
Dispute Resolution

/s/Joseph Garrison

Joseph Garrison, Partner
Garrison & Arterton

/s/Robert D. Manning

Robert D. Manning
Rep., Arbitration Committee of
Labor & Employment Section,
American Bar Association

/s/George H. Friedman

George H. Friedman
Senior Vice President
American Arbitration
Association

/s/Max Zimny

Max Zimny, Co-Chair
General Counsel, International Ladies' Garment Workers'
Union; Rep., Council of Labor
& Employment Section,
American Bar Association

/s/Carl E. VerBeek

Carl E. VerBeek, Partner
Varnum Riddering Schmidt &
Howlett
Rep., Arbitration
Committee of Labor &
Employment Section, American Bar Association

/s/Charles F. Ipavec

Charles F. Ipavec, Arbitrator
Rep., Arbitration Committee
of Labor & Employment
Section, American Bar
Association

/s/Michael F. Hoellering	/s/Lewis Maltby
Michael F. Hoellering	Lewis Maltby
General Counsel	Director—Workplace Rights
American Arbitration	Project, American Civil
Association	Liberties Union

/s/Wilma Liebman
Wilma Liebman
Special Assistant to the
Director, Federal Mediation &
Conciliation Service

[*Editor's Note:* Approved by the Board of Governors on May 24, 1995.]

Appendix G

Online Arbitration Resources

Dispute Resolution in the Workplace: Searchable Database of Annual Proceedings of the National Academy of Arbitrators
http://naarb.org/proceedings/index.asp

Published annually since 1948, the *Proceedings of the National Academy of Arbitrators* provides analysis of issues that affect arbitration by members of the National Academy of Arbitrators (NAA) and invited non-member experts.

In addition to the print volume of the *Proceedings*, published annually by Bloomberg BNA, the NAA makes available on their website without charge a searchable database of all Proceedings since publication of the first volume in 1948, except for the two most recent editions in print. The database has several search options, including keyword, author, and decision, as well as advanced search parameters.

The Art and Science of Arbitration: Interviews from the Video History Collection of the College of Labor and Employment Lawyers
http://www.laborandemploymentcollege.org/products/Video%20History.aspx

This collection of interviews provides background on arbitration and mediation from a variety of key practitioners in the field, including Arvid Anderson, George Cohen, Roberta Golick, James M. Harkless, Theodore Kheel, George Nicolau, and former U.S. Secretary of Labor George P. Shultz. There are also selected highlights from "Fireside Chats" in the annual *Proceedings of the National Academy of Arbitrators,* discussed above, with Frances K. Biarstow, Hon. Harry T. Edwards, Arnold M. Zack, Theodore J. St. Antoine, and Edgar A. Jones, Jr.

Table of Cases

*References are to chapter and footnote number (e.g., **17:** 64, 69 refers to footnotes 64 and 69 in Chapter 17).* App. A *refers to Appendix A.*

Index

*References are to chapter and section number (e.g., **8:** III.4; **16:** IV.2 refers to section III.4 in Chapter 8 and section IV.2 in Chapter 16).*

519

Index

Z

About the Author

Roger I. Abrams is the Richardson Professor of Law at Northeastern University School of Law. He is a graduate of Cornell University and the Harvard Law School, where he served as a Visiting Professor of Law in 2006. He served as dean at Northeastern University from 1999–2002, as dean at Rutgers Law School from 1993–1998, and as dean at Nova University School of Law from 1986–1993. Prior to entering academic life in 1974 as a faculty member at Case Western Reserve University, Professor Abrams practiced labor law in Boston at Foley Hoag & Eliot and clerked for Judge Frank M. Coffin of the U.S. Court of Appeals for the First Circuit. While in practice, Professor Abrams tried the Boston School Desegregation Case for the NAACP.

Professor Abrams is the author of six books on the law, economics, and social history of the sports industry—*Legal Bases: Baseball and the Law* (1998), *The Money Pitch: Baseball Free Agency and Salary Arbitration* (2000), *The First World Series and the Baseball Fanatics of 1903* (2003), *The Dark Side of the Diamond: Gambling, Violence, Drugs and Alcoholism in the National Pastime* (2008), *Sports Justice: The Law and Business of Sports* (2010), and *Playing Tough: The World of Sports and Politics* (2013). He is co-author of the leading sports law casebook, *Sports and the Law: Text, Cases and Problems* (4th ed. 2010). Professor Abrams is regularly asked to comment on legal and economic issues involving the business of sports by the print and electronic media. In 2006, he served as the first Scholar-in-Residence at the National Baseball Hall of Fame and Museum in Cooperstown, New York.

During his almost 40 years as a labor arbitrator, Professor Abrams has been appointed to resolve nearly 2,500 disputes, including Major League Baseball salary arbitration cases starting in 1986. He is the permanent arbitrator at Walt Disney World, the Internal Revenue Service, and the U.S. Customs Service. He was elected a member of the National Academy of Arbitrators in 1982.

Professor Abrams has authored or co-authored more than 40 law review articles on labor arbitration, sports law, and other legal issues in law journals at Harvard University, the University of Michigan, and Duke University, among others. He is an elected member of the American Law Institute and a life member of the American Bar Foundation. In 2004, he was elected a Fellow of the Massachusetts Historical Society.